SHOW POSTERS

SHOW POSTERS

THE ART AND PRACTICE OF MAKING GIG POSTERS

PAT JONES & BEN NUNERY, founders of POWERHOUSE FACTORIES

PRINT
Cincinnati, Ohio
www.printmag.com

 Published by Print Books, an imprint of F+W, A Content + eCommerce Company, 10151 Carver Rd. Blue Ash, Ohio, 45242. First edition.

Distributed in Canada by Fraser Direct
100 Armstrong Avenue
Georgetown, Ontario L7G 5S4
Canada

Distributed in the U.K. and Europe by
F+W Media International, LTD
Pynes Hill Court, Pynes Hill
Rydon Lane
Exeter EX2 5SP, UK
Tel: (+44) 1392 797680

Distributed in Australia by Capricorn Link
P.O. Box 704
Windsor, NSW 2756
Australia

ISBN-13: 978-1-4403-4054-3
ISBN-10: 1-4403-4054-4
eISBN-13: 978-1-4403-4066-6
eISBN-10: 1-4403-4066-8

19 18 17 16 15 5 4 3 2 1

Editor: Scott Francis
Designer: Michelle Thompson
Production Coordinator: Greg Nock
Cover design by Pat Jones and Ben Nunery
Cover images © Lil-Tuffy.com, Lure Design Incorporated,
Powerhouse Factories, Jermaine Rogers, and Andy Vastagh

DEDICATION/ACKNOWLEDGMENTS

This book is dedicated to Matt Tullis, our design professor, and all the other design and art professors who teach the value of process, heritage, and the physical artifact. These three things play a role in everything we do.

CONTENTS

FOREWORD 9

1: A BRIEF HISTORY OF POSTER DESIGN | 10

War Propaganda 11

Postwar WPA Posters 11

Rebirth & Re-Emergence of Show Posters 12

Historic Venues 13

2: DESIGN TOOLS & APPROACHES | 16

Sign Painting 17

Rubylith 18

Stencil Cut & Construction Paper Cut 22

Xerox 26

Fine Art 28

Hand Lettering 33

Software V. Handmade 36

Linocut 36

Offset Lithography 36

Letterpress 37

Screenprinting / Serigraphy 38

Painted Stencil 39

3: POSTER TRENDS & DESIGN STYLES | 40

Oxidized Degradation 41
Halftone Realism 56
Illustrated Ornamentation 67
Iconic Simplification 80
Lowbrow Handbill 94
Flattened Whimsy 100
Rudimentary Quirk 117
Textured Illustration 125
Psychedelic Repetition 133
Graphic Weight 148
Newsprint Collage 170

4: BEING SUCCESSFUL | 188

Meeting and Working with Bands 188
- Bands 188
- Band Management 188
- Club Owners & Promoters 188
- Merch Companies 189
- Full-Commission Deal 189
- Split the Stack 190
- Producing Posters for Free 190

Artist Profiles
- Andy Vastagh (Boss Construction) 191
- Travis Bone (Furturtle Show Prints) 196
- Lil' Tuffy 200
- Aaron May (Powerhouse Factories) 202
- Matt Barnes 204

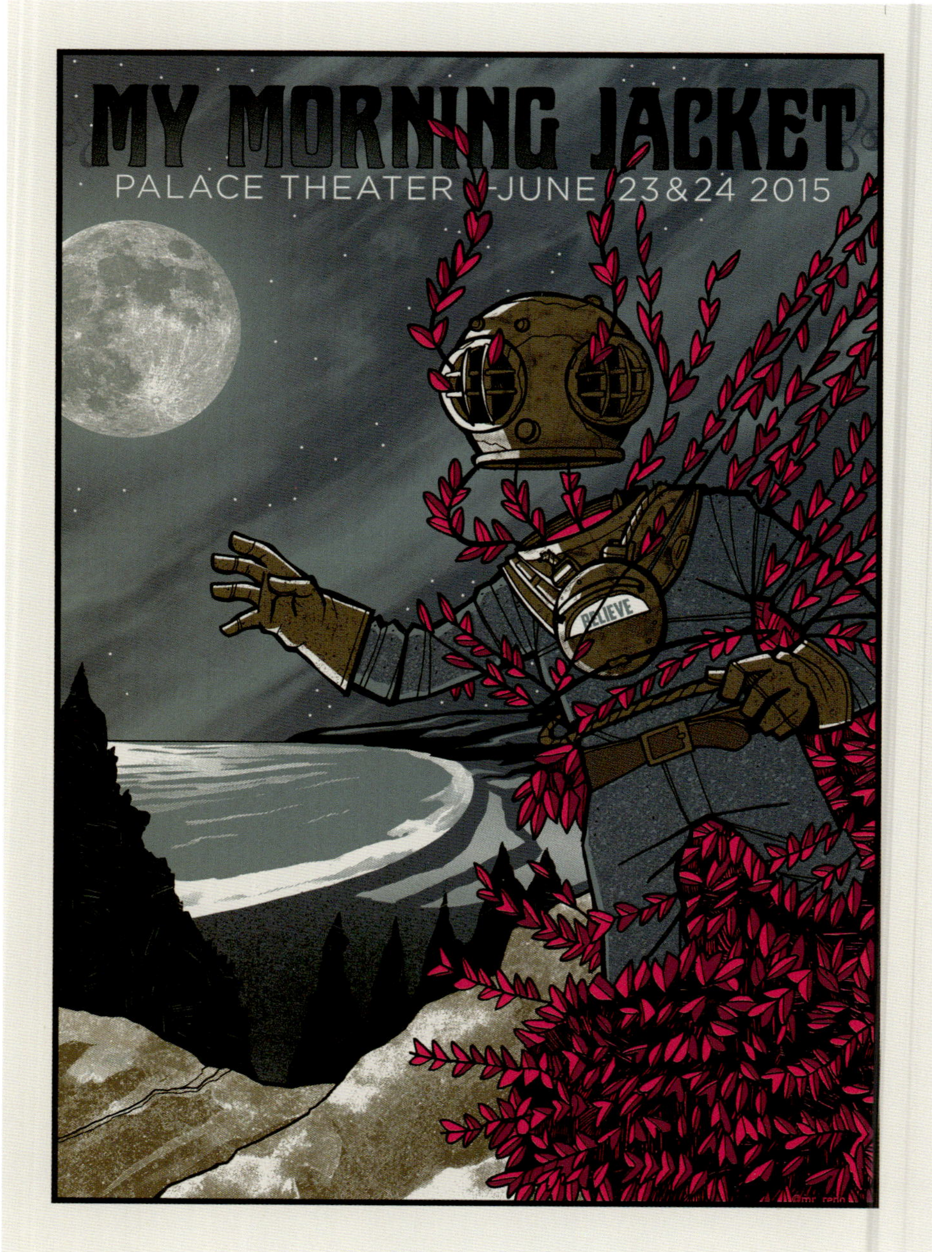

CLIENT: My Morning Jacket
DESIGNER: Clinton Reno
WEBSITE: clintonreno.com

FOREWORD

The poster culture that we [as a band] try to put out there is the same culture that we try to put out musically. We don't like to be painted into a corner and we don't like repetition. When we're making an album we try to create a new environment every time and when it comes to poster art, sticking with one artist might be good for a series, but it's great to have a different look and a different feel for every show—because honestly that coincides with the look and the feel of the show itself. No two shows are the same and that's kinda how we approach the poster culture as well. No two show posters should be the same. The posters should be an extension of the music—an extension of the tour.

We work with visual artists who inspire us, and throughout the years we've tried many different people. Some of the ones I can think of right now are Clinton Reno, Justin Helton, Ron Jasin, Randy Fung, Guy Burwell—fantastic artists who always come to us with designs that challenge and mystify. We collect prints of their other work. They've become friends of ours.

When we're approaching people to design posters for us it's all about "How does this make you feel? Now make a representation of that." I like the show posters that don't have literal elements to them, but somehow encapsulate the feeling of the event, the song, the album. When people design a poster about how the music makes them feel—that's when I feel like I'm walking on air when I look at it. Every song makes you feel a different thing. Some are dark and moody. Some are light and vibrant. If an artist can take those emotions and match them with an appropriate color palette, then that becomes a moment—a feeling. When you look at that poster, you feel something.

Poster artists are collaborators in this whole endeavor. At the end of the day, when the last note dissipates and everybody leaves the show, what's left after everything's all said and done is a piece of visual art that represents that night. I think that's why people hold onto posters with such reverence: They were there that night, and the art encapsulates that moment. It goes to show you how important poster art is. And I think we have a responsibility to put out interesting art to encapsulate those moments. The poster becomes a tether to that experience. As long as they have that show poster they have that memory. It's like looking at a picture of a beautiful moment in your life. Show posters help do that. It's proof. It's evidence. I was there. I'll show you. And they signed it!

—Patrick Hallahan from My Morning Jacket

1 A BRIEF HISTORY OF POSTER DESIGN

The modern poster medium, as we know it, dates back to the mid-1800s when the process of color lithography changed the printing industry, making mass production possible. Around the same time many European countries, such as France, began lifting government censorship of public places. Since then posters have been used for a wide range of promotional purposes, from advertising products and services to propaganda to promoting special events. Their increasing artistry and sophistication has attracted artists of varying levels working in a wide range of styles. Posters have spanned design styles including Art Nouveau, Cubism, Art Deco, Bauhaus, and the psychedelic influences of the 1960s.

Much of what eventually became the poster scene we know and love today was influenced by the work of several French artists who advanced the art of poster design. Artists like Henri de Toulouse-Lautrec and Jules Cheret elevated the creation of poster advertisements to an art form through the introduction of striking colors, innovative typography, and evocative imagery. Posters began to transform the streets of Paris and by the 1890s poster art had spread throughout Europe, ushering in a "golden age" of poster art.

In the United States during this time, poster advertisements and handbills were typically comprised mostly of lettering often created from woodcuts. While brightly colored and charming in their own right, these handbills often lacked imagery, and were much more crudely created without much care given to type placement. Event promoters began to notice highly designed European posters, advertisements, and propaganda. Inspired by the burgeoning new poster art scene, more elaborate event posters began to be made stateside as well and more and more printers began to turn their attention to posters.

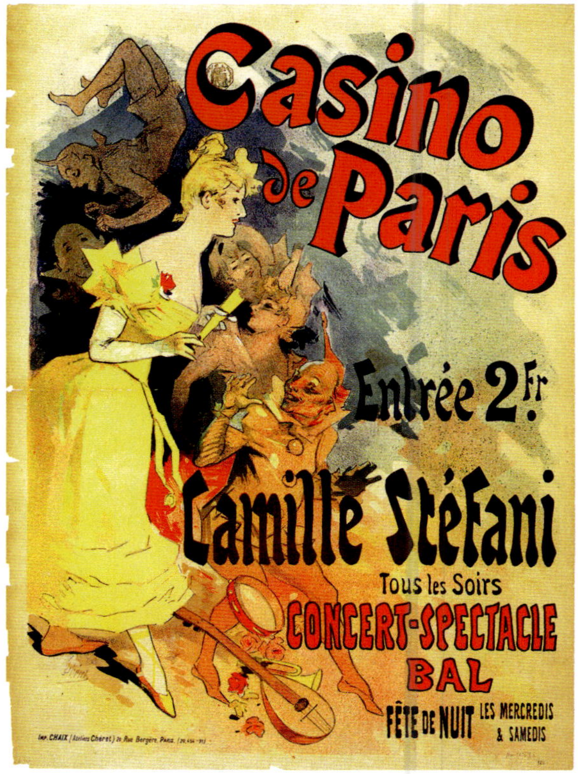

WAR PROPAGANDA

During the early 1900s new modes of advertising began to emerge and come to the forefront. Mass-market magazines, radio, and billboards began to compete with posters for advertising budgets. Posters were suddenly no longer a primary medium for advertisement. Political messaging and propaganda began to emerge as the prevalent subject matter for posters.

World War I marked the first time that illustrated posters were widely used for political messaging. Recruitment posters and posters promoting war bond drives all but replaced commercial uses for posters.

POSTWAR WPA POSTERS

The Works Progress Administration (later renamed the Work Projects Administration and commonly called the WPA) was created by President Franklin D. Roosevelt in 1935 as part of a response to the Great Depression. The WPA employed millions of people for public works projects, such as road construction and public building projects. One of the projects sponsored by the WPA was the Federal Art Project. The WPA employed struggling artists and artisans to create public works of art including murals, sculptures, graphic art, and posters. During this time the WPA created posters to publicize local exhibits, theater productions, and health and educational programs. The posters have become popular collectors' items and reproductions.

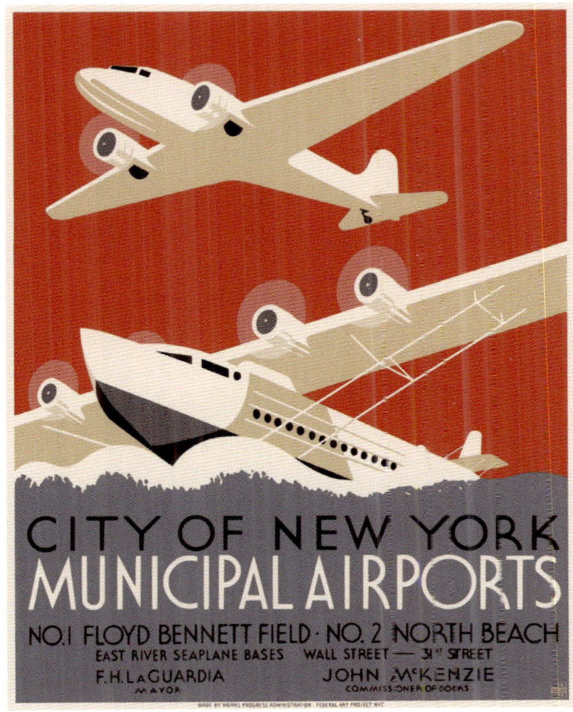

REBIRTH & RE-EMERGENCE OF SHOW POSTERS

Around the mid-1960s the use of posters to promote events re-emerged as part of a broader counter culture movement. What most people consider "contemporary" or the beginning of the rock poster tends to be associated with the Fillmore (a San Francisco concert venue that gave away posters at every show) and the promotion company known as the Family Dog.

The Family Dog was comprised of rock promoter Chet Helms and a group of artists including Stanley Mouse, Alton Kelley, Rick Griffin, Wes Wilson, and Victor Moscoso. Together they created some of the most memorable posters in rock 'n' roll history.

The Fillmore and the San Francisco scene is probably the most well-known example of this art explosion that was occurring at the time; however, the same thing was happening in Austin with the Vulcan Gas Company and later the Armadillo World Headquarters. They had posters made for every show just like the Fillmore but Vulcan Gas Co. predated the Bill Graham–era Fillmore West by a year. The Armadillo Art Squad included Gilbert Shelton, Jim Franklin, Guy Juke, Kerry Awn, Ken Featherston, Henry Gonzalez, Danny Garrett, Sam Yeates, Micael Priest, G.L. McElhaney, Jack Jaxon, and later on Nels Jacobson (who helped form Flatstock and the API with Geoff Peveto, Frank Kozik, Jeff Kleinsmith, Jay Ryan, Clay Hayes, and Rene DeBos in 2002).

The use of posters seemed to fade out a bit between the late 1970s and early 1990s. Aside from the punk rock flyers and underground show posters, the style of posters we are accustomed to now weren't as prevalent. However, some designers began pushing the art of poster making and ignited a new movement in contemporary show posters. Art Chantry was quietly making very highly designed rock posters in the Pacific Northwest and applying styles more akin to theater than music to his work.

Chantry made it cool or acceptable to "design" a rock poster versus the psychedelic styles that dominated the 1960s. Then a designer named Frank Kozik came on the scene in Austin and changed the model for making posters. Kozik flipped the whole process on its ear by approaching bands and offer to make a poster, give them part of the run, and then sell the rest of them to make his money back. This was contrary to the typical way for poster artists to do business up to that point, which was paying for the design and production and then getting a stack of posters to do whatever they want with.

Other artists like Derek Hess, Coop, and Mark Arminski were also making a name for themselves during this new era of poster making and changing the landscape of what people considered a "rock poster." Their styles were wildly contrasting and they set the stage for an entire movement of artists that would shape the new landscape for the contemporary rock poster. Poster artists began popping up in cities around the country that were known for their live music scenes. Firehouse in San Francisco, Mike King and Gary Houston in Portland, and Jeff Kleinsmith in Seattle were all around in the early 1990s making really great work. Not long after, Steve Walters and Jay Ryan began establishing their own unique poster styles in Chicago and quickly became known as the godfathers of the Chicago poster scene. Aesthetic Apparatus was another hugely influential studio out of Minneapolis that began breaking down poster design to minimal two-color, highly successful posters. Geoff Peveto and The Decoder Ring were also garnering lots of praise for pushing the boundaries of show posters with nontraditional media. It was also during this time that The Decoder Ring, and others, began doing entire series of posters for bands like Built to Spill, Modest Mouse, and Queens of the Stone Age.

If we call that era "old school," then when we talk about the "new school" scene—say, 2000 to present—the difference seems to be access. The Internet and social media afford access to bands, to venues, to materials, to studios, and to information that was more difficult to obtain a couple of decades ago. This accessibility that anyone and everyone has in this day and age makes it easy for people to claim they are a "poster artist." It doesn't make them talented or qualified, but they have immediate access to all the components that make up generating a poster and negotiating a deal. This is a specific difference in how things get done today versus yesterday. The old-school scene was a completely different network. It was based on artist collectives who worked centric to where they lived. For example, the Armadillo guys typically worked for beer and food at the local show venues.

With regard to style, the new school also has the same impact of access. Because of the Internet and social media your spectrum of influence can be infinite now. Where the old school's circle of influence might have just existed with your immediate peers, you can visit GigPosters.com now and see thousands of styles. That pool of visual influence has pushed styles and mediums of what people would traditionally consider a rock poster. It also generates some healthy competition for creating the next new thing in terms of style or approach.

HISTORIC VENUES

THE FILLMORE

Originally named the Majestic Hall, the Fillmore Auditorium is a historic music venue in San Francisco. Along with other venues opened by promoter Bill Graham under the Fillmore franchise (Fillmore West and Fillmore East), the Fillmore has been a well-loved concert venue for major music acts throughout its history. During the 1960s the Fillmore Auditorium was a counter culture hub and played a huge role in the psychedelic music scene, hosting such bands as the Grateful Dead, Jefferson Airplane, the Doors, Jimi Hendrix Experience, and many others. As time marched on, the Fillmore hosted many acts ranging from psychedelic to blues to jazz to punk to indie rock.

A mainstay tradition of the Fillmore during all of this was its elaborate concert posters. To this day, attendees of a show at the Fillmore receive that night's poster free upon exiting the show.

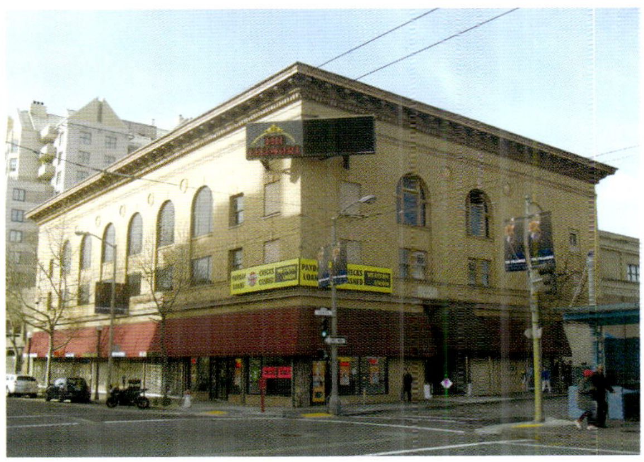

THE RYMAN AUDITORIUM

This historic auditorium located in Nashville hosted concerts by the biggest country music acts during the genre's golden age. For a time it was also the stage for the Grand Ole Opry radio show.

There was no back stage at the Ryman—performers often had to wait in the halls to perform and changed in cramped bathrooms. While the lack of dressing rooms was a source of much misery for many performers, the Ryman was a place where music simply sounded good. The acoustics of the Ryman Auditorium have been heralded as among the best in the world.

The Ryman and Hatch Show Print have always had a close relationship (for a long time Hatch was located directly behind the Ryman). Hatch's Ryman posters continue to be highly collectible today.

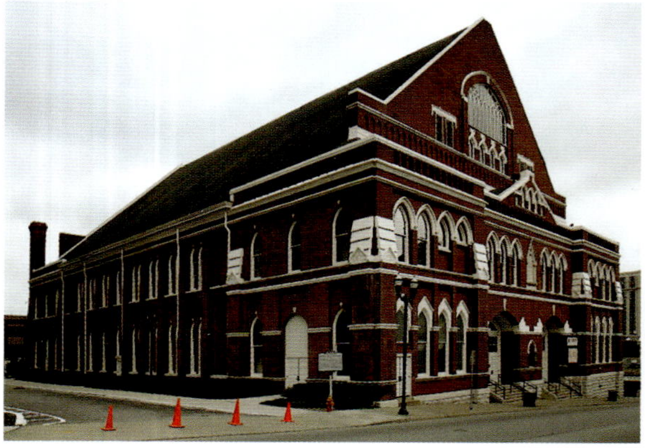

CBGB

CBGB (which stands for country, bluegrass and blues) was a music club opened by Hilly Kristal in the East Village in 1973. Previously a biker bar, CBGB soon became a well-known venue for new wave and punk rock acts including Talking Heads, Patti Smith Group, Blondie, and, of course, the Ramones. During the 1980s the venue became known for its hardcore punk shows, a reputation that continued until the venue finally closed its doors in 2006 after a long, drawn-out dispute over allegedly unpaid rent.

CBGB was well loved in the punk community and many of the shows performed there are the stuff of legend. The art surrounding CBGB is impressive and offers fantastic examples of punk, hardcore, post punk, and metal show posters. The posters from CBGB showcase some of the biggest punk rock acts in history and are sought-after collectibles.

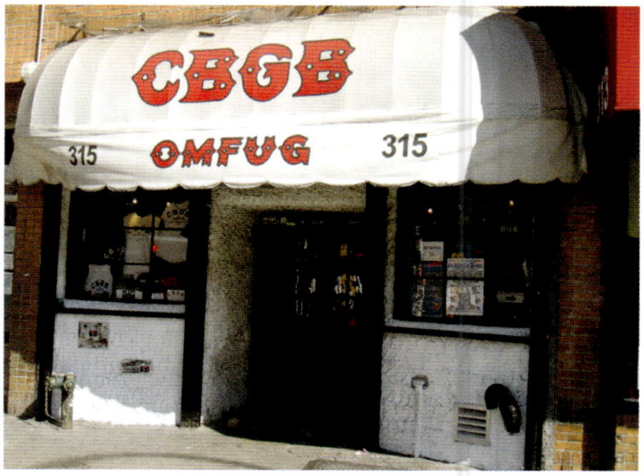

HATCH SHOW PRINT

One of the most well-known printers is Hatch Show Print of Nashville, TN. Started in 1879 by Charles and Herbert Hatch, sons of Wisconsin printer William T. Hatch who taught them the family business, the business was originally named CR and HH Hatch. Their first print job was a handbill announcing a speaking appearance by Reverend Henry Ward Beecher, the brother of author Harriet Beecher Stowe. From there Hatch began a legacy that is woven into Southern culture and the history of American entertainment.

Eventually changing its name to Hatch Show Print so as to not be confused as a hatchery, Hatch created posters for all kinds of acts in show business from vaudeville acts to circuses to carnivals to minstrels. During the 1920s Charles's son Will T. Hatch took over the business and ushered in a golden age for the printer by working with countless country music performers.

Legendary venues like the Grand Ole Opry and the Ryman Auditorium filled their seats due to promotional posters from Hatch Show Print. The printer went on to create posters for other musical acts and newer forms of entertainment including jazz and blues. It wasn't until rock 'n' roll appeared in the '50s that Hatch's business began to struggle. The shop went through three name changes and five ownership transitions until the '80s when Paul Ritscher got the shop in good running order before appointing Master Printer Jim Sherraden to take over. Sherraden began restriking old original Hatch prints, fostering new interest in the print shop and earning new customers. Today Hatch remains a bustling print shop, printing posters and limited edition merchandise, not only for fans of classic country music, but also the hottest bands across all kinds of genres. Hatch Show Print designs and prints approximately 600 posters per year and houses a museum that showcases their historical posters. Hatch also has a dedicated classroom and workshop space for teaching visitors and clients through hands-on printing.

2 DESIGN TOOLS & APPROACHES

There are an unlimited number of tools people have used over the years to create imagery and type for designs and for gig posters. Many of these methods have been used for many years. Designers use different tools and techniques to achieve different looks and combine them in various ways for even more looks. Some techniques that have been popular in gig poster design are stencil cutting, use of traditional fine-art tools, hand lettering, and even the use of old machines to purposefully degrade image quality.

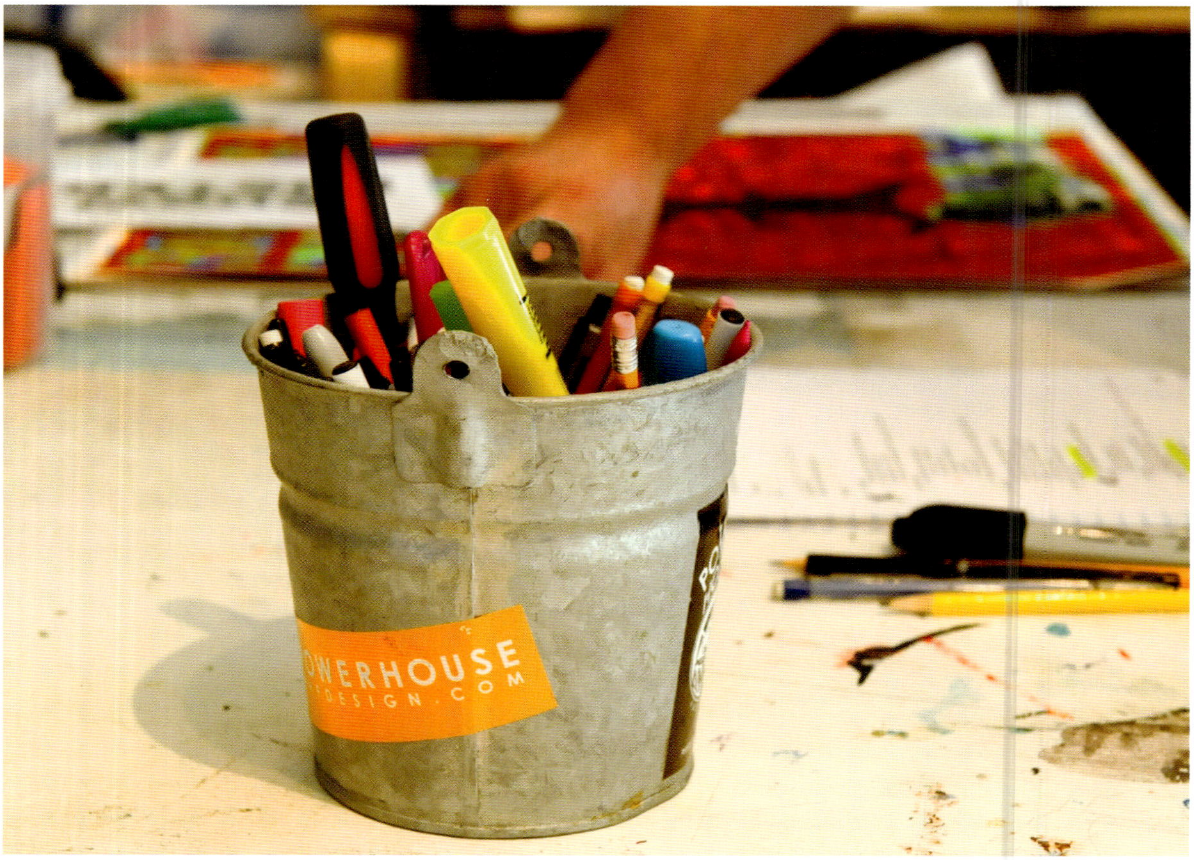

SIGN PAINTING

Sign painters are considered the first graphic designers because of their need to display a message around a service or product that caught people's attention as well as symbolized the differentiation of a brand (service or product). Originally known as the art of painting on buildings and signs, sign painting grew out of the need to communicate services, products, and events. During the 1970s and '80s, sign painting began to slowly be replaced by new advances in printing: digital layout machines, vinyl printers, and die cutters. It saw resurgence as people began to look at hand lettering and typographic illustration to add a human touch to advertisements. Sign painting allowed businesses a chance to create "one-off" typography and iconography that carried an air of authenticity. And now, sign painting is still used contemporarily because of its unique look and its tie to the idea of Americana as well as its industrious nature (hand done, time spent, and a human value). A hand-painted sign shows a human quality—it gives the reader a sense of someone telling you something important one on one. And that is something a machine mass-producing a sterile message can never do. Hand lettering and hand-done type styles are born out of sign painting.

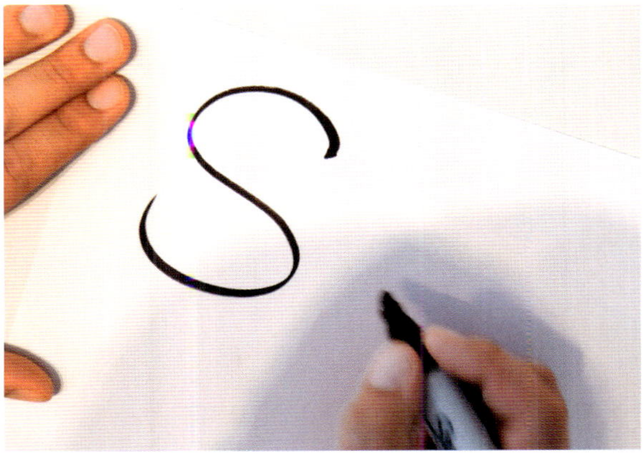

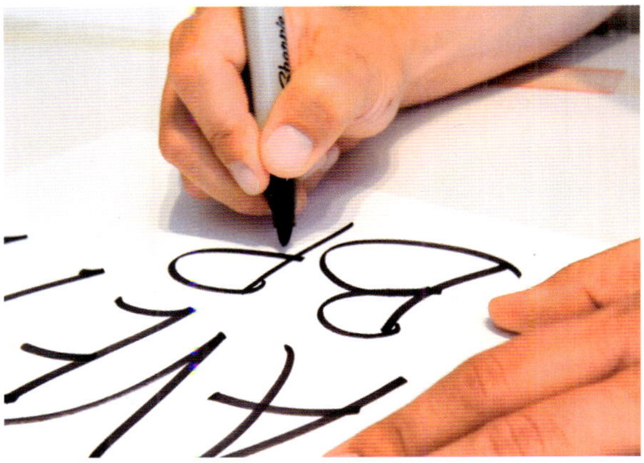

Thick marker/chisel tip conveys a sign-painting type of quality.

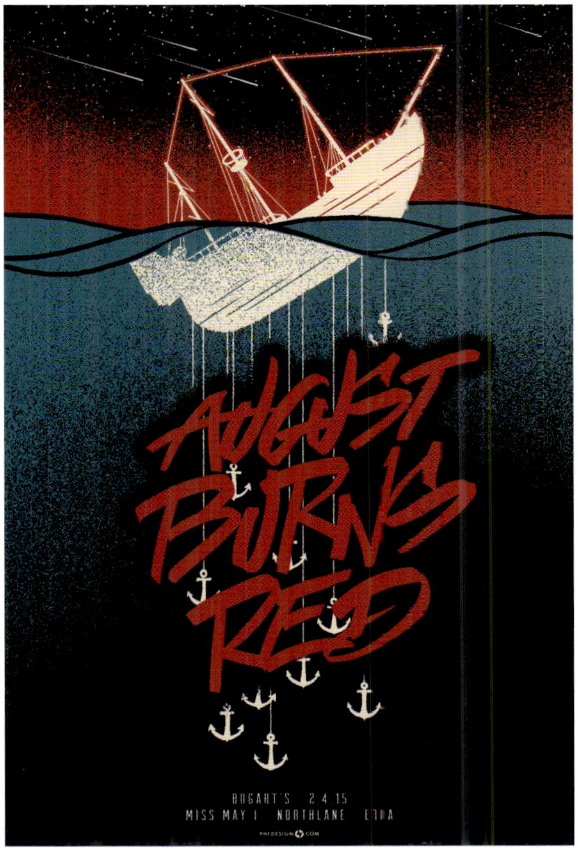

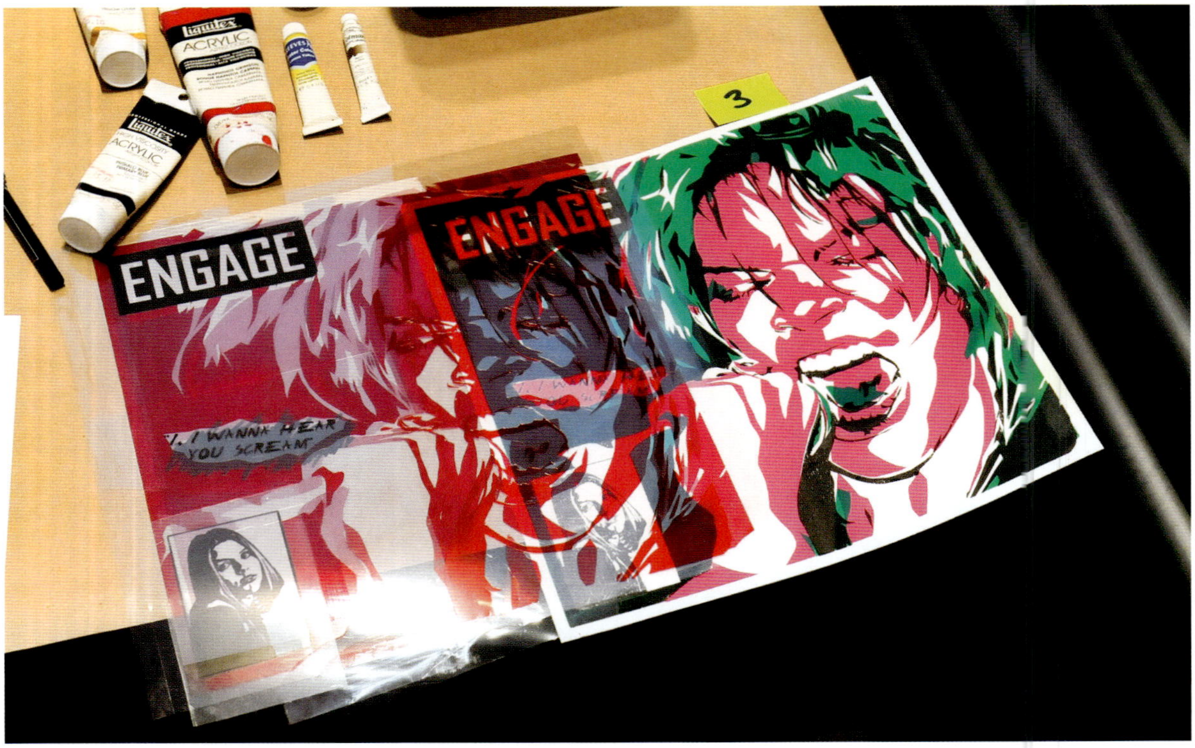

Rubylith creates a smooth, "vector" line that looks as if it were painted or cut vinyl.

RUBYLITH

This mask-making technique was born out of necessity before digital printers were invented (in printmaking). Rubylith, a brand of masking film invented by the Ulano Corporation, helped artists and book makers create multiple copies of a work quickly from a mold that wasn't constrained to pre-existing imagery and type that could be laid out with letterpress. It was used to create screens in screenprinting or plates for offset lithography. Using Rubylith you could create large areas of color in printmaking before you could digitally output a film.

Rubylith allows you to draw layers of shadowing, but with a knife versus a pencil, which gives you free flow decision-making. To create an image, layers of the masking film are built upon one another and a screen is shot for each. Layers of colors are trimmed away to create an image. On the first layer you cut away all but the lightest lights and white. Depending on the number of colors, multiple layers are built on top, each cutting away the next level of "light color." The last layer will be the darkest darks or black in the image. Ultimately, the technique creates a smooth, "vector" line that looks as if it were painted or cut vinyl.

Rubylith is still used today to create low-color-number designs that still show form shading and depth. It is commonly used in portraiture or to show a posterized version of a person, place, or thing (a good example of this is the work of Shepard Fairey). Rubylith is still made by Ulano as a "masking film" but is less used as a print process tool. Today it is used more as an illustration tool that limits you to just a few layers of depth. Similar tools are Amberlith (a yellow-colored masking film), which has been discontinued by Ulano. Amberlith blocks less light than Rubylith, but still blocks much of the UV spectrum.

In terms of overall visual style, Rubylith is similar to the stencil cut. However, Rubylith produces a perfectly printed line where stencil cutting depends on the quality of the way it is applied—spray-painted, stamped—and the distance from stencil to substrate.

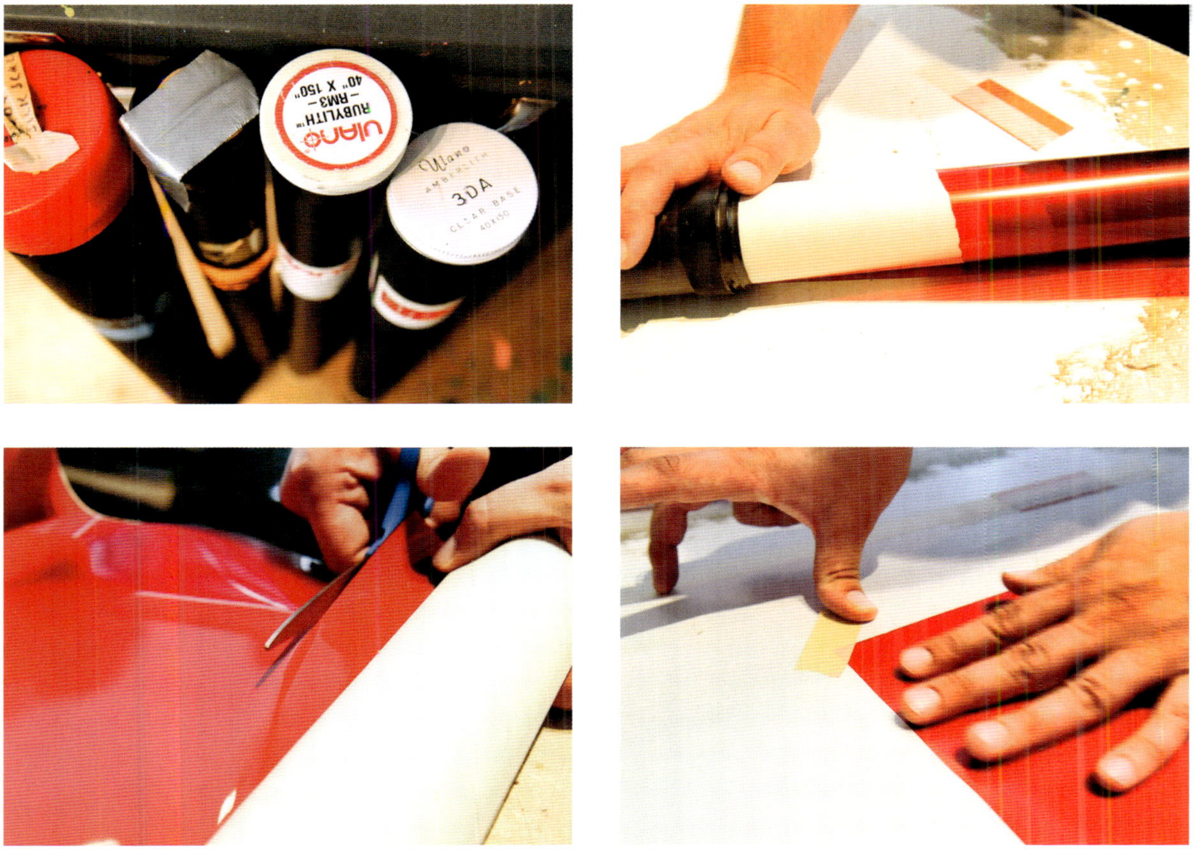

Remove Rubylith from tube, cut the amount you need, and position it over your black-and-white image.

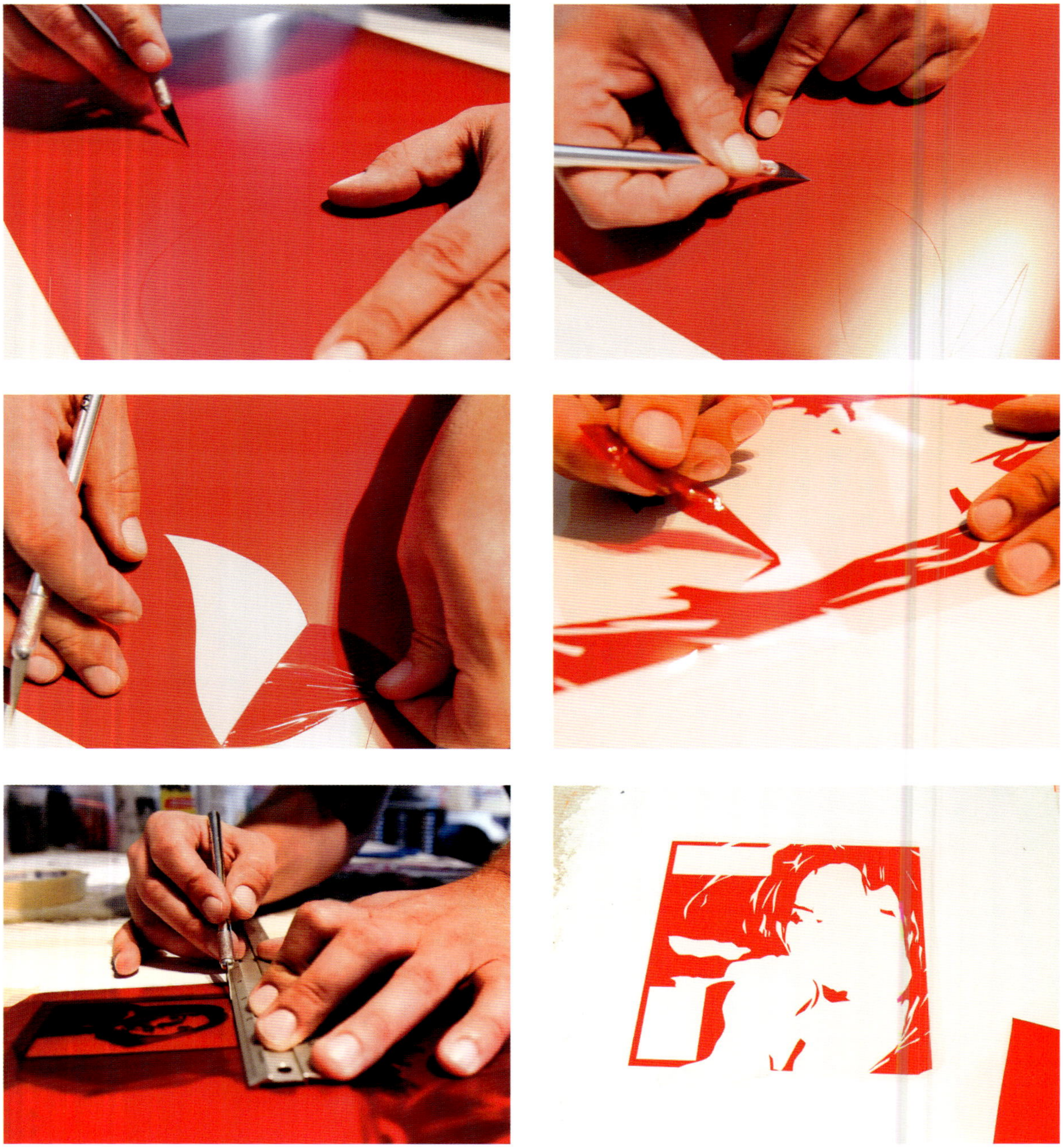

Layers of film are trimmed away to create an image.

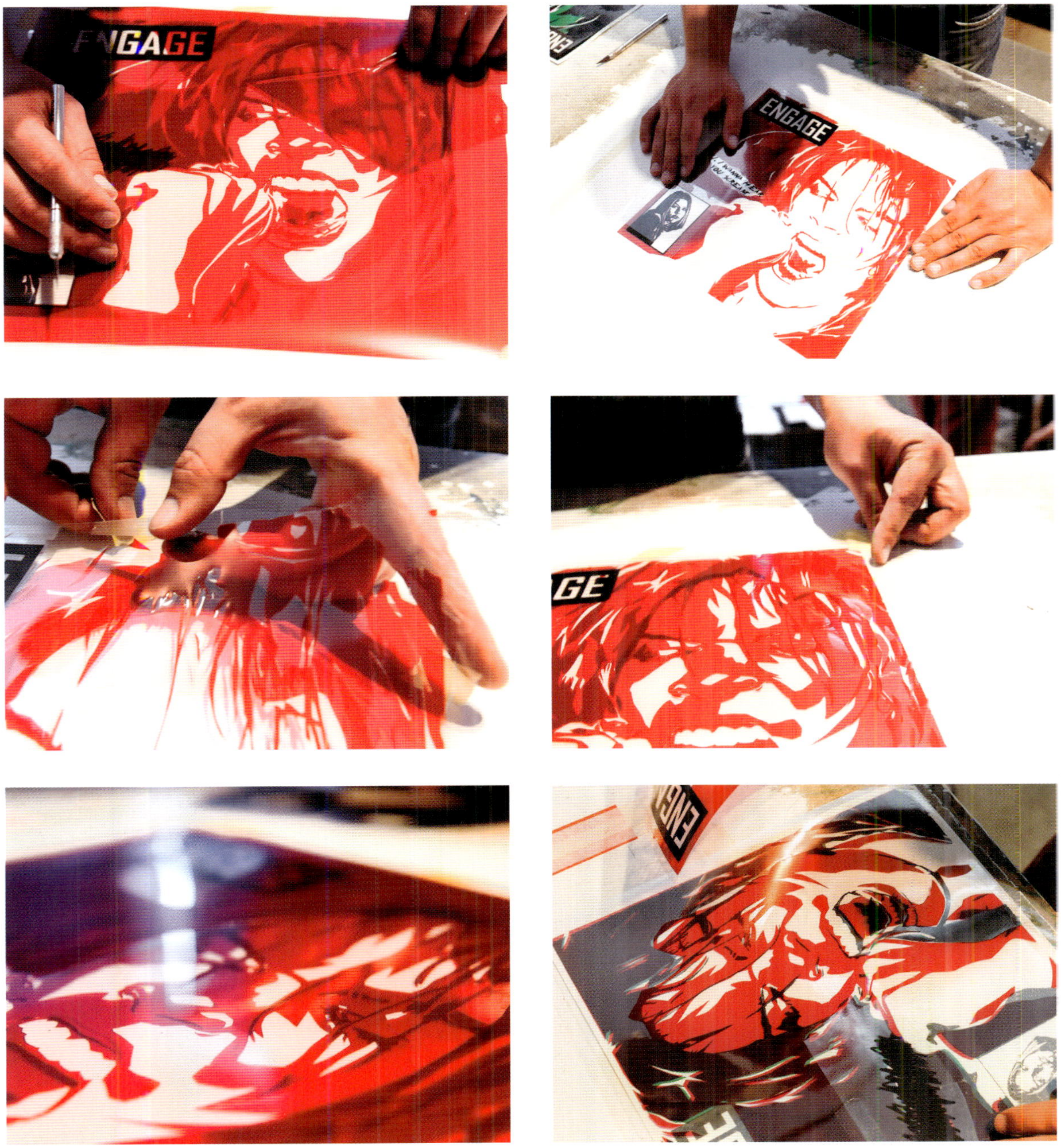

Layers of the masking film are built upon one another and a screen is shot for each.

STENCIL CUT & CONSTRUCTION PAPER CUT

The process of stencil cutting goes all the way back to cave-man drawings and hasn't changed too much to this day. The process involves rubbing pigment, ink, paint, charcoal, etc. through a mask to produce an image. Stencils were used before screenprinting was invented as a means of mass-producing books. And for decades graffiti artists have used stencils to quickly and stealthily create works of street art, often displaying multiples of the same image, message, or tag in major metropolitan areas. Stencils are used contemporarily to show quick design decision-making, DIY quality, and a handmade aesthetic.

The construction paper cut is a similar method. The main difference between the two is that stencil cutting is the first step in a masking and application process and construction paper cut is the positive or reversed version. Instead of cutting away the positive and painting, printing, or drawing through the mask, construction paper cut uses the positive image or paper as the image itself. Construction paper cut refers to the rudimentary tool (construction paper) and process (like a child could do) that creates a particular look that is quickly made, which is often made with whatever is available.

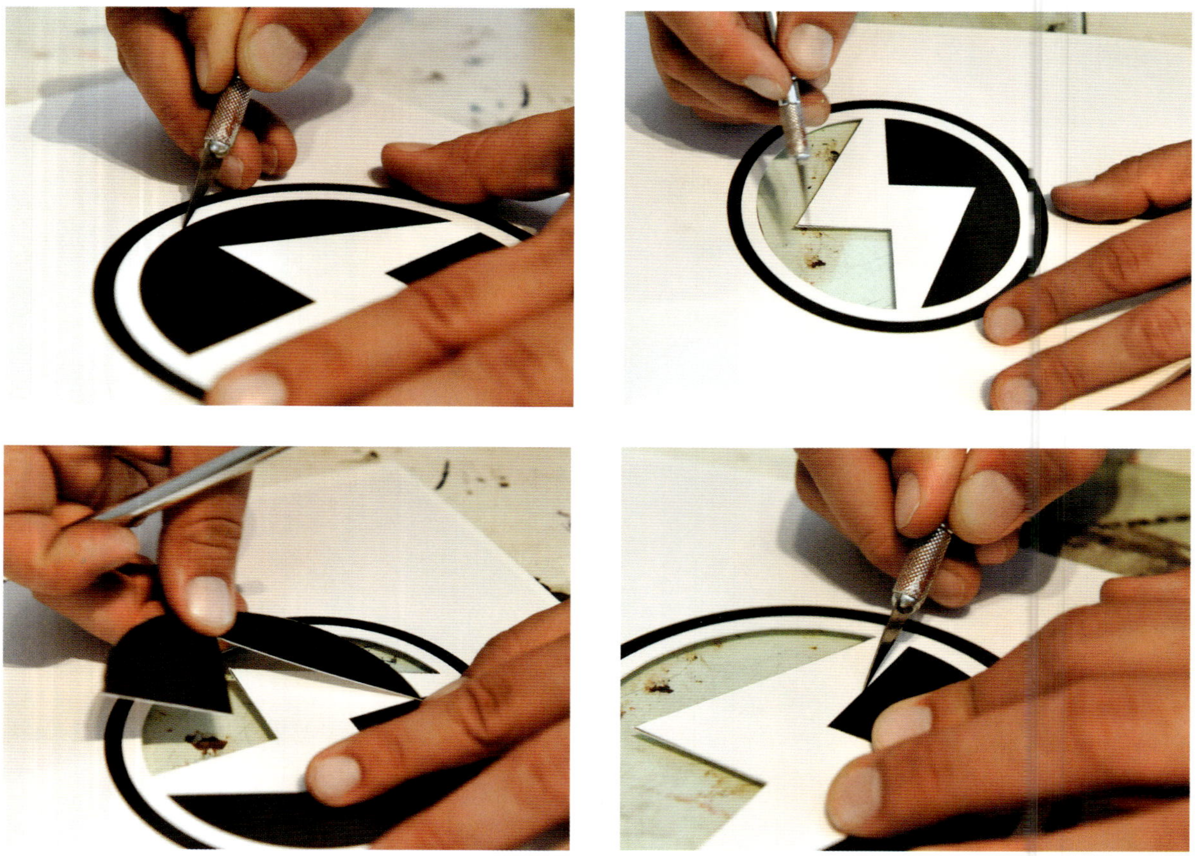

Create a stencil by cutting away the positive space in your image.

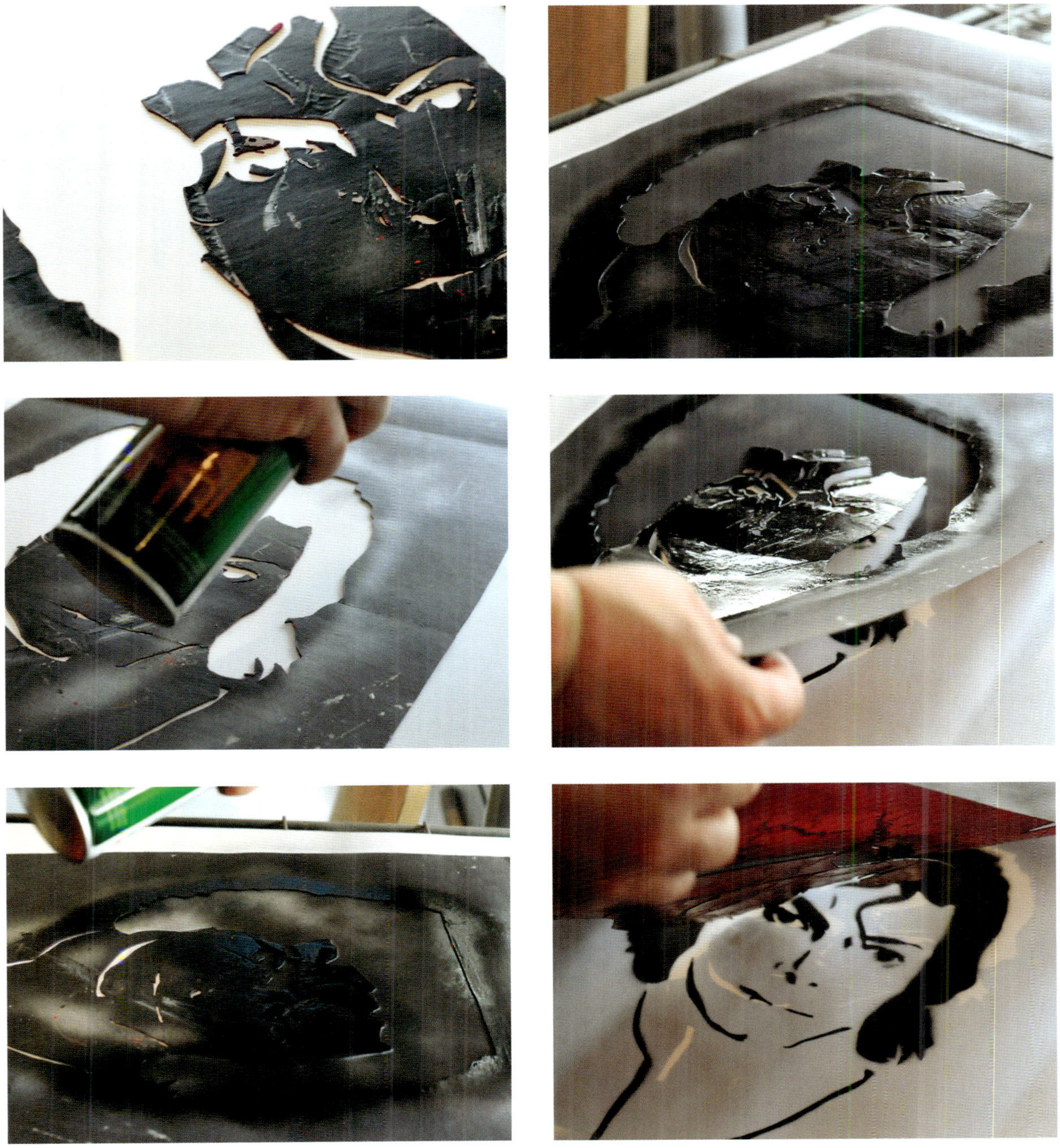

This series of photos shows the process of using a stencil and spray paint to quickly create an image.

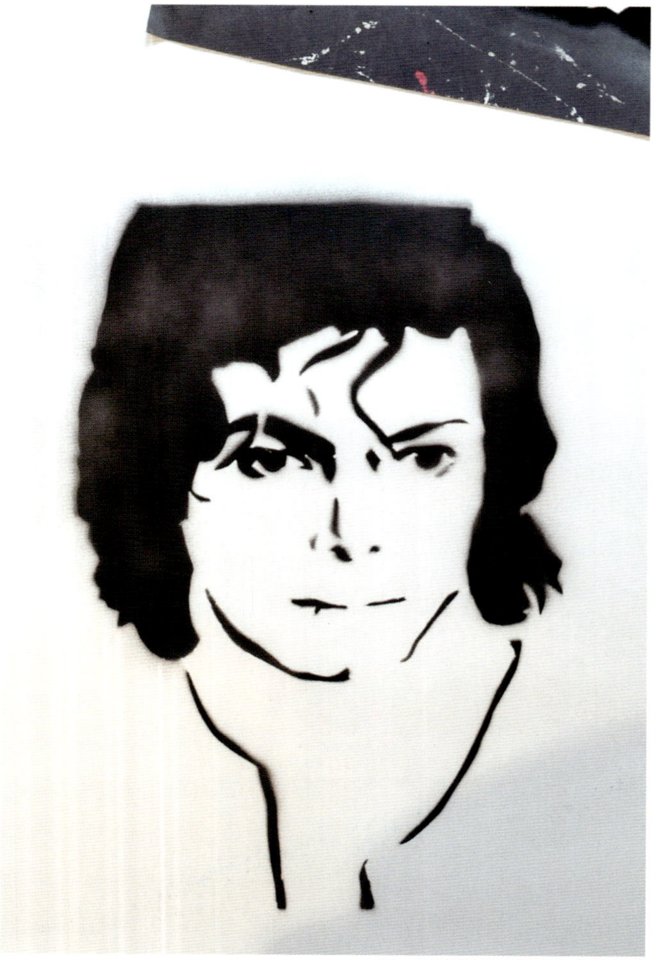

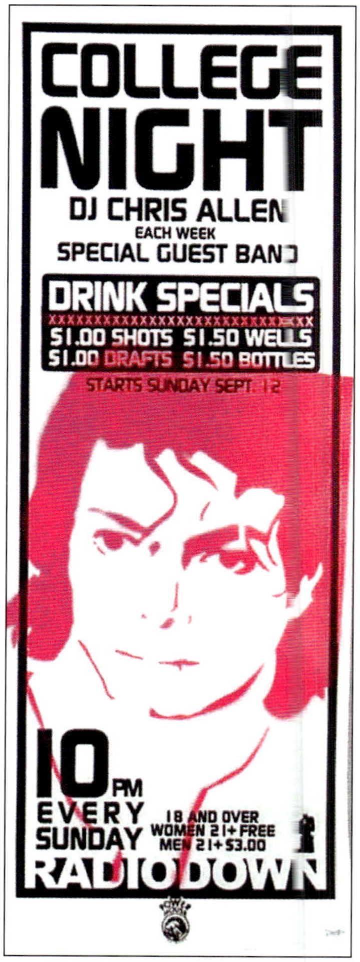
COLLEGE
NIGHT
DJ CHRIS ALLEN
EACH WEEK
SPECIAL GUEST BAND
DRINK SPECIALS
$1.00 SHOTS $1.50 WELLS
$1.00 DRAFTS $1.50 BOTTLES
STARTS SUNDAY SEPT. 12
10PM
EVERY
SUNDAY
18 AND OVER
WOMEN 21+ FREE
MEN 21+ $3.00
RADIODOWN

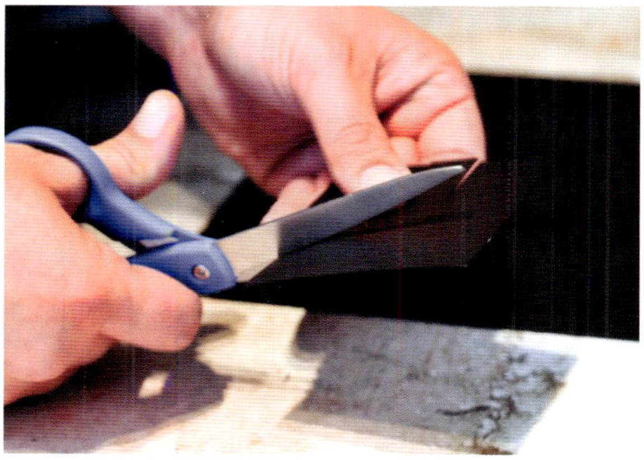

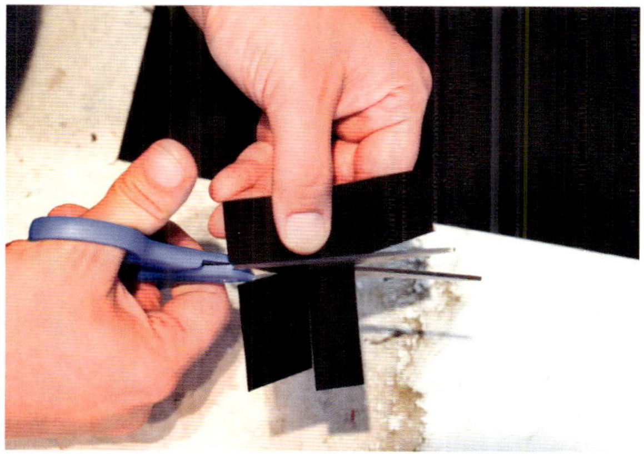

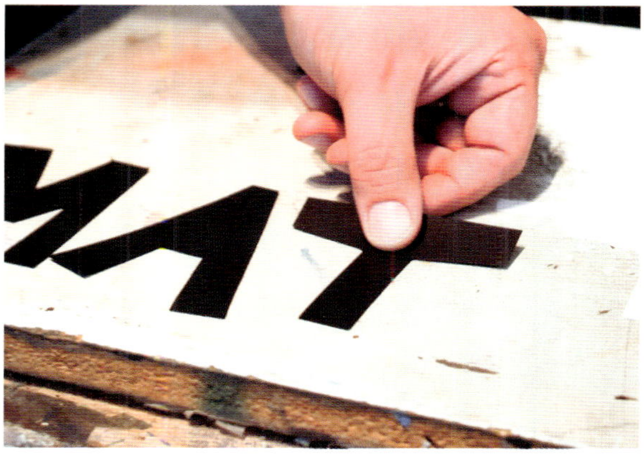

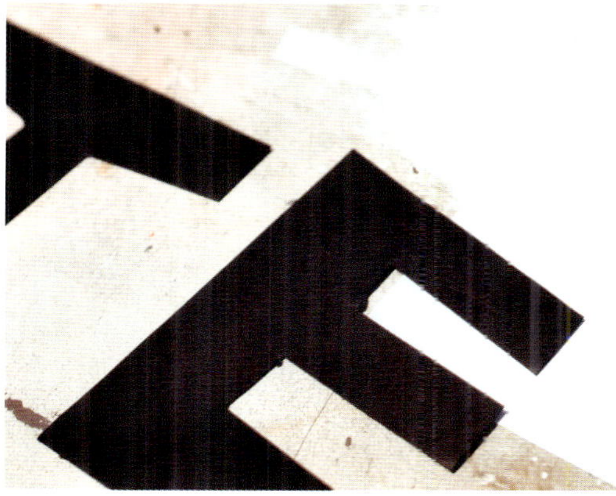

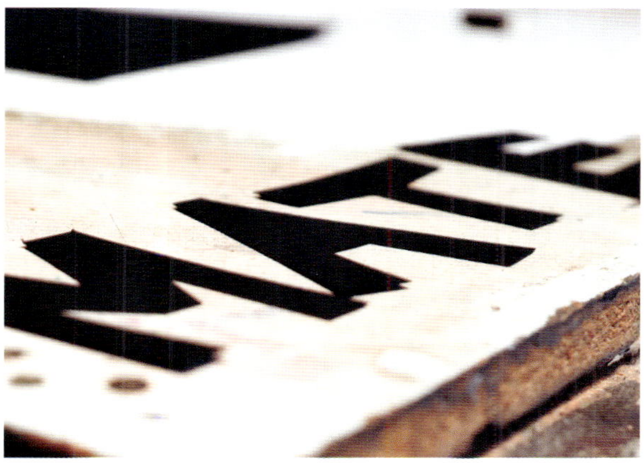

Construction paper cut uses the positive image or paper as the image itself.

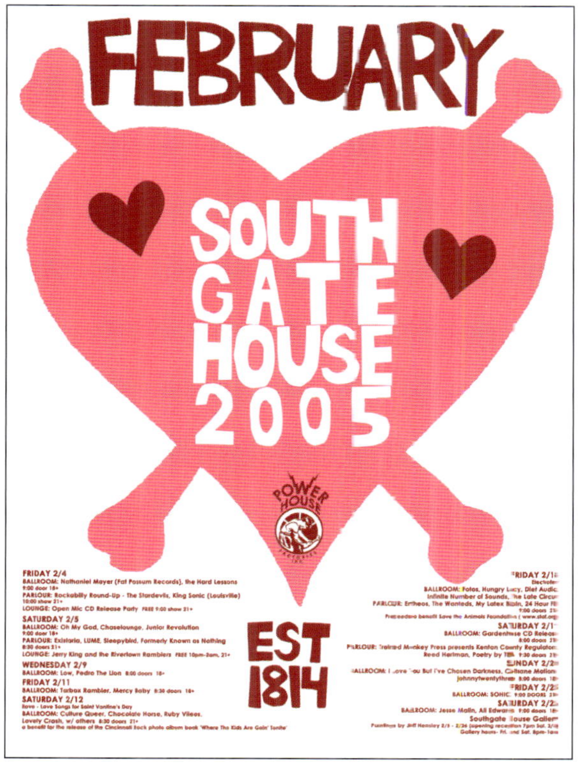

XEROX

Xerox machines or filters in Photoshop that emulate an old Xerox machine's output allow designers to show a low quality that can actually resonate more with their consumers than a professional, clean design and output. This type of production value shows the grit and handmade DIY quality that is associated with punk rock music and the tools that were available in the 1970s and 1980s.

Xerox machines were originally used in design and marketing because of their ability to do super cheap reproductions of anything and everything. Eventually this look became desirable as a design technique to show DIY, low-rent reproduction. The look communicated that an idea or event wasn't a "paid for" or corporately funded effort. This "low-rent" aesthetic is used to showcase a purposefully rudimentary level of effort, which equates to a legitimately honest event. This look is often used by the punk community because of its low cost and communication of legitimacy. Typically even when there is money to promote an event, this design style and low-quality aesthetic is still used because it has come to symbolize the punk community and their objection to large marketing budgets to promote their events. Punk art still uses these tools almost exclusively when creating fliers, pamphlets, posters, albums, and other designs. Use of an old Xerox machine (the older the better) produces degradation and a grittiness that is associated with punk music and the punk lifestyle. Collage and ransom note lettering are highly leveraged in this technique, again, to symbolize the rugged, lawless, and insubordinate qualities of punk.

The overall look of this Xerox approach is similar to posterization except the machine makes the decision versus cutting with the human hand.

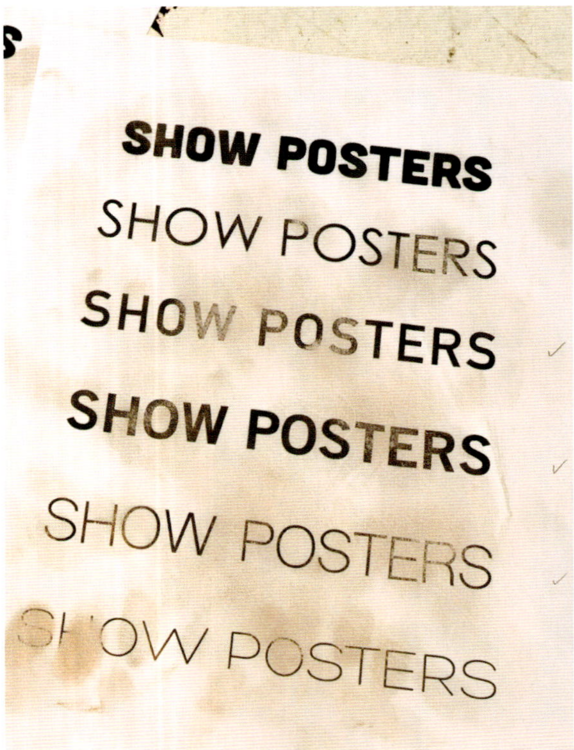

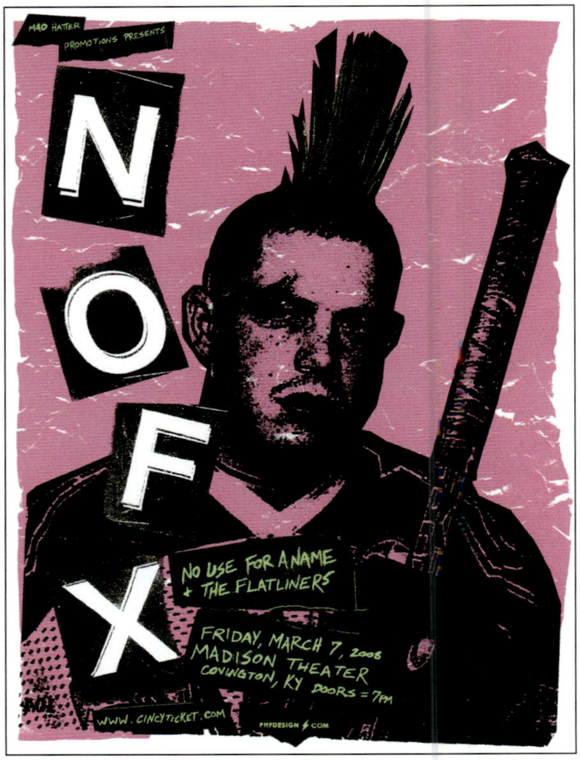

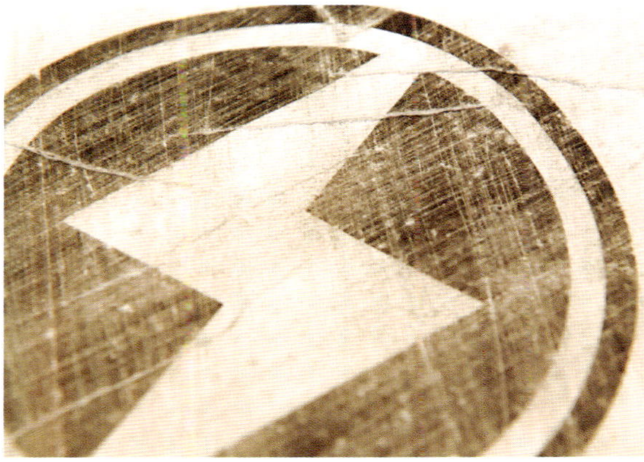

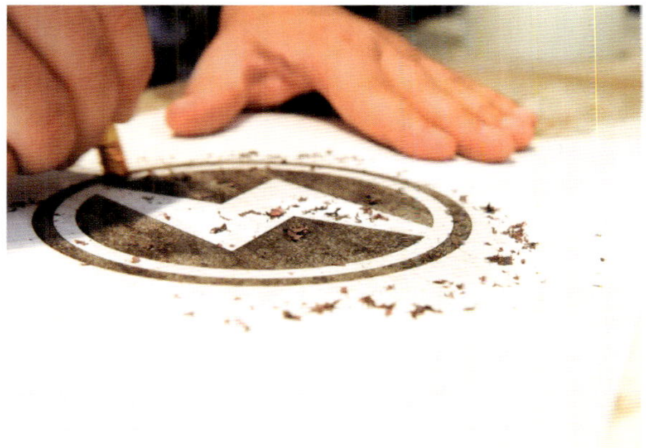

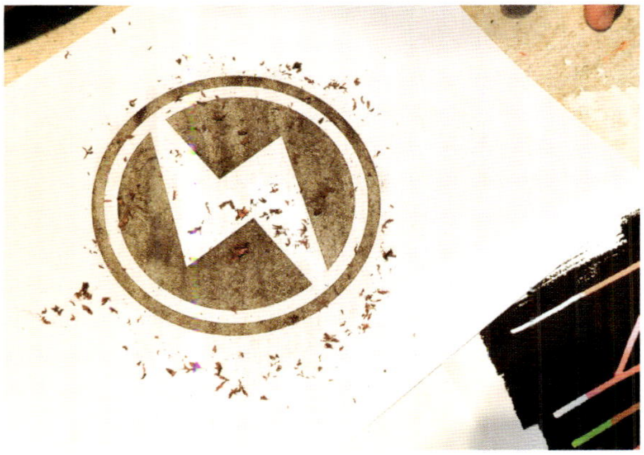

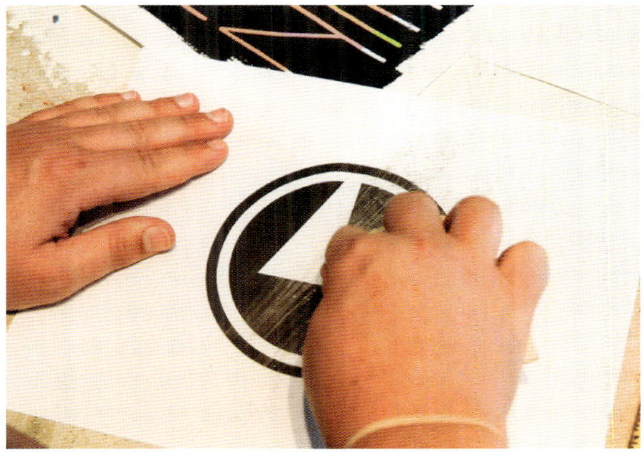

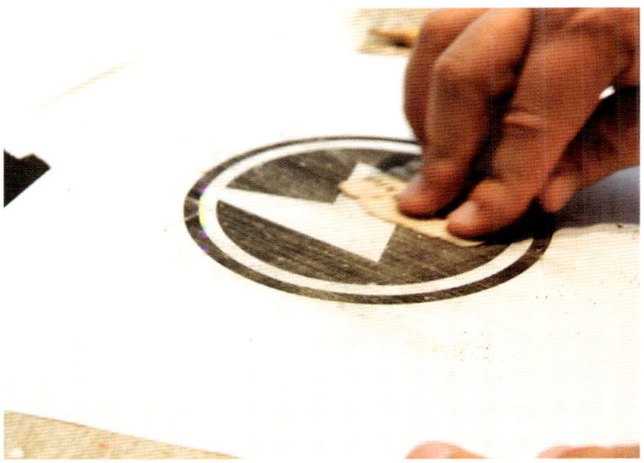

It's possible to mimic the degradation you get with a Xerox machine by hand. Hand-done degradation can be achieved by roughing up the the image or by erasing some of the image from the paper surface and then scanning.

FINE ART

This category broadly refers to the use of tools commonly found in the fine-art world to create gig posters. These are items you would find in an art supply store including many different types of brushes, pencils, pens, charcoal, watercolor, Conté crayon, ink, etc. Each tool allows the poster artist to create a piece in a specific classic style of art that can then be scanned and manipulated in Photoshop to output a film. Sometimes multiple fine-art techniques/approaches are used together—like collaging—for their combined beauty or to help visualize a particular concept.

Layers are created separately and are typically done with a black medium on a white substrate, which makes it easier to scan. The layers are created separately so that screenprinting inks can be laid down one by one to create the same colors and overlay effects that the fine-art medium would. Printed solid, opaque colors emulate the look of oil paint or charcoal, and translucent, light colors emulate the cloudiness and color-mixing qualities of watercolor painting.

Specific drawing styles fit into this category as well, regardless of what tool was used. Examples include cross-hatching, scratchboard, and pen and ink technical drawing.

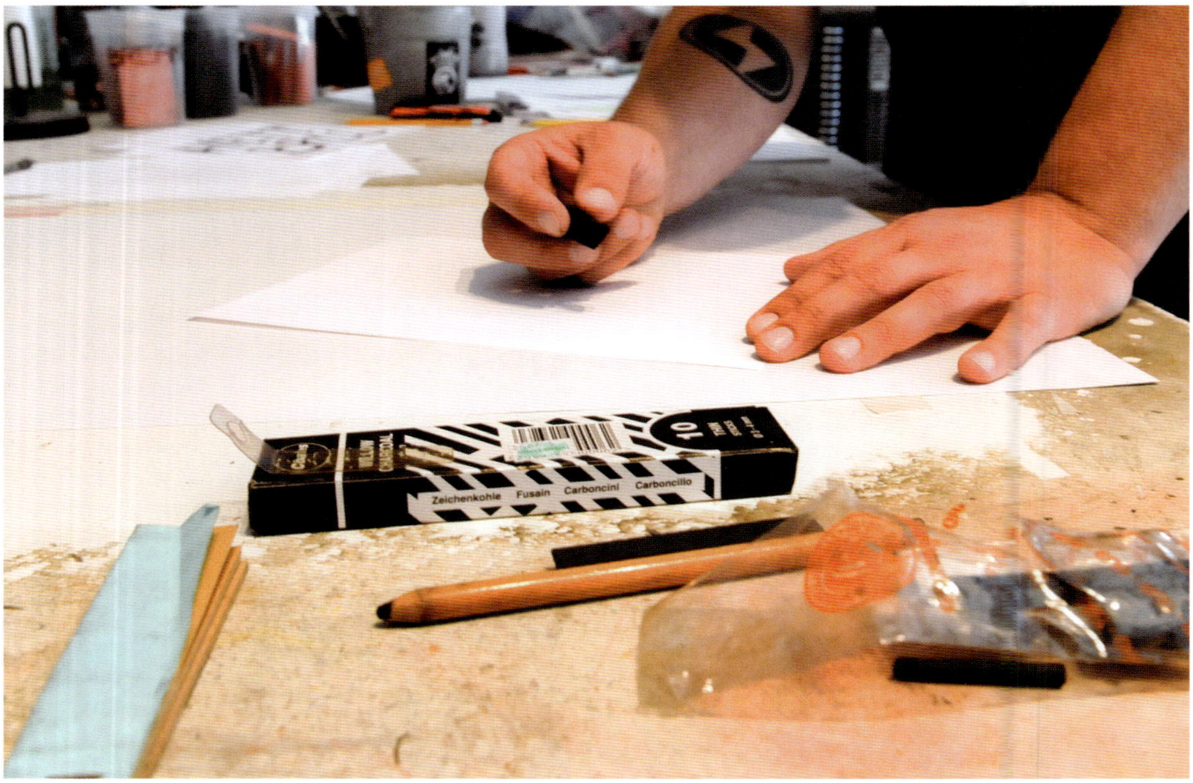

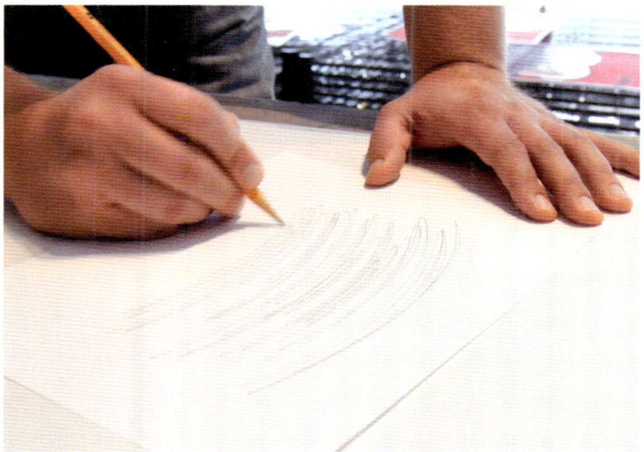

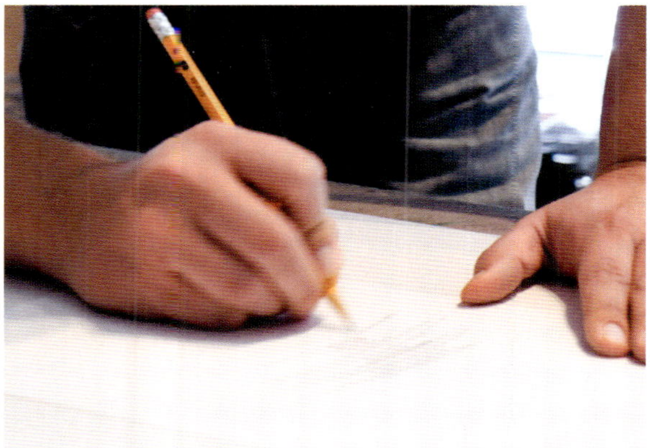

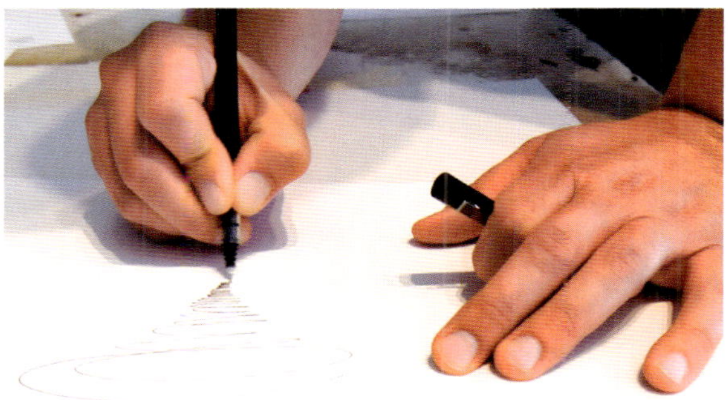

Showing motion

EXAMPLES OF PEN AND PENCIL TECHNIQUES

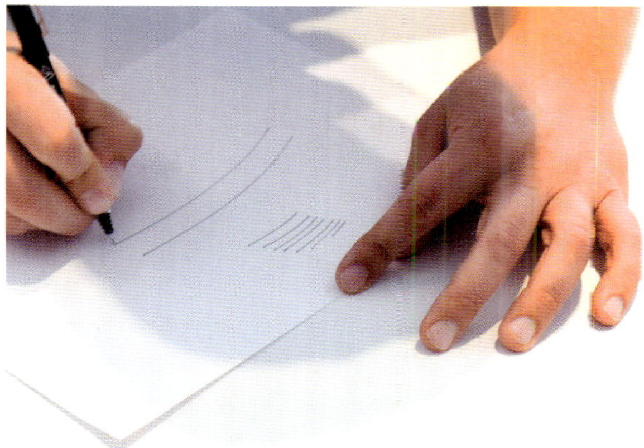

Thin line weight from pen

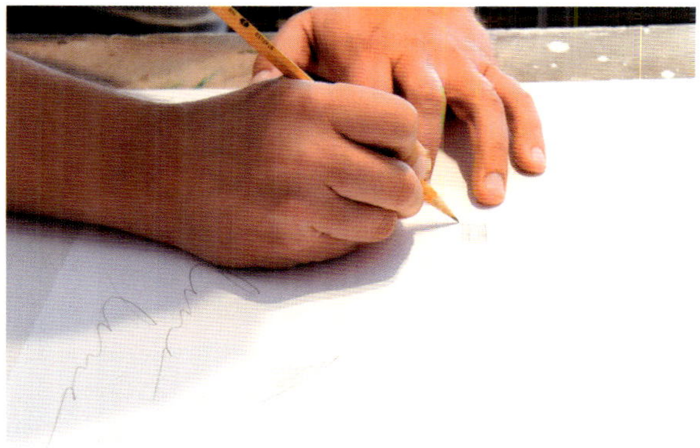

Different pencils for different line weights

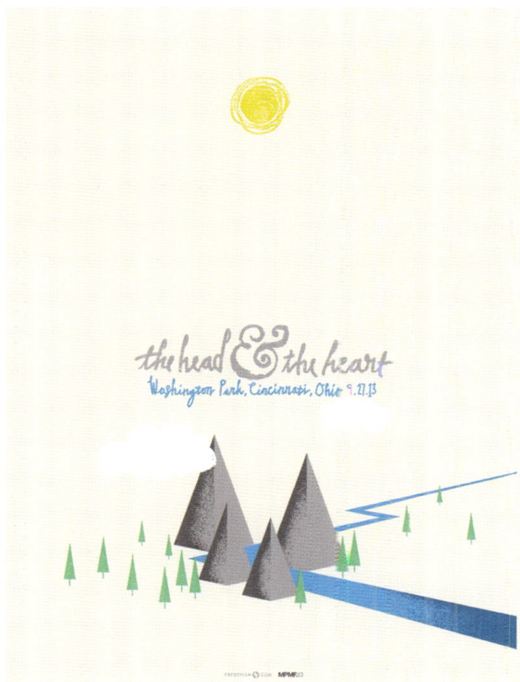

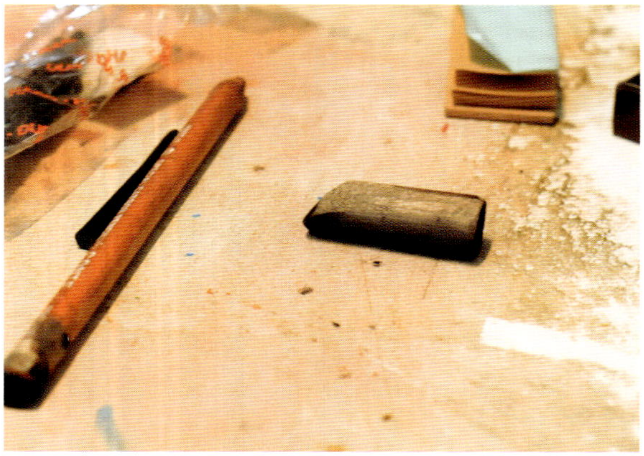

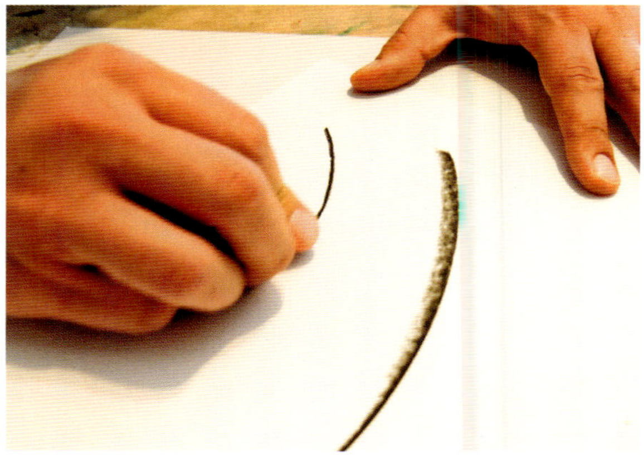

Tools of the trade

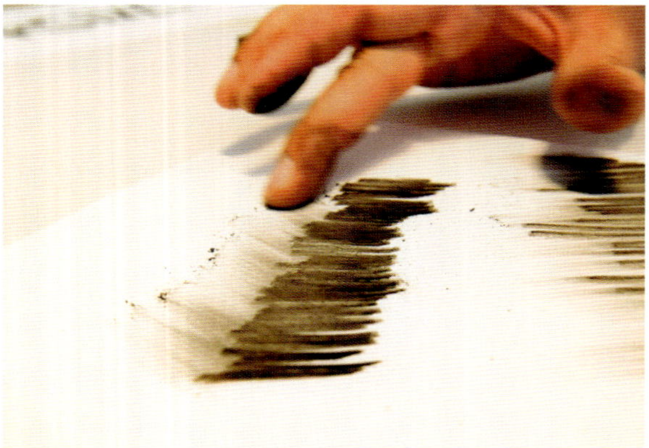

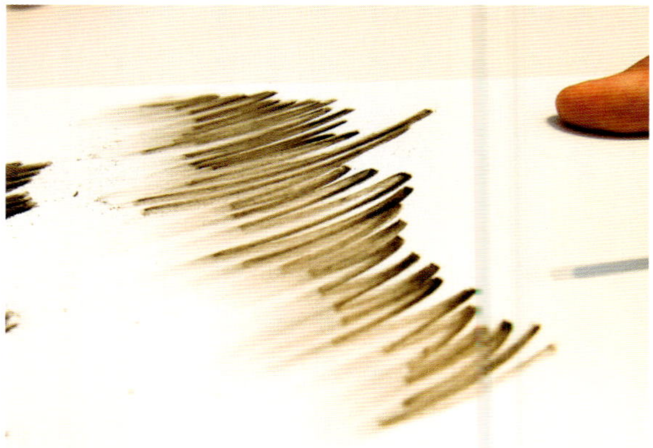

Create fading and gradients by smearing the charcoal with your finger.

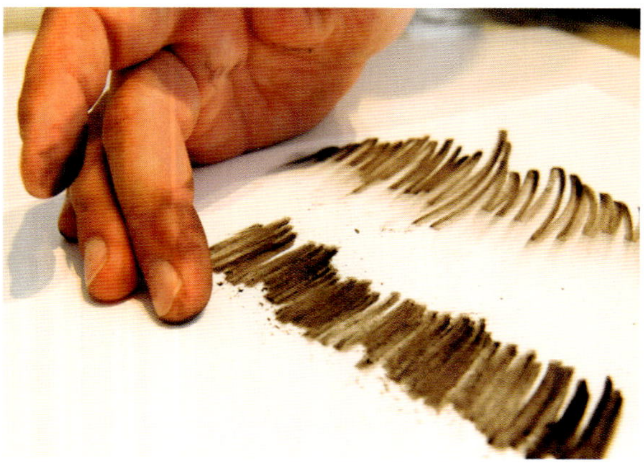

Use the charcoal shake for dirt or noise.

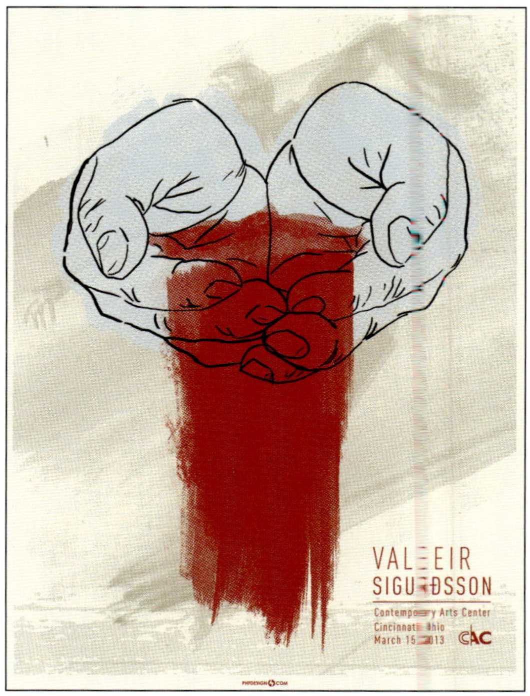

EXAMPLES OF WORKING WITH CHARCOAL

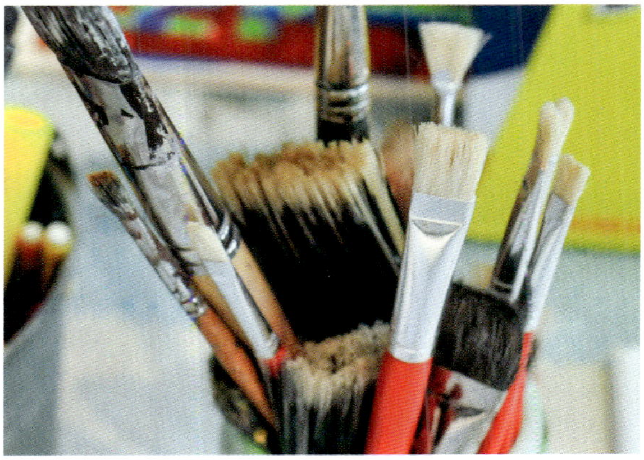

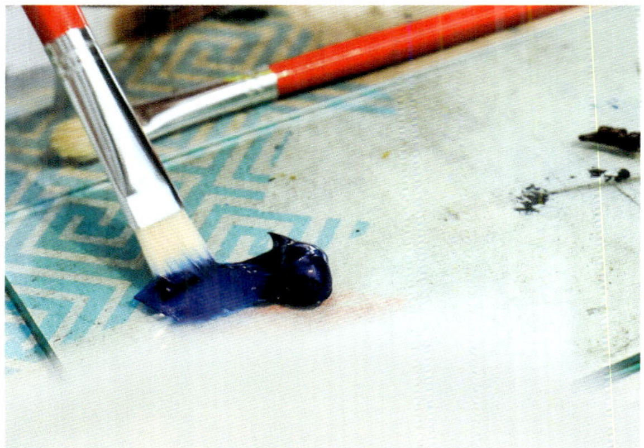

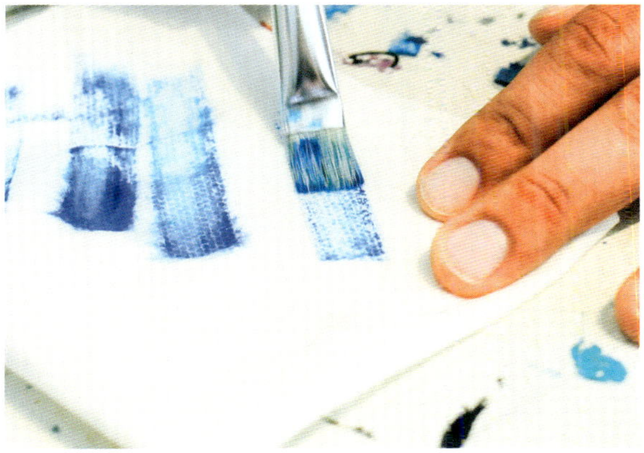

Dry brushing technique

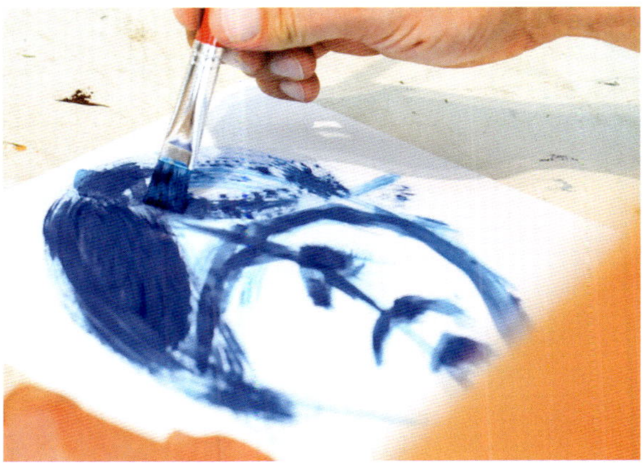

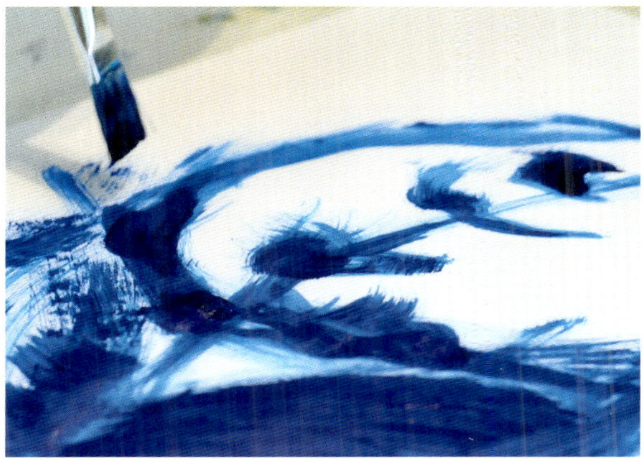

A VARIETY OF WATERCOLOR BRUSH TECHNIQUES

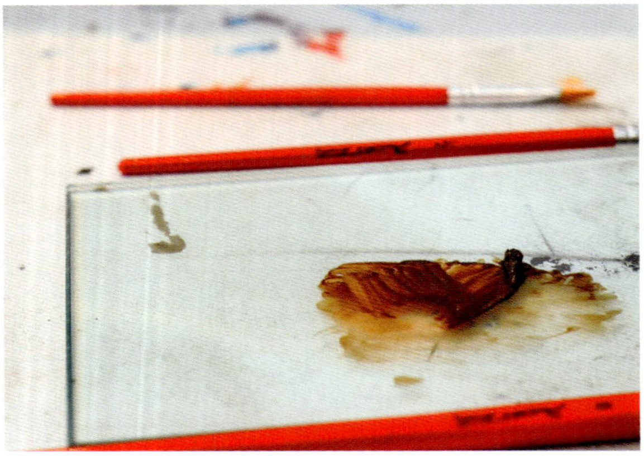

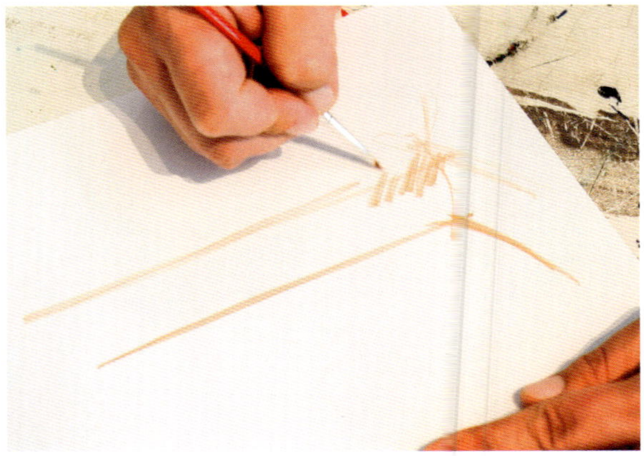

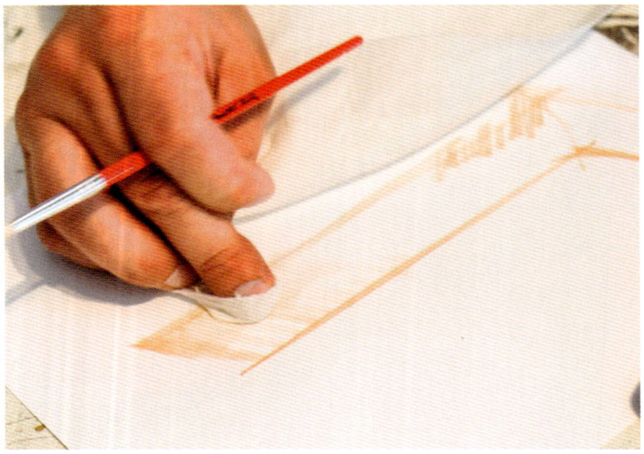

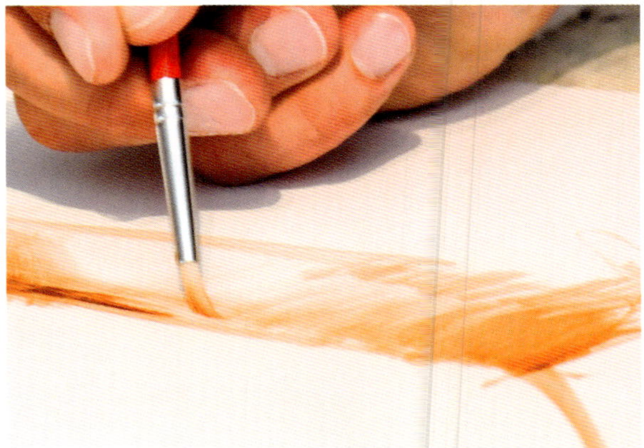

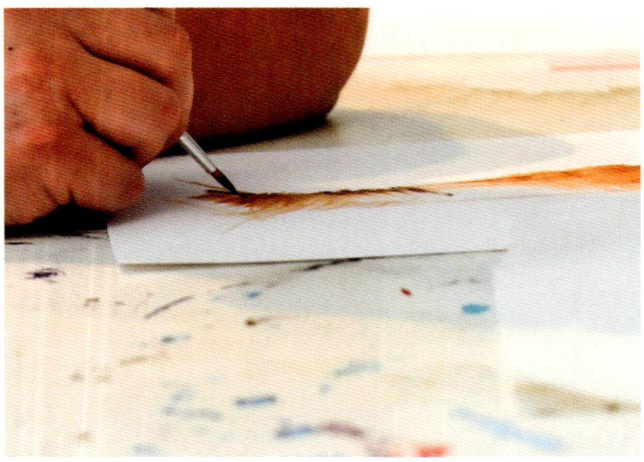

Layer up watercolor to show more detail though layers of tone.

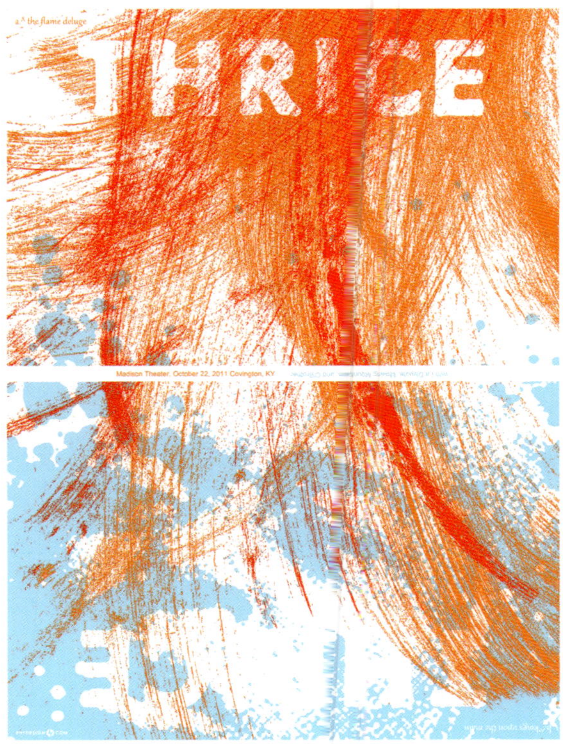

HAND LETTERING

Hand lettering, by definition, is the art of drawing letters. The history of hand lettering is extensive because of people's need to communicate messages before printing was created. Hand lettering's origins lie with calligraphy in the Middle East and Asia and also the work of royal scribes of the Middle Ages in Europe. With the advent and evolution of printing, hand lettering was still used to show formality or professionalism because of its customized nature and the amount of time it required. A good example of this is hand calligraphy used in wedding invitations.

Today hand lettering is the specific combination of letterforms crafted for a single use and purpose. Inspired by sign painting, hand lettering encompasses a large range of approaches and many different styles from formal and fancy to rough and rugged. Calligraphy is often used to communicate a sense of formality or sophistication. Shaky handwritten lettering may be used to communicate a sense of urgency. Overdone scratch letters can indicate a punk style. Sign painting–style, thick letterforms offer a visual call to action and may be used to advertise a sale or big event. No matter the approach or style, hand lettering adds a human element to a poster design.

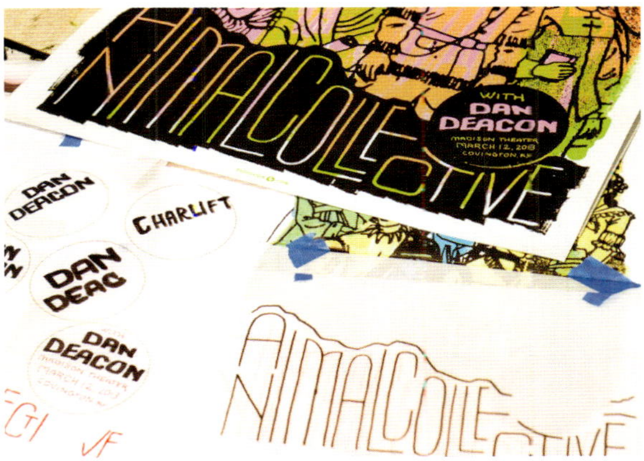

Initial sketch for a hand-lettered poster

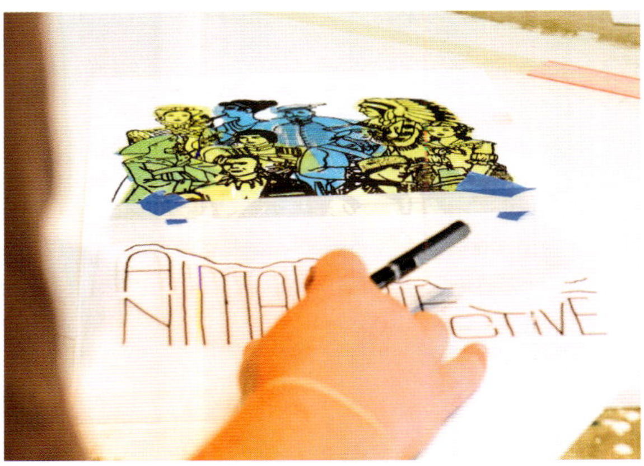
Tracing paper refinements

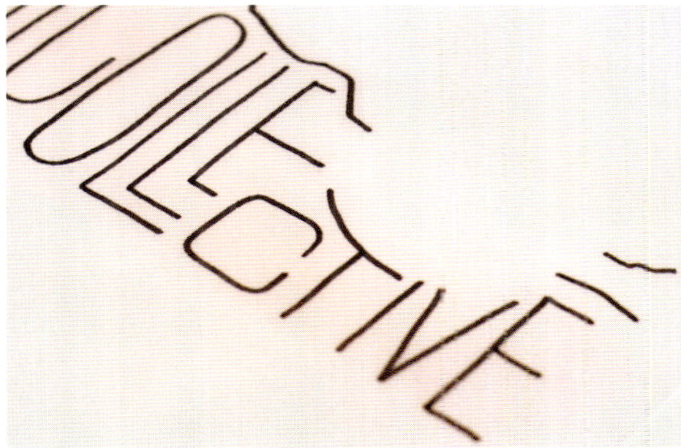
Final type illustration ready for scanning

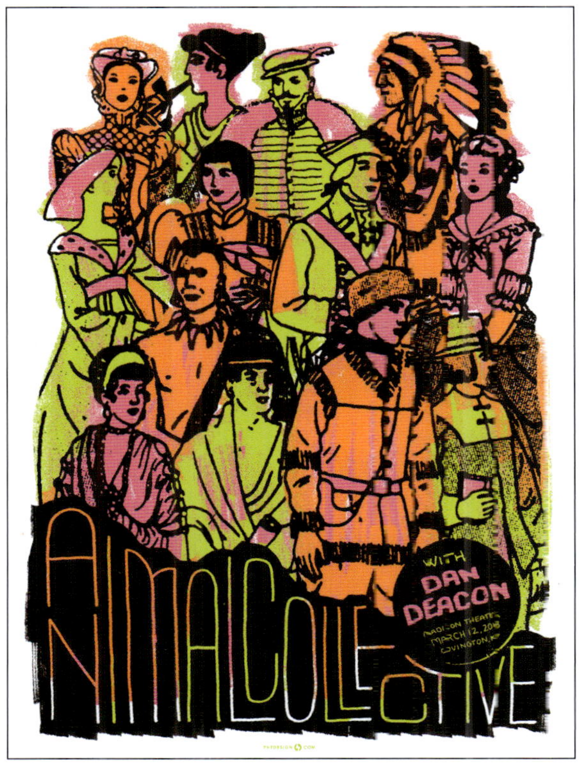

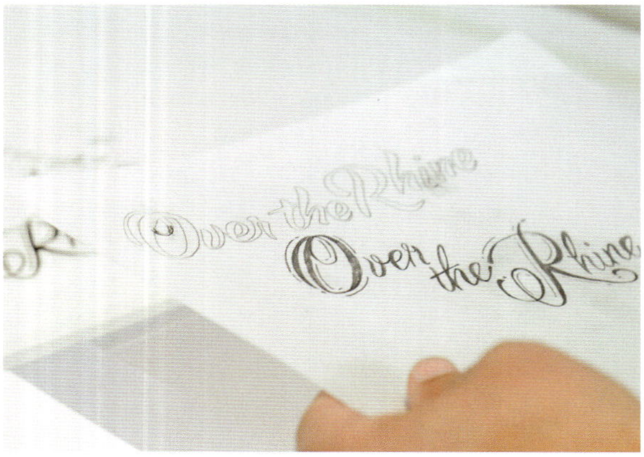

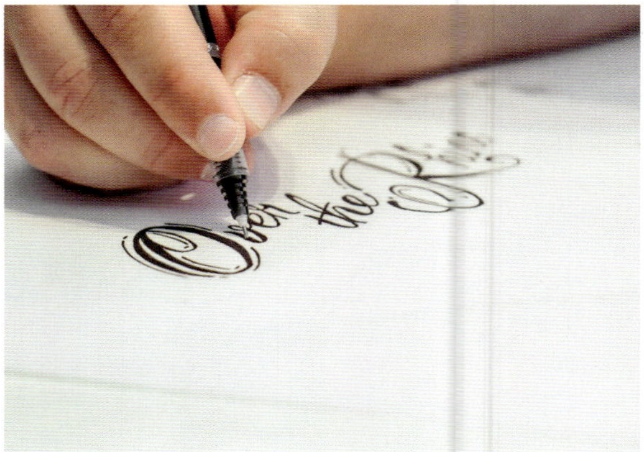

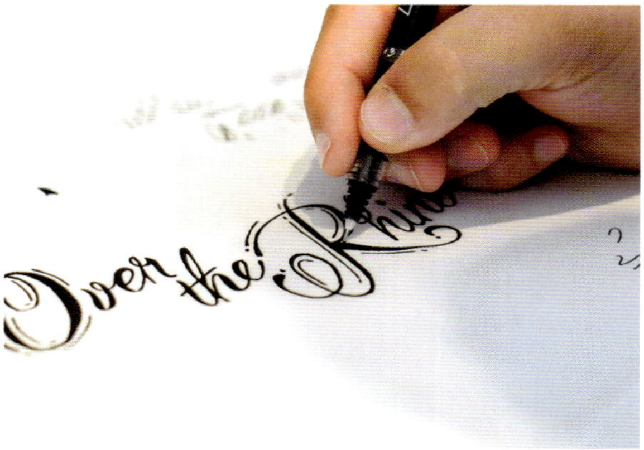

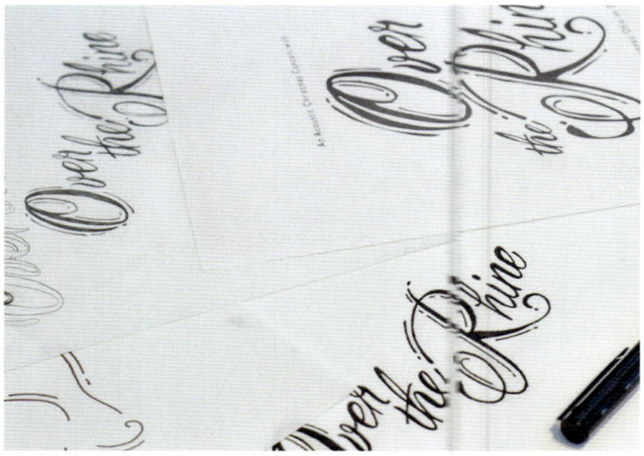

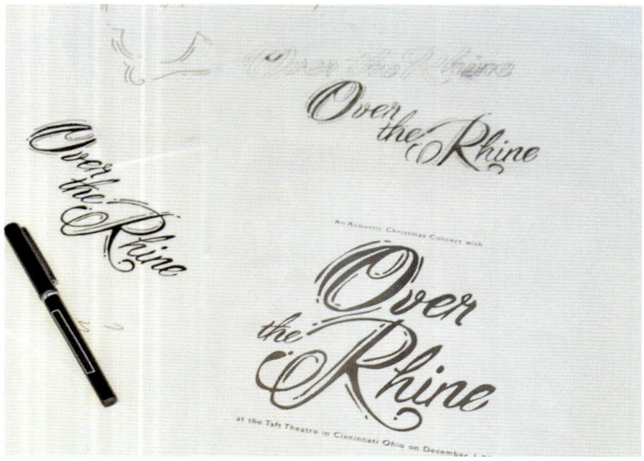

Calligraphy can be used to convey a sense of formality.

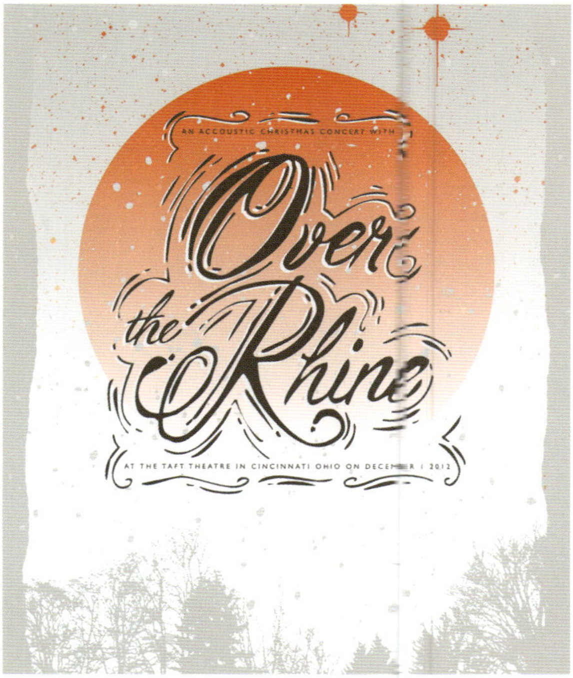

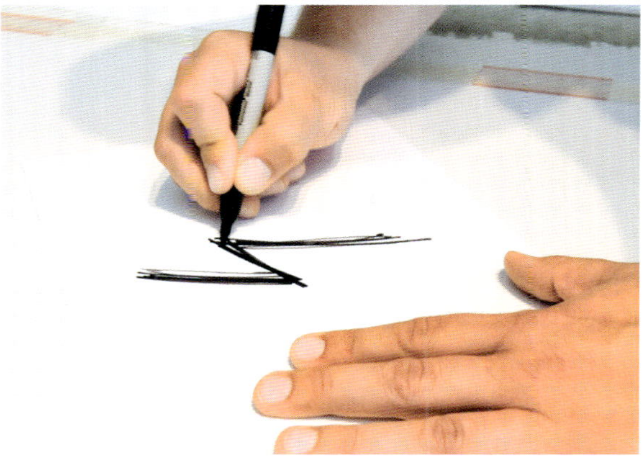

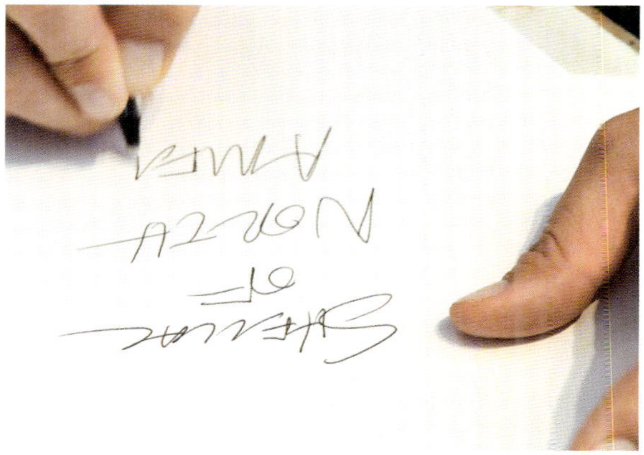

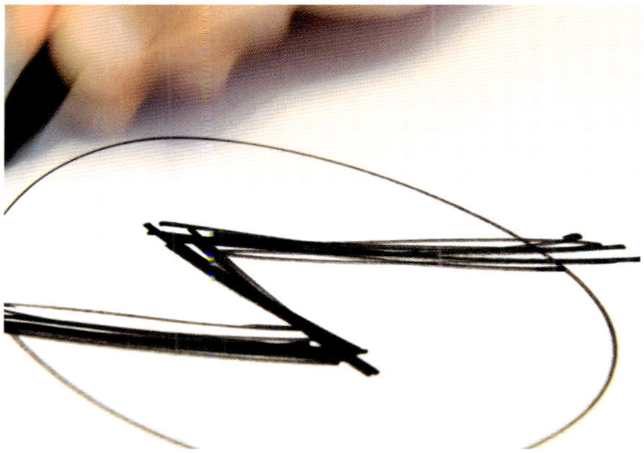

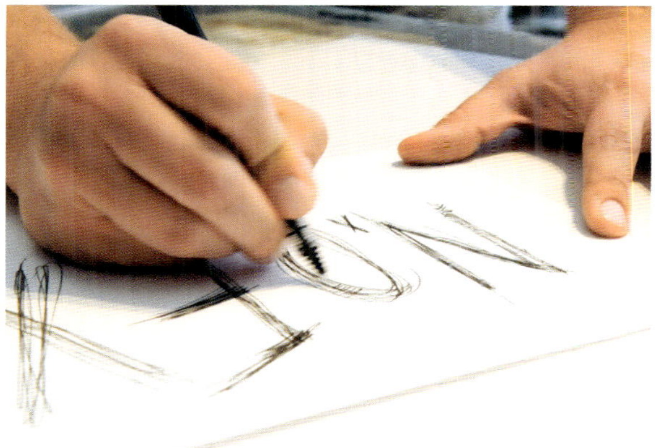

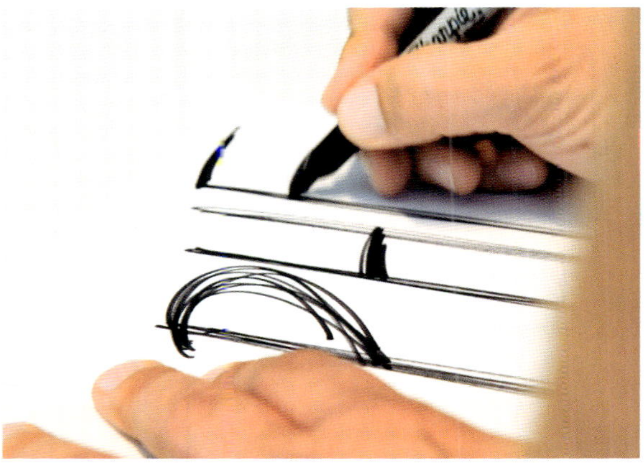

Overdone scratch letters are often used for a punk style.

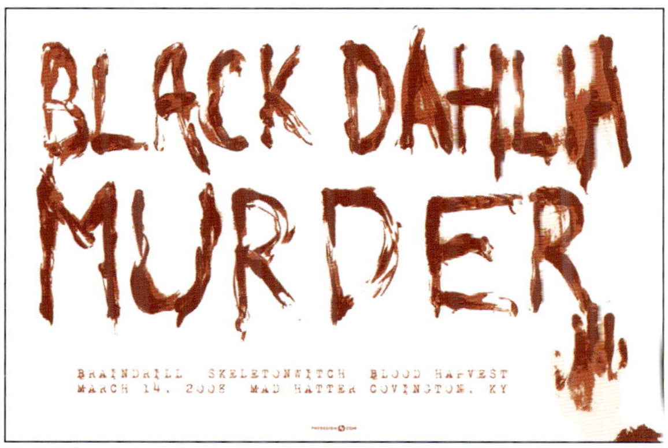

A quick note style conveys a sense of urgency.

SOFTWARE V. HANDMADE

Even though show posters are the tangible, tactile artifacts of rock shows, that doesn't necessarily mean the artwork was created through tactile processes. In the long history of poster making, many methods have emerged to create them, but since the mid-1990s one of the more widely used methods of creating artwork for posters has been through the use of digital software like Adobe Photoshop and Adobe Illustrator. Programs such as these have opened the door to a wide range of styles that had previously not been available through handmade processes and allowed the possibility for much faster imagery manipulation. However, that's not to say that the use of digital programs has eclipsed other methods. Software merely offers another tool in a vast toolbox of methods for creating and manipulating artwork for the purposes of printmaking. Some poster artists still use hand tools as part of the design process, creating imagery or type by hand and then scanning it into the computer to manipulate it and output a film. And of course, some use hand tools exclusively and stay out of the computer altogether, using Rubylith and copy machines to create their films.

LINOCUT

Historically used as a wallpaper-printing technique, Linocut is a classic handmade method for creating artwork. It is a printmaking technique, very similar to woodcut, in which a sheet of linoleum is used as the relief surface. A knife, chisel, or gouge is used to cut into the surface to create the design. The raised or uncarved areas represent the negative or mirror image of the parts that show when printed. The linoleum sheet is inked with a roller and either impressed on the substrate or rolled with a press. Because it is an intricate and time-consuming process it is a lesser-used approach in the rock poster community these days.

OFFSET LITHOGRAPHY

Offset lithography is by far the most commonly used printing technique for high-volume, commercial printing in which color matching is precise and color registration is often flawless. Most of the printed material that you come across (outside of the show poster scene) is printed using this offset technique. Newspapers, magazines, brochures, and the like are all printed with offset lithography. It's the most efficient and cost-effective way of mass-producing high-quality printed material. This method probably requires the most amount of "prepress" work in order to ensure proper transfer of the image to the printing plates; the image is then transferred to a rubber blanket and then to the printing surface. Offset presses are often huge machines that can print continuously while paper is fed through. With so much prepress work and massive machinery, low-volume print jobs typically don't make sense for offset litho and are printed digitally in smaller runs.

LETTERPRESS

Letterpress is a relief-printing technique where a worker composes and locks moveable type blocks and artwork in the bed of a printing press. The blocks are then inked and pressed against paper to transfer the ink from the blocks to the paper creating an impression on the paper.

The letterpress printing process dates back to the 1400s when Johannes Gutenberg invented the first moveable type printing press. For centuries it was the primary method for printing and distributing information. It was instrumental in giving people equal access to the written word and subsequently spreading information and ideas. Gutenberg's process remained largely unchanged until the 1950s when it was overtaken by commercial offset printing, leaving letterpress a more artistic endeavor. By then, letterpress had already entered the golden era for country music and letterpress posters were the primary method for informing people about shows. Letterpress became part of the fabric of the country music scene, eventually branching out into other genres like jazz and blues. Today, letterpress remains a niche style, but still captures the essence of Southern culture while promoting shows of all types.

'90S DESKTOP PUBLISHING

Around the 1990s there was a surge of PC ownership and people had instant access to design, illustration, and layout tools. With the advent of desktop publishing, suddenly anyone could try on the hat of a designer and then print multiple copies of his or her work at home. This hurt the practice of graphic design initially, but later allowed trained designers to differentiate their work and its quality. Desktop publishing exposed the use of shitty fonts, the use of wingdings, and poor type layout, kerning, leading, and contrast for what it was. The use of computers and digital printers, initially thought to be a death knell for screenprinting, ultimately offered the ability to build and manipulate imagery in the computer and then output a film that actually made screen-printing cheaper and easier.

Today 1990s desktop publishing–style fonts and approaches are used to show another type of low-rent, easy-to-create style—similar to Xerox/punk. This type of aesthetic looks like it was quickly created in Windows 98 with little to no regard for foundational design principles. Many Internet memes offer a good example of this simple, ironic style.

SCREENPRINTING / SERIGRAPHY

Screenprinting is a stencil method in which a nylon screen is used to transfer ink onto a substrate. The image is transferred onto clear film that is then used in combination with intense UV light to transfer that image onto the nylon mesh. Ink is then pressed through the screen with a rubber blade called a squeegee and then transferred onto the paper or cloth substrate.

Screenprinting is by far the most common printing technique used in the rock poster community. Because of its DIY nature and the fact that you don't have to use an expensive press or piece of machinery, screenprinting is a far more accessible technique for designers and illustrators. A kid in his parents' garage can produce a stack of rad screenprinted posters with the right tools and a little effort. For this reason it has become the technique of choice for rock poster designers all over the world. Not only is it highly accessible, but also the process's similarity to the down-and-dirty DIY nature of rock 'n' roll makes it the clear choice for artists to create one-of-a-kind artifacts for the music they love.

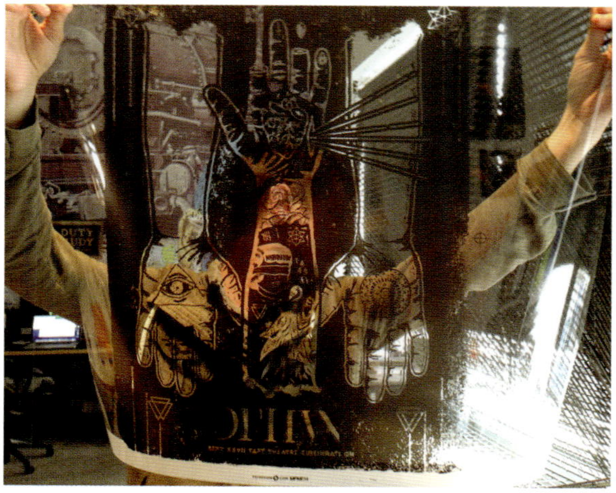

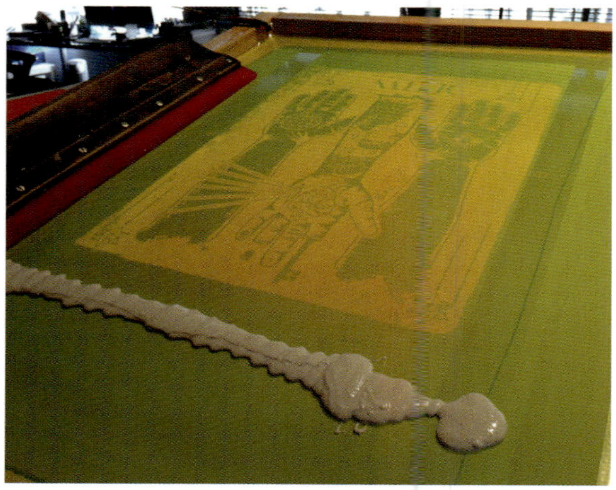

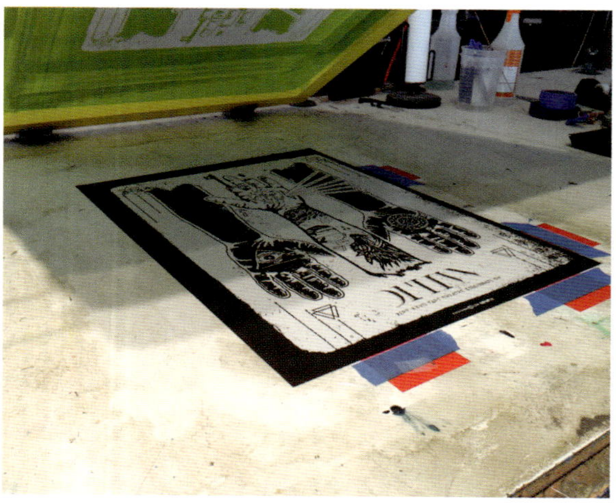

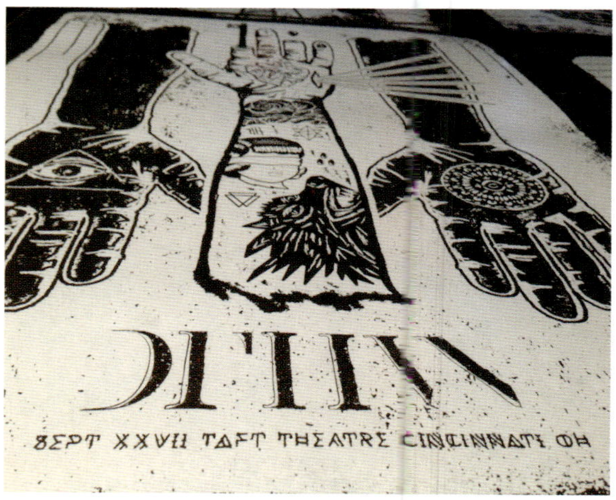

A screenprinted poster by Aaron May of Powerhouse Factories

PAINTED STENCIL

Painted stencil is a technique in which ink is passed over holes cut in various materials. It penetrates the holes and is transferred onto another surface. The stencil can then be used over and over to re-create the same image.

The painted-stencil method of printing dates back 37,000 years to some examples of Neanderthal cave art found in Spain. It is believed that these early humans would place their hand on the wall of a cave and blow natural pigments onto their hands, leaving an outline of their hand on the wall.

The use of stenciling spread throughout the ancient world; examples of it can be found from ancient Egypt to first-century China. The main advantage of stenciling is the ability to reproduce the same image over and over again, creating intricate patterns. Stencils still have many practical applications today in industrial, commercial, and artistic settings.

In recent years, stencil artwork has often taken the form of graffiti art in urban settings, giving the artist the ability to quickly reproduce an image in areas where graffiti is illegal.

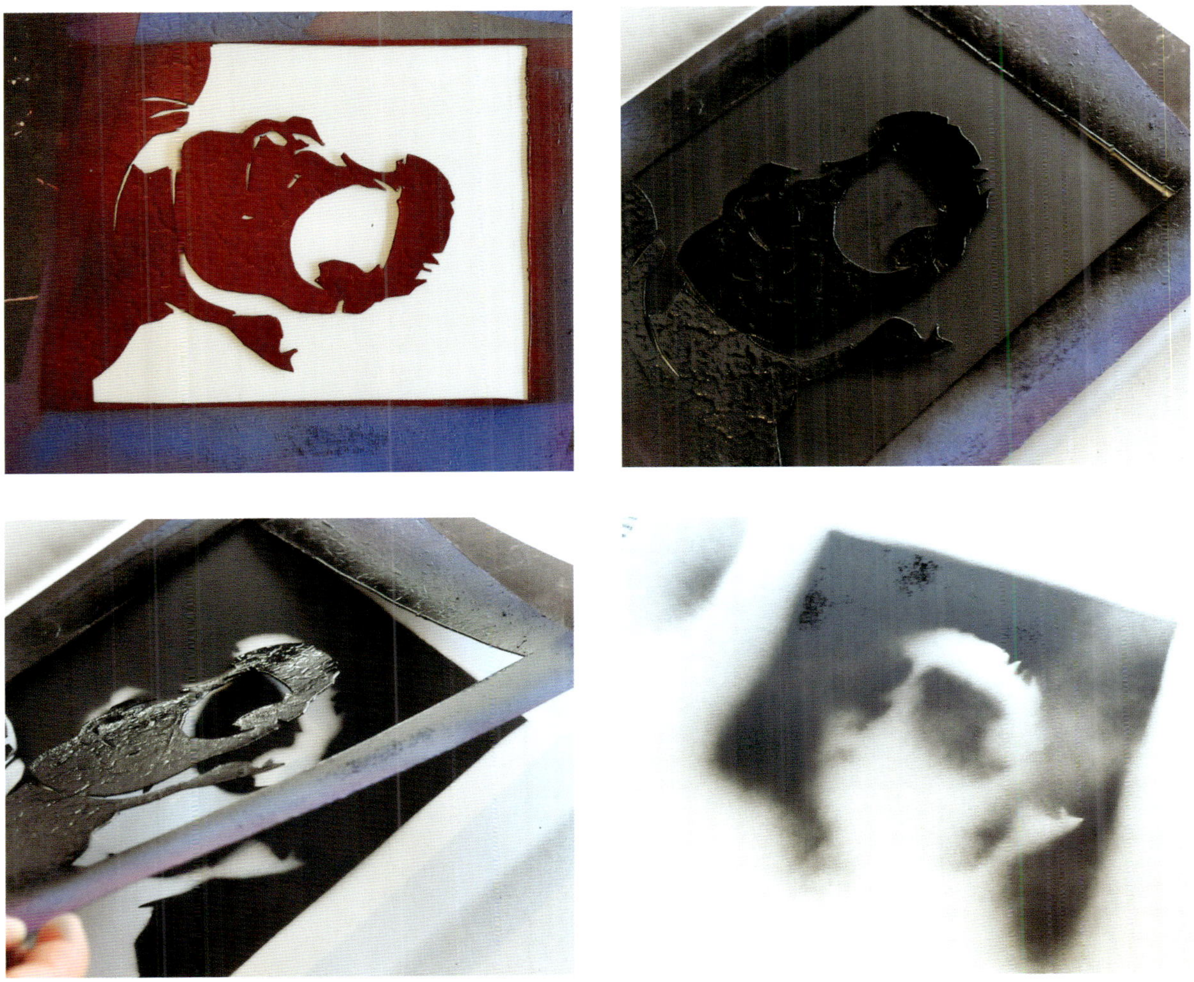

An example of a painted stencil

3 POSTER TRENDS & DESIGN STYLES

Trends come and go and pigeonholing someone's art into a "design style" can be incredibly tricky. Style is subjective and nuanced—often walking the line between one thing or another. One has to take into account where an illustrator or designer draws inspiration and what medium he or she chooses to work in, and all of that can be difficult or nearly impossible to classify.

Still, in order to study different poster designs and designers, it is helpful to group them in some sort of meaningful way to help frame the discussion. The design styles discussed here should be just that: a way of grouping things in order to study them but with the understanding that artists and designers draws from many different sources of inspiration and may shift and combine mediums in their efforts to convey a visual message.

Oxidized Degradation

This style puts an emphasis on the process used to create the print itself by bringing elements of the art techniques to the forefront. Multiple layers may be used or portions of the work may look washed-out, overprinted, or misregistered. The overall effect may look like a mistake or printing error at first blush, but ultimately this style puts an emphasis on texture, layering, and the printing process used to create the piece.

KEY STYLE CHARACTERISTICS

- Almost looks misprinted or miscut, like items were thrown together on the page
- Combines multiple illustration and design styles, sometimes even within one piece
- Sometimes made to look like a test print, meaning it's mis-registered and has a high number of layers
- Heavy use of texture
- Often shows the process of screenprinting in the work—this calls attention to the handmade quality of the poster and lends authenticity

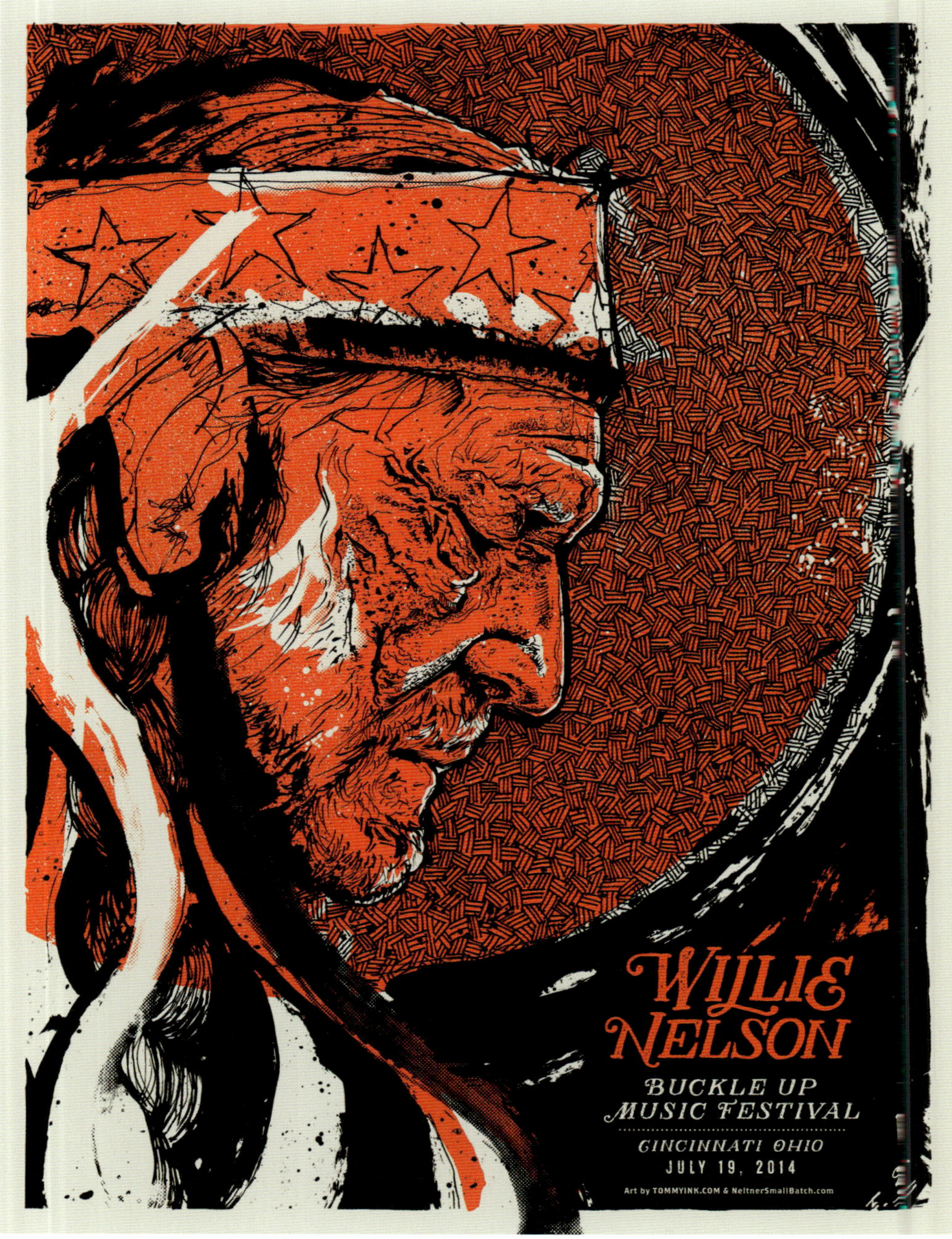

CLIENT: Willie Nelson
DESIGNER: Keith Neltner
DESIGN FIRM: Neltner Small Batch
WEBSITE: neltnersmallbatch.com

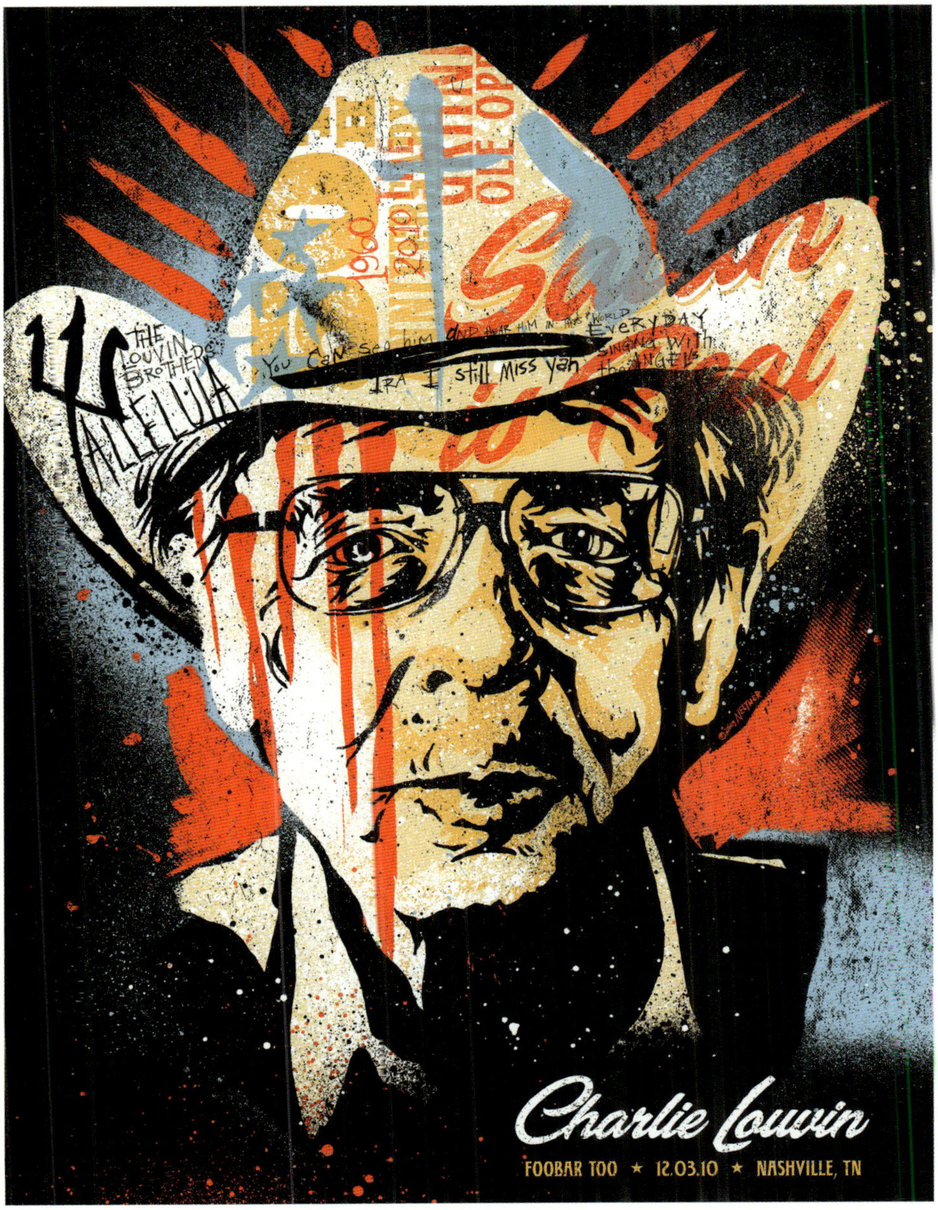

CLIENT: Charlie Louvin
DESIGNER: Keith Neltner
DESIGN FIRM Neltner Small Batch
WEBSITE: neltnersmallbatch.com

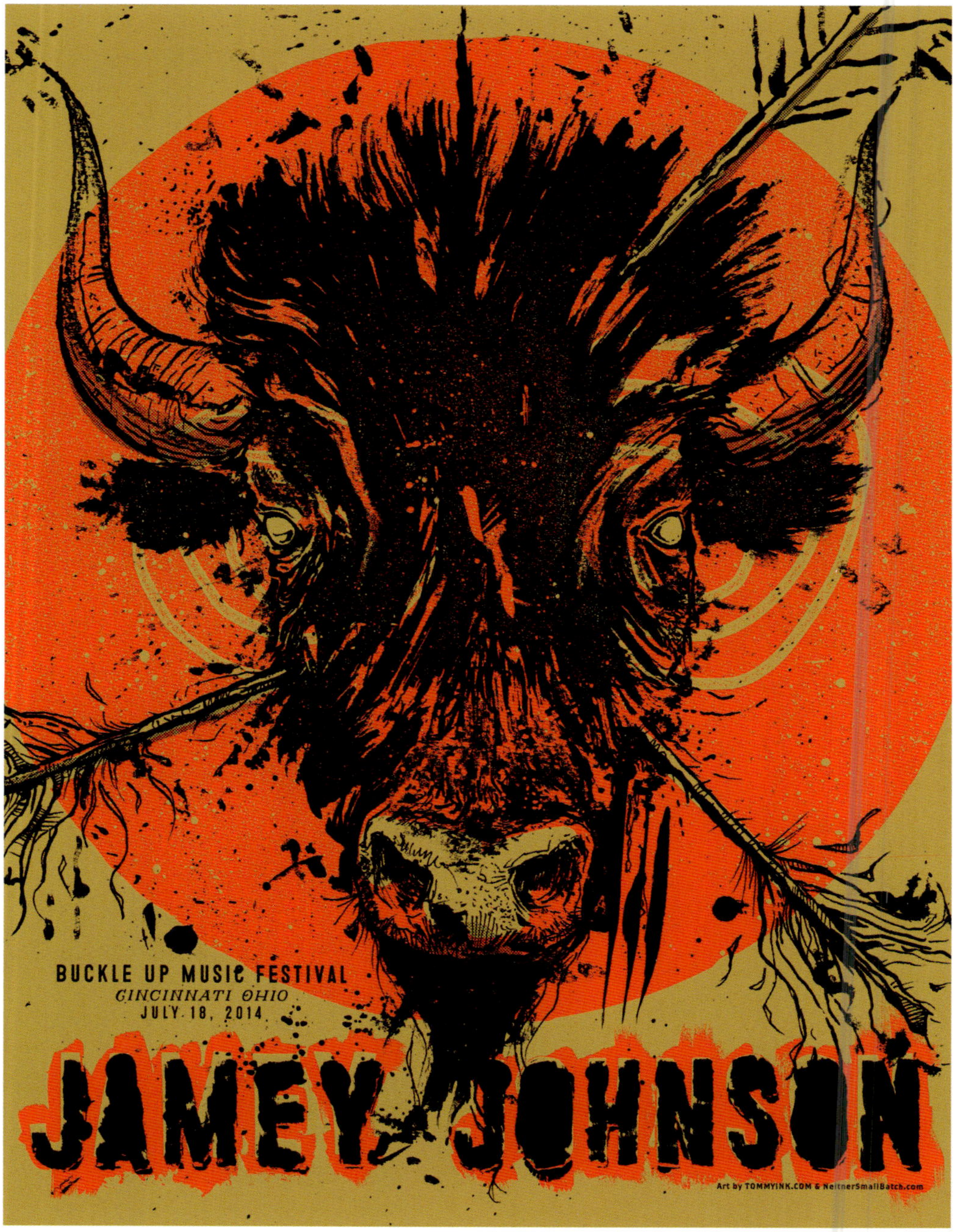

CLIENT: Jamey Johnson
DESIGNER: Keith Neltner
DESIGN FIRM: Neltner Small Batch
WEBSITE: neltnersmallbatch.com

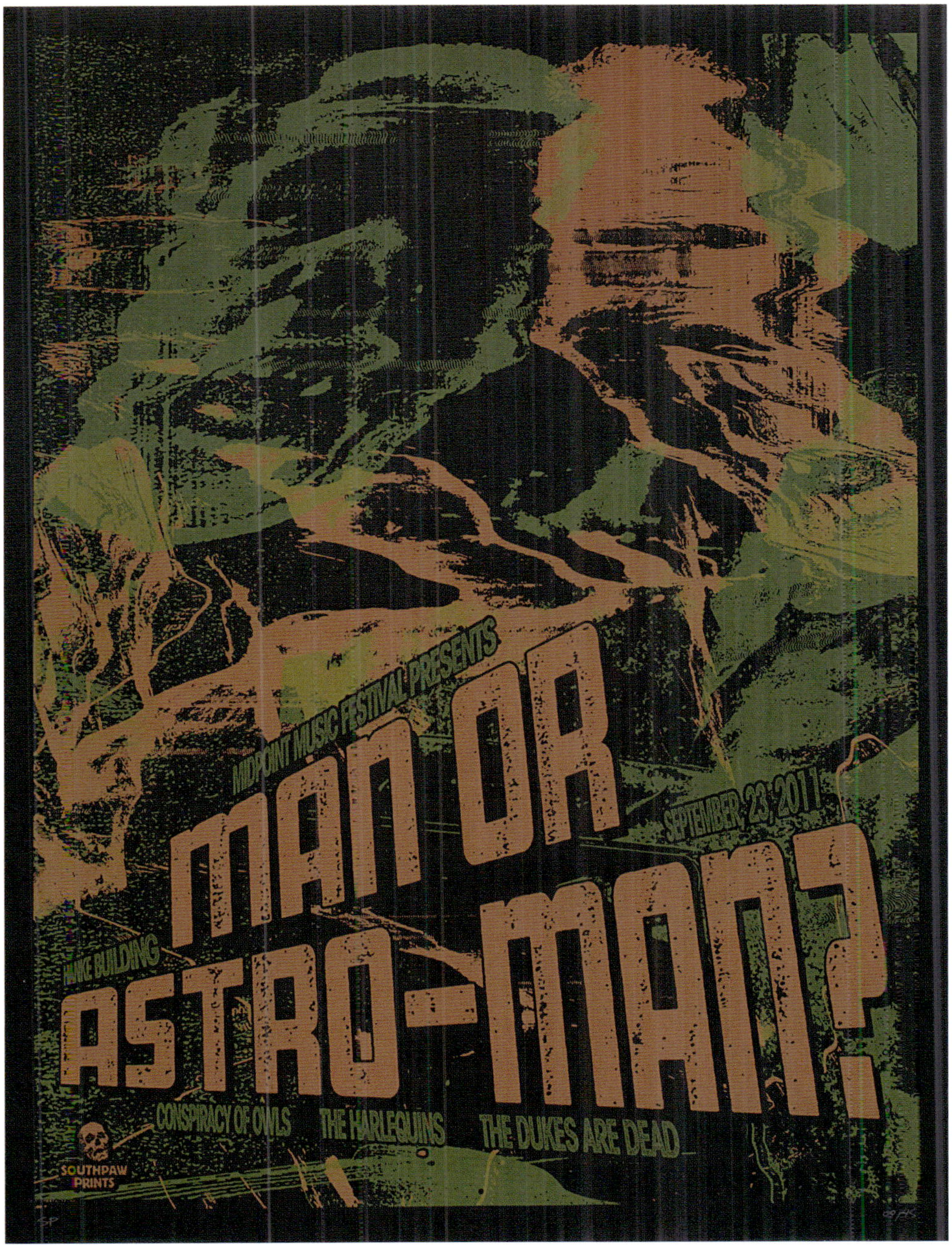

CLIENT: Man or Astro-Man?
DESIGNER: Southpaw Prints
WEBSITE: southpawprints.com

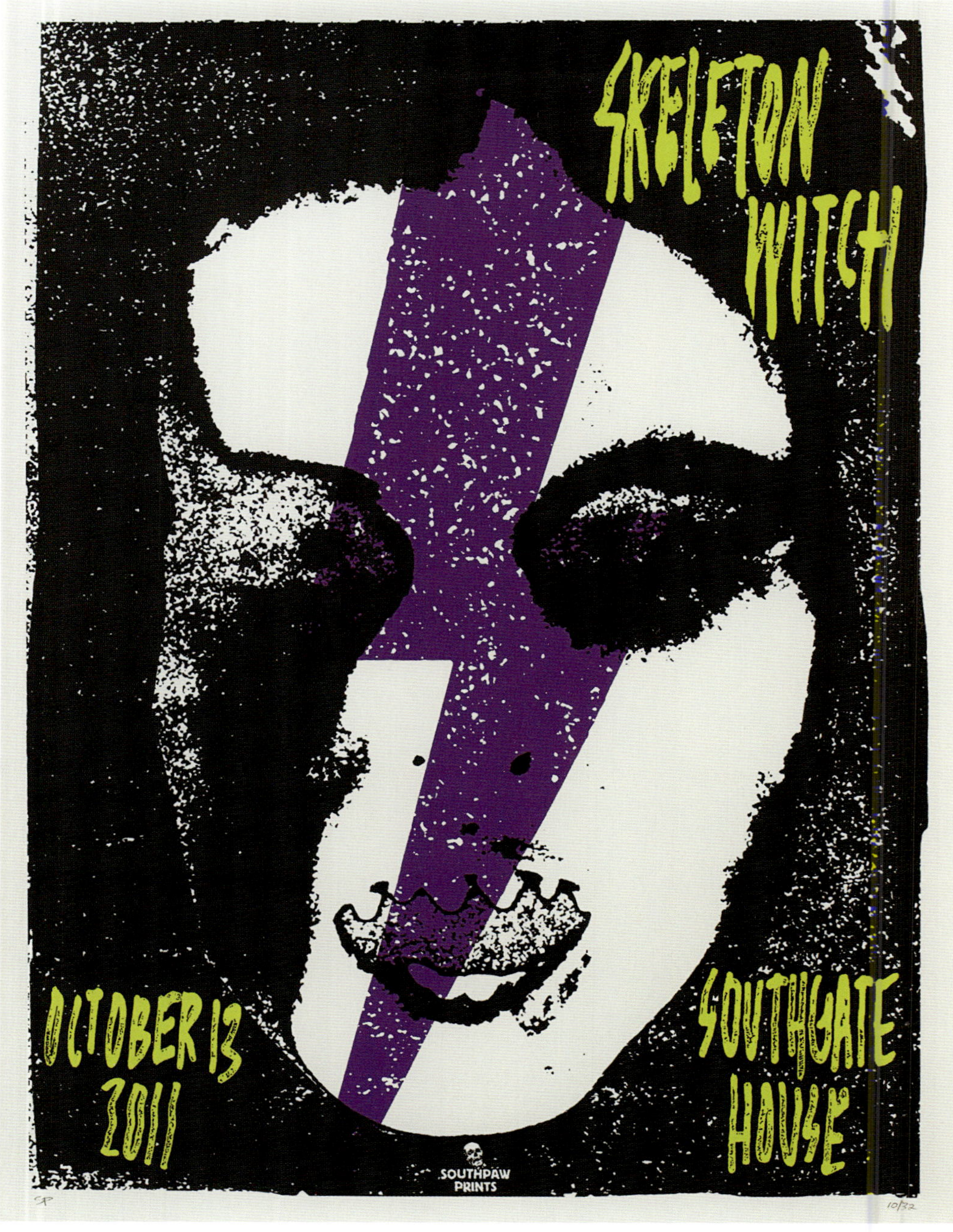

CLIENT: Skeletonwitch
DESIGNER: Southpaw Prints
WEBSITE: southpawprints.com

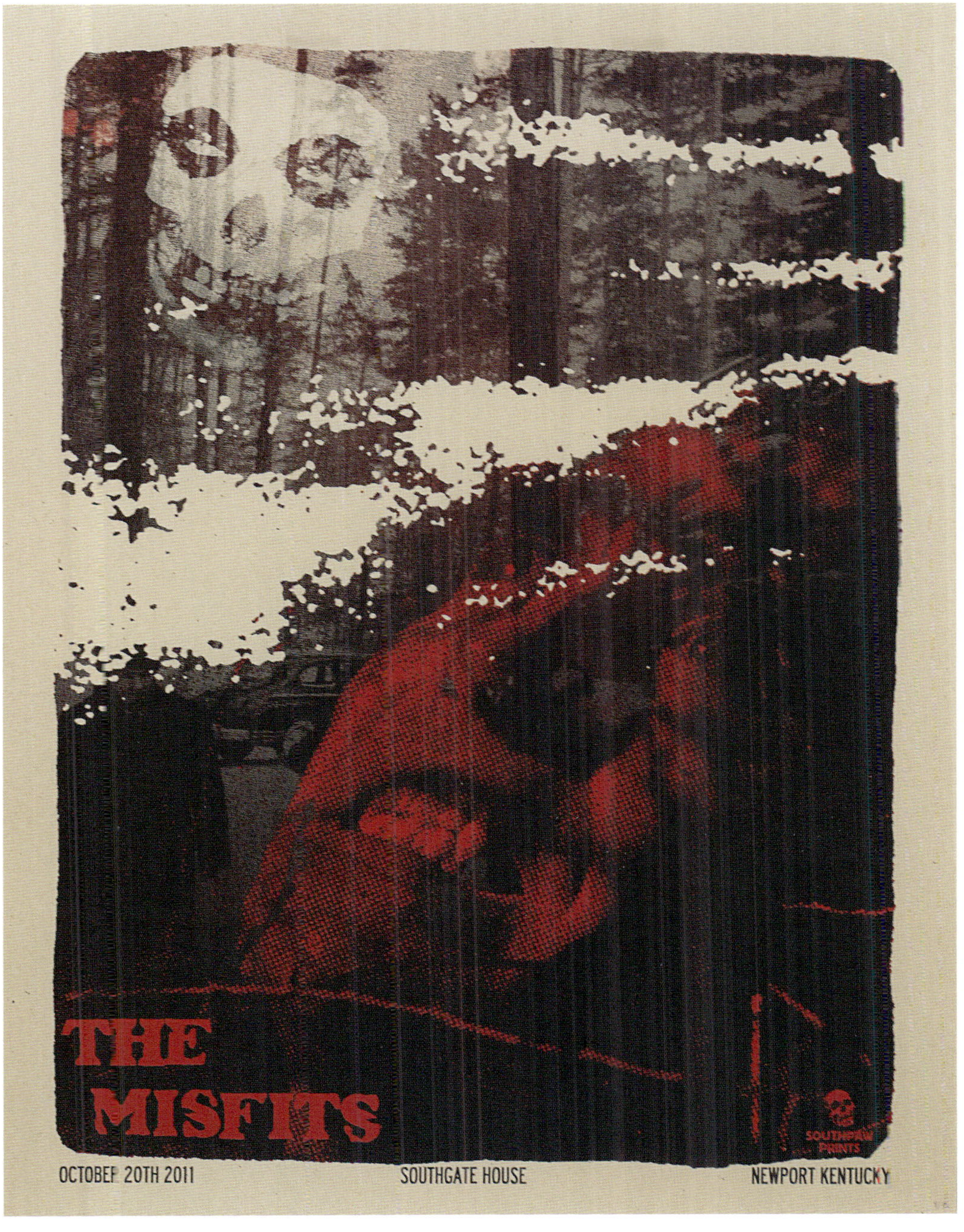

CLIENT: The Misfits
DESIGNER: Southpaw Prints
WEBSITE: southpawprints.com

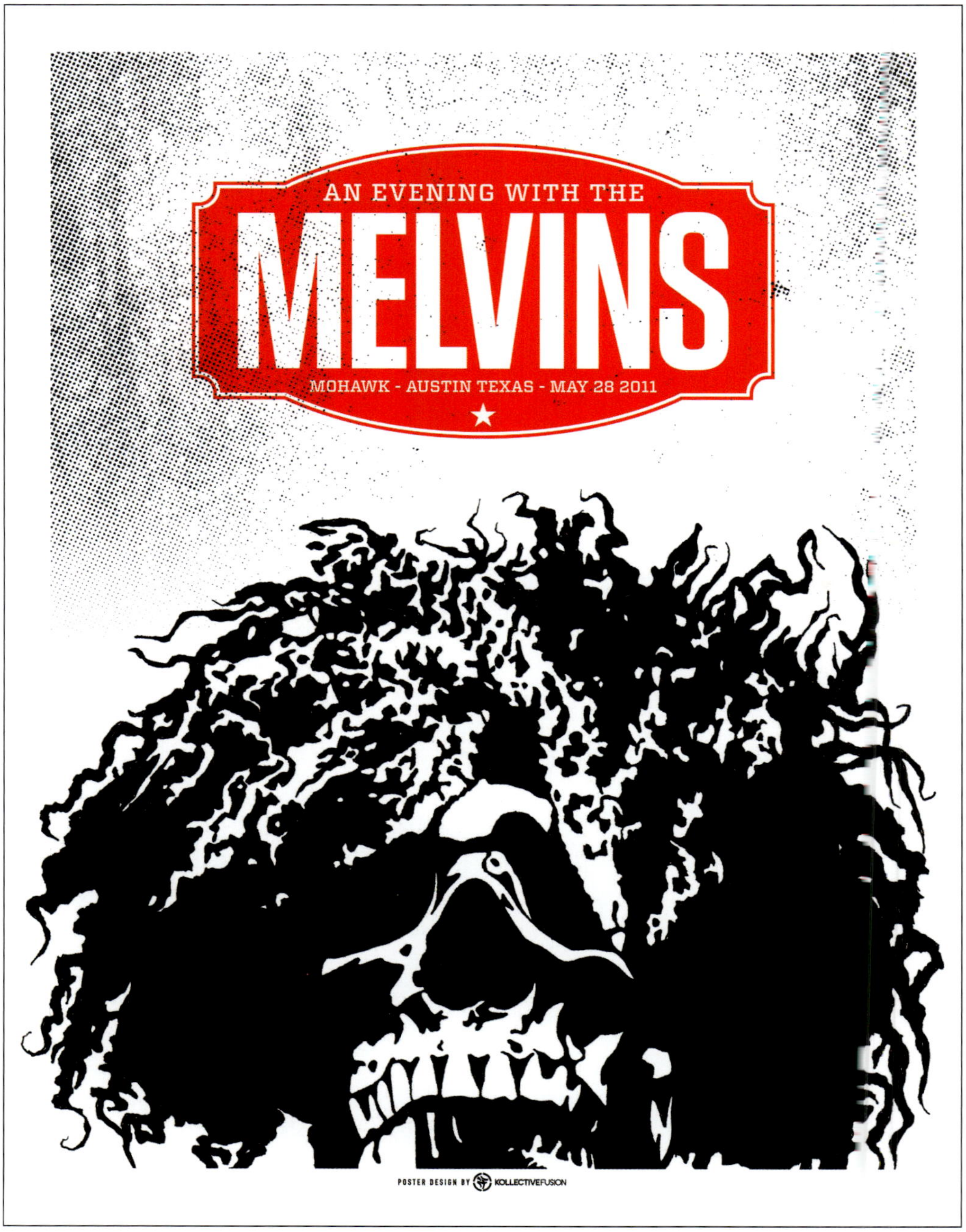

CLIENT: Melvins
DESIGNER: Bobby Dixon
DESIGN FIRM: Kollective Fusion
WEBSITE: etsy.com/shop/kollectivefusion

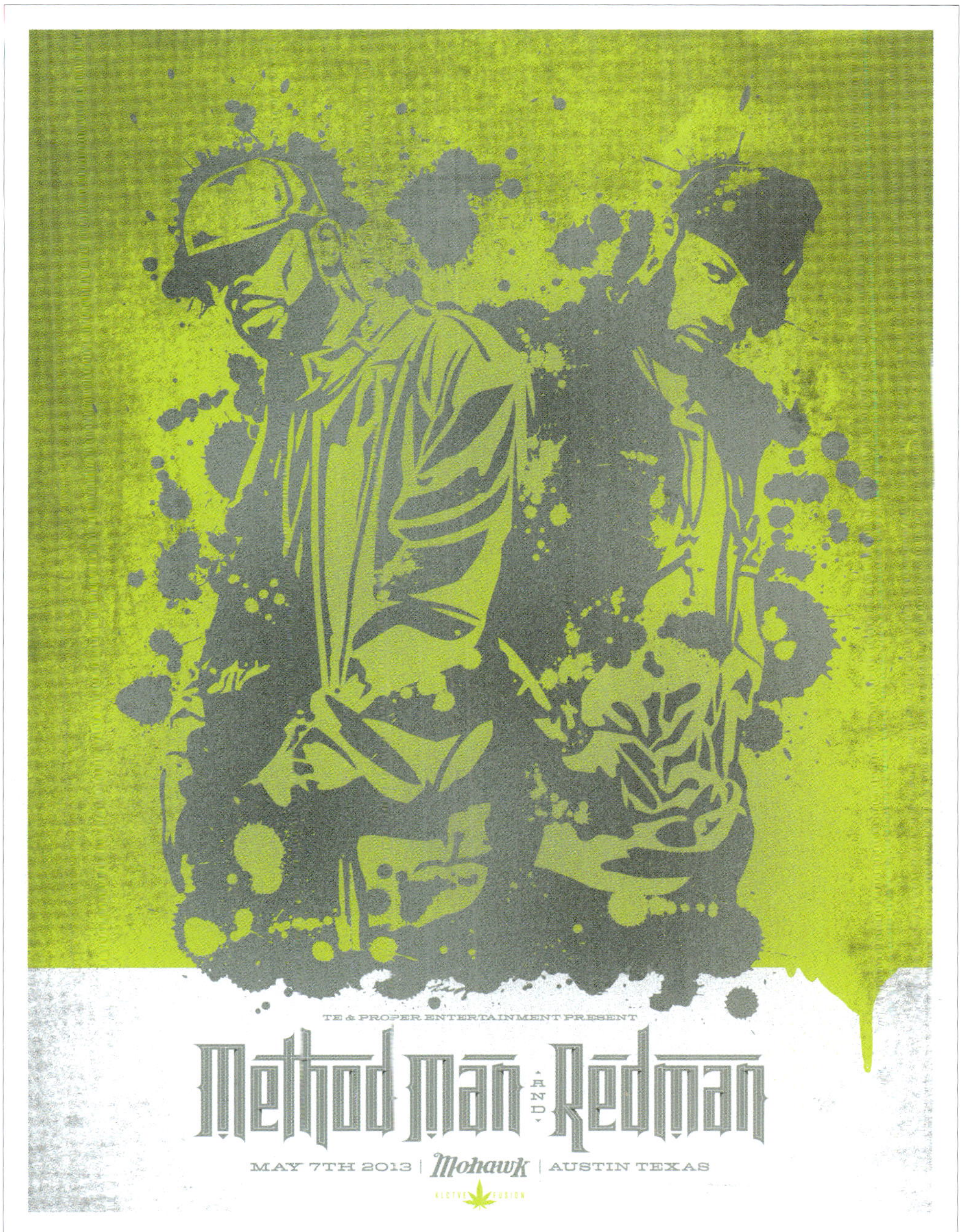

CLIENT: Method Man and Redman
DESIGNER: Bobby Dixon
DESIGN FIRM: Kollective Fusion
WEBSITE: etsy.com/shop/kollectivefusion

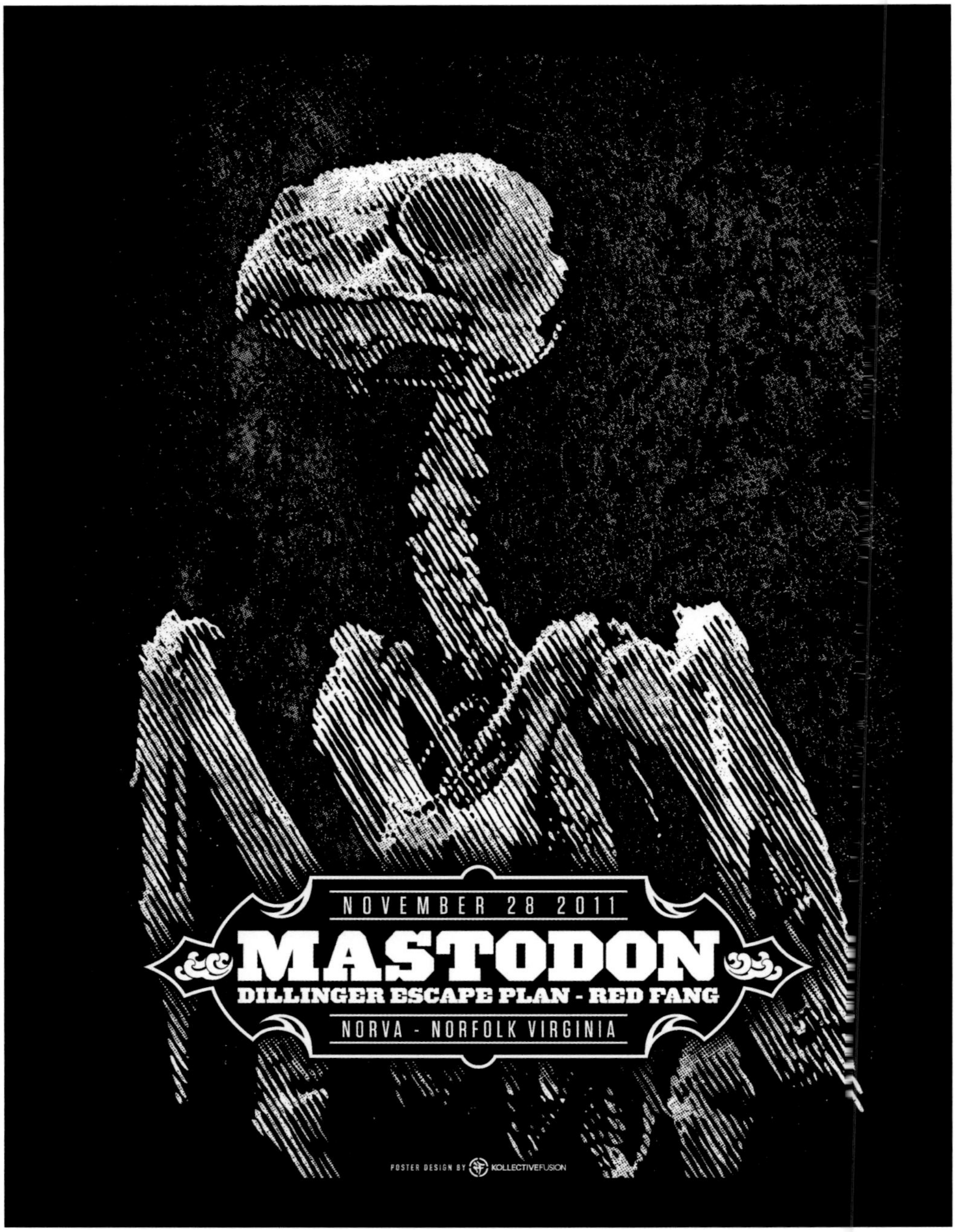

CLIENT: Mastodon
DESIGNER: Bobby Dixon
DESIGN FIRM: Kollective Fusion
WEBSITE: etsy.com/shop/kollectivefusion

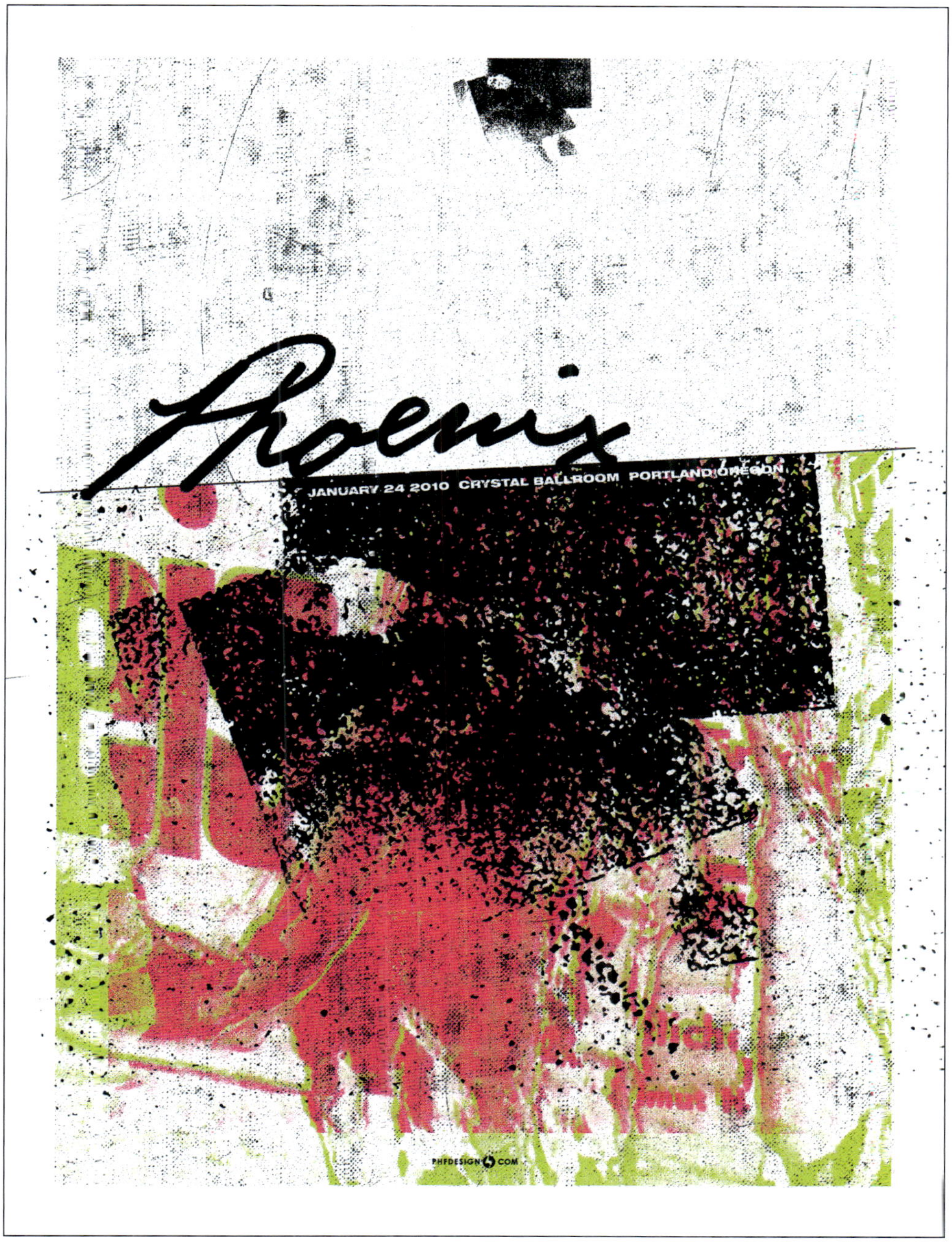

CLIENT: Phoenix
DESIGNER: Ben Nunery
DESIGN FIRM: Powerhouse Factories
WEBSITE: powerhousefactories.com

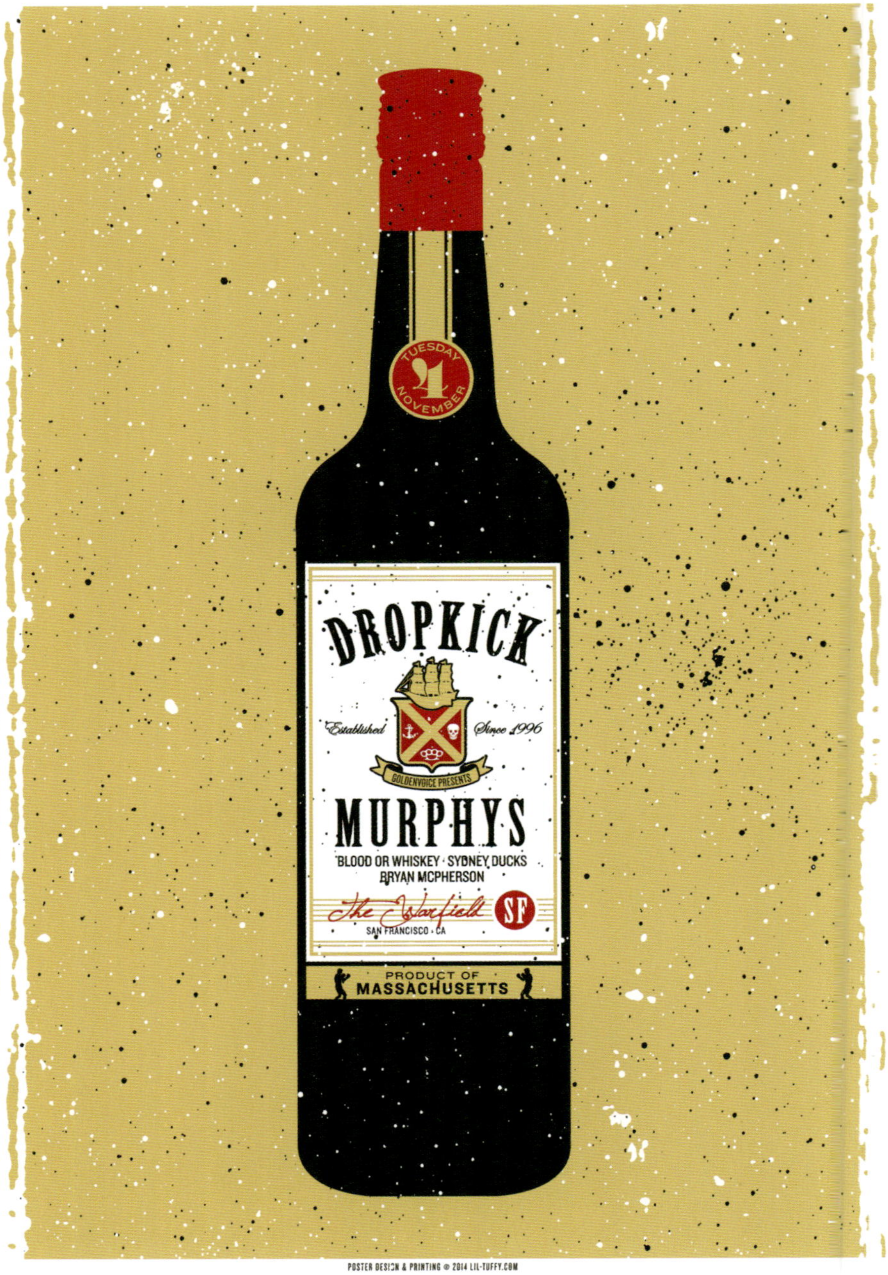

CLIENT: Dropkick Murphys
DESIGNER: Terrence Ryan
DESIGN FIRM: Lil' Tuffy
WEBSITE: lil-tuffy.com

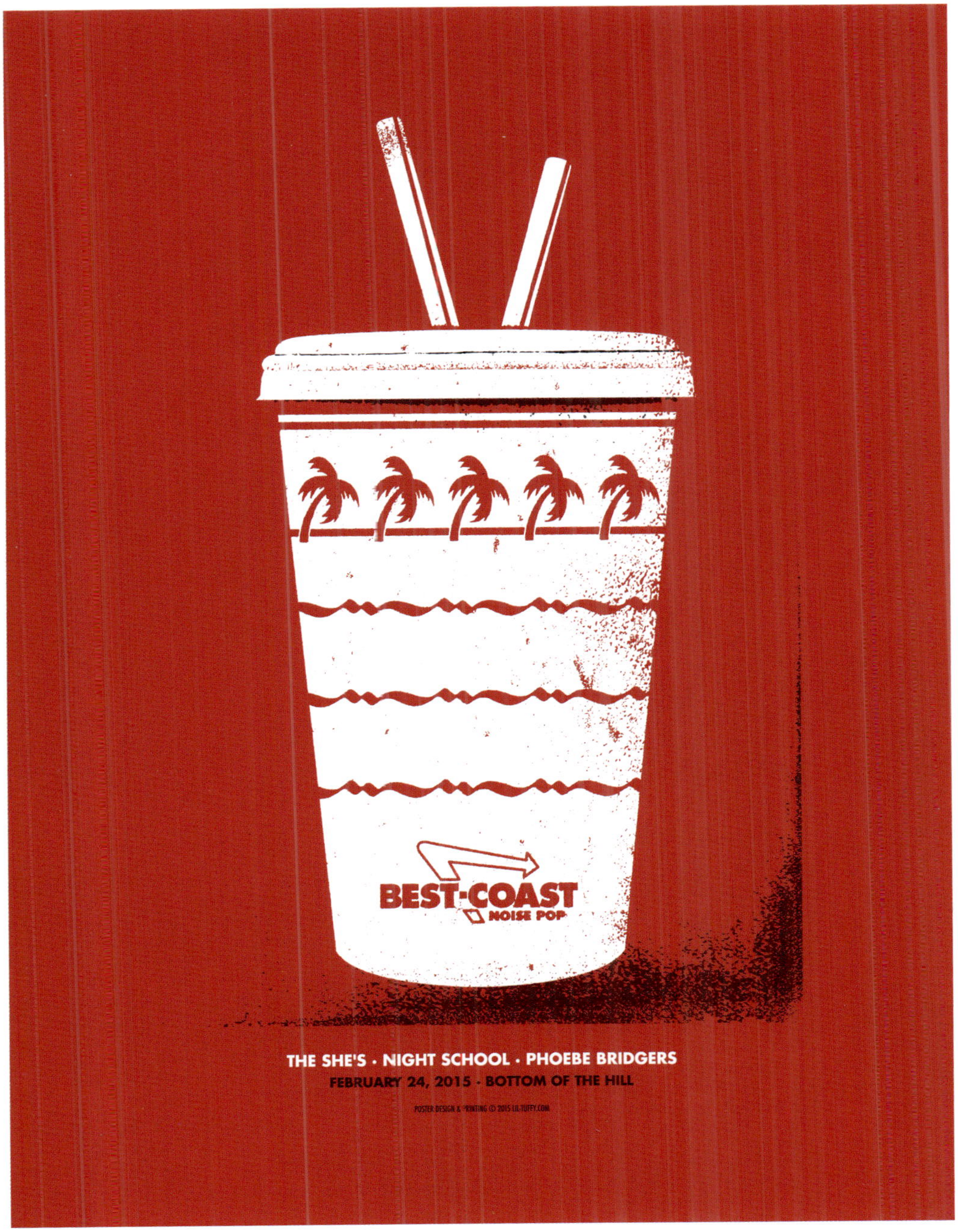

CLIENT: Best Coast
DESIGNER: Terrence Ryan
DESIGN FIRM: Lil' Tuffy
WEBSITE: lil-tuffy.com

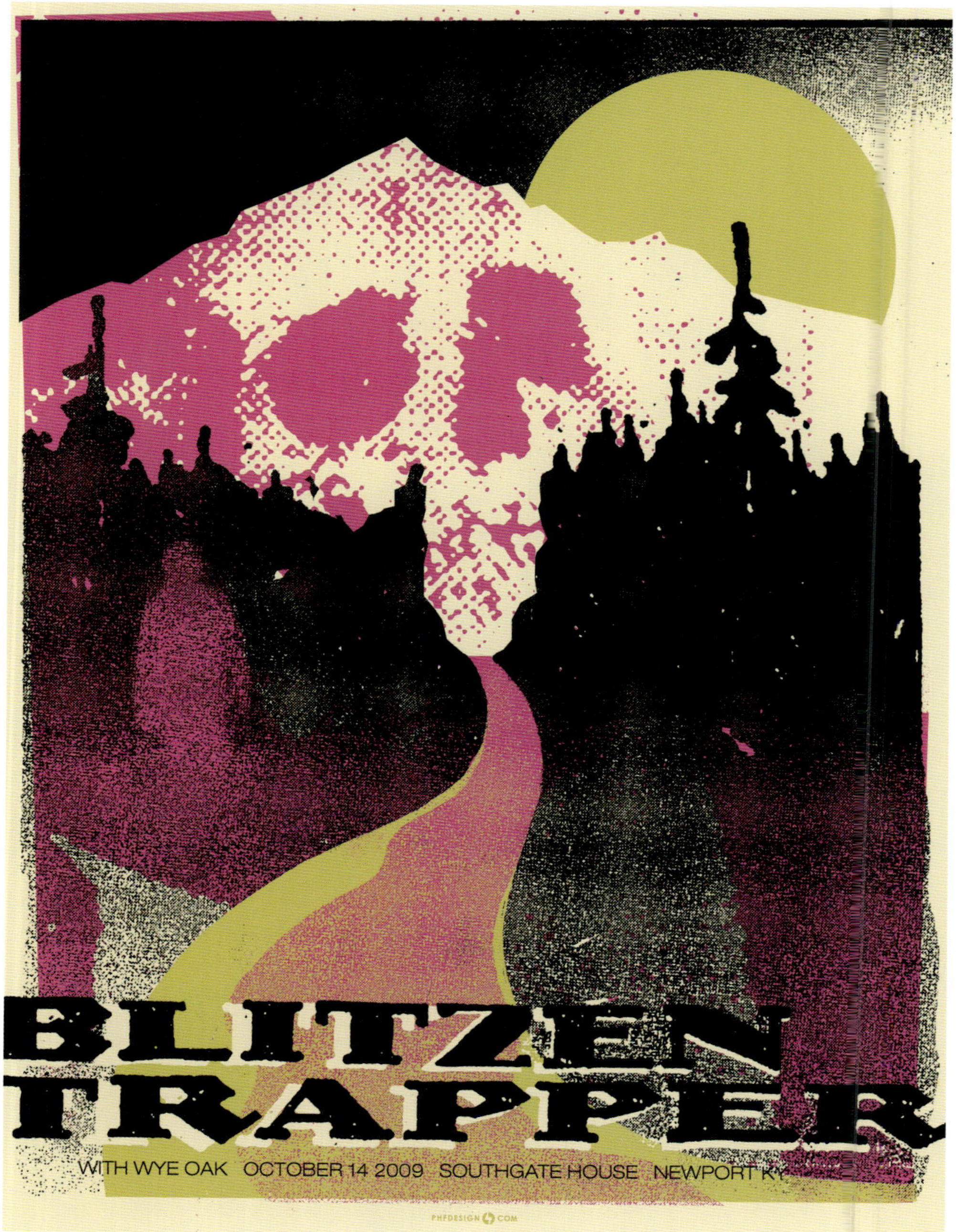

CLIENT: Blitzen Trapper
DESIGNER: Ben Nunery
DESIGN FIRM: Powerhouse Factories
WEBSITE: powerhousefactories.com

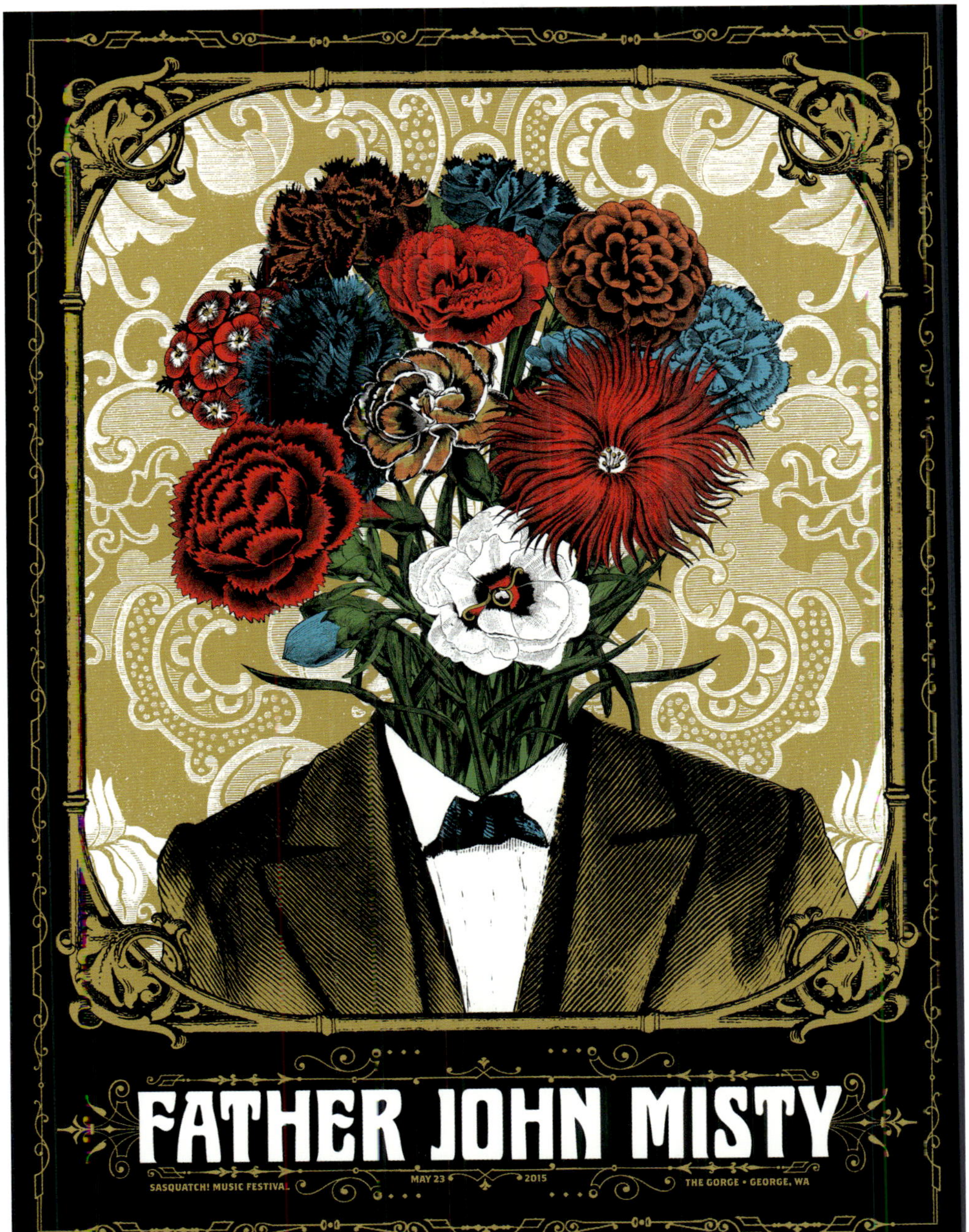

CLIENT: Father John Misty
DESIGNER: Nate Duval
WEBSITE: nateduval.com

Halftone Realism

This style utilizes halftones to recreate photographs in a way that looks very realistic—so much so that at first the piece may be mistaken for digital recolor of a photograph. Landscapes and settings are used to convey message with type integrated into the piece. The ultimate effect is reminiscent of movie posters or book covers.

KEY STYLE CHARACTERISTICS

- Halftones are used to re-create a photograph for a print that is very realistic and high quality
- Use of high contrast adds to photographic quality and realism
- Photography processes and color breakdown/separations are used to show realism
- While not overly colorful or bright, a lot of colors are printed to add depth and detail
- Landscapes and setting of a scene are often used to convey the message and focal point
- Type is often integrated into the landscape and/or piece
- Compositions are reminiscent of movie posters or book covers

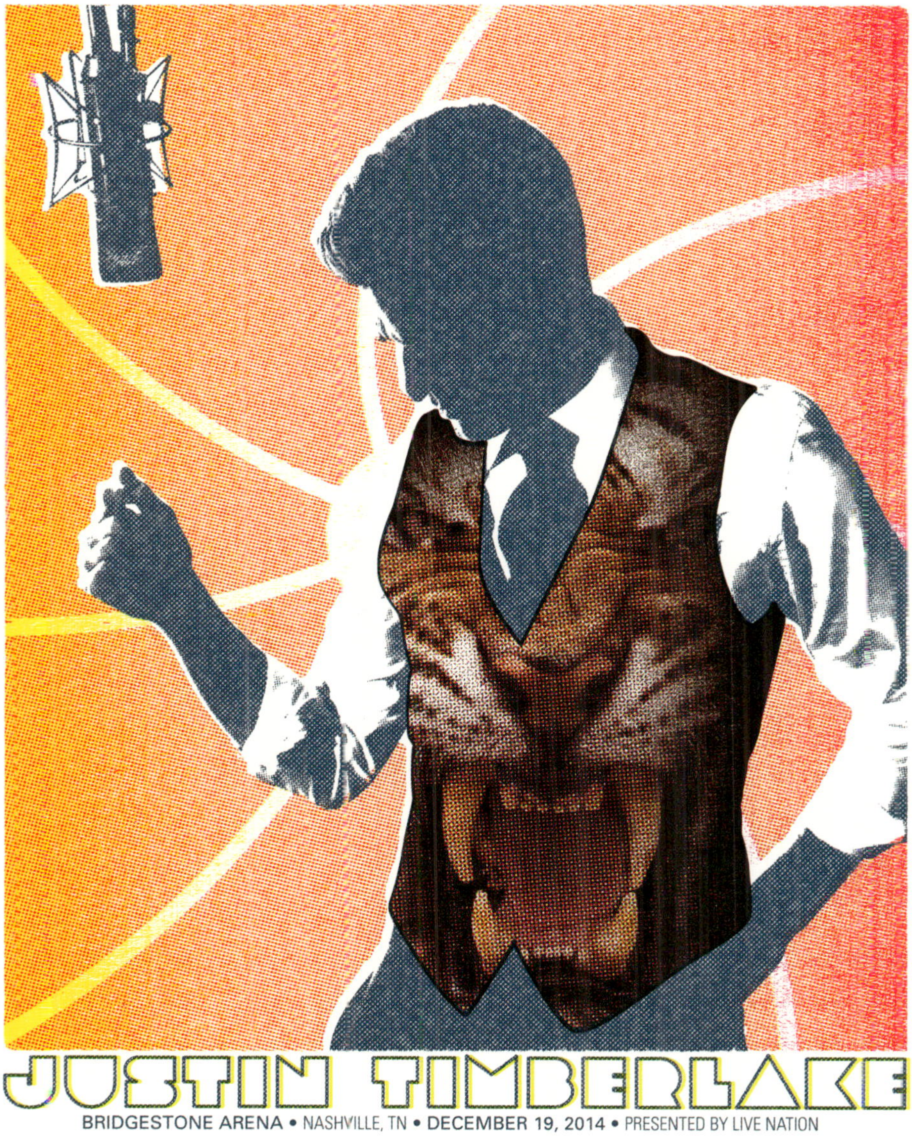

CLIENT: Justin Timberlake
DESIGNER: Andy Vastagh
DESIGN FIRM: Boss Construction
WEBSITE: bossconstruct.com

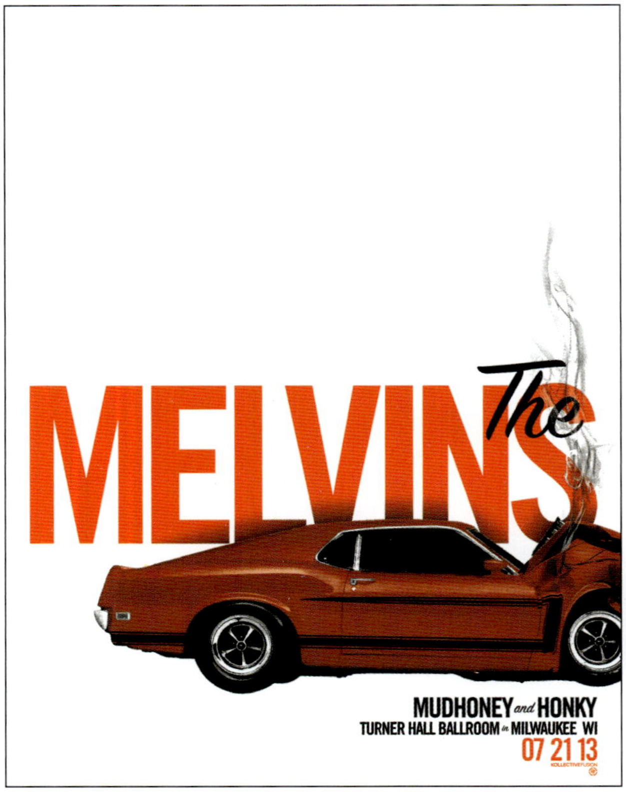

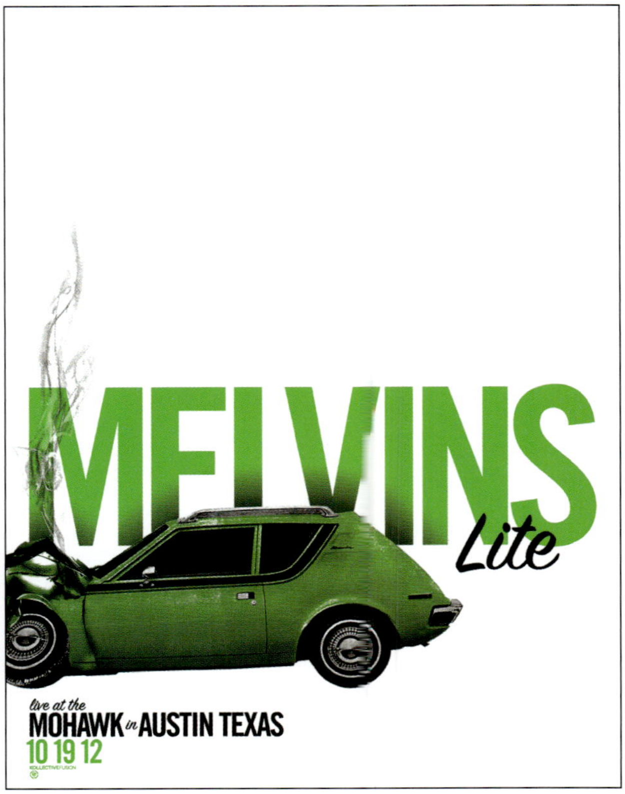

CLIENT: Melvins
DESIGNER: Bobby Dixon
DESIGN FIRM: Kollective Fusion
WEBSITE: etsy.com/shop/kollectivefusion

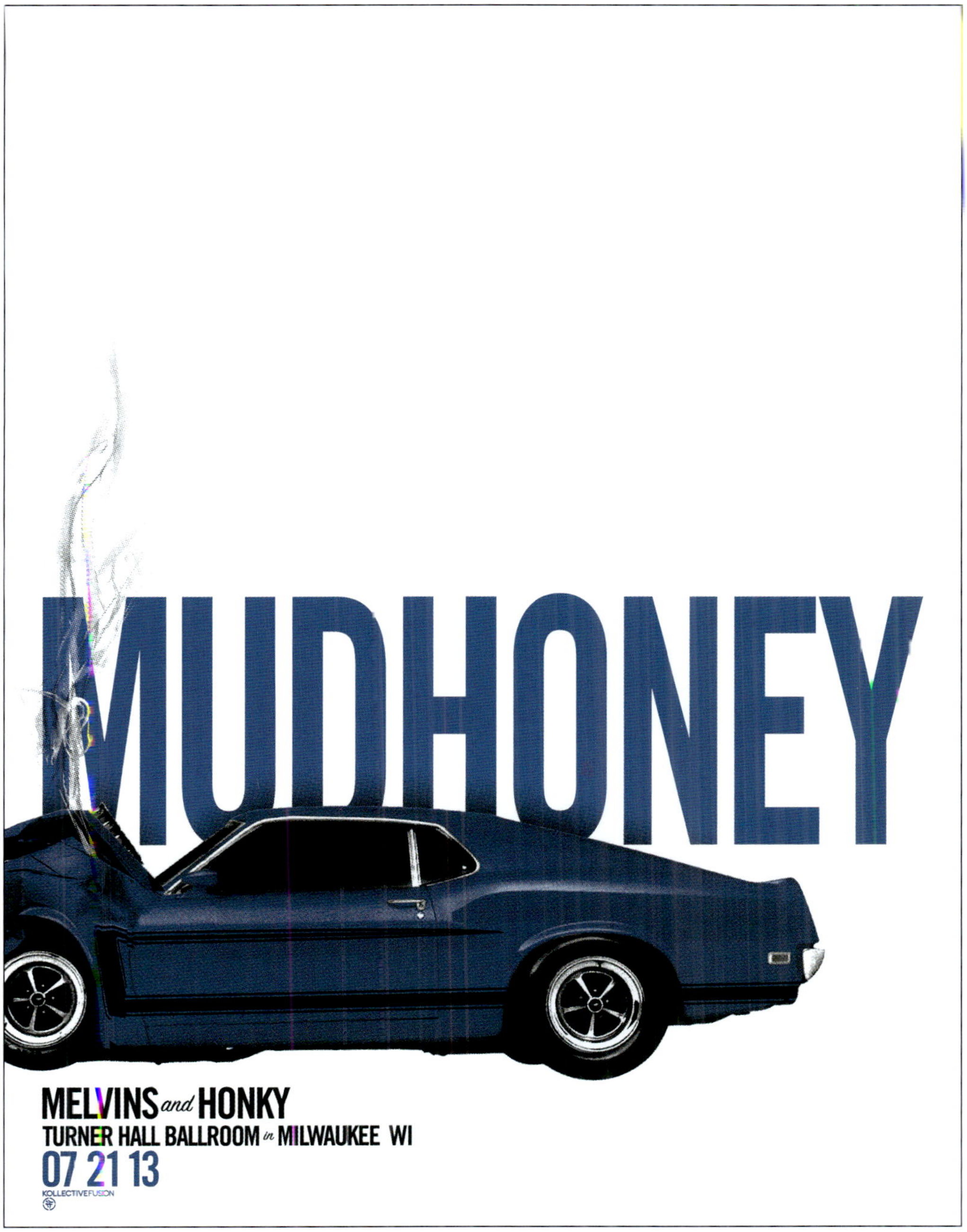

CLIENT: Mudhoney
DESIGNER: Bobby Dixon
DESIGN FIRM: Kollective Fusion
WEBSITE: etsy.com/shop/kollectivefusion

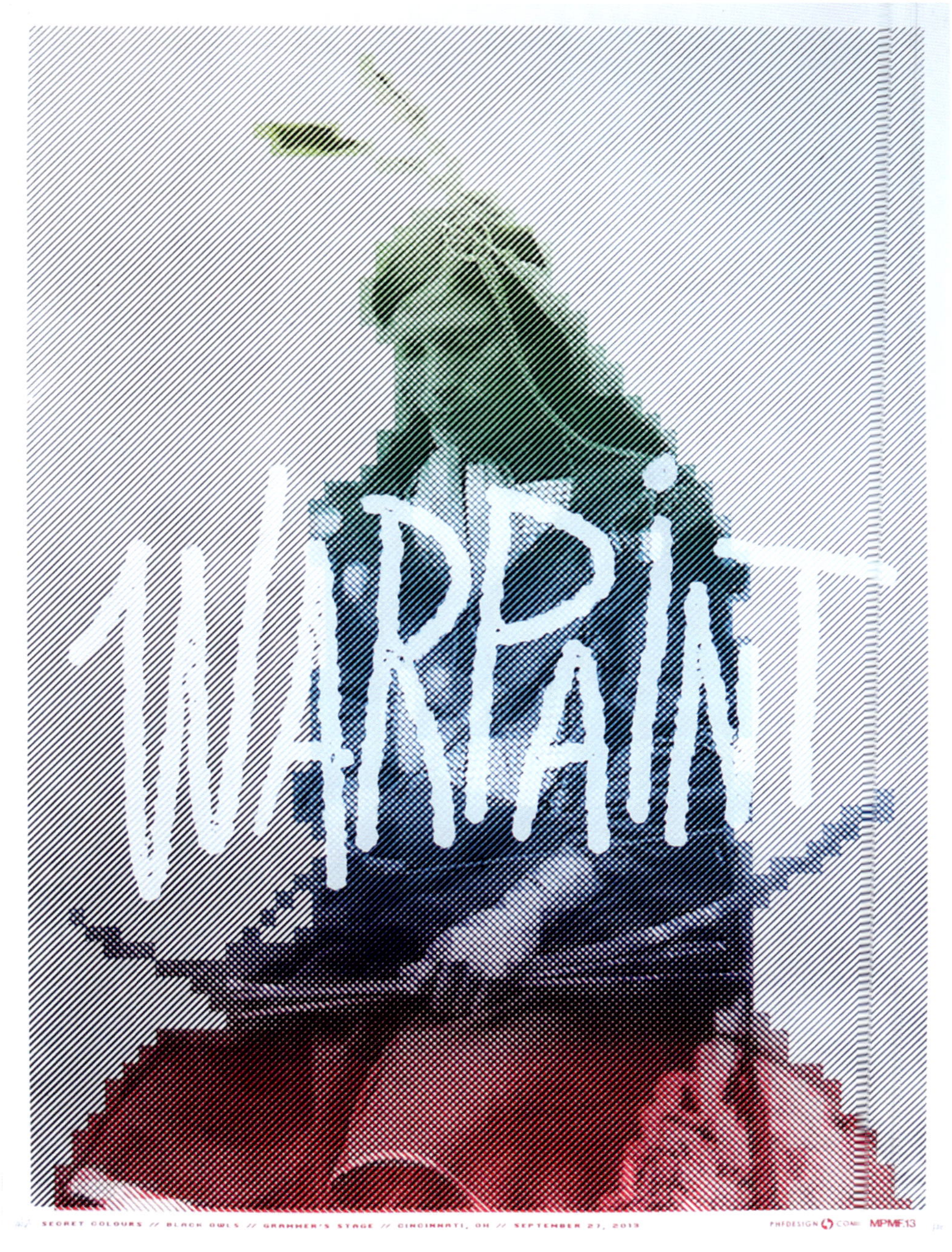

CLIENT: Warpaint
DESIGNER: John Matthew Overwine
DESIGN FIRM: Powerhouse Factories
WEBSITE: powerhousefactories.com

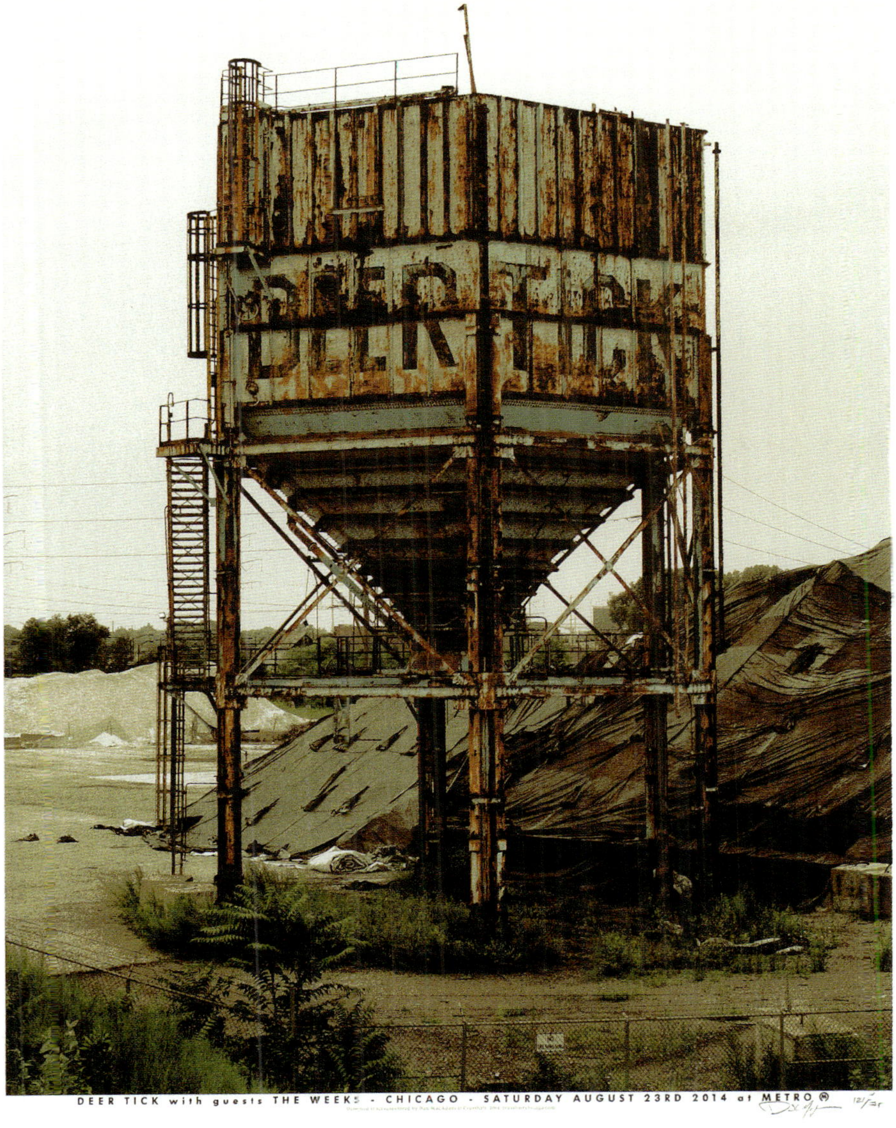

CLIENT: Deer Tick
DESIGNER: Daniel MacAdam
DESIGN FIRM: Crosshair
WEBSITE: crosshairchicago.com

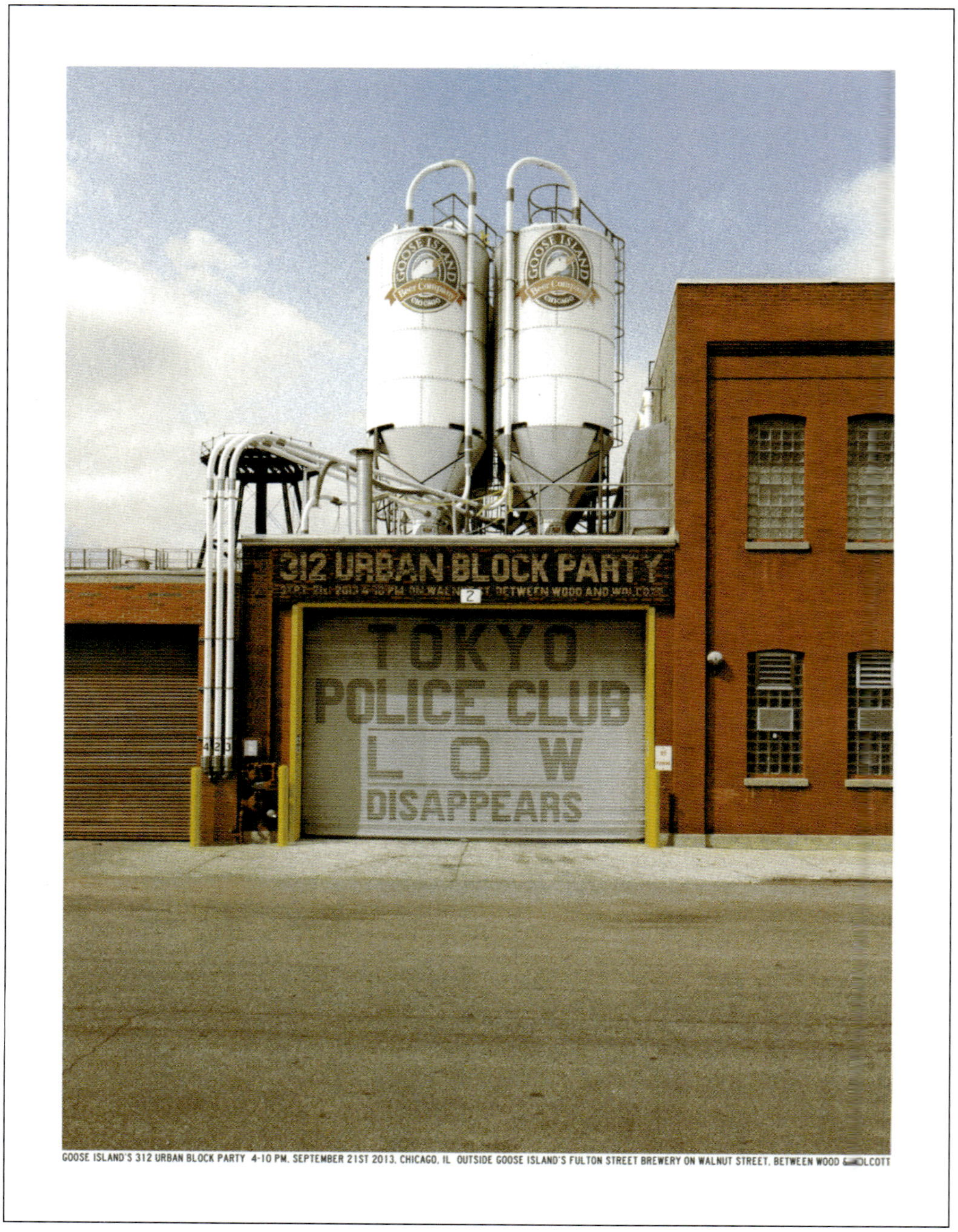

CLIENT: 312 Urban Block Party
DESIGNER: Daniel MacAdam
DESIGN FIRM: Crosshair
WEBSITE: crosshairchicago.com

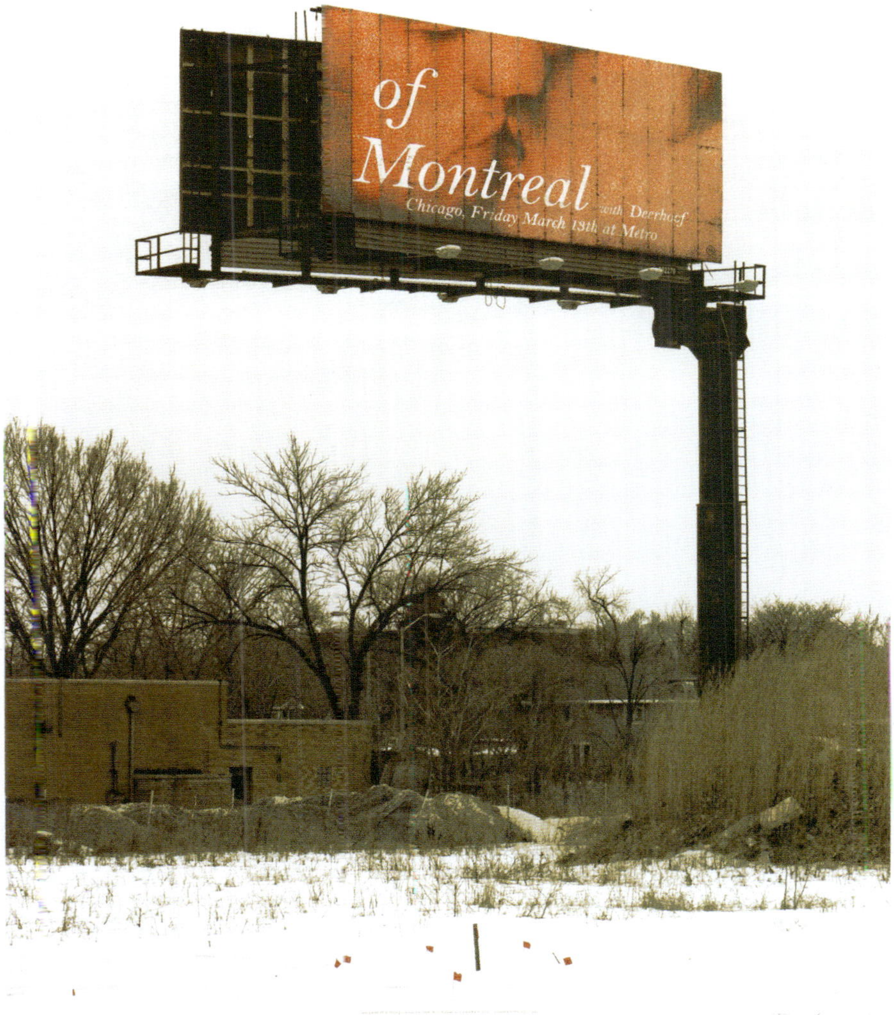

CLIENT: Of Montreal
DESIGNER: Daniel MacAdam
DESIGN FIRM: Crosshair
WEBSITE: crosshairchicago.com

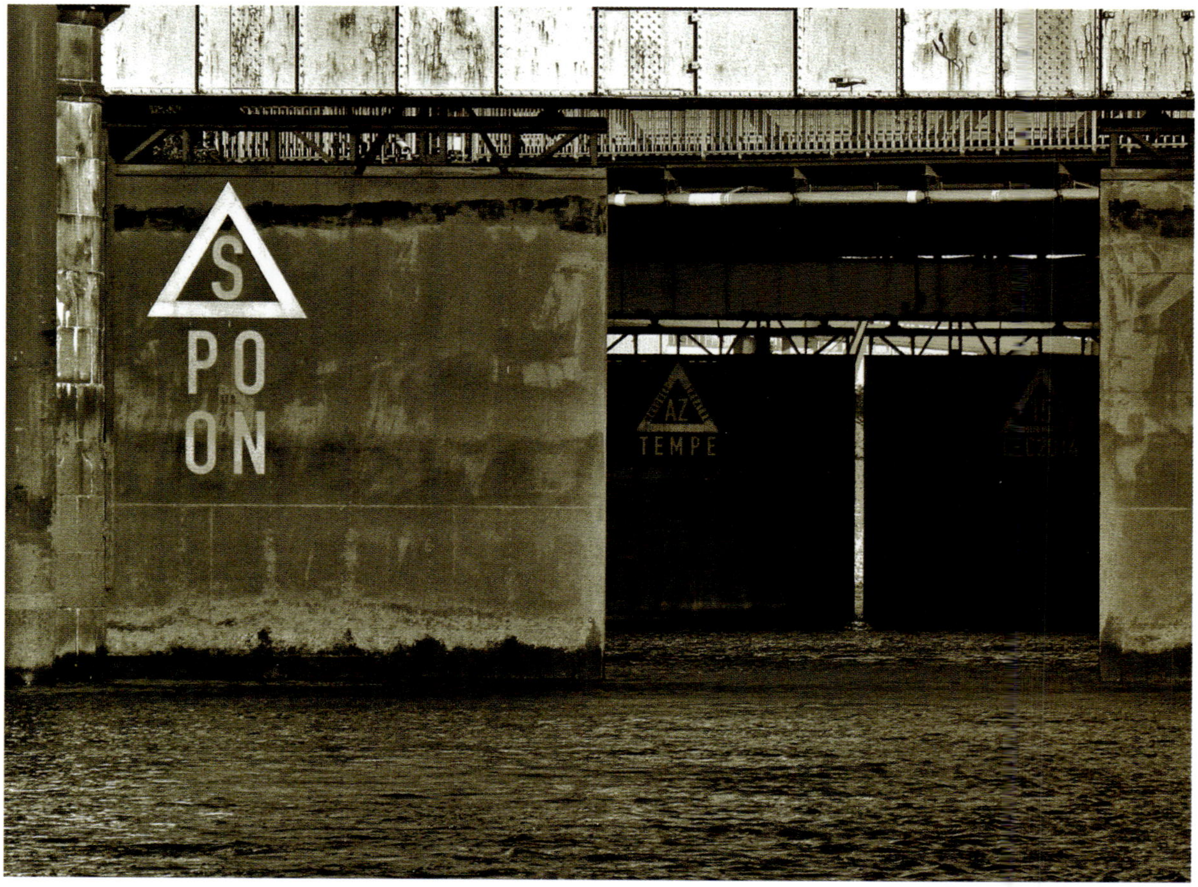

CLIENT: Spoon
DESIGNER: Daniel MacAdam
DESIGN FIRM: Crosshair
WEBSITE: crosshairchicago.com

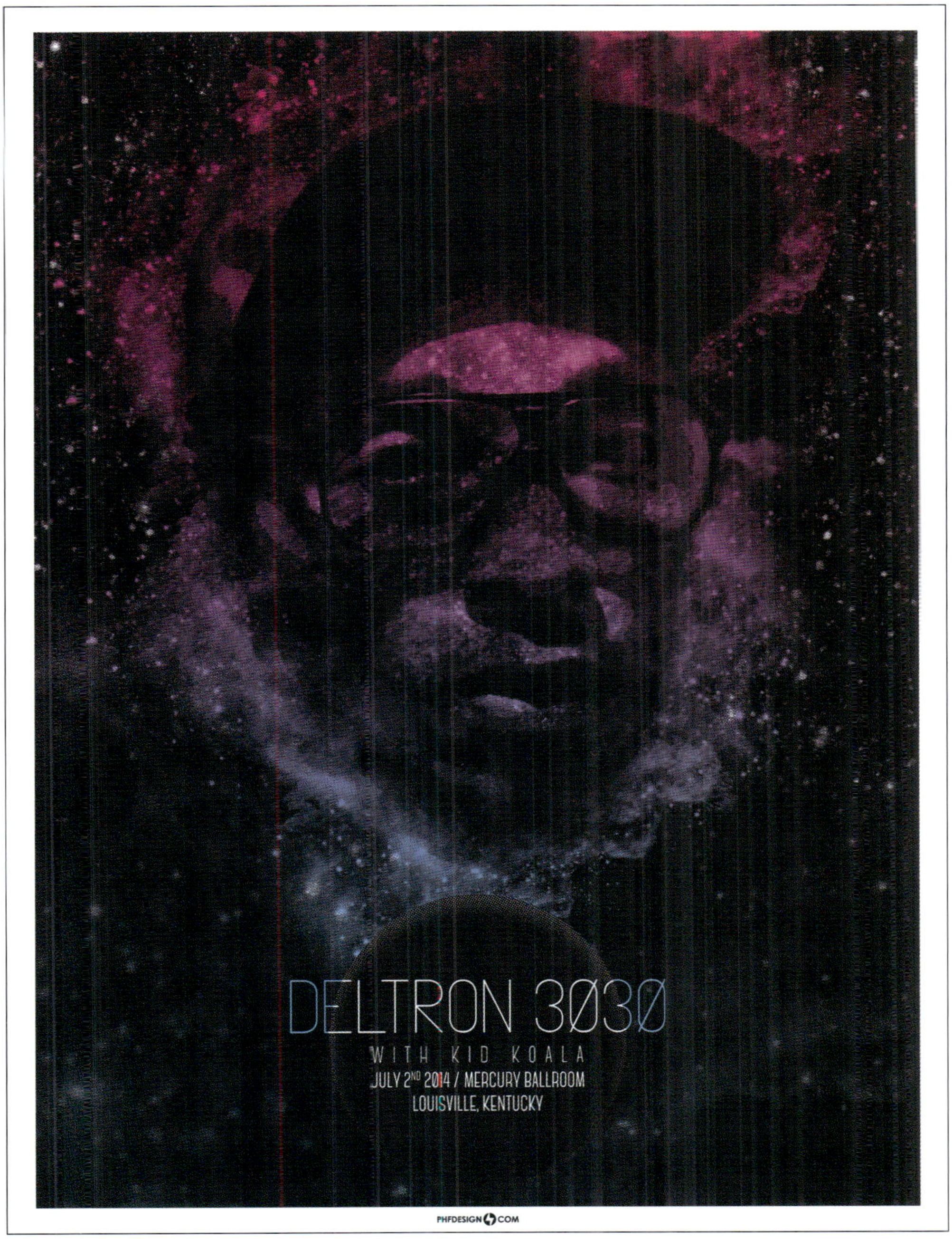

CLIENT: Deltron 3030
DESIGNER: Tim Engel
DESIGN FIRM: Powerhouse Factories
WEBSITE: powerhousefactories.com

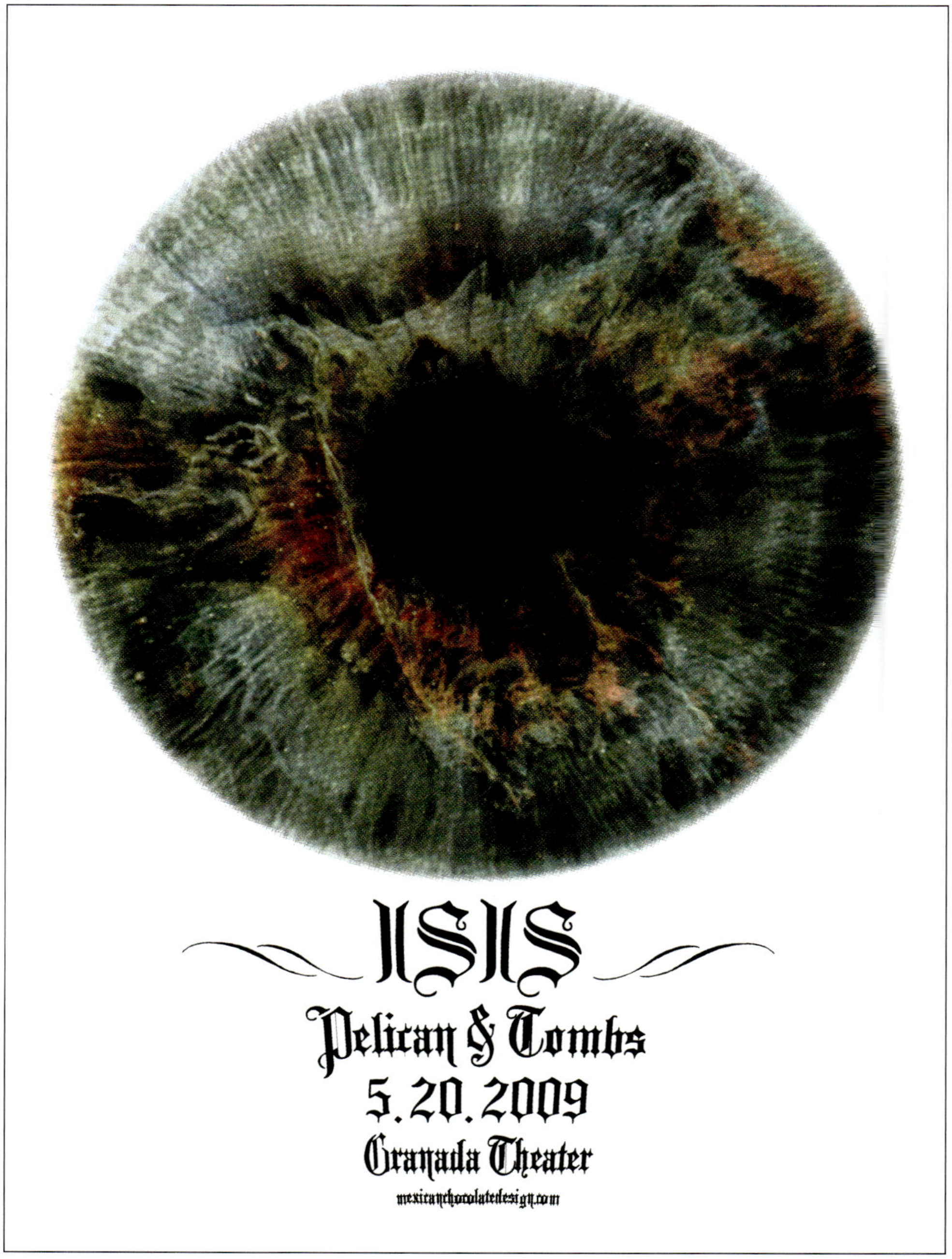

CLIENT: ISIS
DESIGNER: Jared Connor
DESIGN FIRM: Mexican Chocolate Design
WEBSITE: mexicanchocolatedesign.com

Illustrated Ornamentation

At times reminiscent of the classic realist painters, this highly illustrated style incorporates strong imagery that borders on realism. Out-of-this-world, larger-than-life subjects are often portrayed very realistically through painstaking detail and fine ornamentation.

KEY STYLE CHARACTERISTICS

- This style tends to showcase very strong illustration skills in this category
- Subjects are portrayed in a realistic manner
- Utilizes complex scale and composition; uses foreshortening and realistic forms
- Ornamental use of color and type
- Fine detail and ornamentation in this style indicates heavy time and effort spent creating these pieces
- Subject matter tends to be out of this world/larger than life (while portrayed in a highly realistic manner)

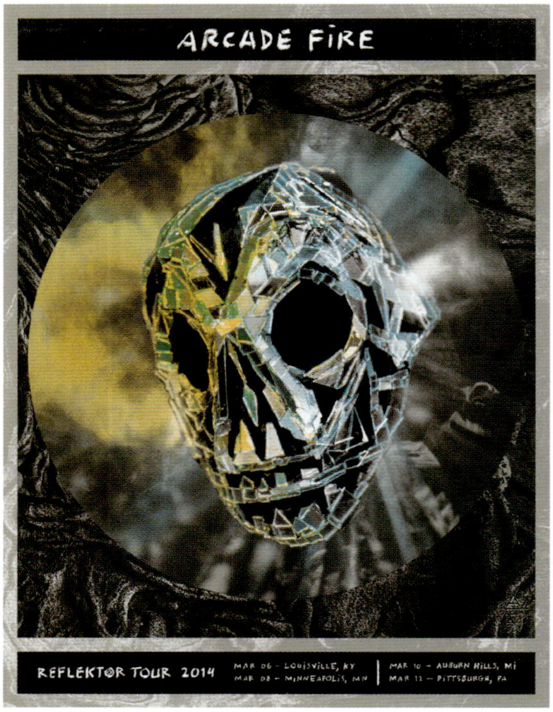

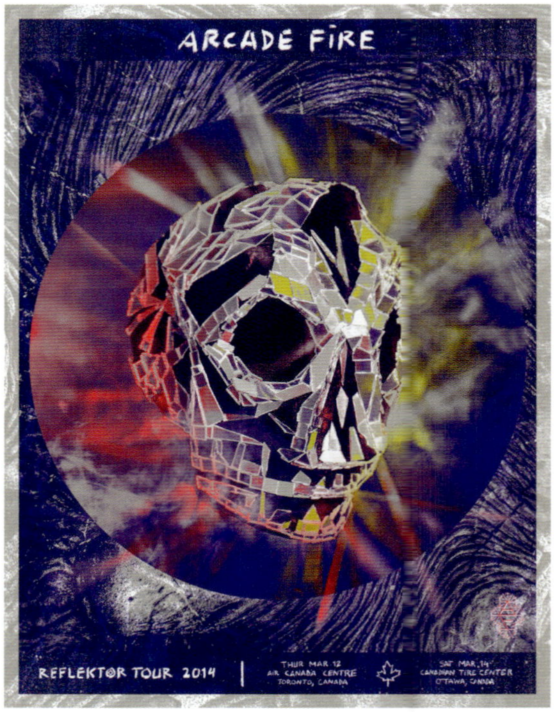

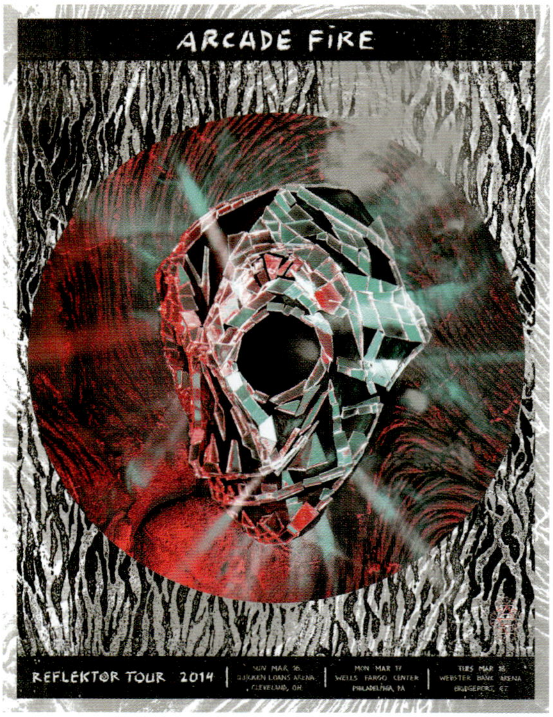

CLIENT: Arcade Fire
DESIGNER: Mike Davis
DESIGN FIRM: Burlesque of North America
WEBSITE: burlesquedesign.com

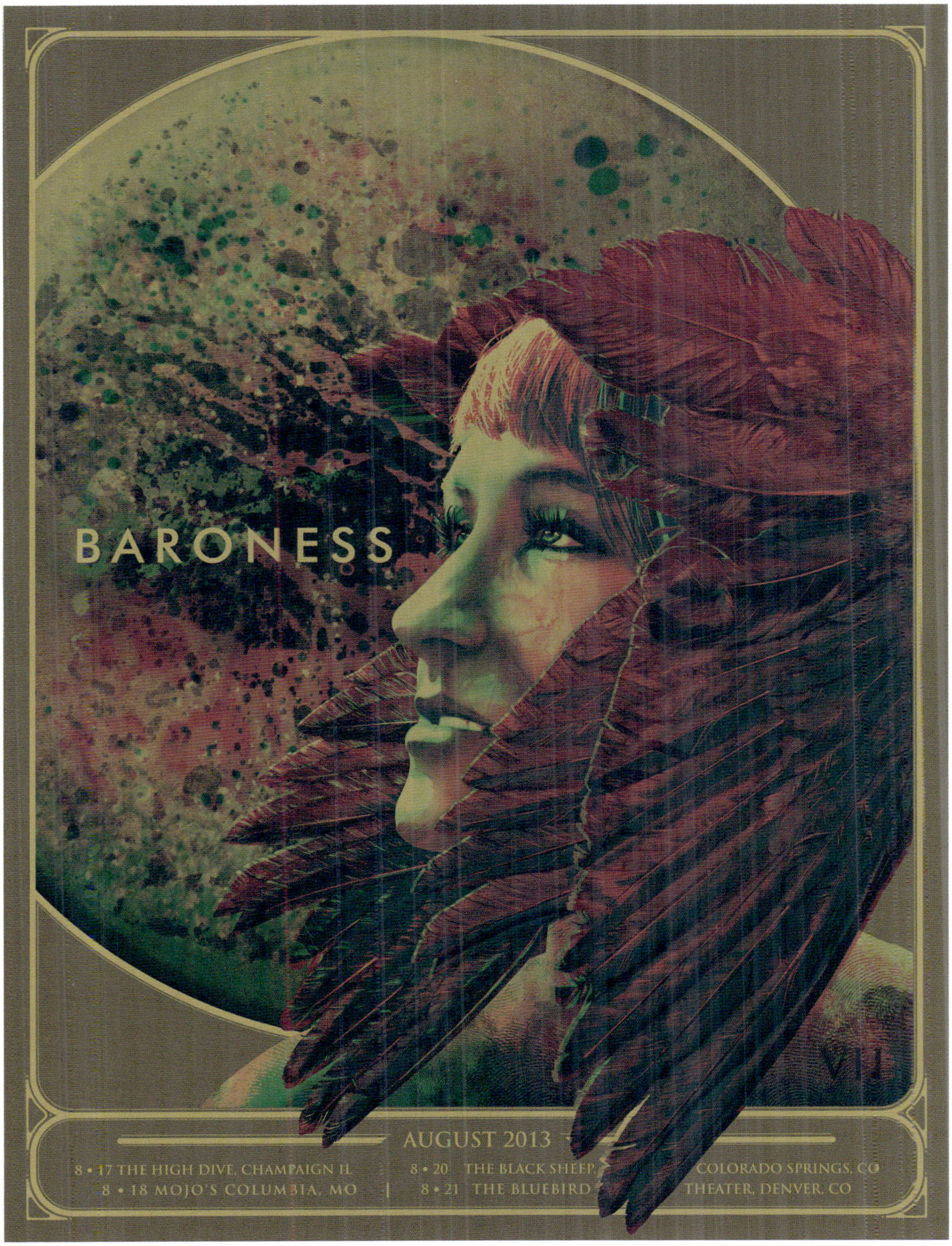

CLIENT: Baroness
DESIGNER: Mike Davis
DESIGN FIRM: Burlesque of North America
WEBSITE: burlesquedesign.com

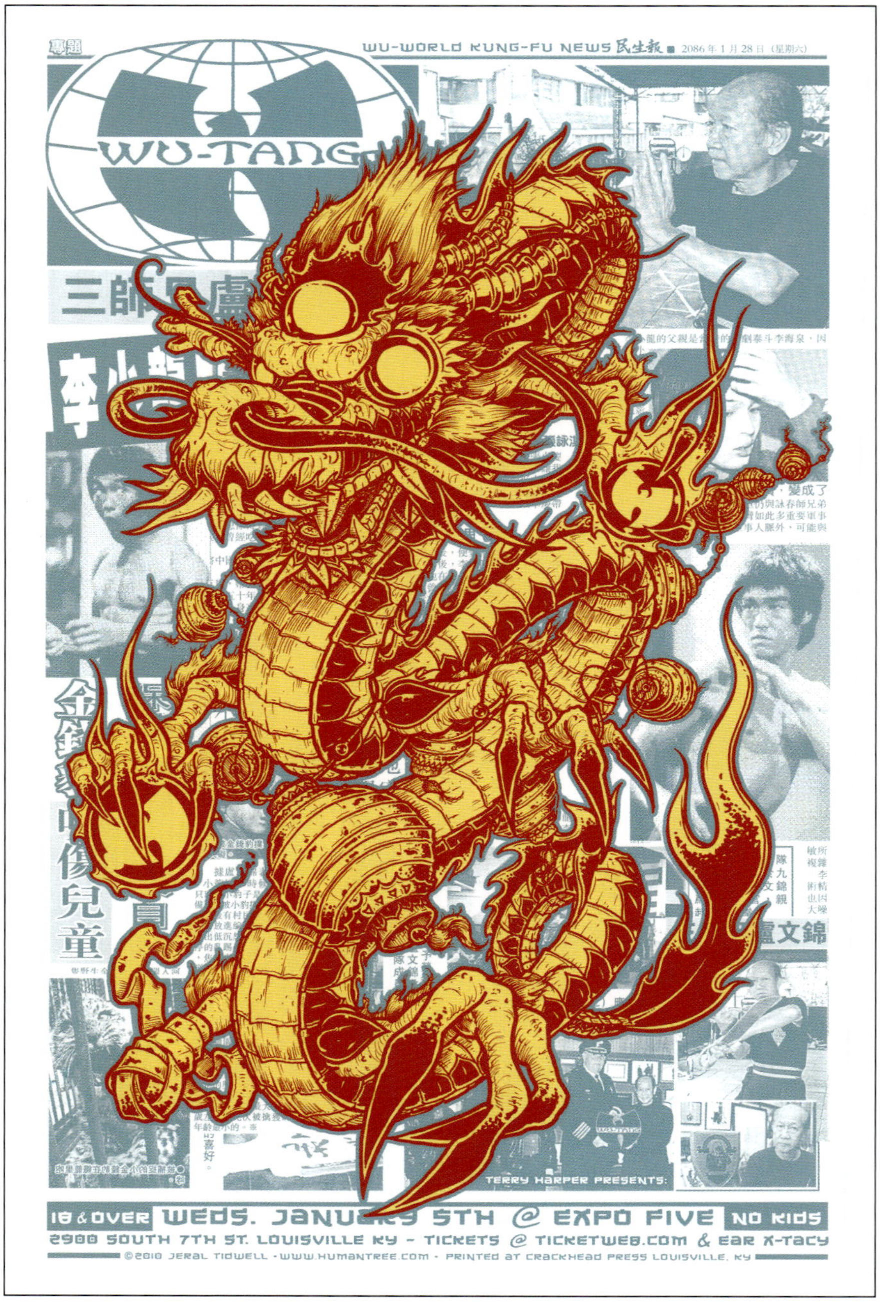

CLIENT: Wu-Tang
DESIGNER: Jeral Tidwell
DESIGN FIRM: Humantree
WEBSITE: humantree.com

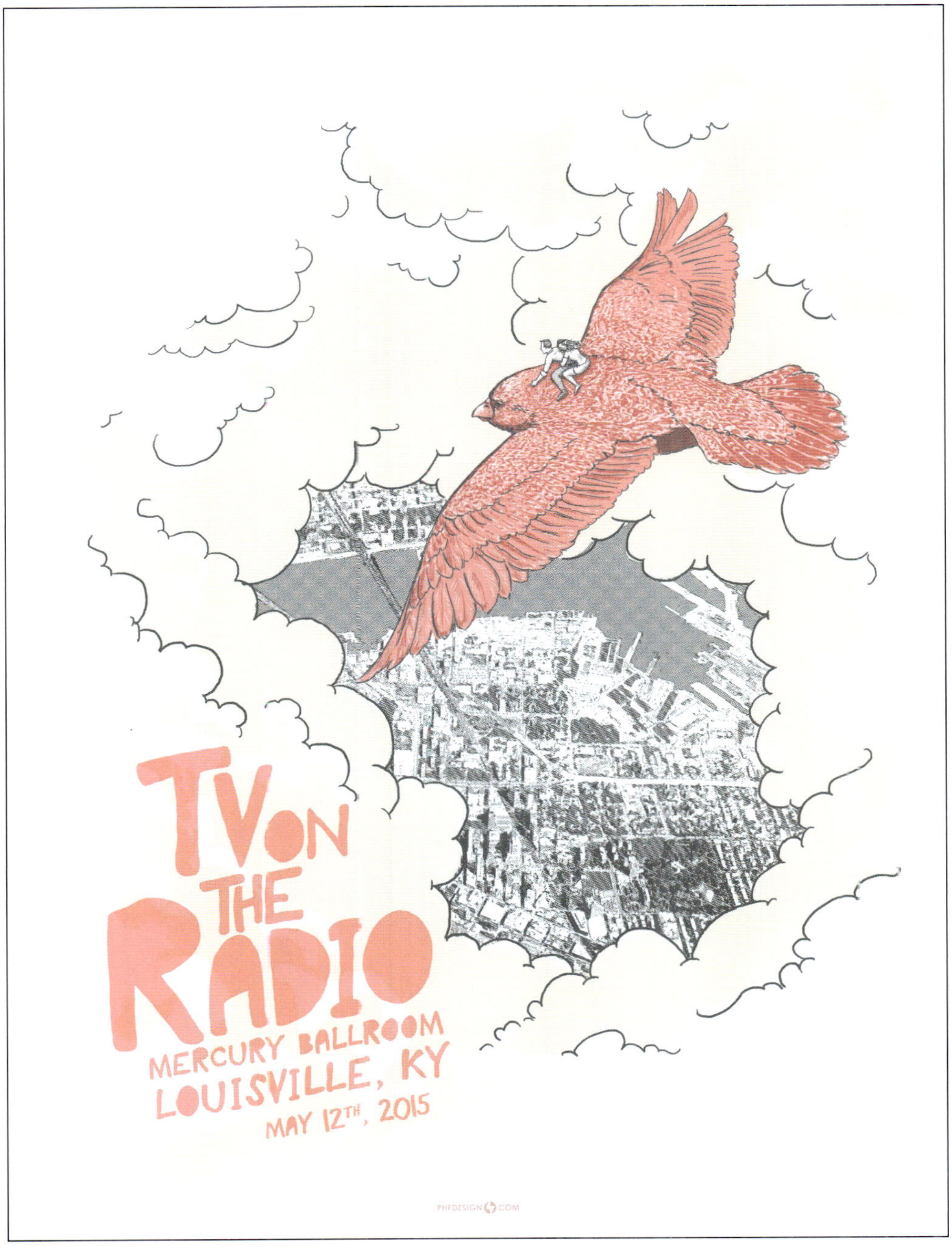

CLIENT: TV on the Radio
DESIGNER: Tim Engel
DESIGN FIRM: Powerhouse Factories
WEBSITE: powerhousefactories.com

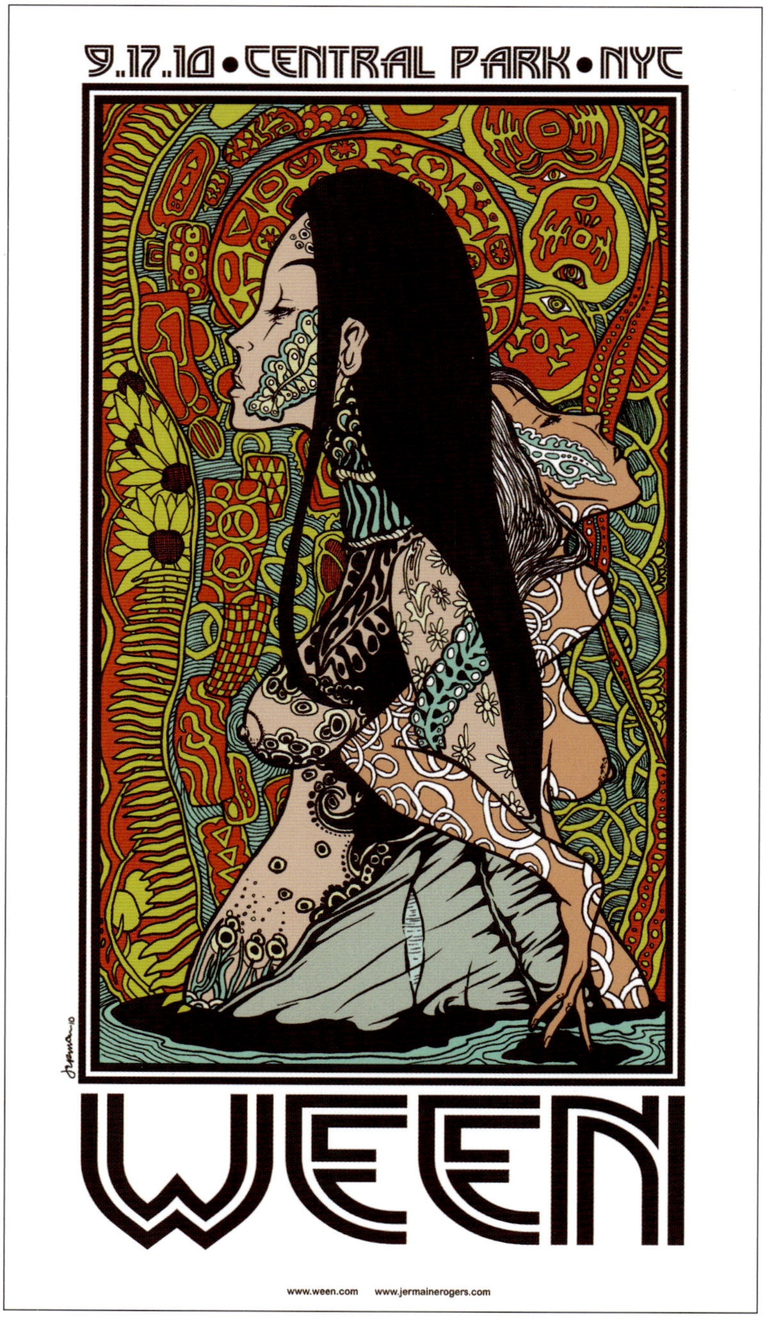

CLIENT: Ween
DESIGNER: Jermaine Rogers
WEBSITE: jermainerogers.com

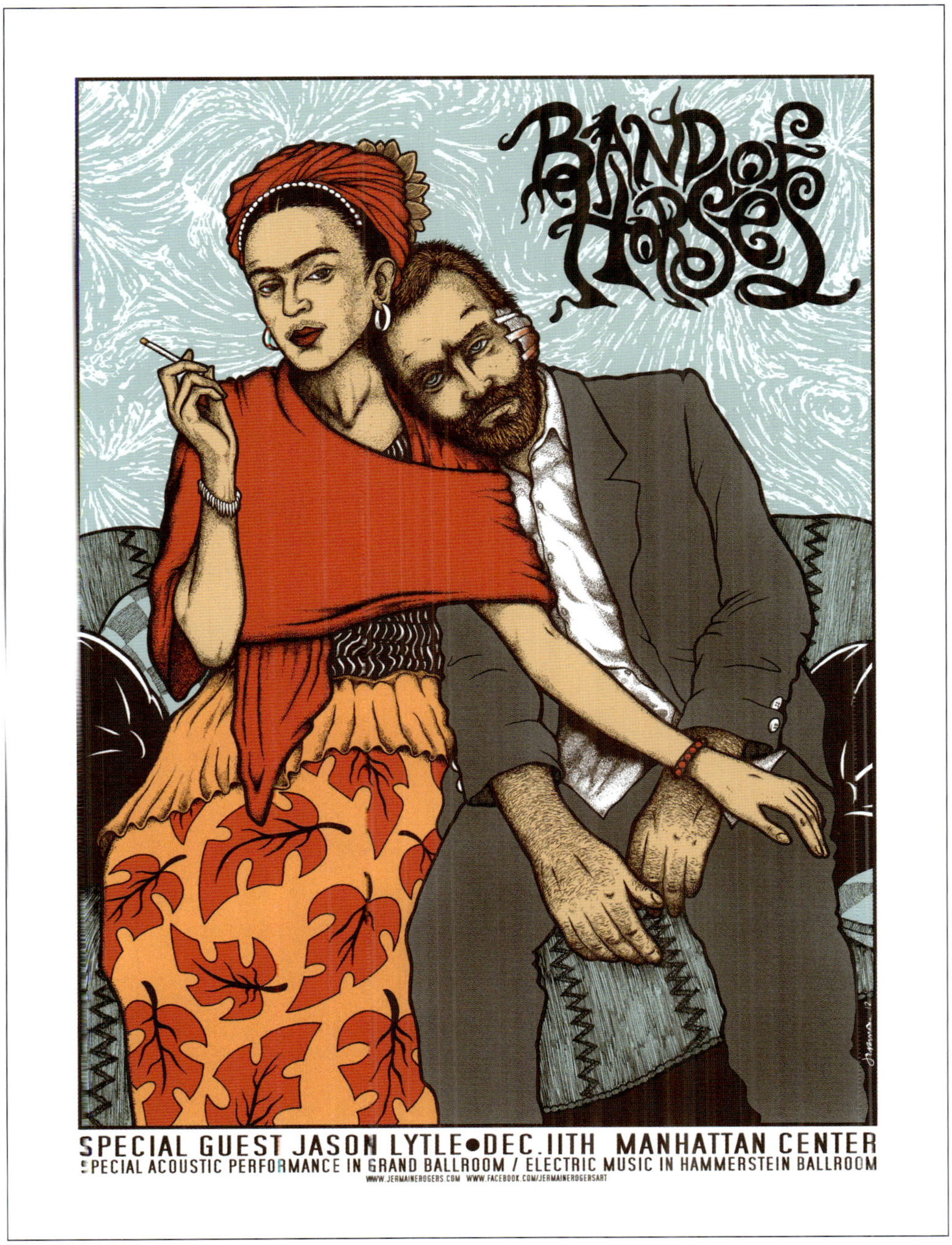

CLIENT: Band of Horses
DESIGNER: Jermaine Rogers
WEBSITE: jermainerogers.com

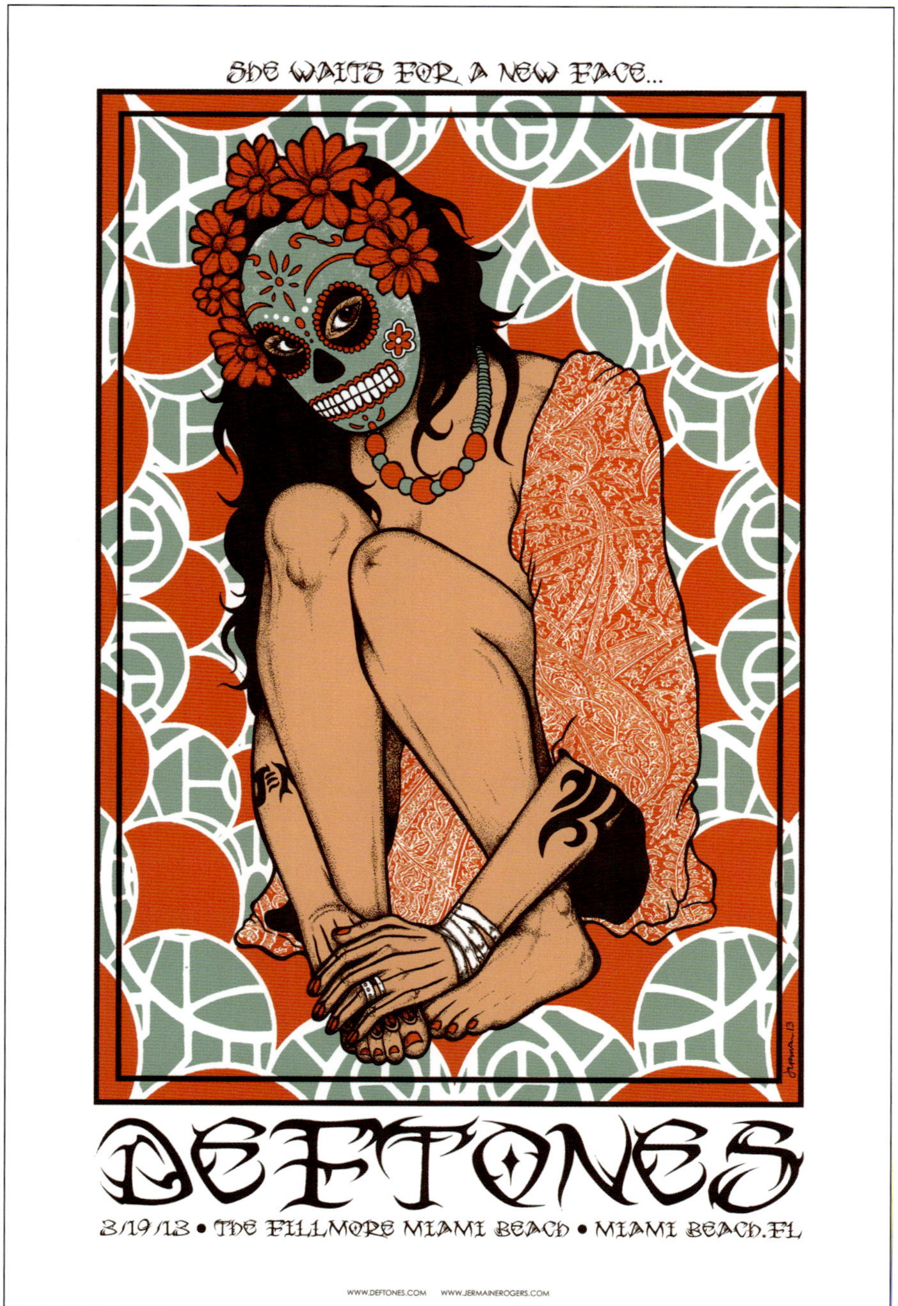

CLIENT: Deftones
DESIGNER: Jermaine Rogers
WEBSITE: jermainerogers.com

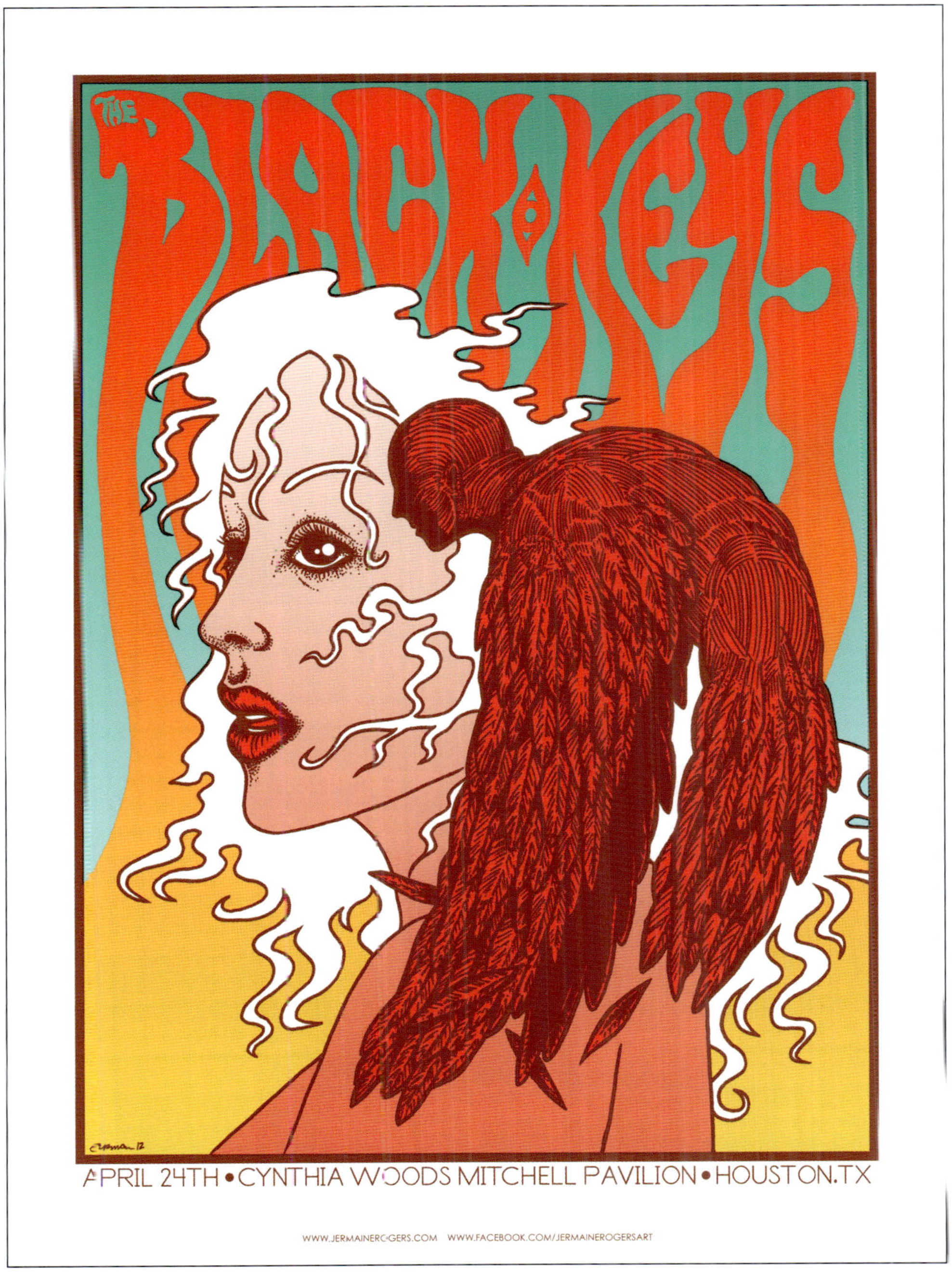

CLIENT: The Black Keys
DESIGNER: Jermaine Rogers
WEBSITE: jermainerogers.com

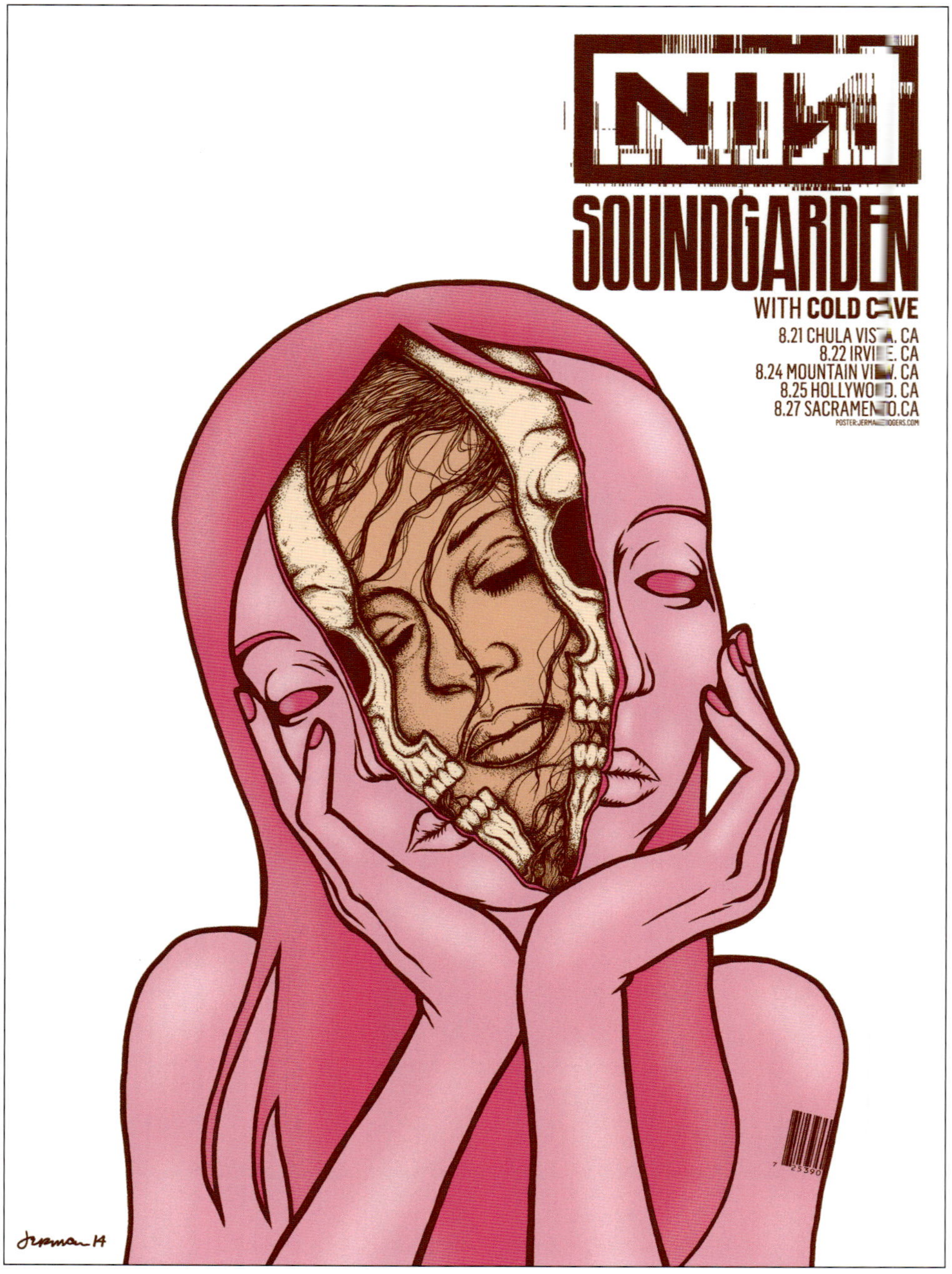

CLIENT: NIN / Soundgarden
DESIGNER: Jermaine Rogers
WEBSITE: jermainerogers.com

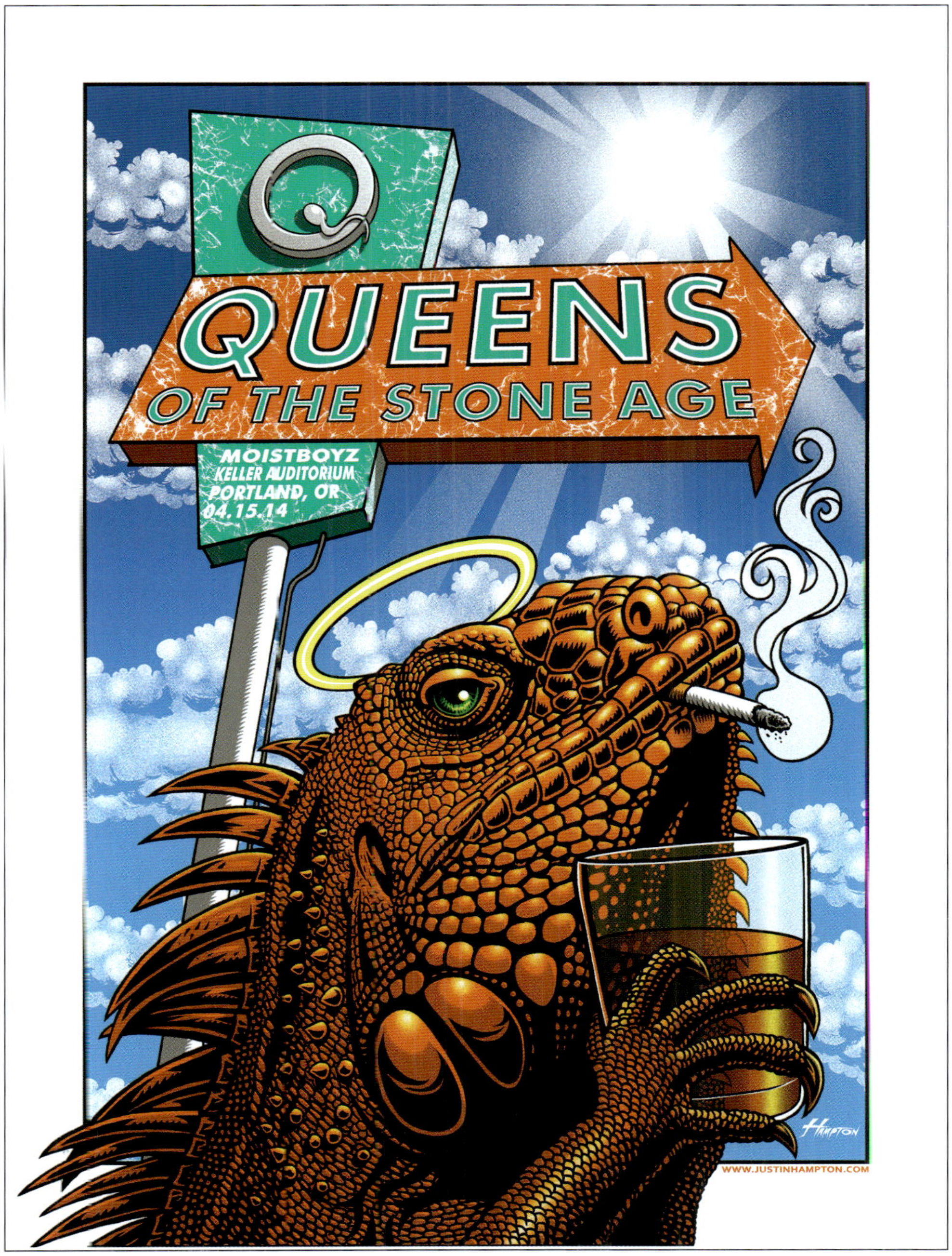

CLIENT: Queens of the Stone Age
DESIGNER: Justin Hampton
WEBSITE: justinhampton.com

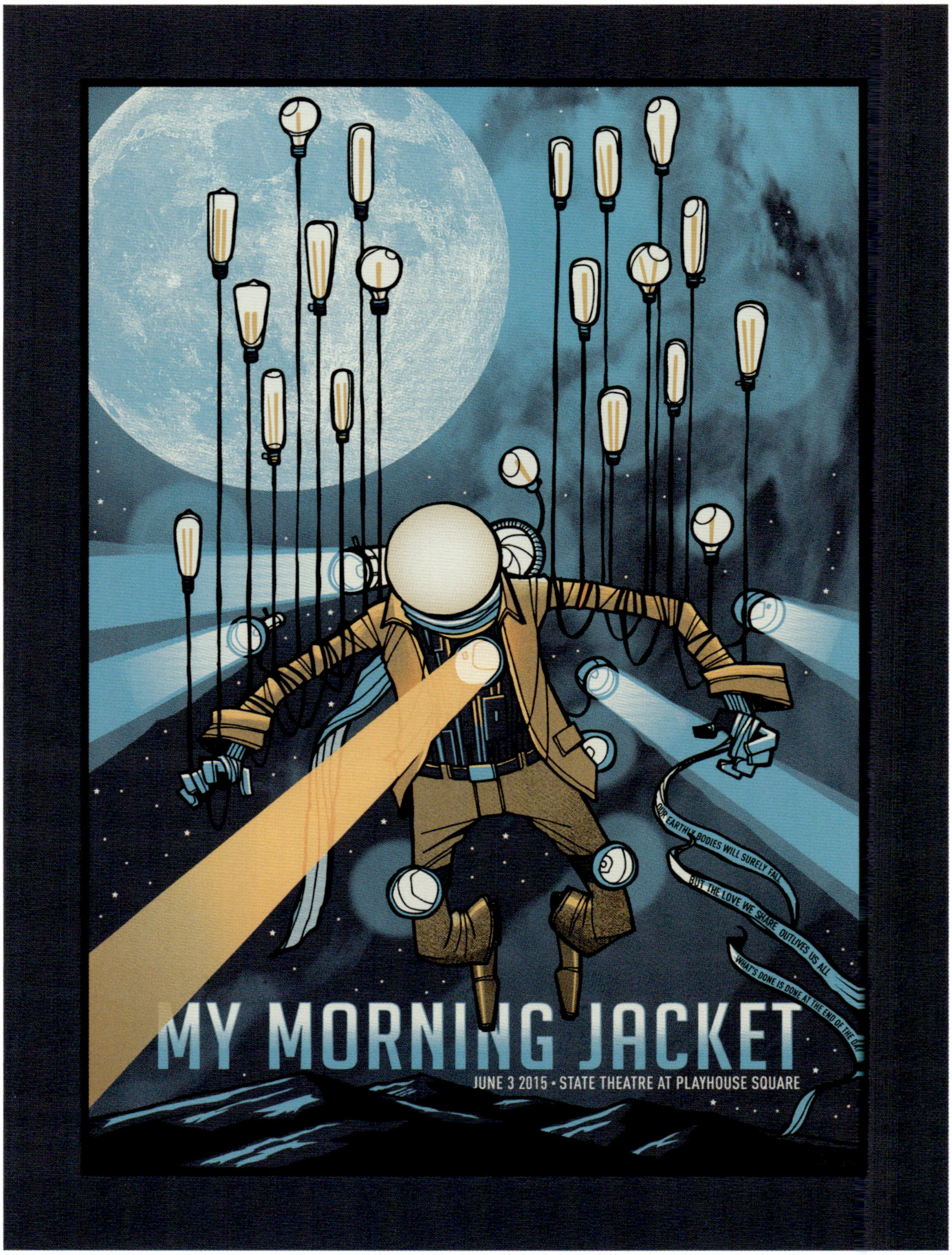

CLIENT: My Morning Jacket
DESIGNER: Clinton Reno
WEBSITE: clintonreno.com

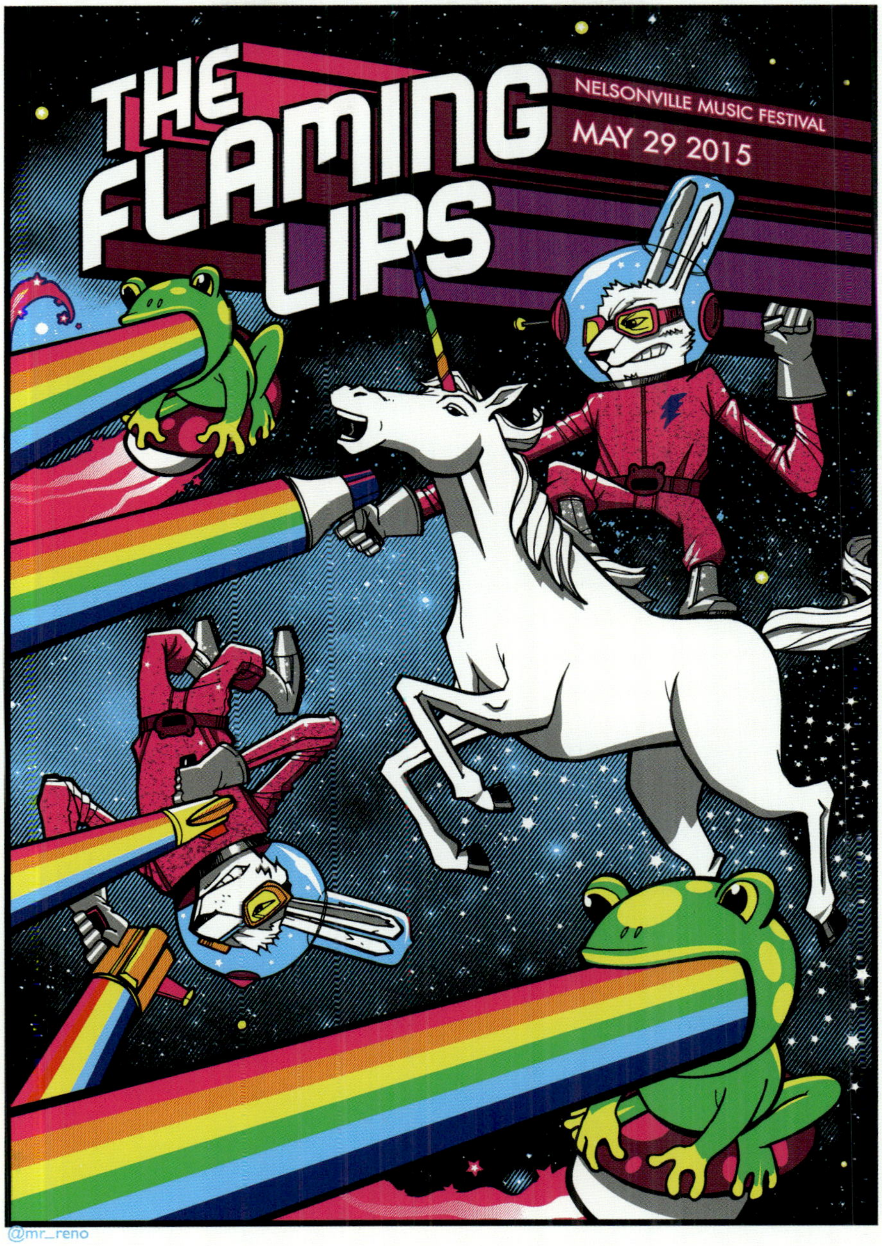

CLIENT: The Flaming Lips
DESIGNER: Clinton Reno
WEBSITE: clintonreno.com

Iconic Simplification

Iconic simplification attempts to mimic "classic" design and illustration styles. You'll see obvious nods to old print ads from the 1940s, '50s, and '60s and art will typically be created in multiple tones of one hue, such as duo-tone or tri-tone. Large fields and simple geometric shapes characterize the style.

KEY STYLE CHARACTERISTICS

- Utilizes multiple tones of one hue or color, like duo-tone or tri-tone
- Employs a flat graphic style that mimics cut construction paper
- Incorporates sophisticated compositions and type
- Light use of line, heavier use of shapes and positive/negative space
- The simple illustrations in this style walk the line between graphic design and illustration
- Inspired by old "classic" design and illustration styles (such as the work of Charly Harper and old print ad's from the 1940s-1960s)
- Storytelling and narrative qualities of simple illustration leveraged, similar to a storybook
- Compared to other gig poster styles this one is very narrative
- Draws inspiration from a storybook cover, info graphics, textbooks, old instructional video graphics

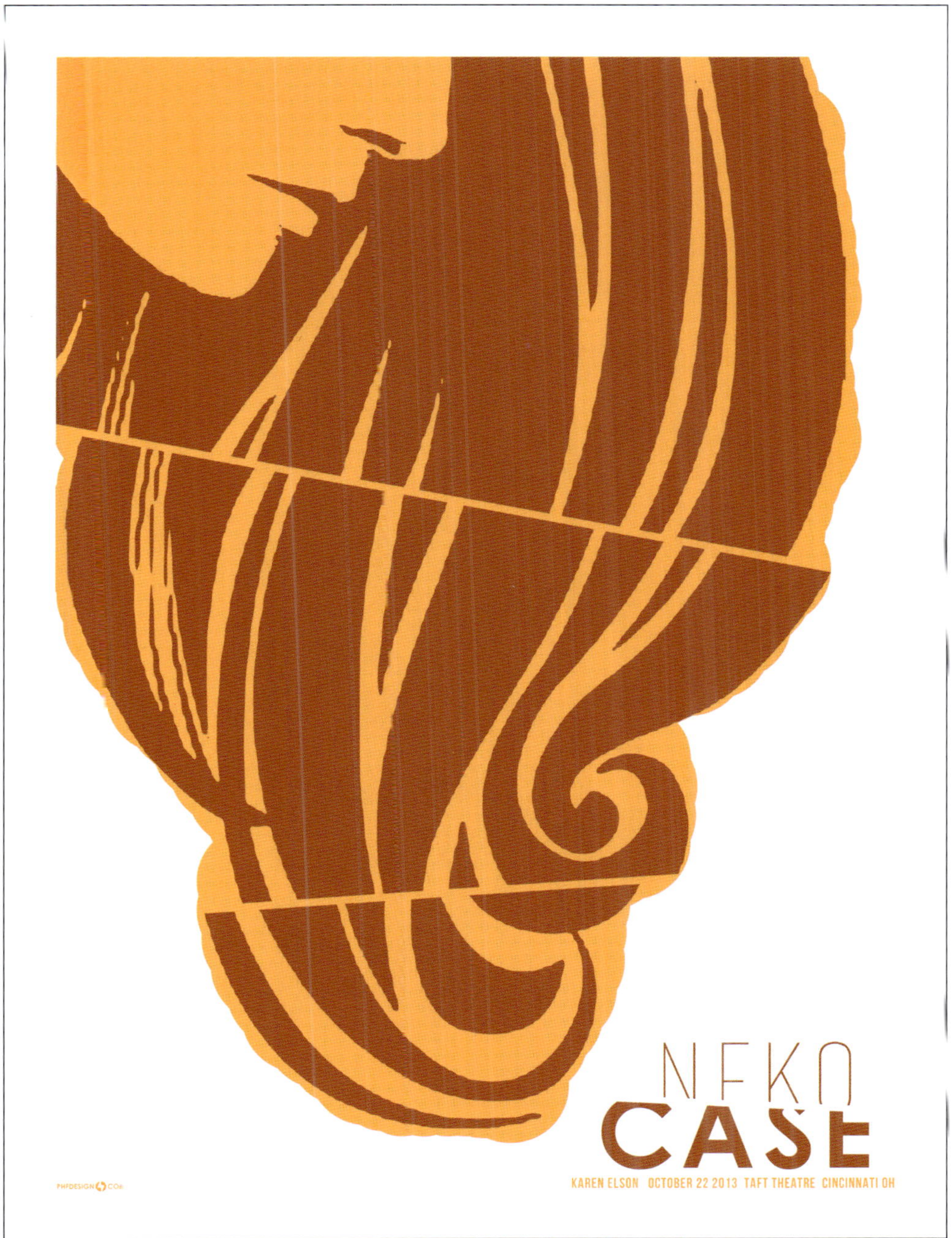

CLIENT: Neko Case
DESIGNER: Ben Nunery
DESIGN FIRM: Powerhouse Factories
WEBSITE: powerhousefactories.com

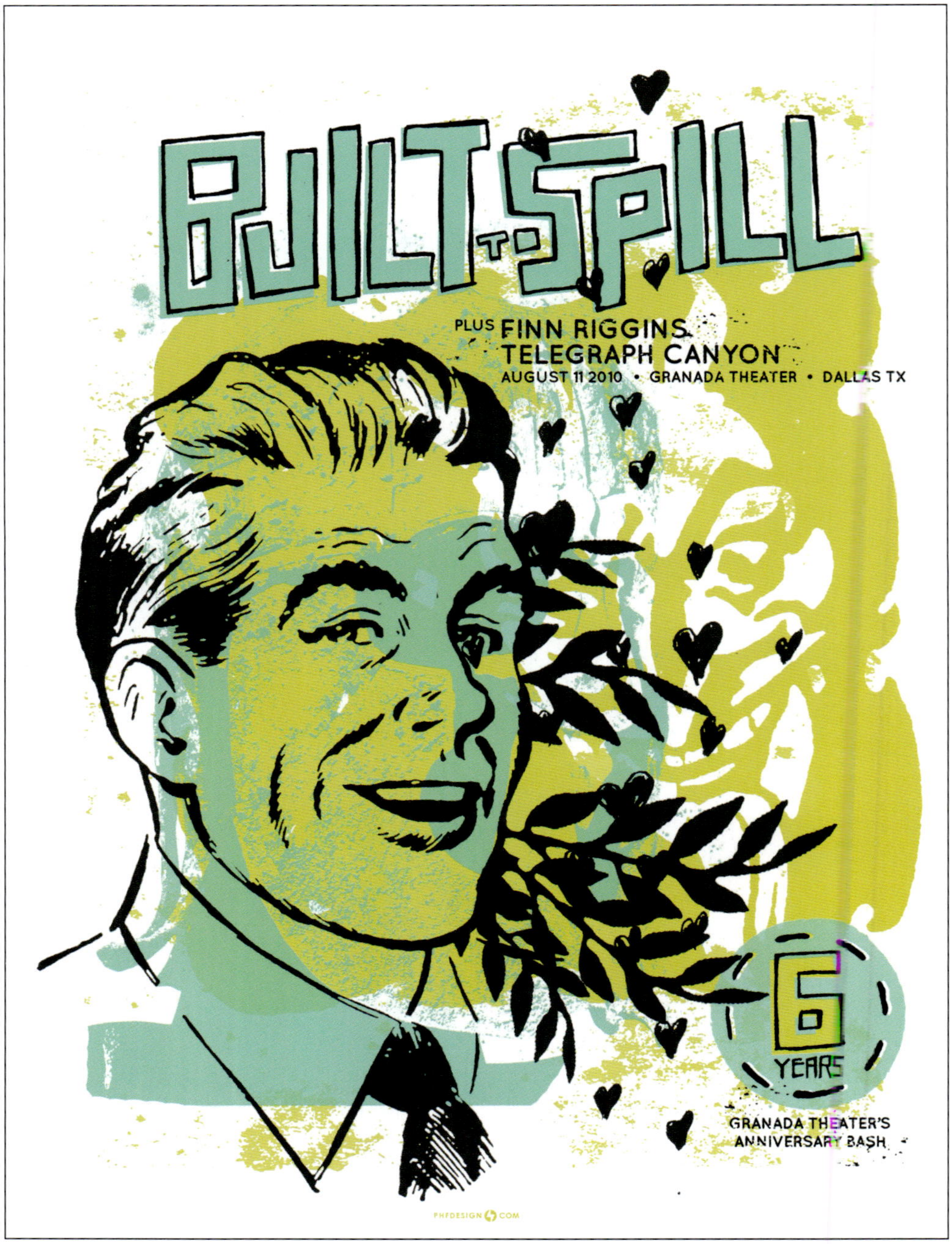

CLIENT: Built to Spill
DESIGNER: Ben Nunery
DESIGN FIRM: Powerhouse Factories
WEBSITE: powerhousefactories.com

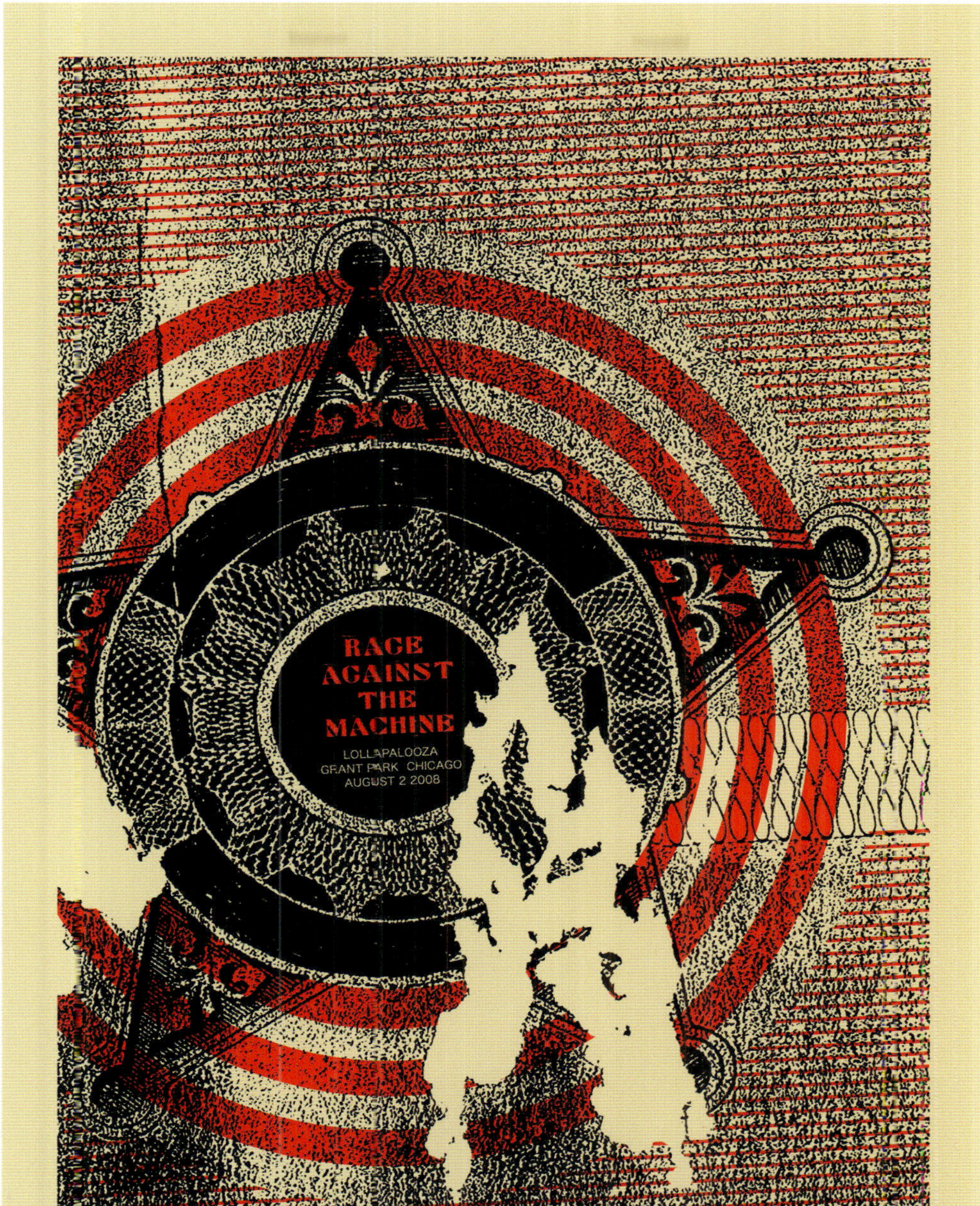

CLIENT: Rage Against the Machine
DESIGNER: Ben Nunery
DESIGN FIRM: Powerhouse Factories
WEBSITE: powerhousefactories.com

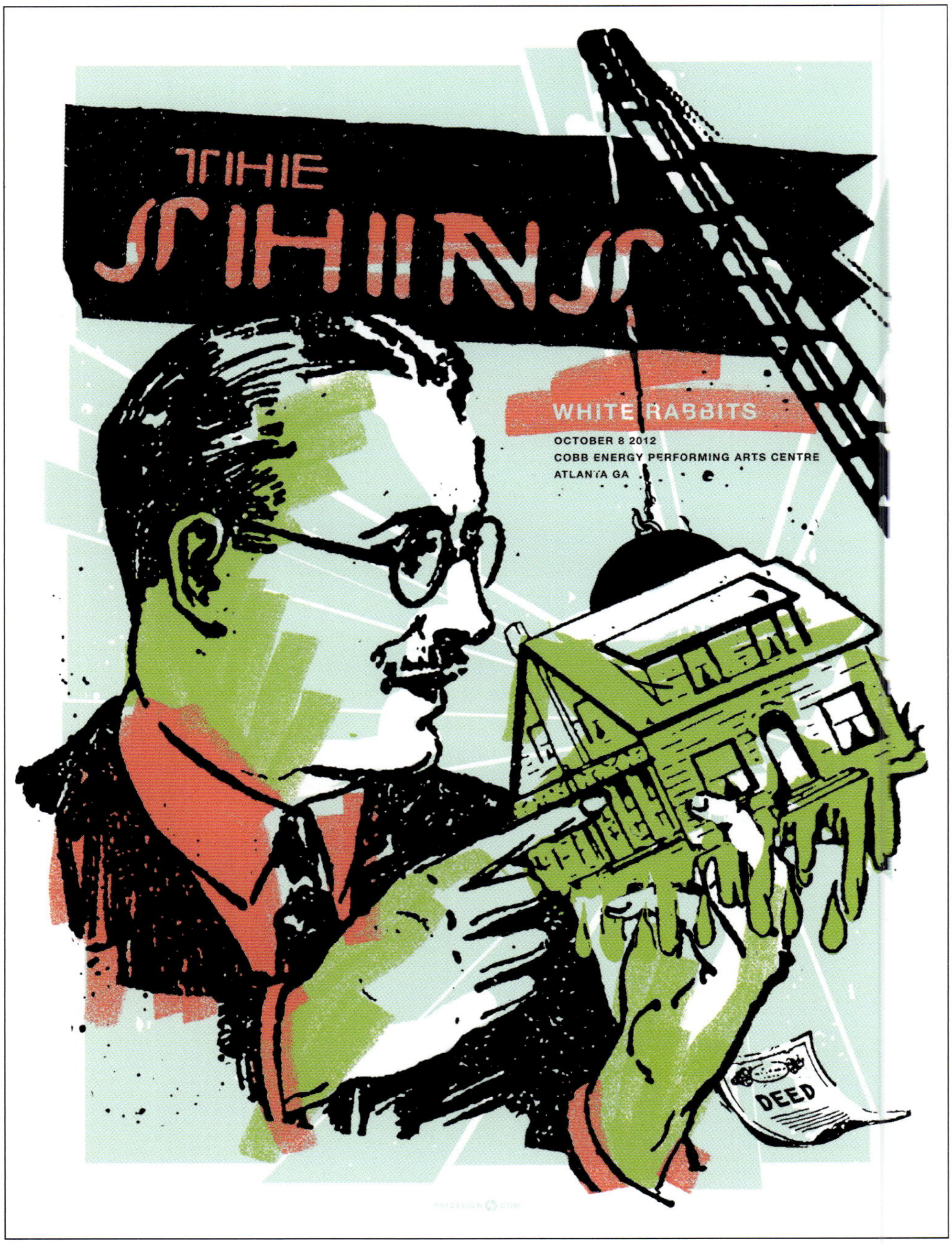

CLIENT: The Shins
DESIGNER: Ben Nunery
DESIGN FIRM: Powerhouse Factories
WEBSITE: powerhousefactories.com

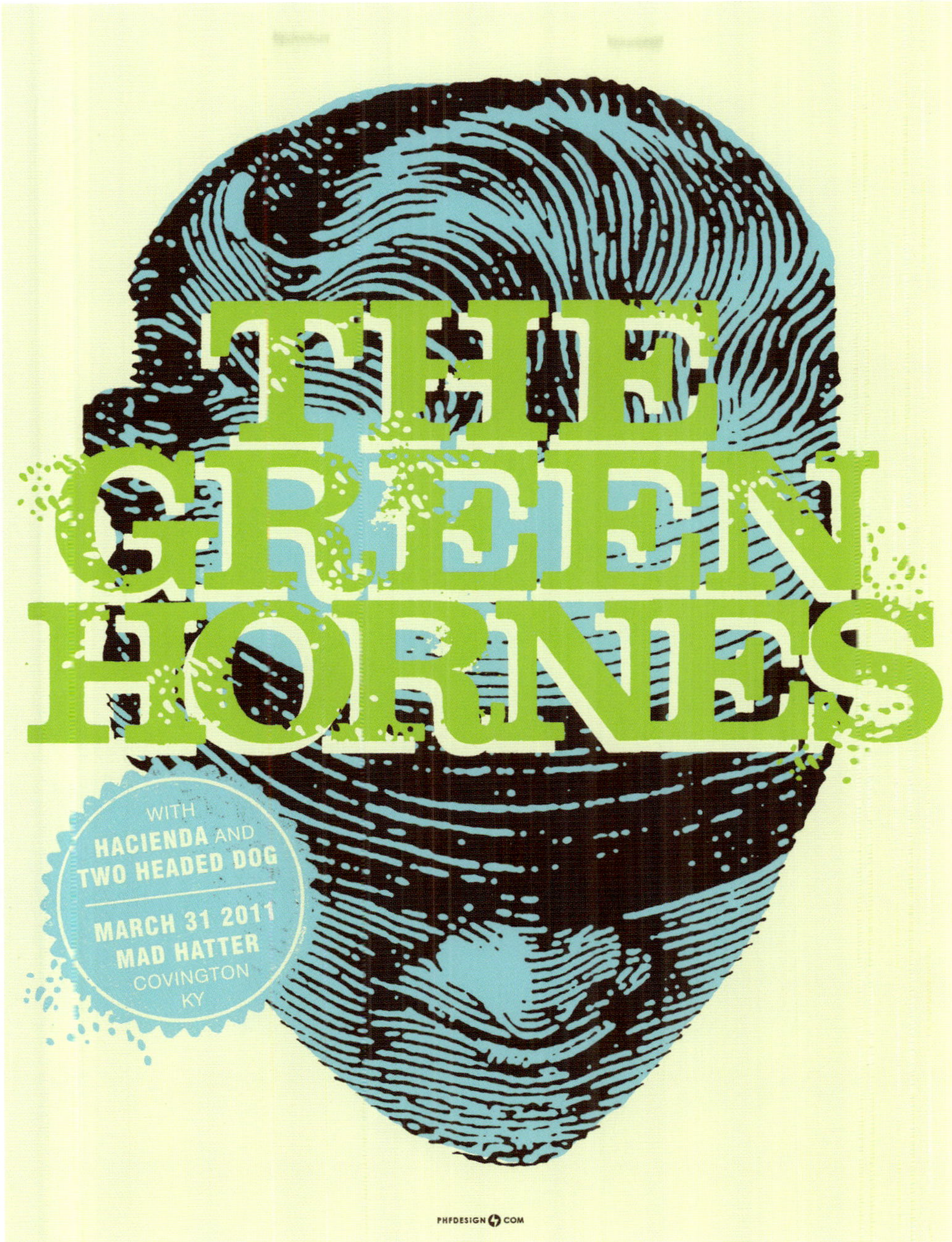

CLIENT The Greenhornes
DESIGNER: Ben Nunery
DESIGN FIRM: Powerhouse Factories
WEBSITE: powerhousefactories.com

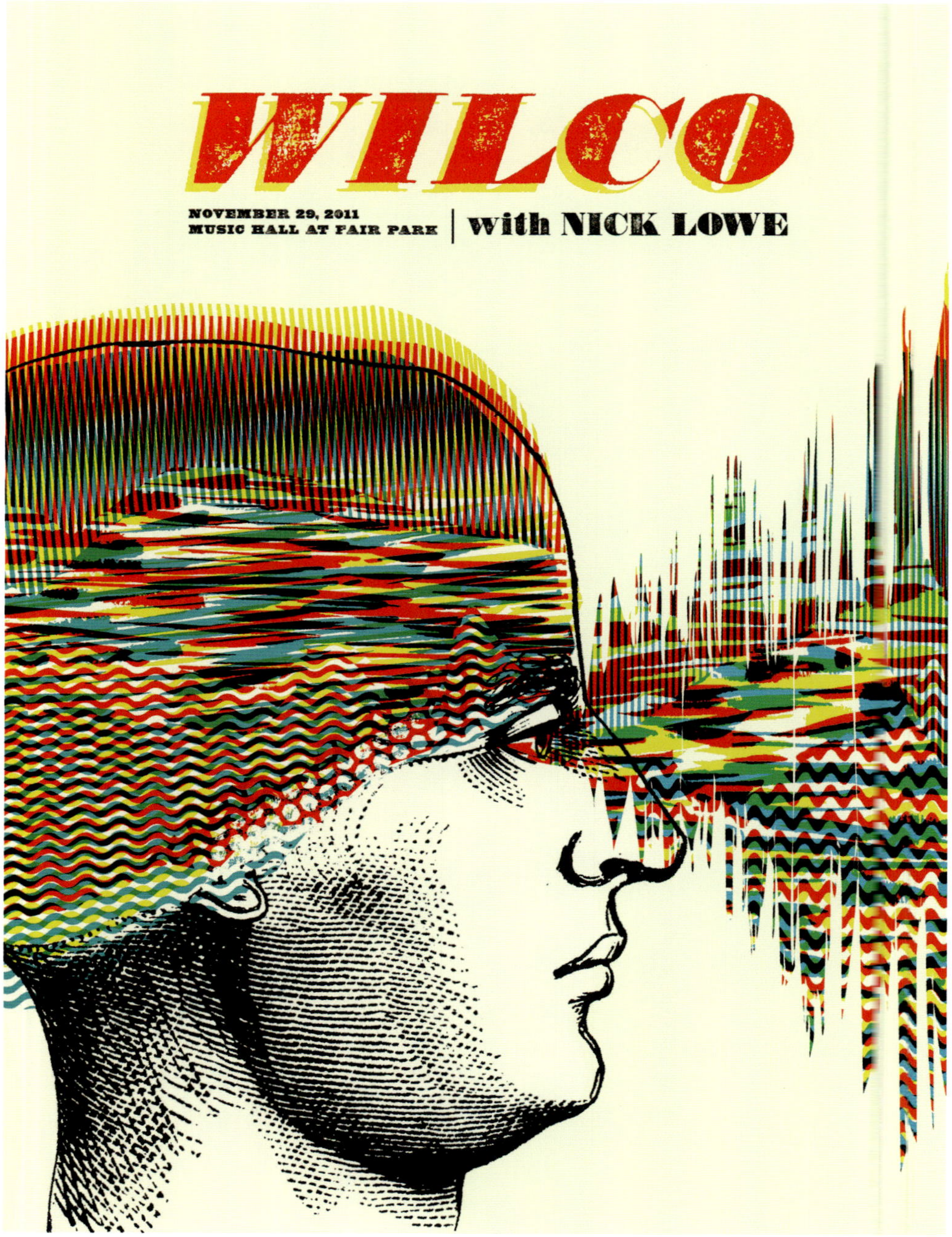

CLIENT: Wilco
DESIGNER: Jeff Matz
DESIGN FIRM: Lure Design Incorporated
WEBSITE: luredesigninc.com

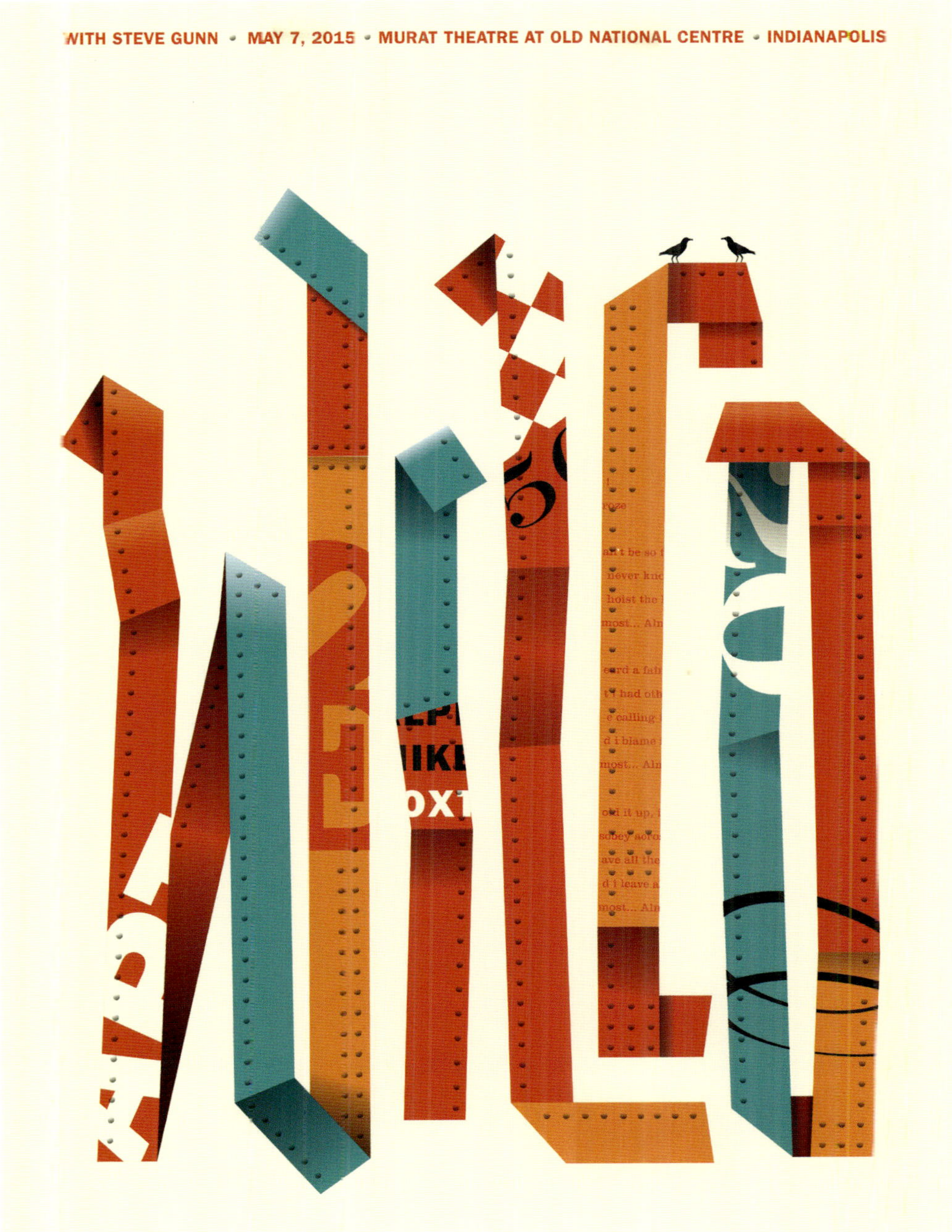

CLIENT: Wilco
DESIGNER: Jeff Matz
DESIGN FIRM: Lure Design Incorporated
WEBSITE: luredesigninc.com

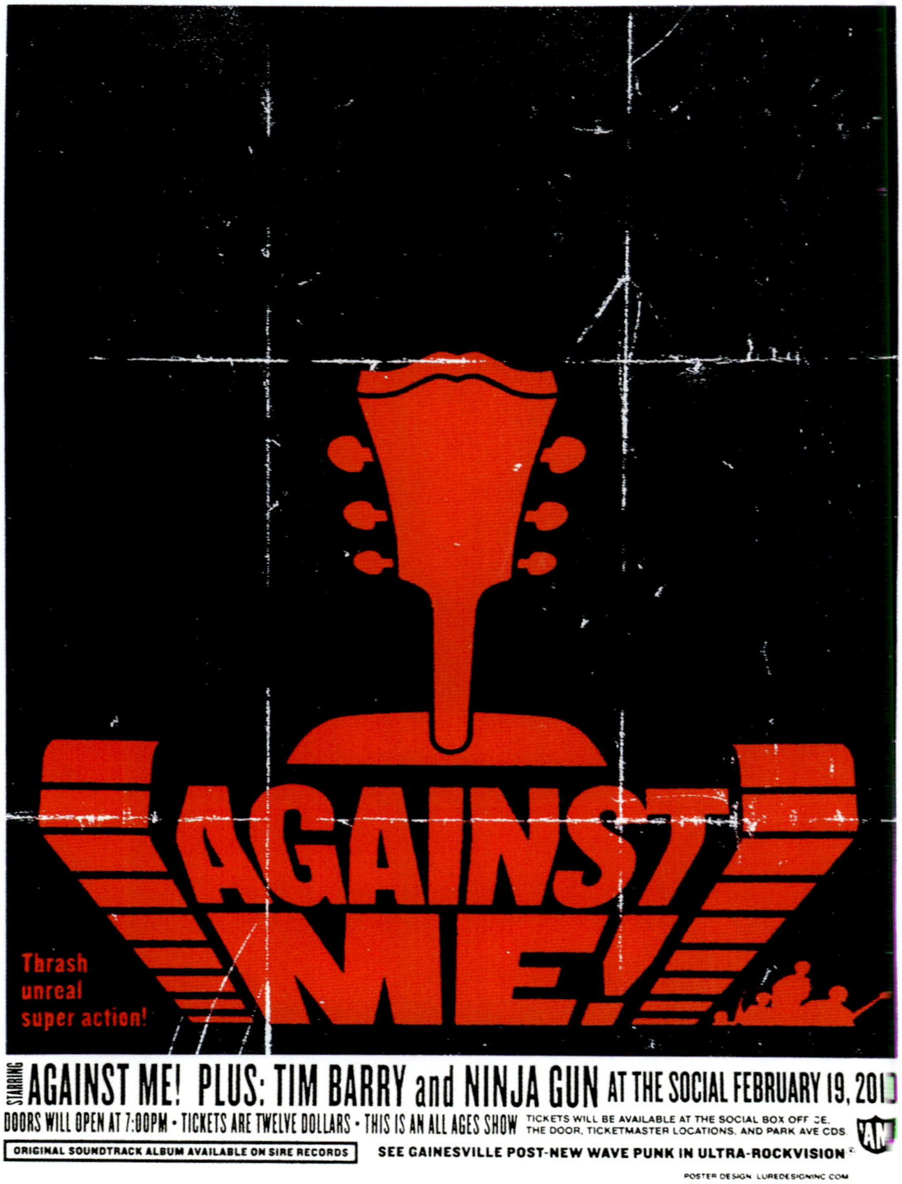

CLIENT: Against Me!
DESIGNER: Jeff Matz
DESIGN FIRM: Lure Design Incorporated
WEBSITE: luredesigninc.com

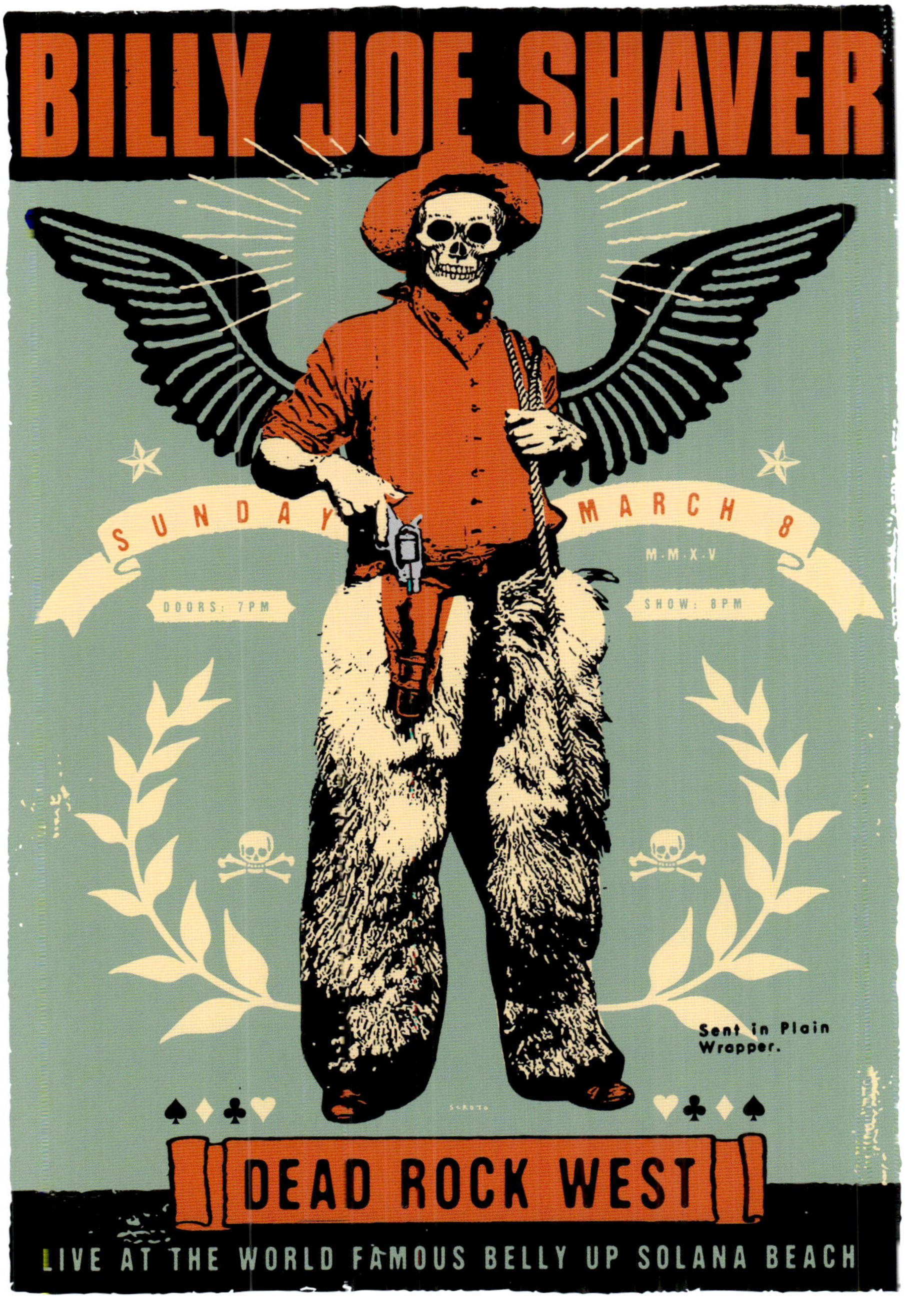

CLIENT: Billy Joe Shaver
DESIGNER: Scrojo
WEBSITE: scrojo.com

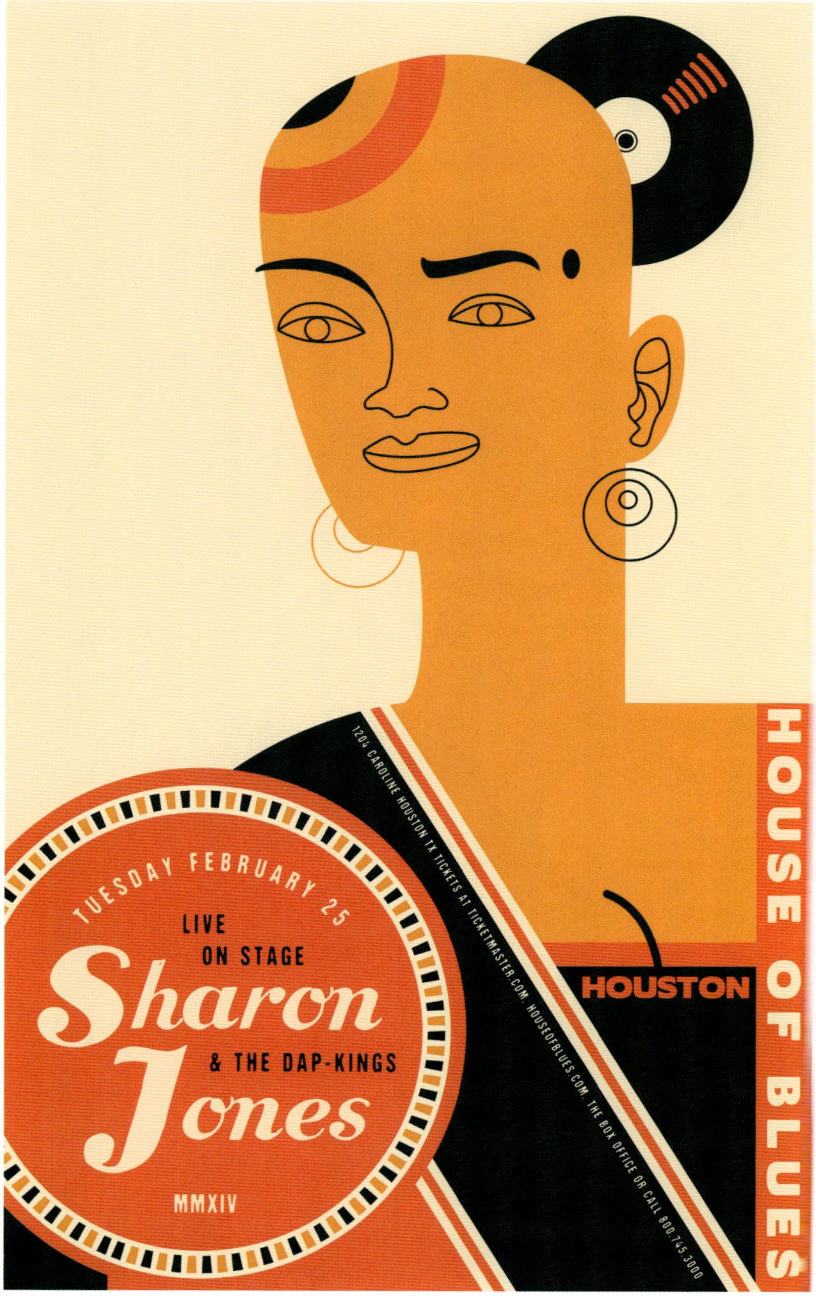

CLIENT: Sharon Jones & the Dap-Kings
DESIGNER: Scrojo
WEBSITE: scrojo.com

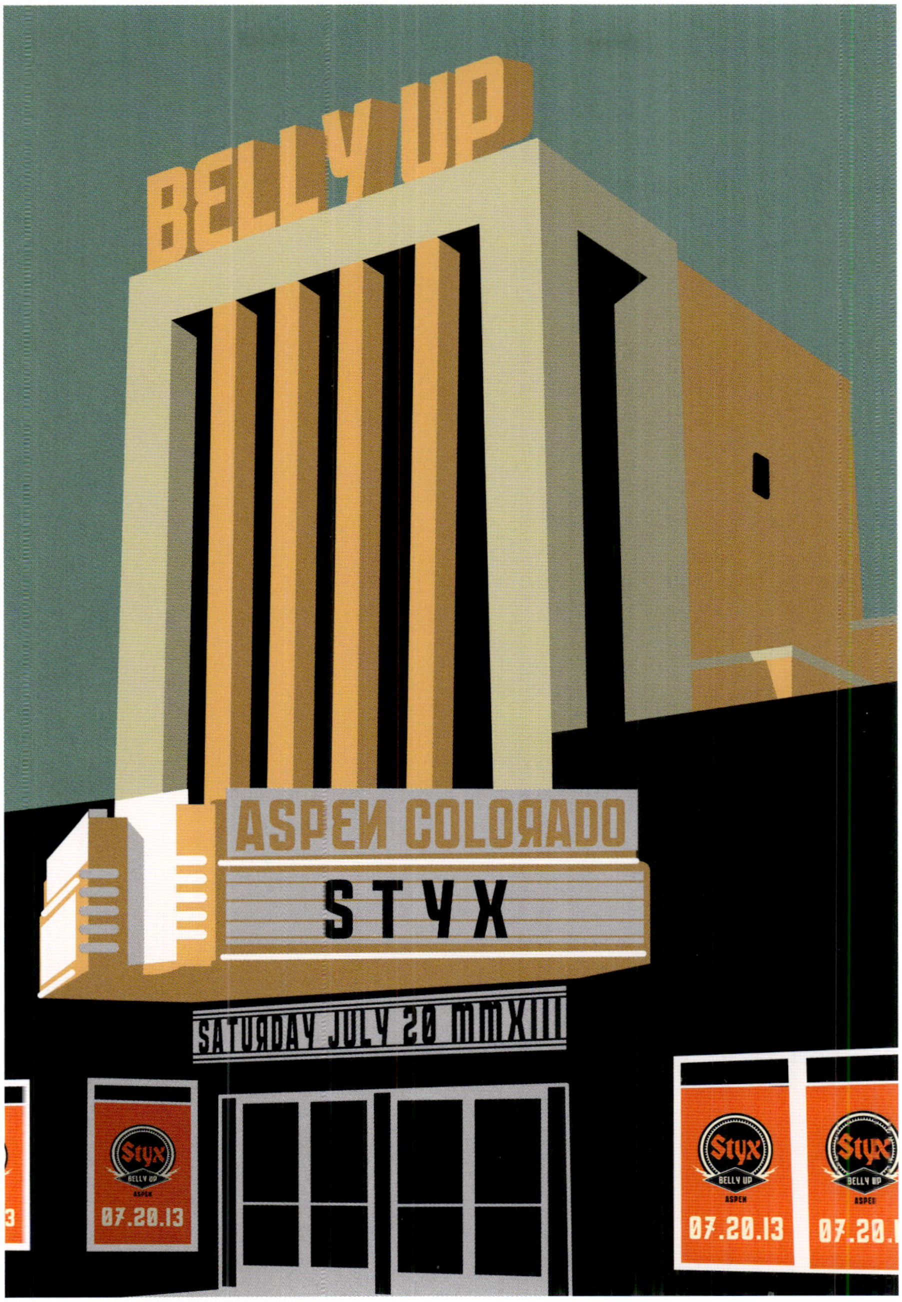

CLIENT: Styx
DESIGNER: Scrojo
WEBSITE: scrojo.com

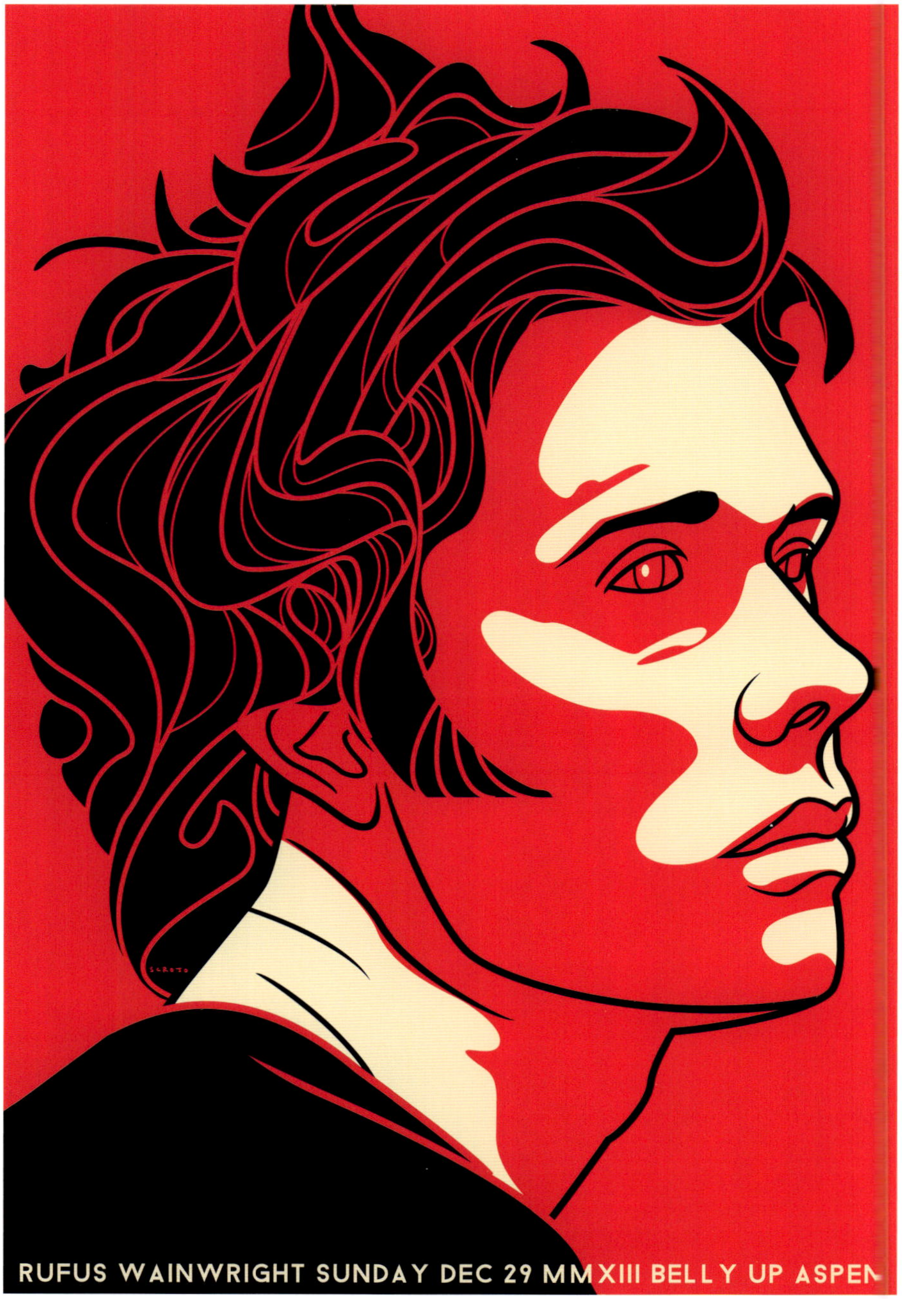

CLIENT: Rufus Wainwright
DESIGNER: Scrojo
WEBSITE: scrojo.com

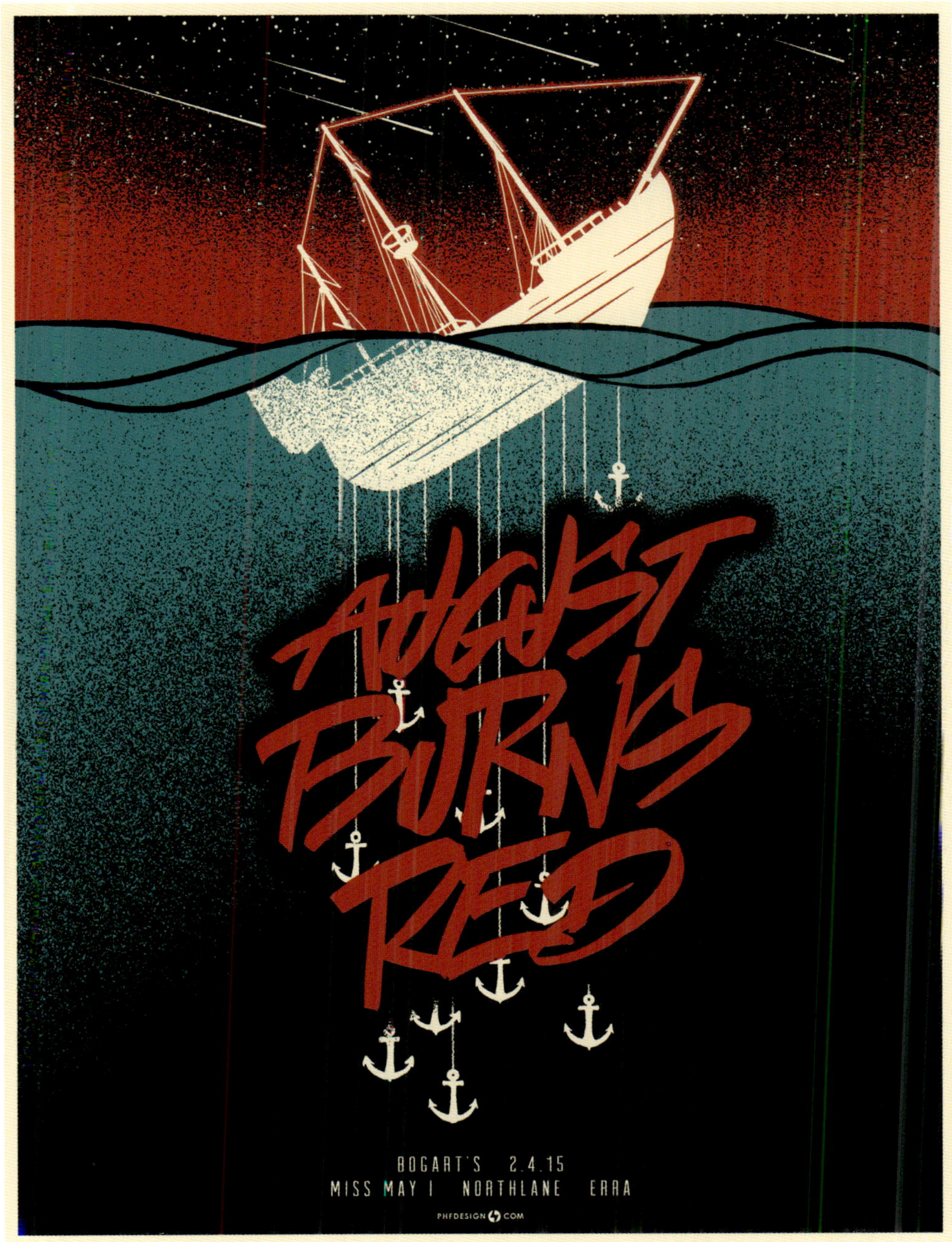

CLIENT: August Burns Red
DESIGNER: Nathan Meyer
DESIGN FIRM: Powerhouse Factories
WEBSITE: powerhousefactories.com

Lowbrow Handbill

While the music may seem different upon first impression, punk and old-school country movements have much in common upon closer examination. Both styles are meant to represent their fans in an authentic way. This grassroots aesthetic shows up in everything related to these styles, including the artwork. Posters created in this style often incorporate the qualities of old-school letterpress handbills (even when created by other means). Type is often at the forefront of this style as a primary graphic element. A handmade quality is embraced, so some accidents in the printing process are often embraced or even intentional.

KEY STYLE CHARACTERISTICS

- Features letterpress qualities or a handmade aesthetic
- Controlled "accidents" are often incorporated in the design
- Often uses the raw machine to create graphic elements and compositional choices for the piece
- Heavy focus on type and ornamentation
- Type used as a primary graphic element
- Employs simple, classic poster/sign composition and organization
- Limited use of color, often focusing on primary colors
- Repurposes old type, pictures, design elements, and even entire compositions
- Often mimics specific eras
- Although the computer is used a lot in the process, many if not all elements are handmade in the lowbrow handbill style
- Illustration quality is limited; silhouettes or rudimentary, low-level hand drawing

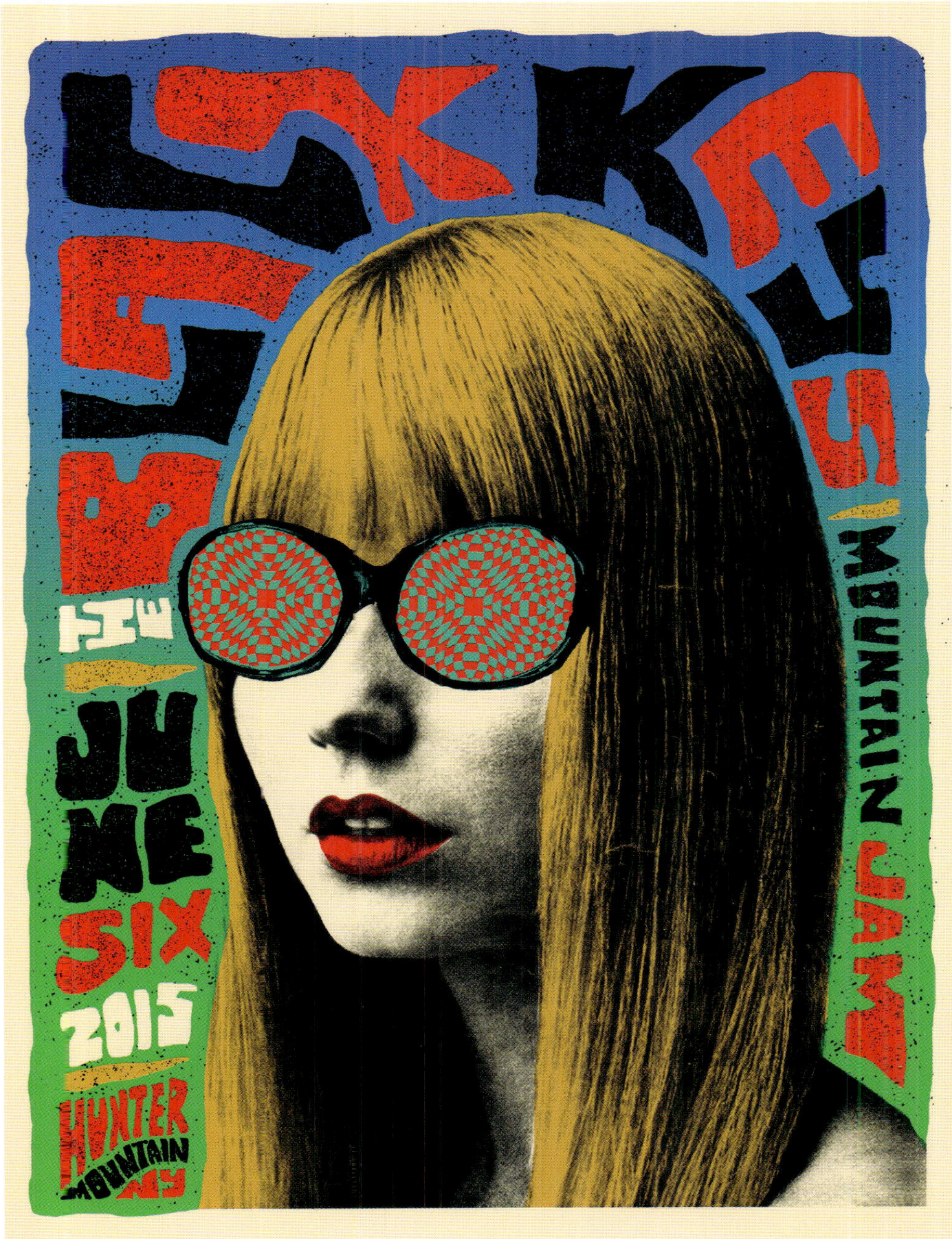

CLIENT: The Black Keys
DESIGNER: Nate Duval
WEBSITE: nateduval.com

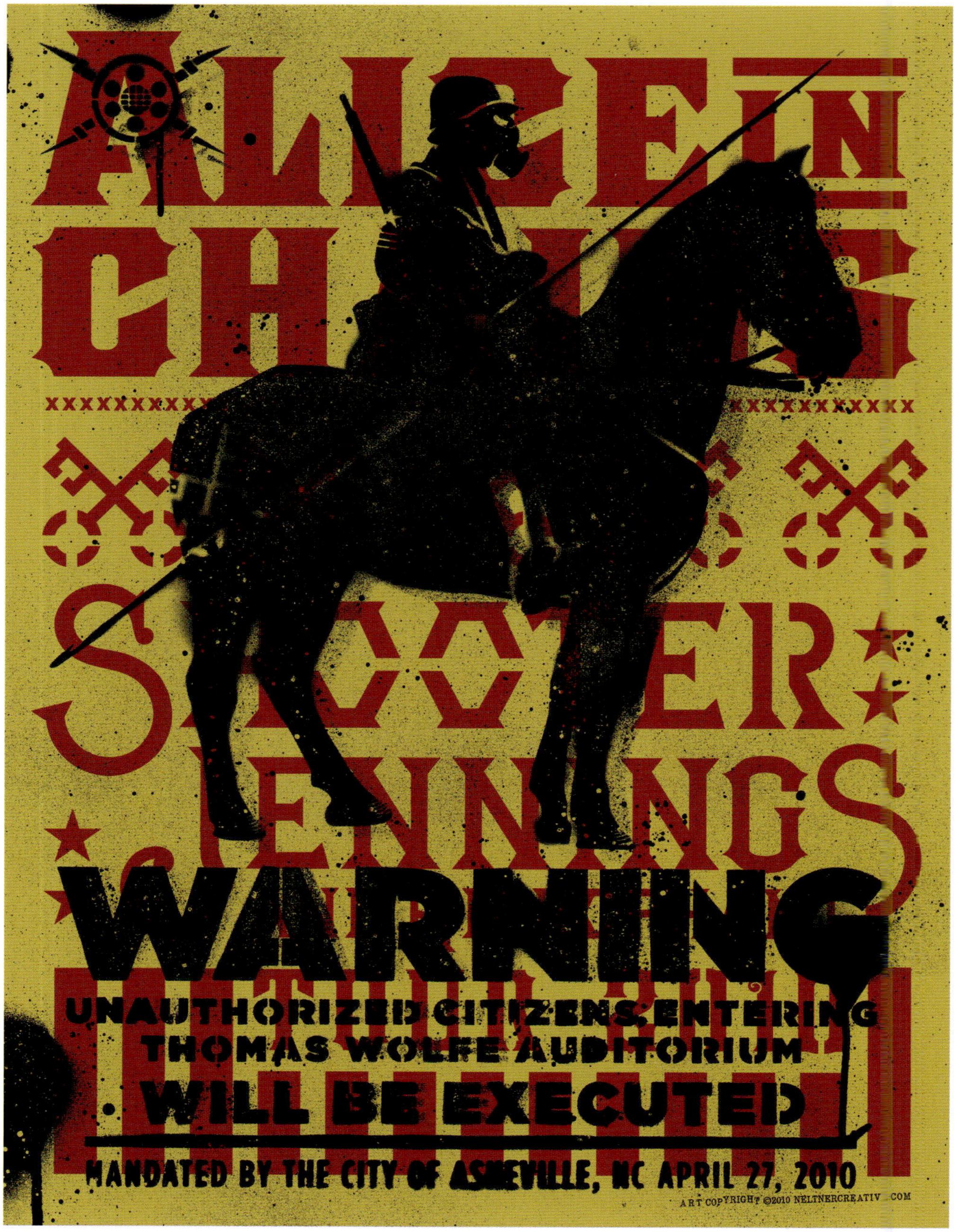

CLIENT: Alice in Chains
DESIGNER: Keith Neltner
DESIGN FIRM: Neltner Small Batch
WEBSITE: neltnersmallbatch.com

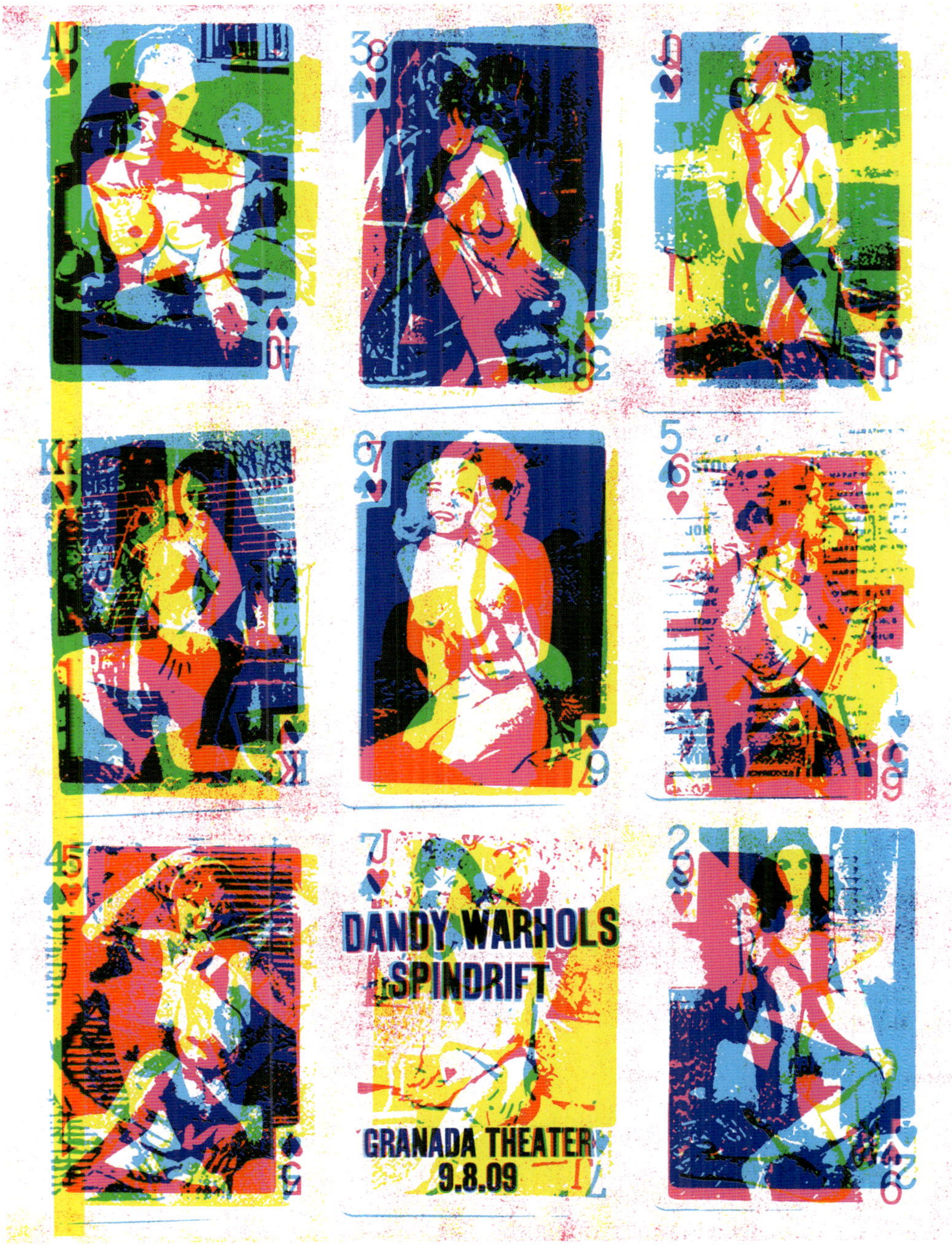

CLIENTS: The Dandy Warhols / Spindrift
DESIGNER: Jared Connor
DESIGN FIRM: Mexican Chocolate Design
WEBSITE: mexicanchocolatedesign.com

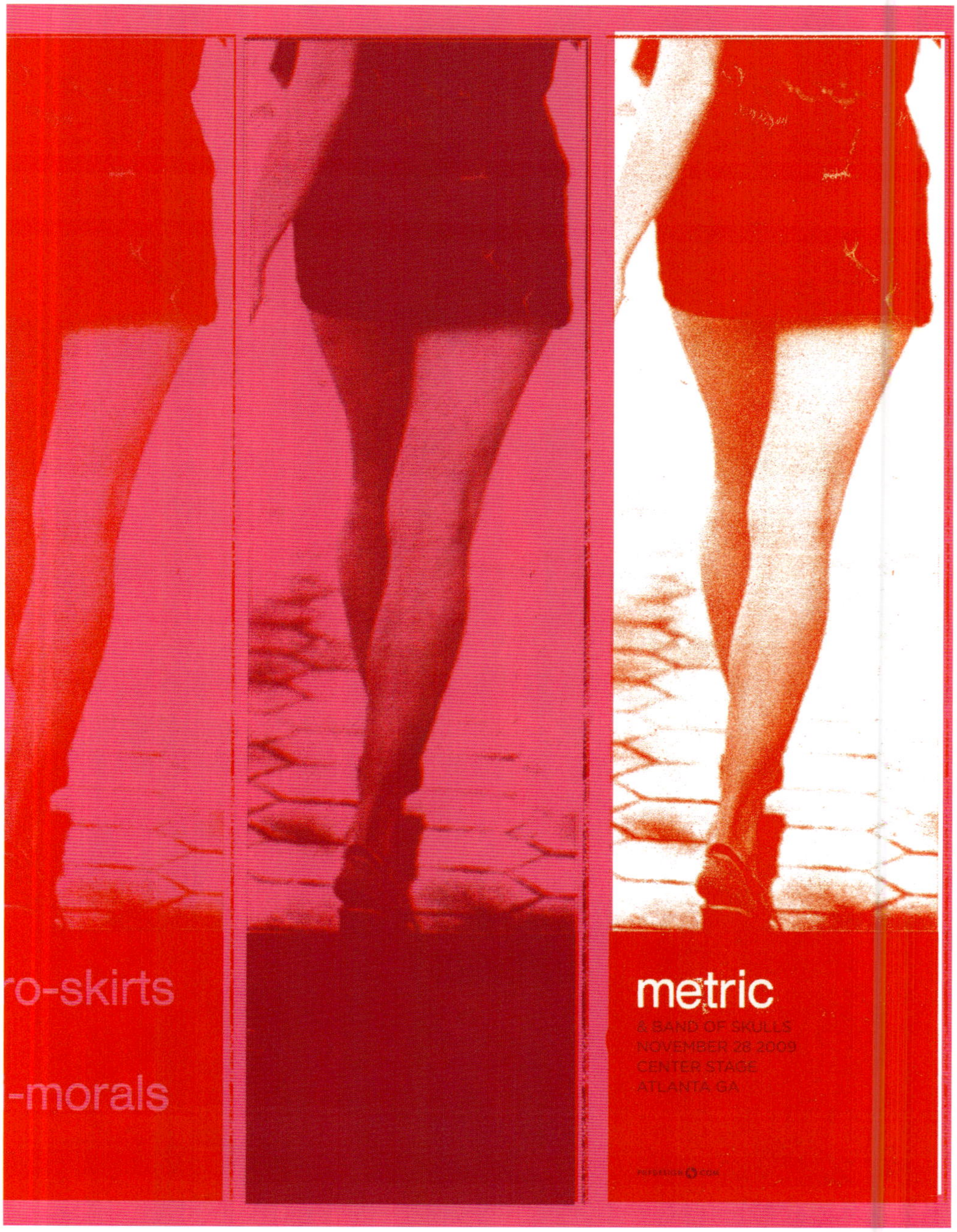

CLIENT: Metric
DESIGNER: Pat Jones
DESIGN FIRM: Powerhouse Factories
WEBSITE: powerhousefactories.com

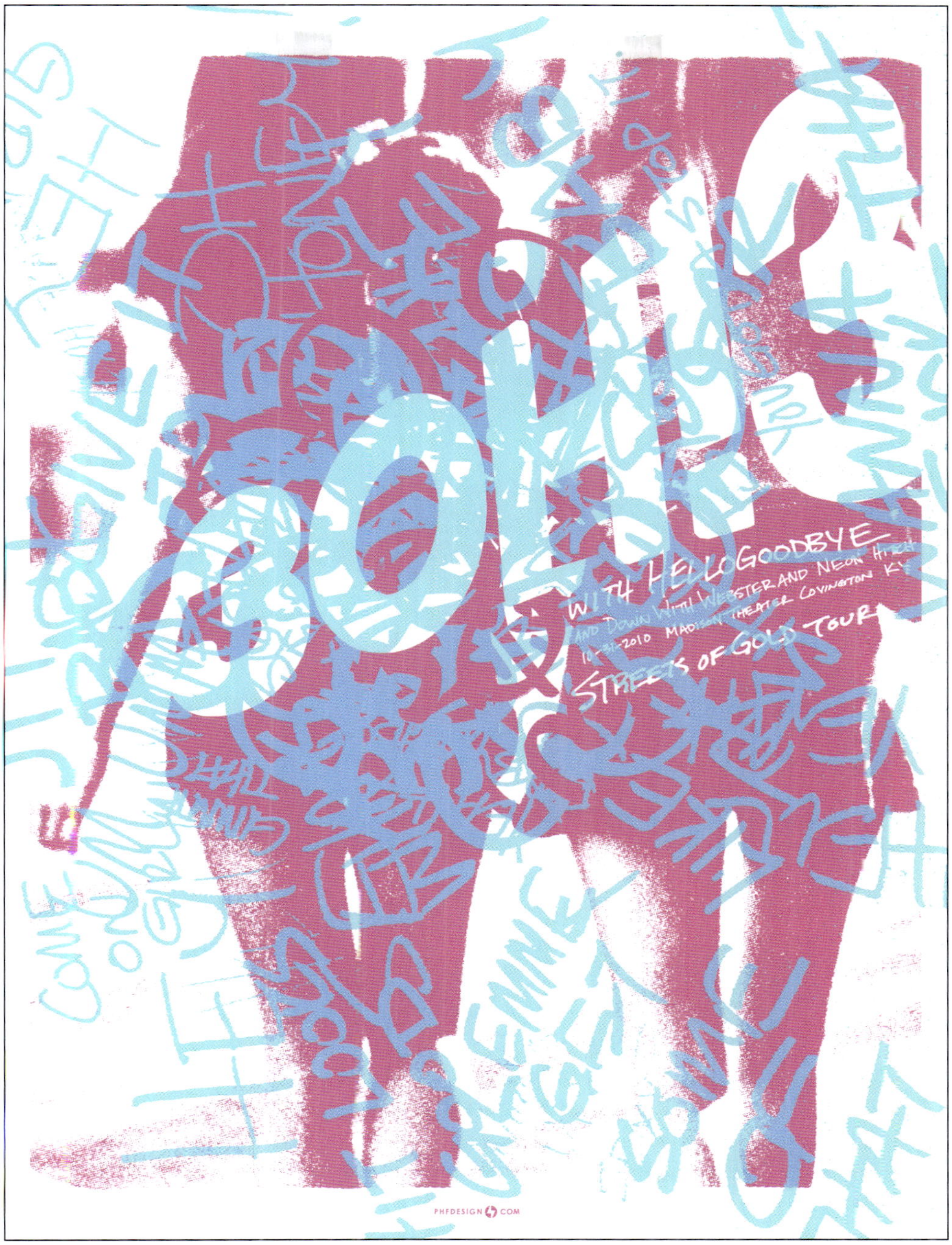

CLIENT: 3OH!3
DESIGNER: Pat Jones
DESIGN FIRM: Powerhouse Factories
WEBSITE: powerhousefactories.com

Flattened Whimsy

This fun and eclectic style uses simple shapes and flat colors to convey a lighthearted tone. There is a childlike simplicity to the style that is reminiscent of children's storybook illustrations. While the style is simple with minimal use of patterns, shading, or ornamentation, it is also quite imaginative. Movement and depth are conveyed through line weight, color variation, and multilevel tones. The ultimate effect is a narrative quality that can portray even serious or frightening topics in a childlike way that softens the visual.

KEY STYLE CHARACTERISTICS

- Simple shapes used in combination to make beautiful characters and/or landscapes
- Similar to storybook illustration in that it is very narrative and imagination driven
- Flat colors and little to no shading, but conveys movement and depth by using line weight, color variation, and multilevel tones
- Minimal use of pattern or ornamentation
- Employs high-quality illustrations and relies heavily on use of shape and line
- Type is commonly played into the narrative landscape
- Conveys a lighthearted or childlike tone (often creating a juxtaposition when portraying more serious subject matter)

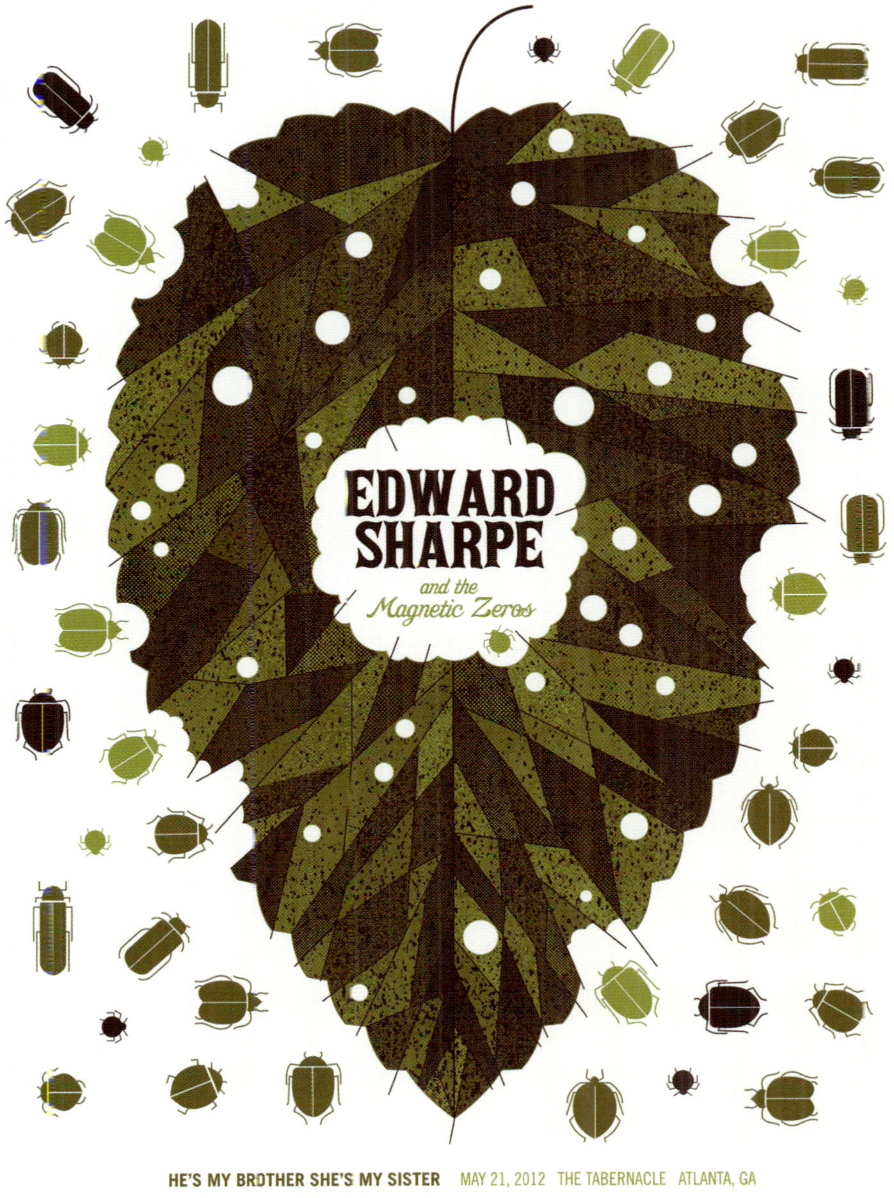

CLIENT: Edward Sharpe and the Magnetic Zeros
DESIGN FIRM: Methane Studios
WEBSITE: methanestudios.com

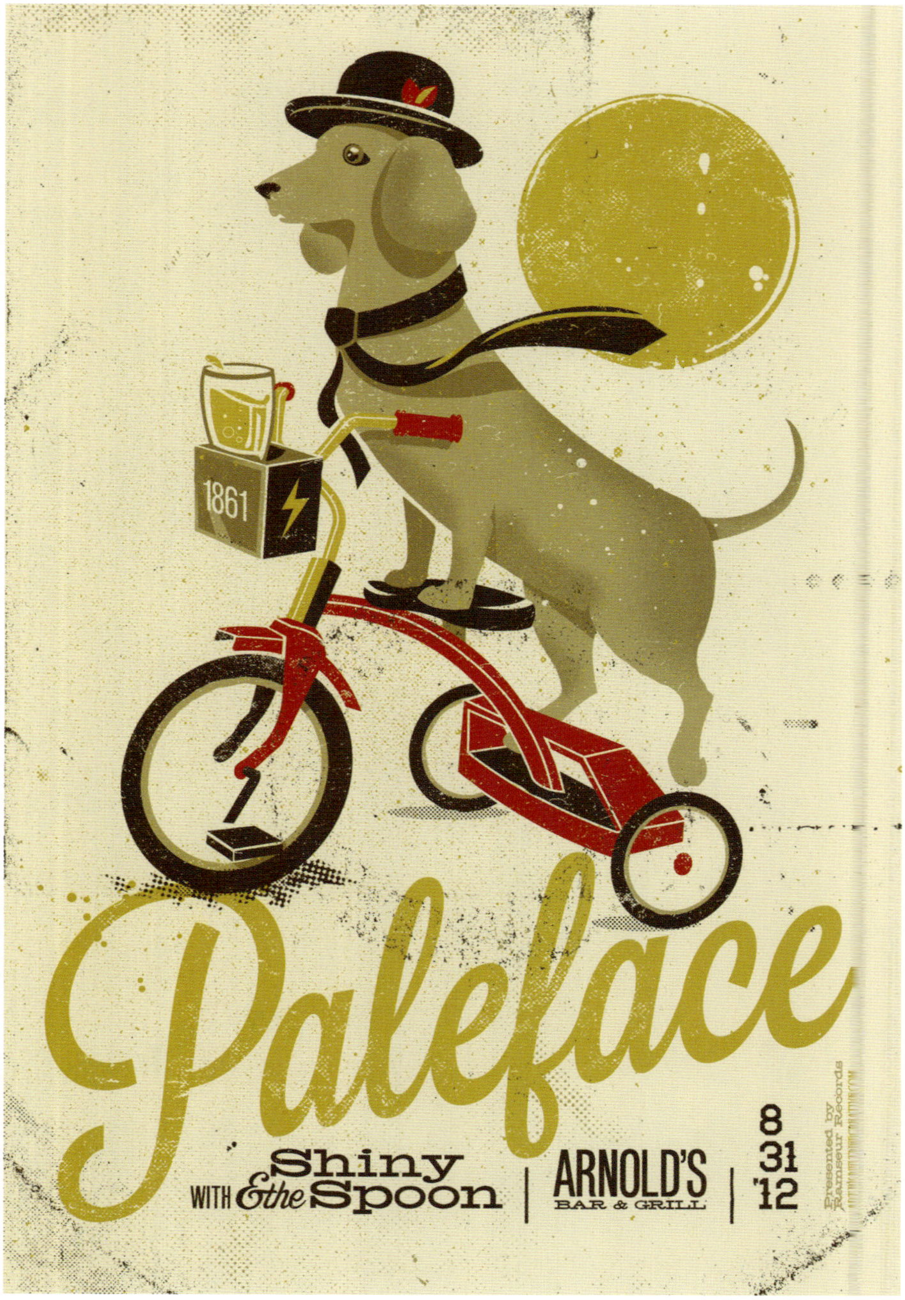

CLIENT: Paleface
DESIGNER: Keith Neltner
DESIGN FIRM: Neltner Small Batch
WEBSITE: neltnersmallbatch.com

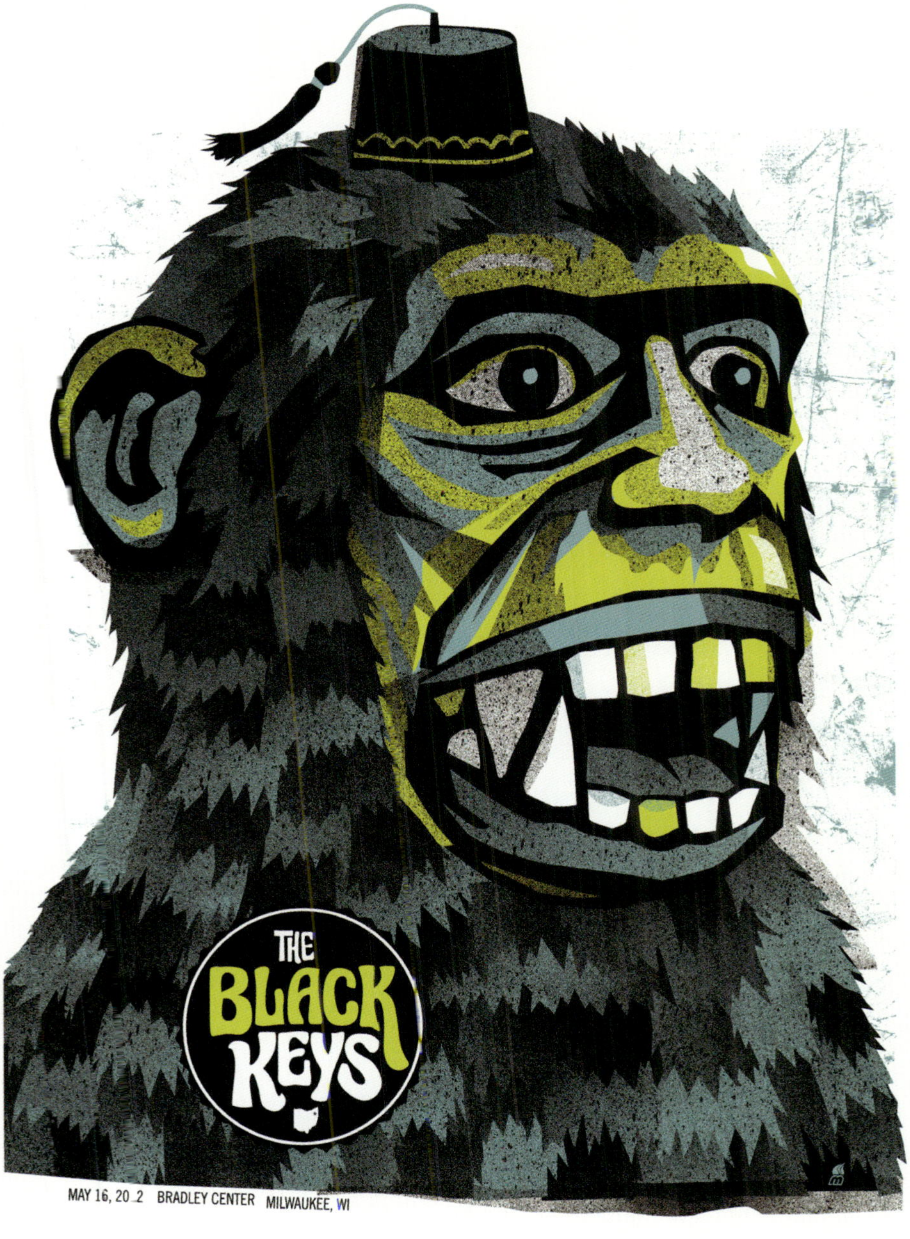

CLIENT: The Black Keys
DESIGN FIRM: Methane Studios
WEBSITE: methanestudios.com

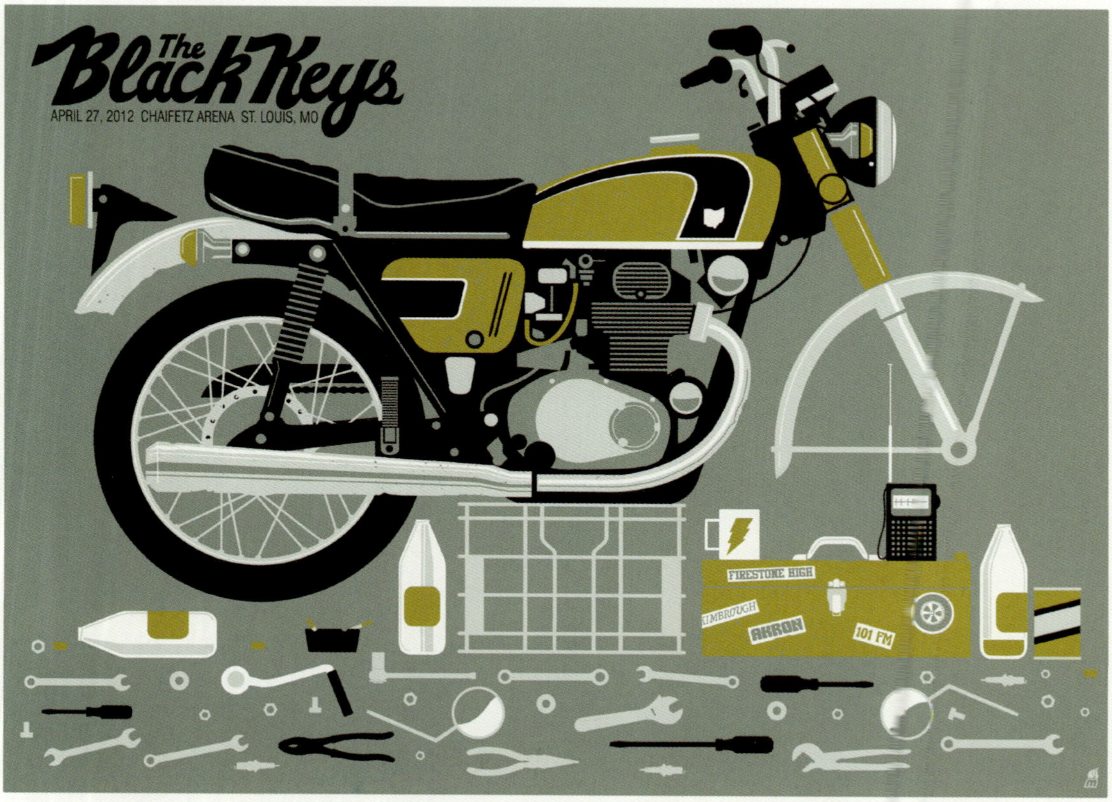

CLIENT: The Black Keys
DESIGN FIRM: Methane Studios
WEBSITE: methanestudios.com

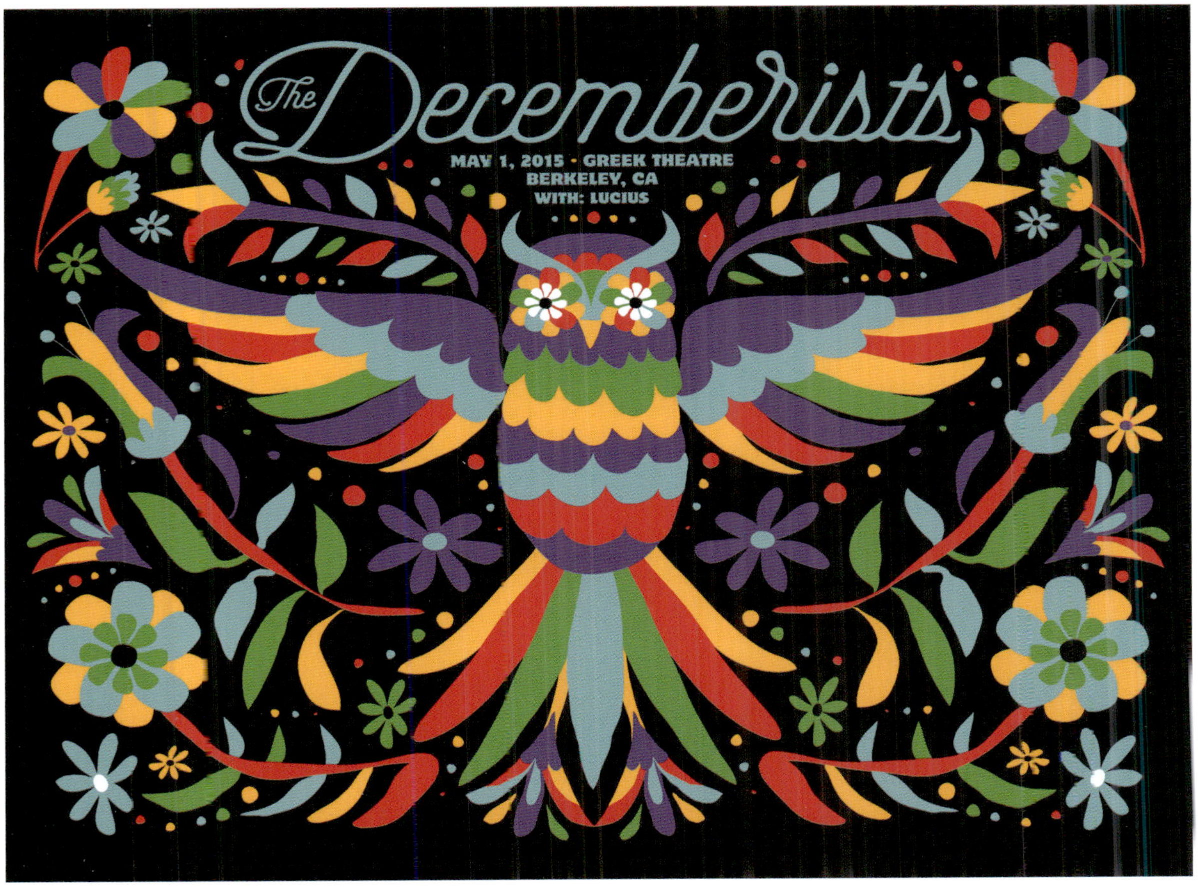

CLIENT: The Decemberists
DESIGNER: Nate Duval
WEBSITE: nateduval.com

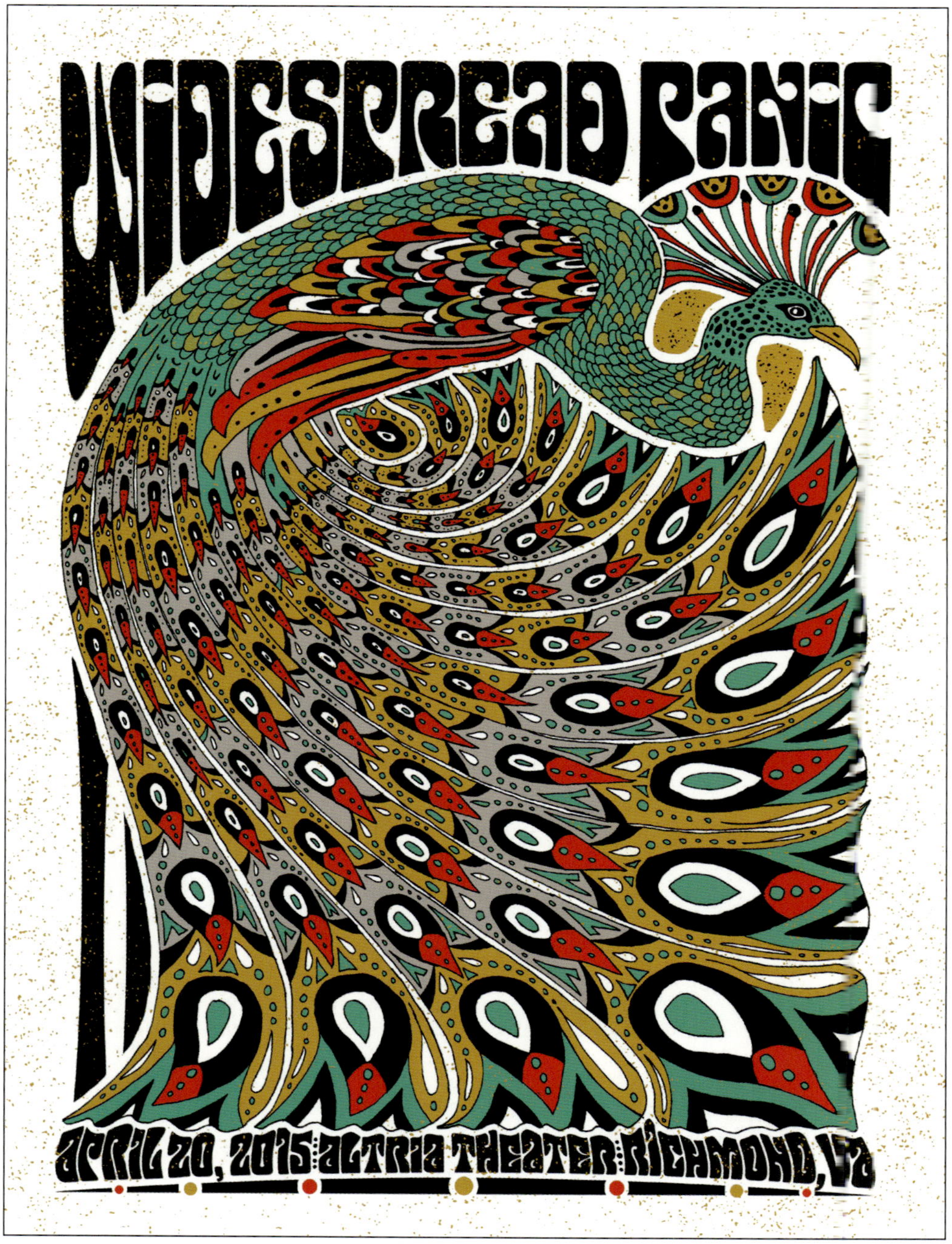

CLIENT: Widespread Panic
DESIGNER: Nate Duval
WEBSITE: nateduval.com

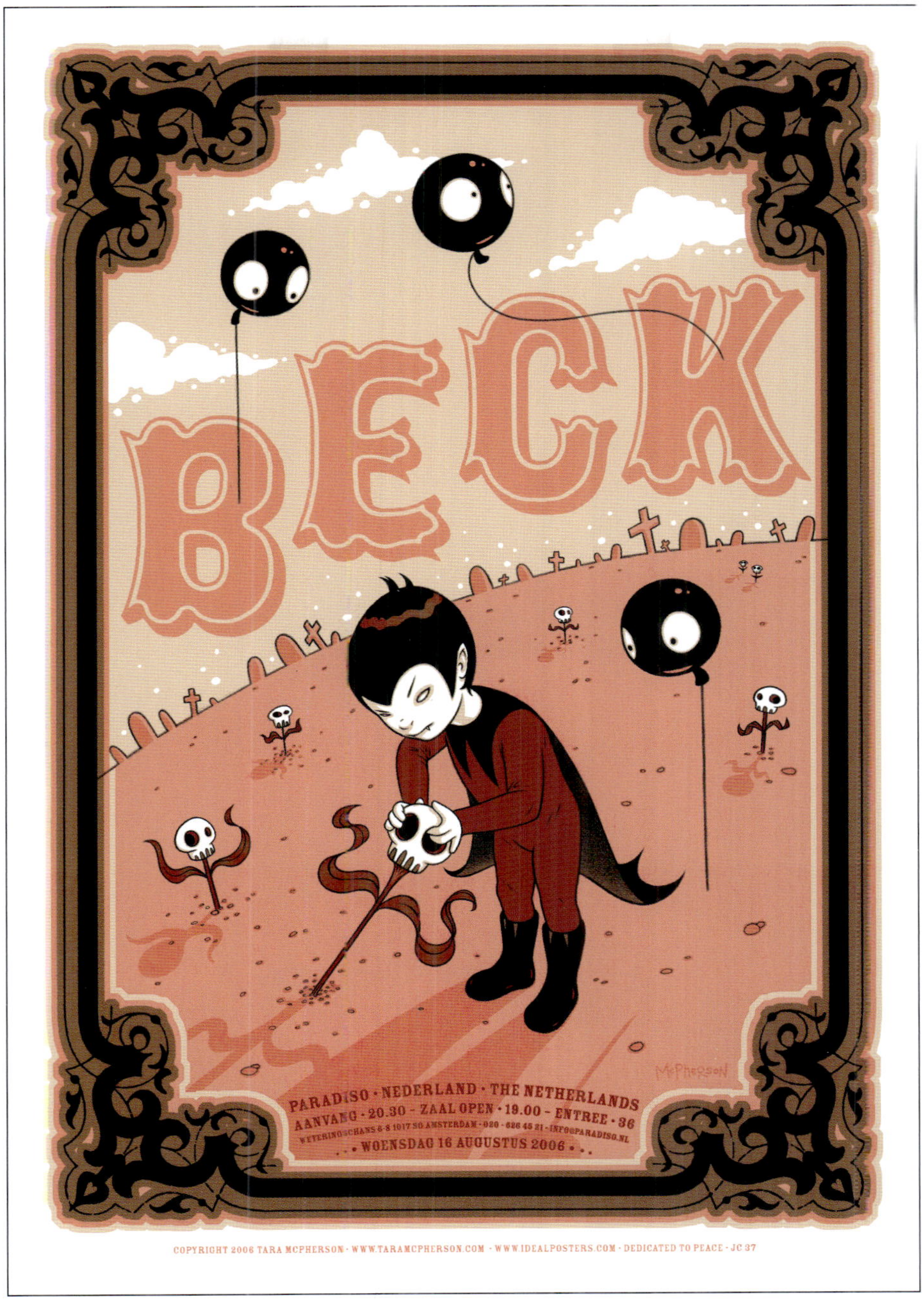

CLIENT: Beck
DESIGNER: Tara McPherson
WEBSITE: taramcpherson.com

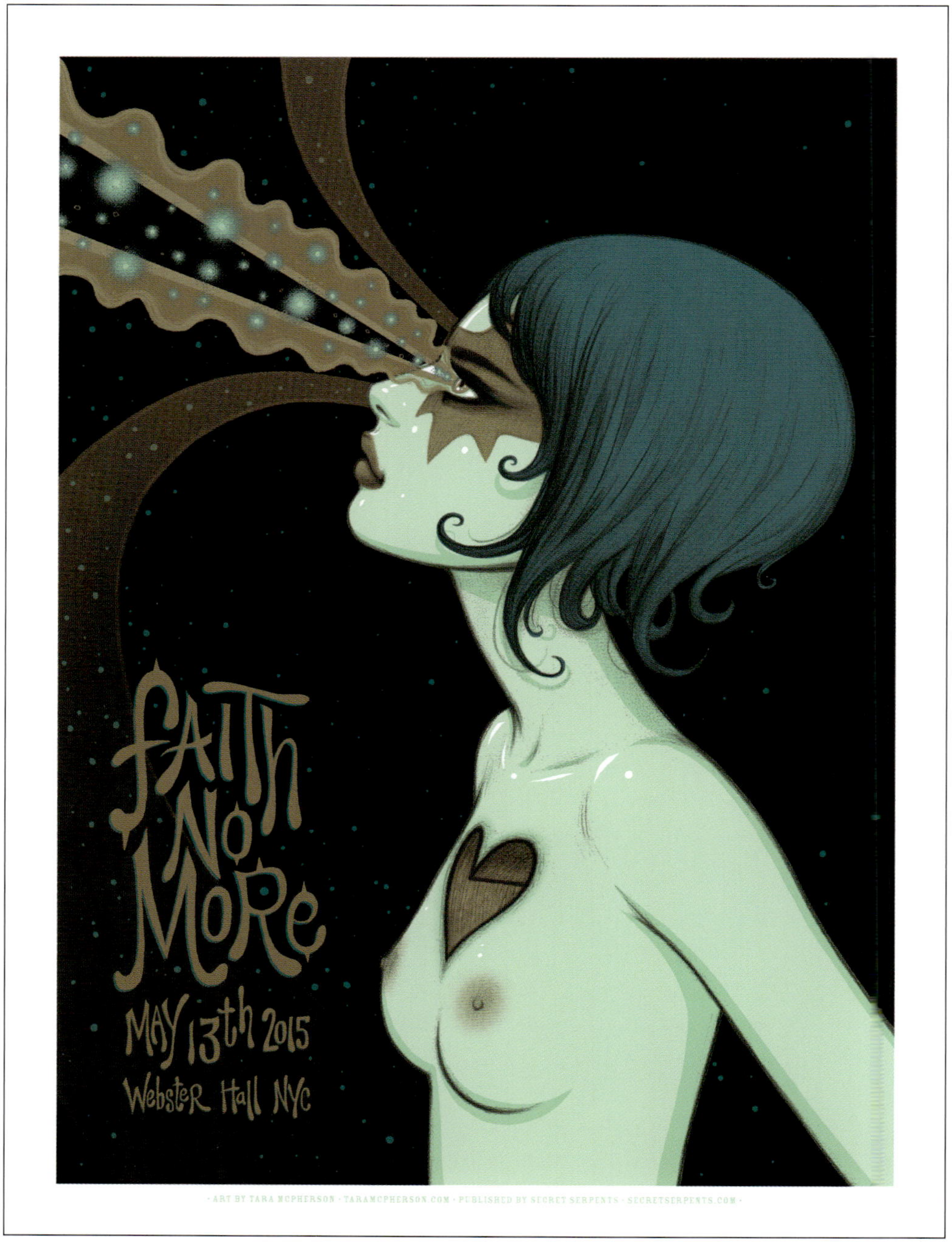

CLIENT: Faith No More
DESIGNER: Tara McPherson
WEBSITE: taramcpherson.com

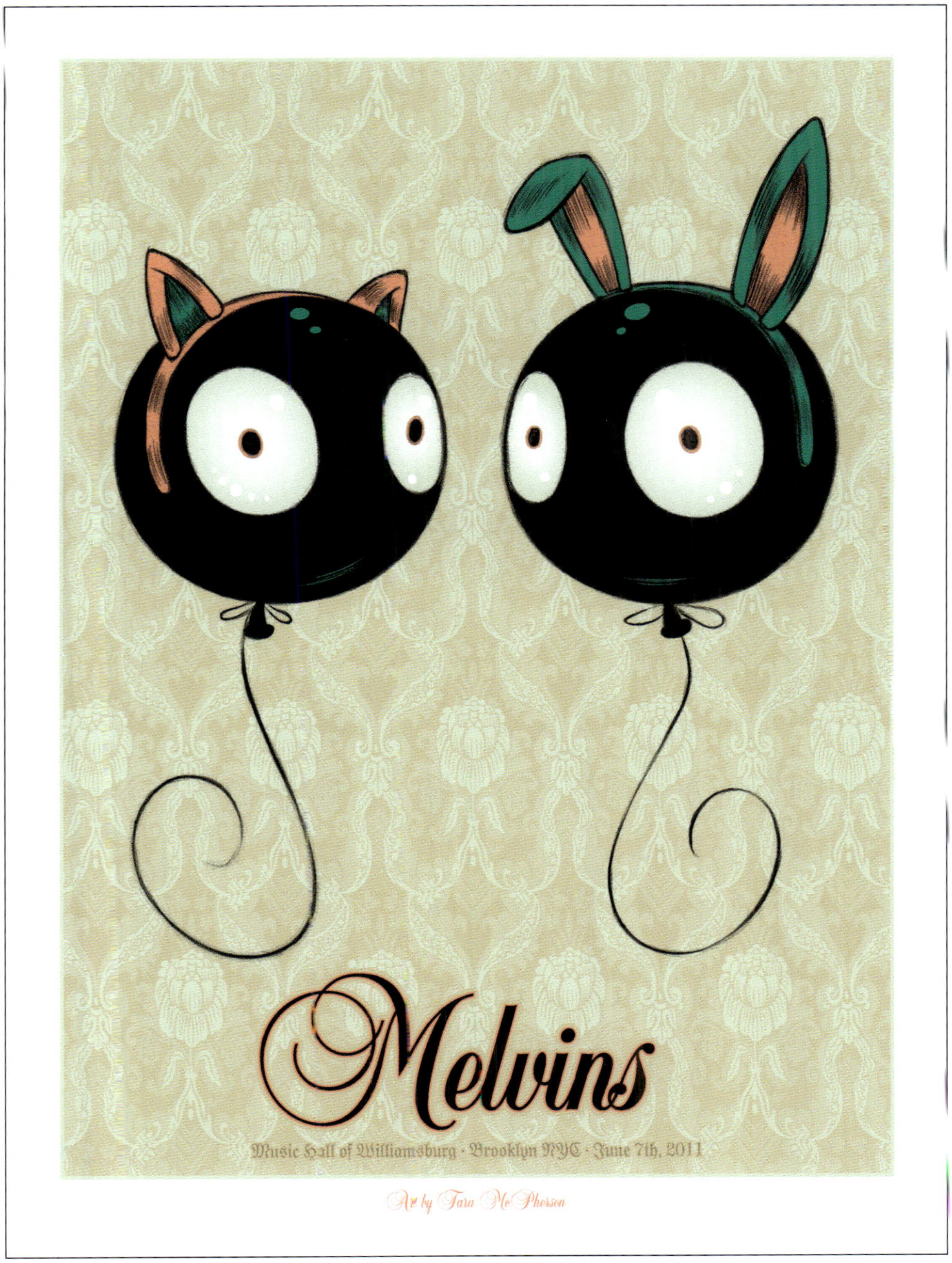

CLIENT: Melvins
DESIGNER: Tara McPherson
WEBSITE: taramcpherson.com

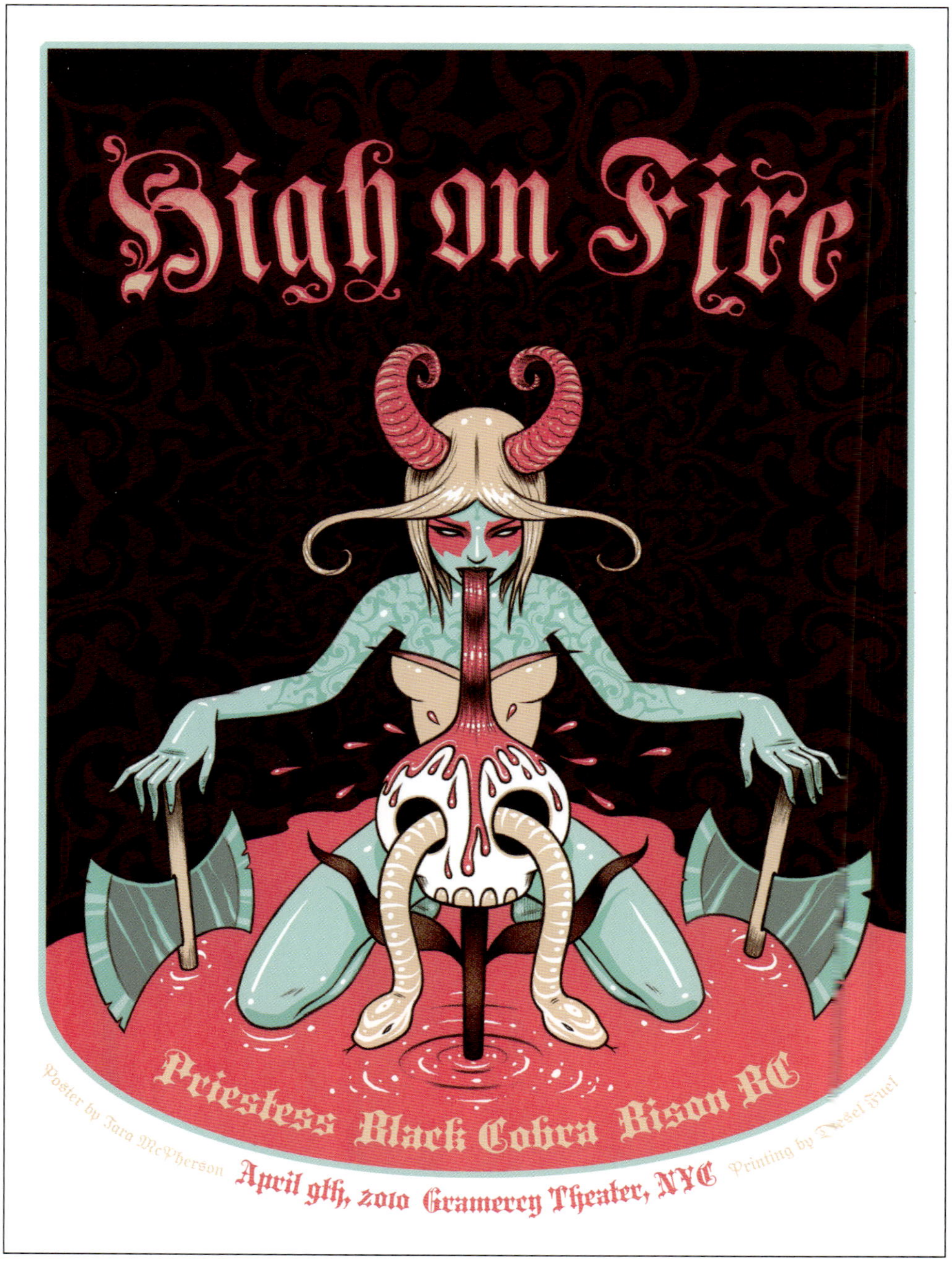

CLIENT: High on Fire
DESIGNER: Tara McPherson
WEBSITE: taramcpherson.com

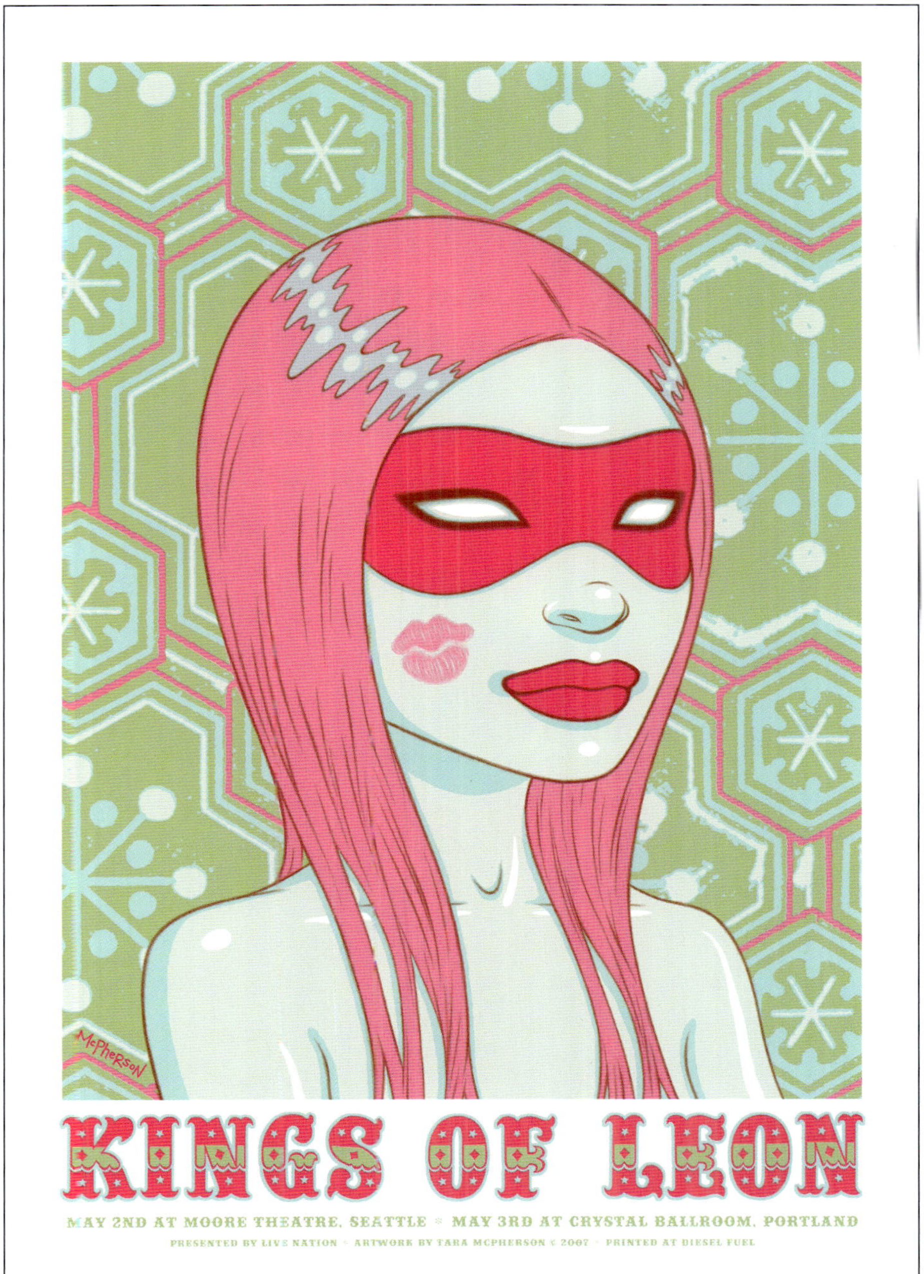

CLIENT: Kings of Leon
DESIGNER: Tara McPherson
WEBSITE: taramcpherson.com

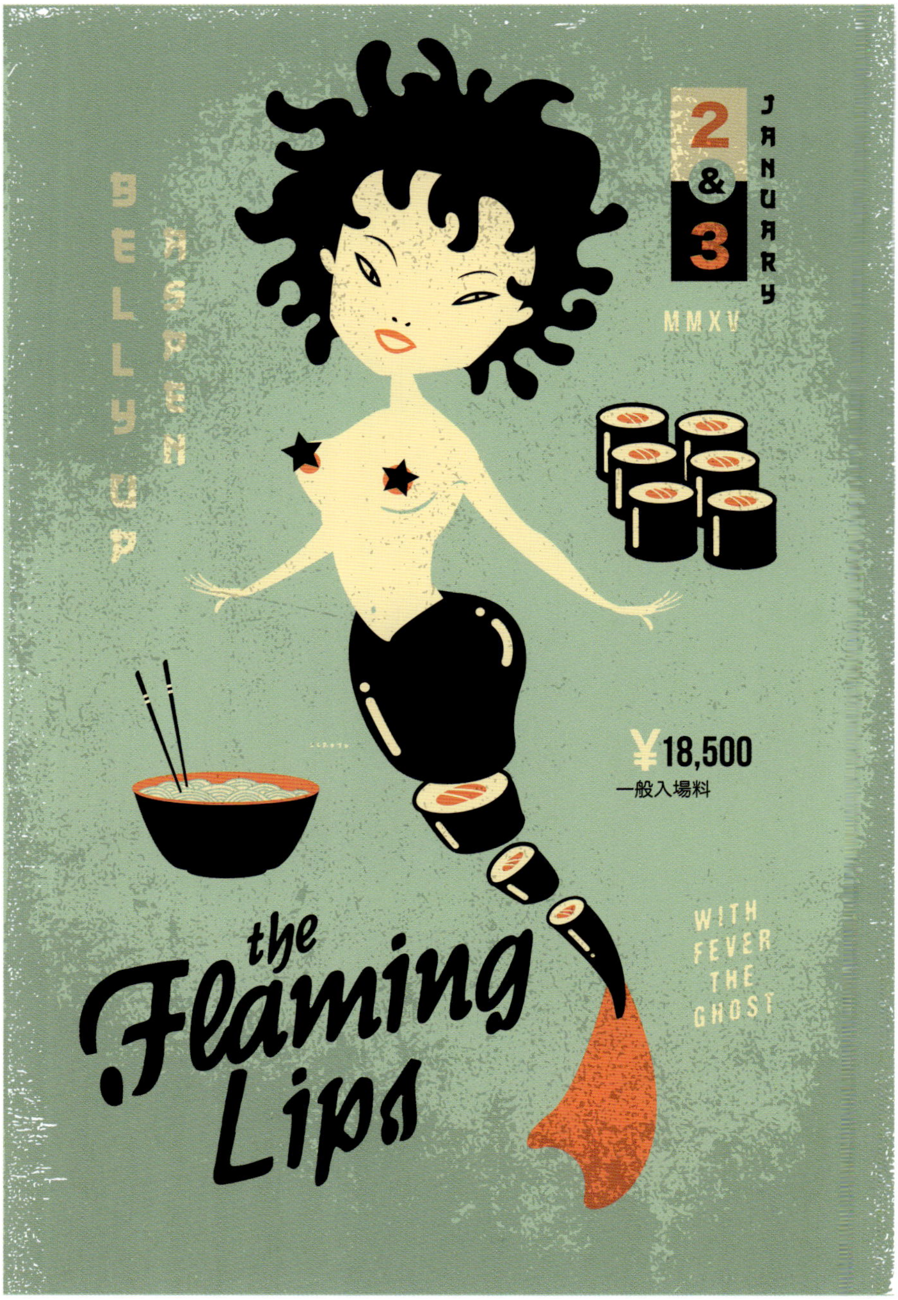

CLIENT: The Flaming Lips
DESIGNER: Scrojo
WEBSITE: scrojo.com

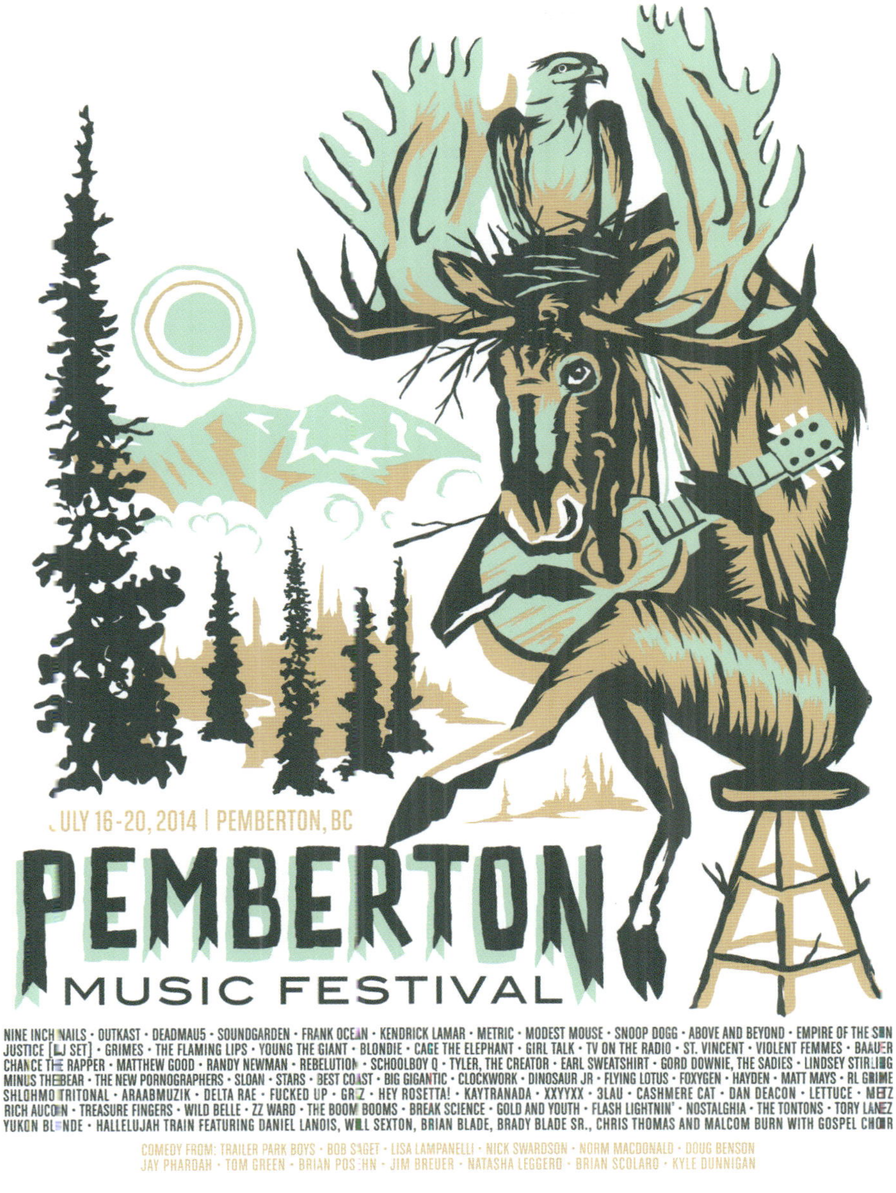

CLIENT: Pemberton Music Festival
DESIGNER: Travis Bone
DESIGN FIRM: Furturtle Show Prints
WEBSITE: furturtle.com

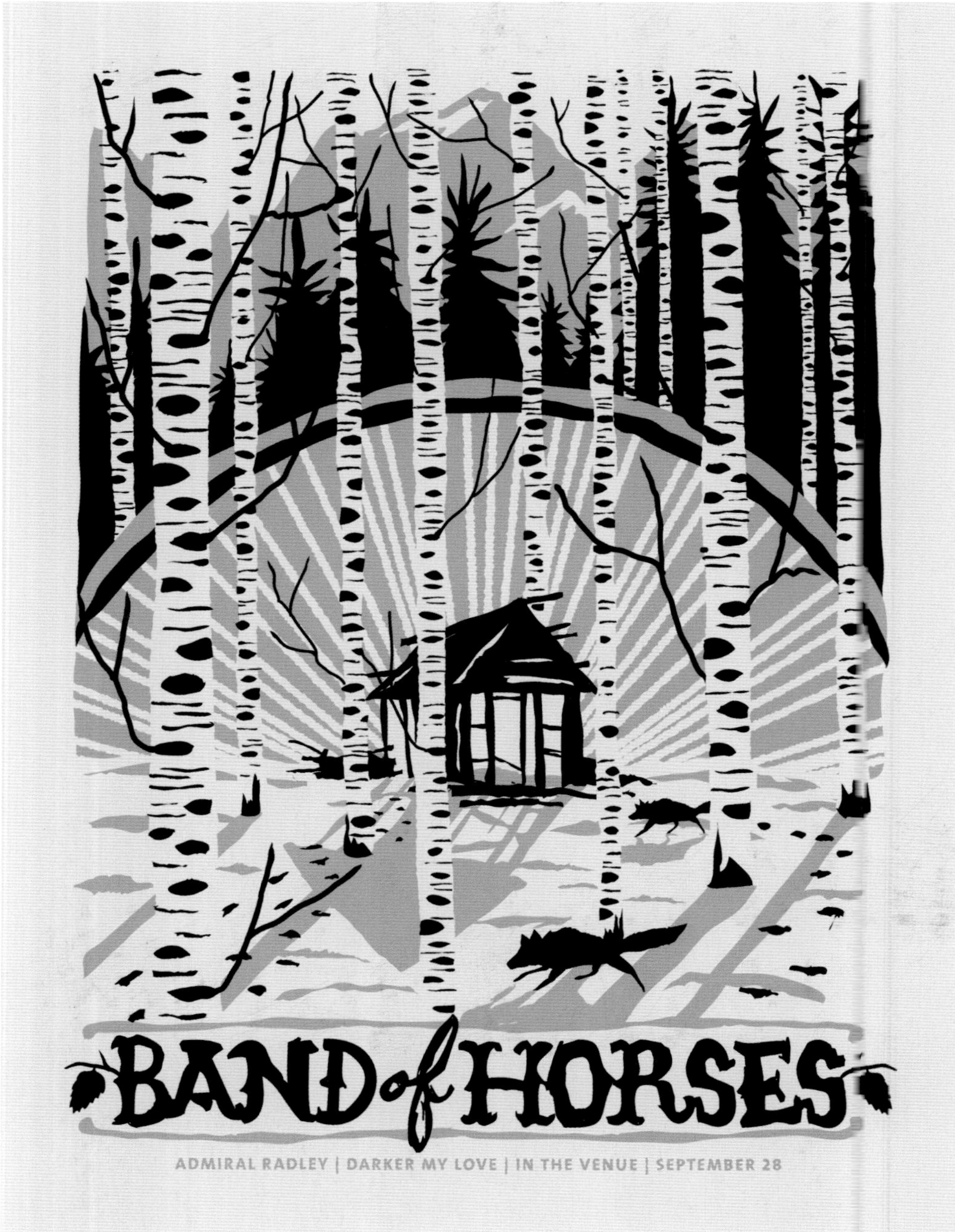

CLIENT: Band of Horses
DESIGNER: Travis Bone
DESIGN FIRM: Furturtle Show Prints
WEBSITE: furturtle.com

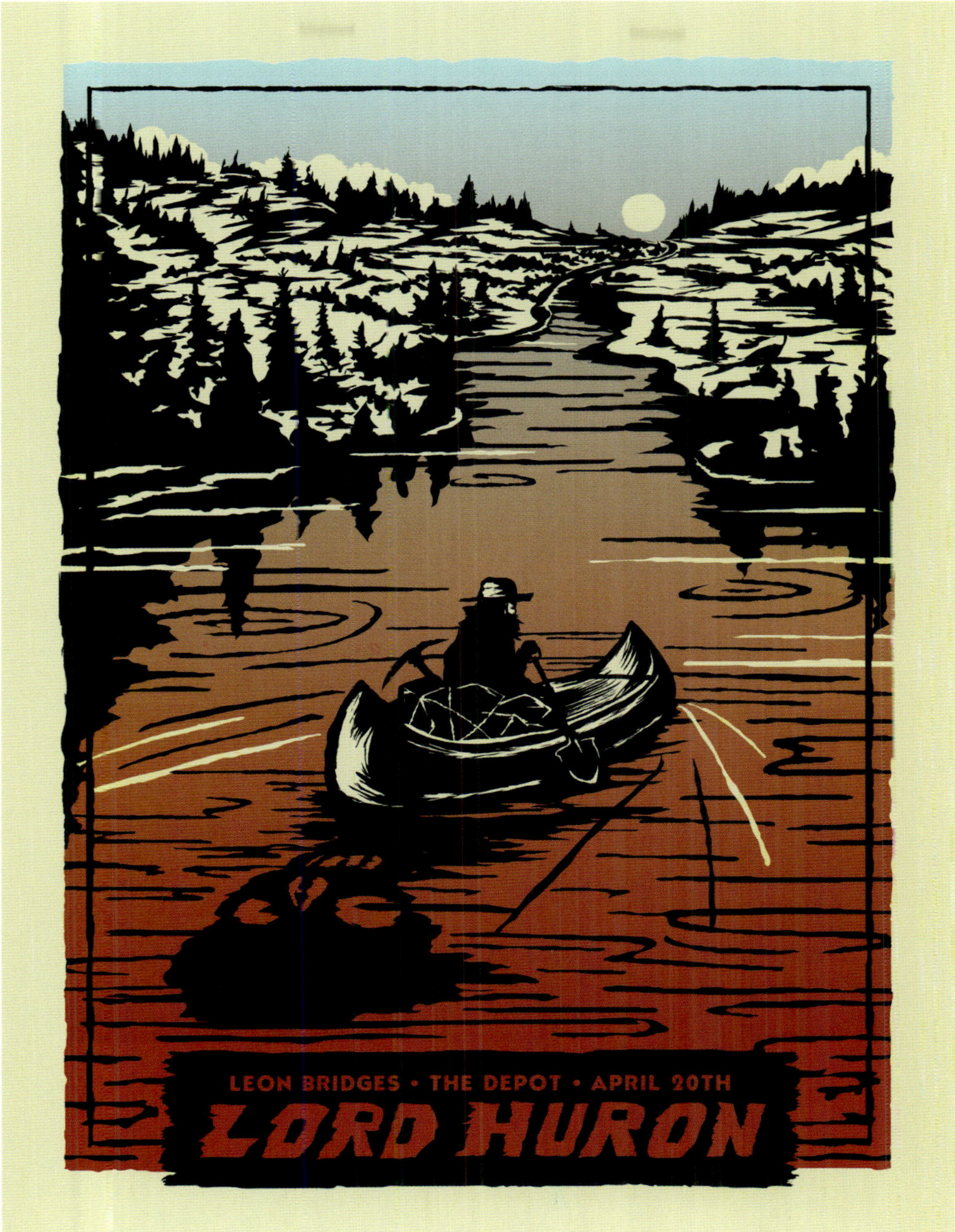

CLIENT: Lord Huron
DESIGNER: Travis Bone
DESIGN FIRM: Furturtle Show Prints
WEBSITE: furturtle.com

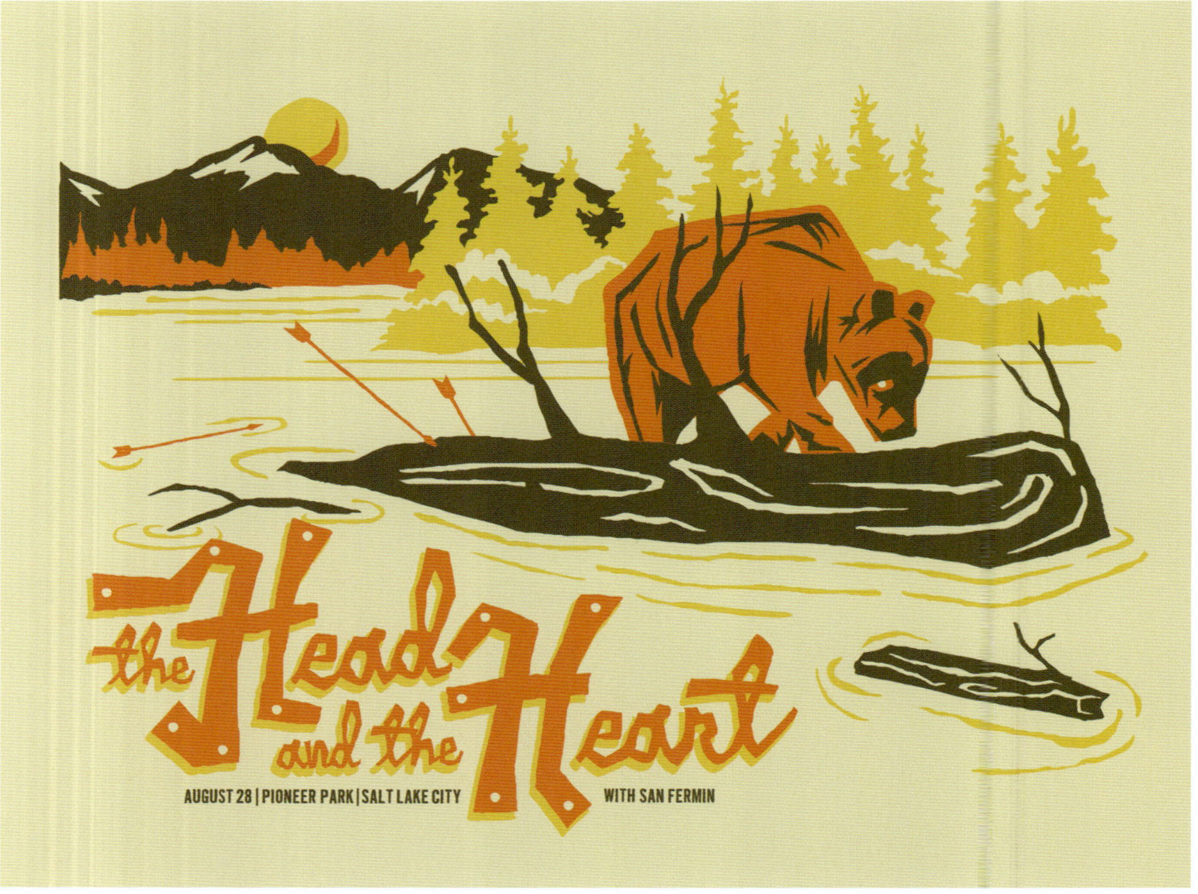

CLIENT: The Head and the Heart
DESIGNER: Travis Bone
DESIGN FIRM: Furturtle Show Prints
WEBSITE: furturtle.com

Rudimentary Quirk

This style uses quickly drawn forms to convey a "young adult" tone. Letterforms are hand drawn or appear to be scissor-cut. At first glance the impression is of something quickly slapped together. Closer inspection of the forms and color palettes reveals that while simplified and relying on basic principles, the style still employs correct technique, foreshortening, and good use of line weight to achieve the overall effect.

KEY STYLE CHARACTERISTICS

- Utilizes quickly drawn forms that are purposefully rudimentary; forms and color palettes are simplified but still well illustrated
- Type often appears hand drawn or like scissor-cut construction paper letters
- Composition purposefully forced into places it will fit giving the impression that the artist is working with whatever is available

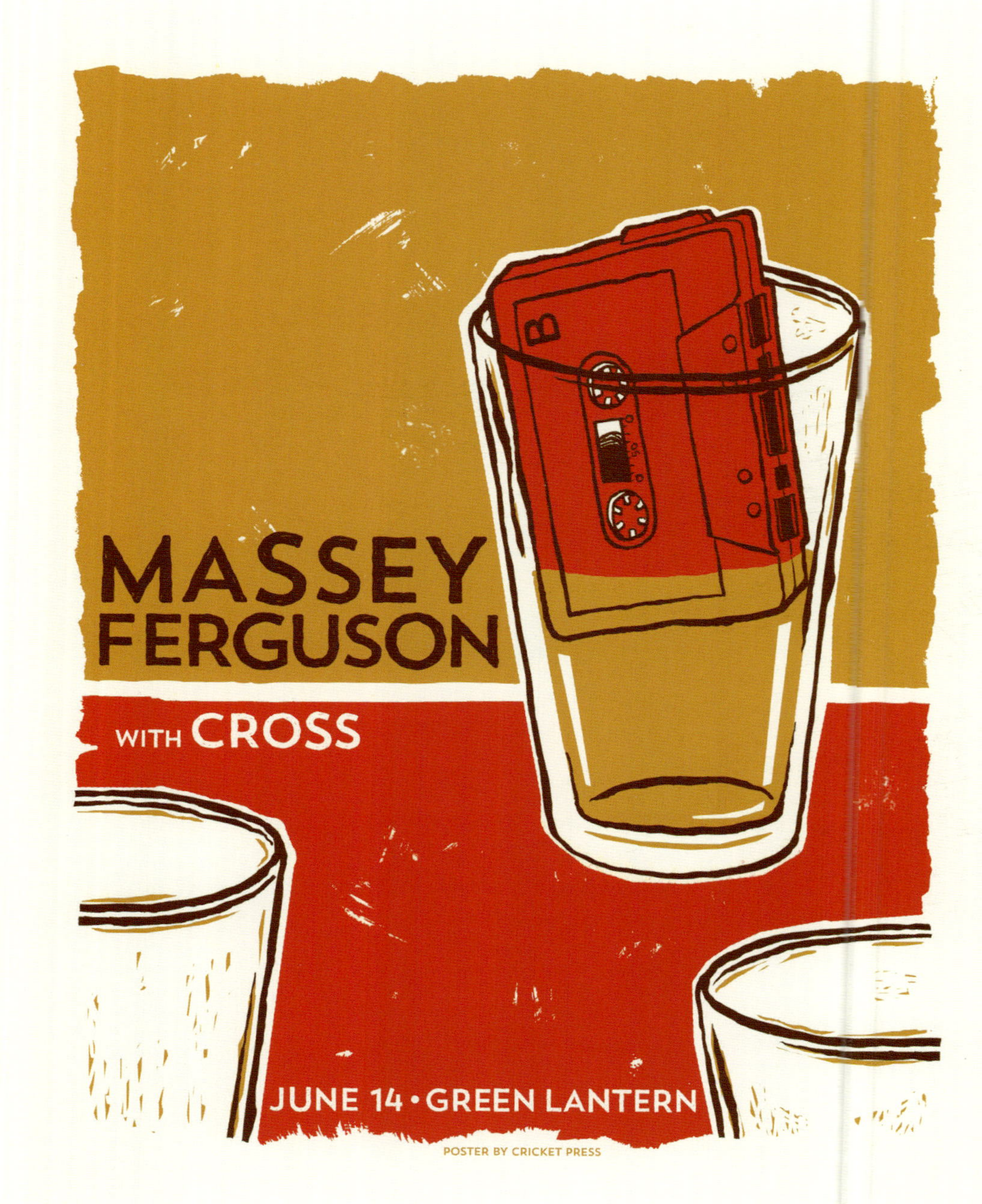

CLIENT: Massey Ferguson
DESIGNER: Brian Turner
DESIGN FIRM: Cricket Press
WEBSITE: cricket-press.com

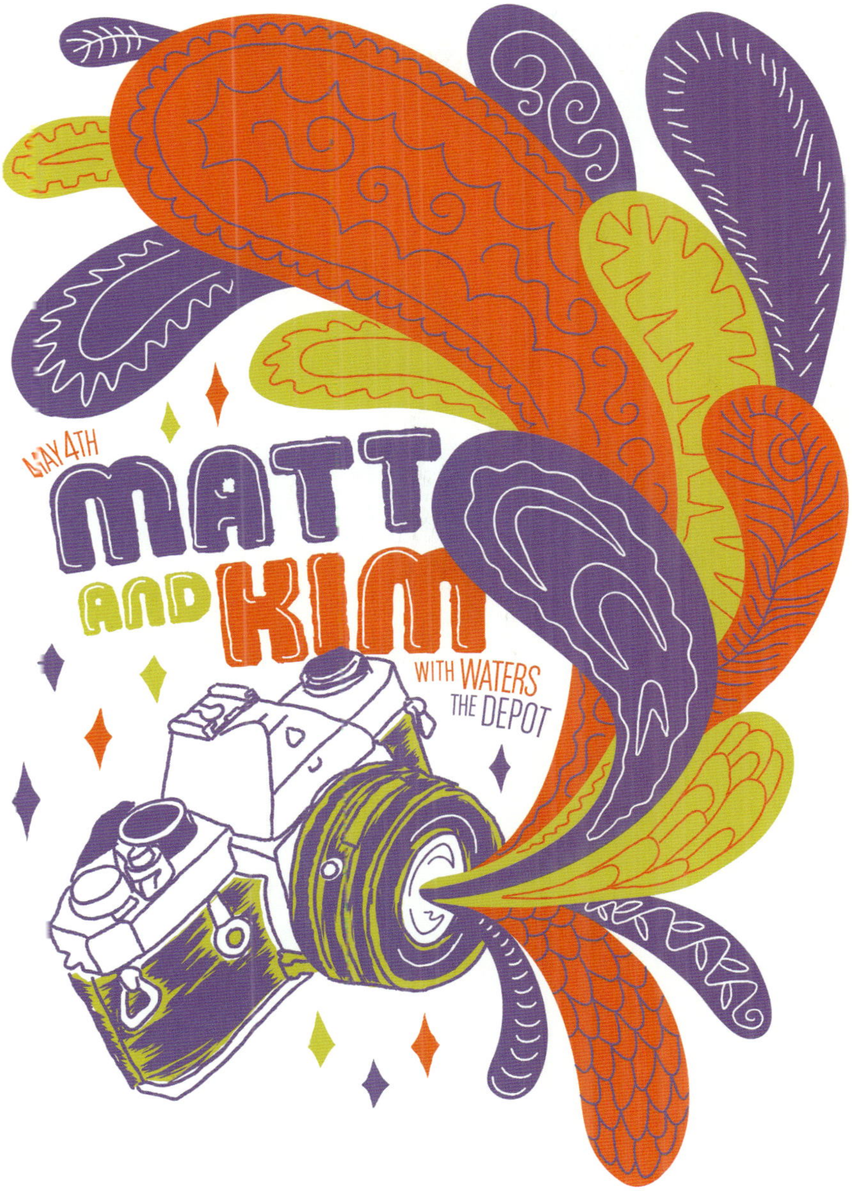

CLIENT: Matt and Kim
DESIGNER: Travis Bone
DESIGN FIRM: Furturtle Show Prints
WEBSITE: furturtle.com

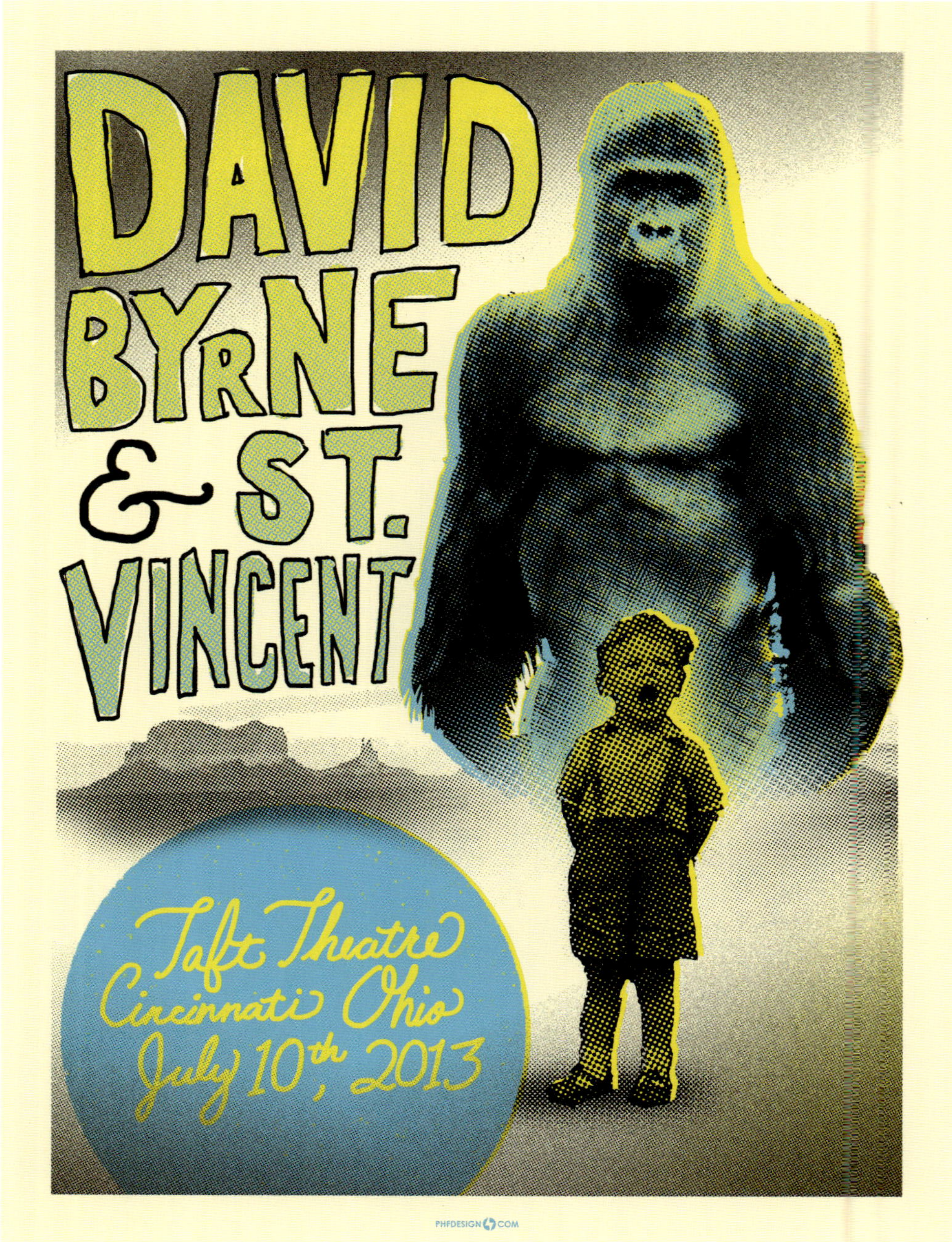

CLIENT: David Byrne & St. Vincent
DESIGNER: Tim Engel
DESIGN FIRM: Powerhouse Factories
WEBSITE: powerhousefactories.com

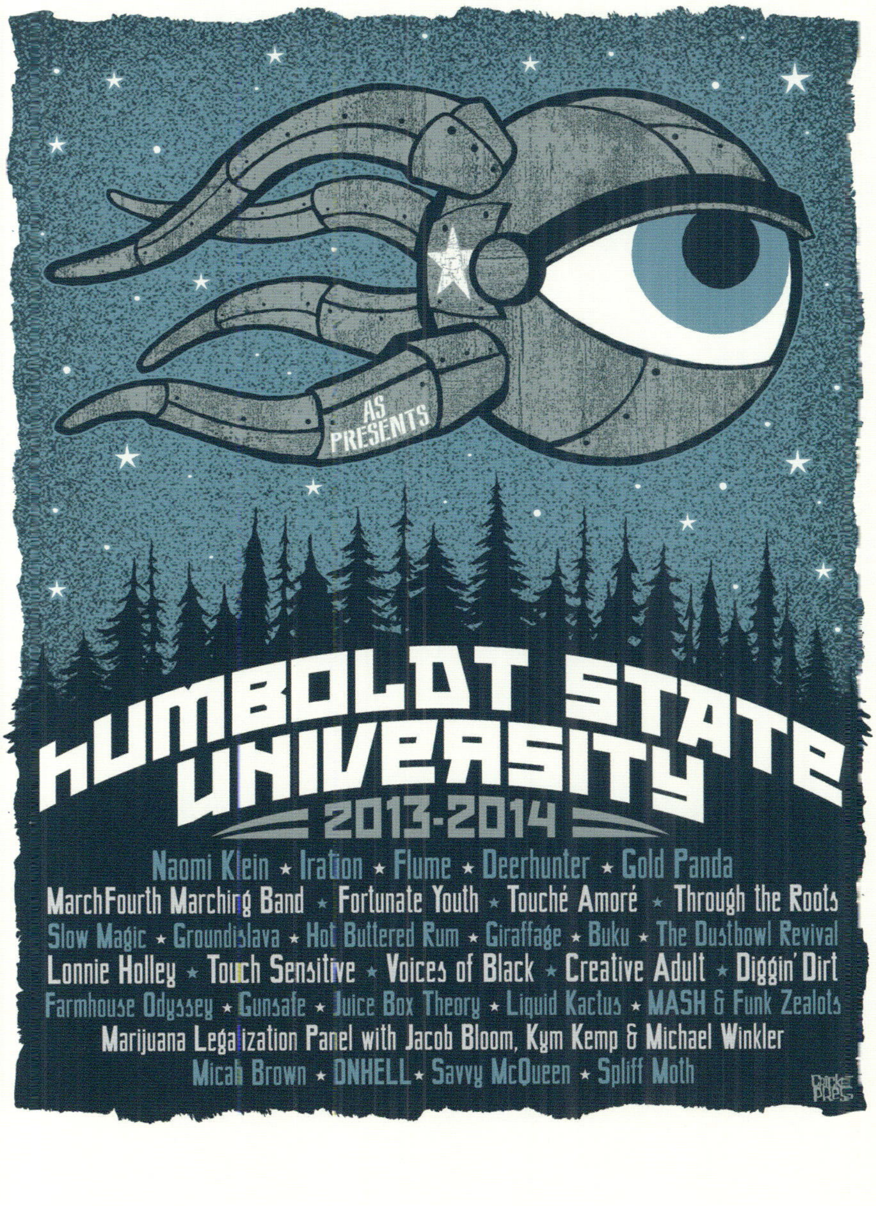

CLIENT: Humboldt State University
DESIGNER: Brian Turner
DESIGN FIRM: Cricket Press
WEBSITE: cricket-press.com

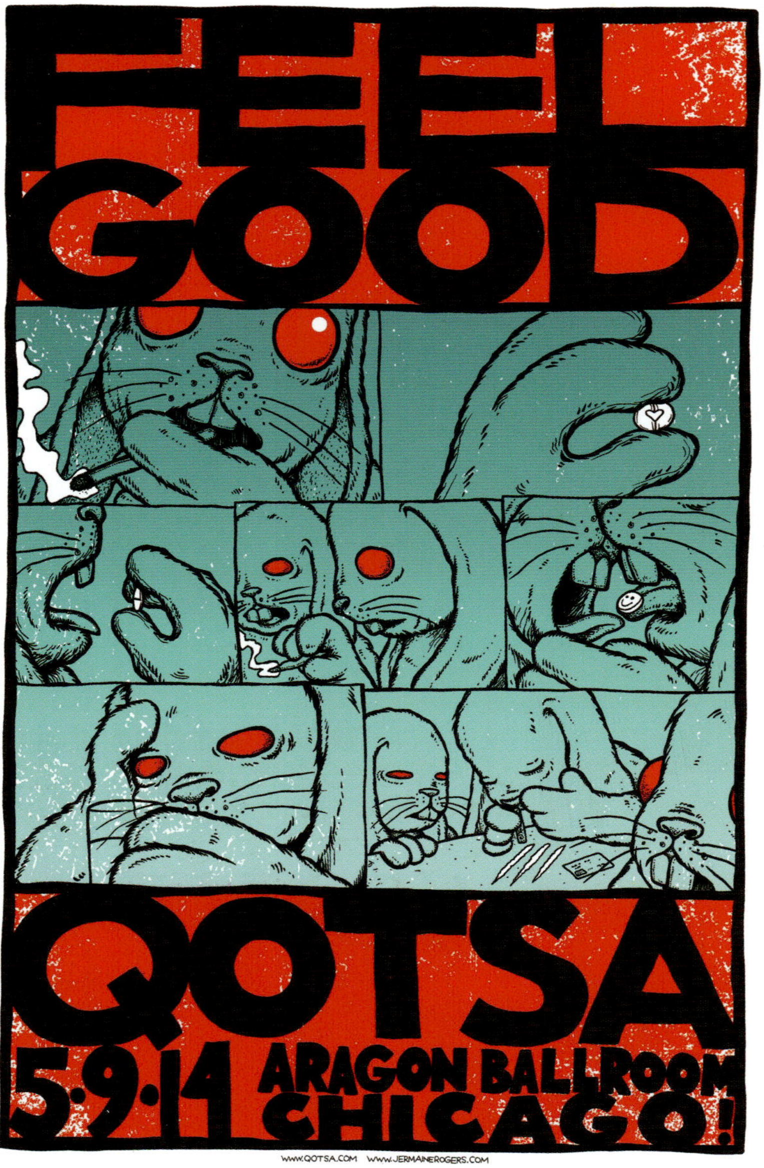

CLIENT: Feelgood / QOTSA
DESIGNER: Jermaine Rogers
WEBSITE: jermainerogers.com

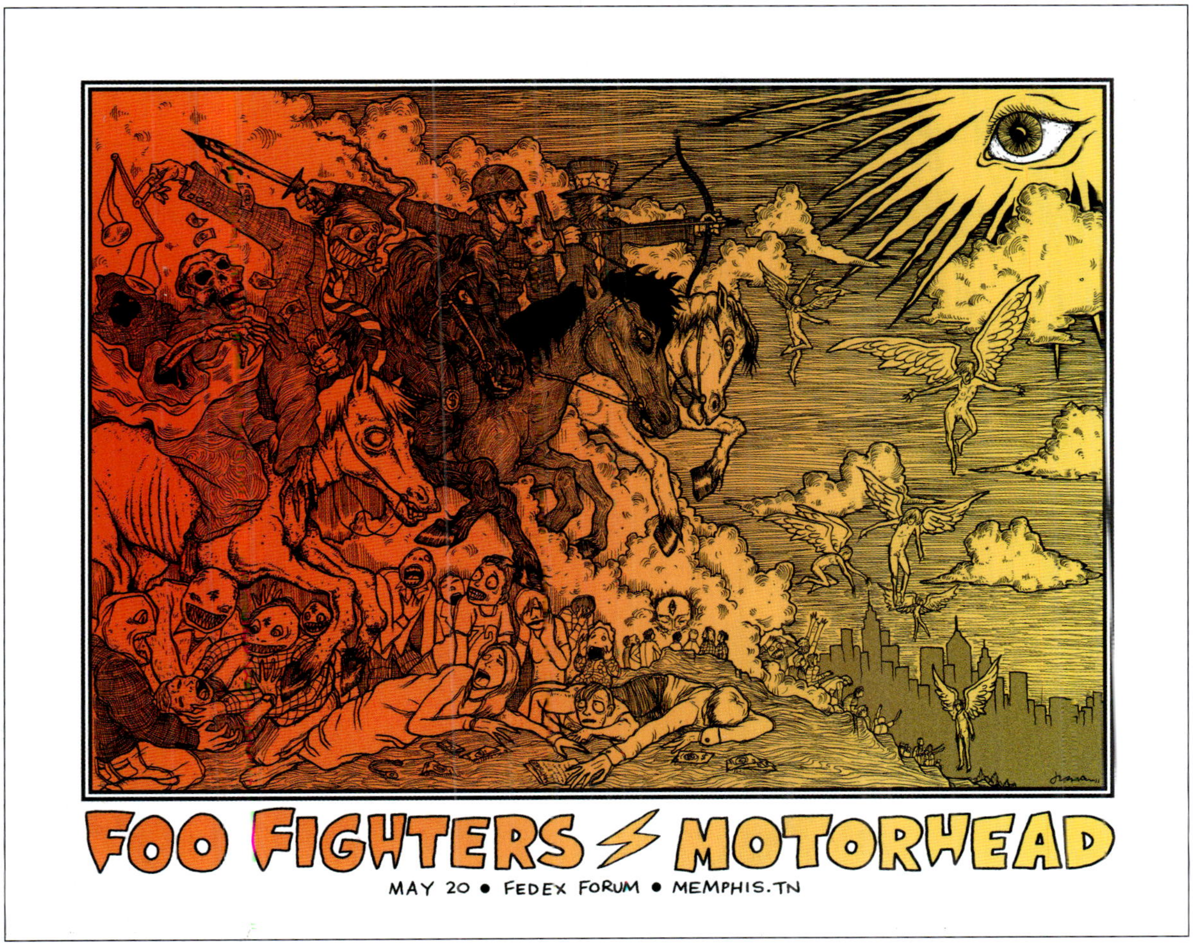

CLIENT: Foo Fighters / Motörhead
DESIGNER: Jermaine Rogers
WEBSITE: jermainerogers.com

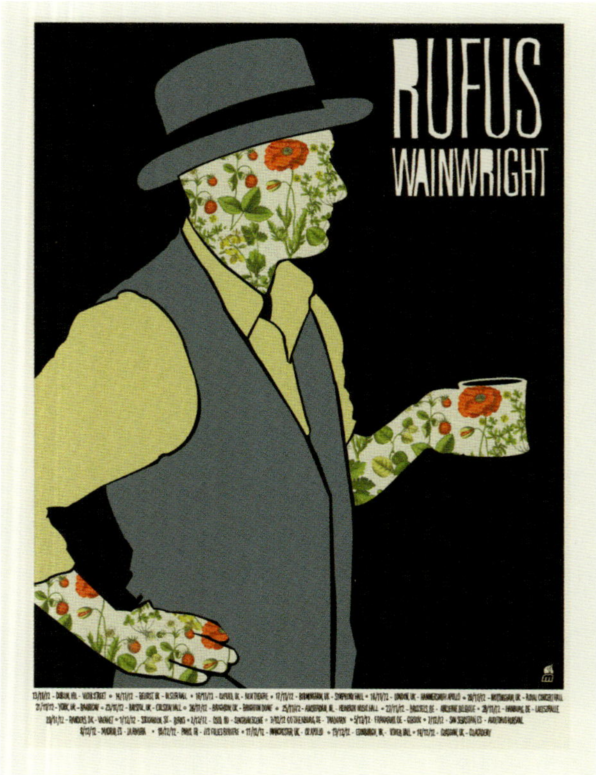

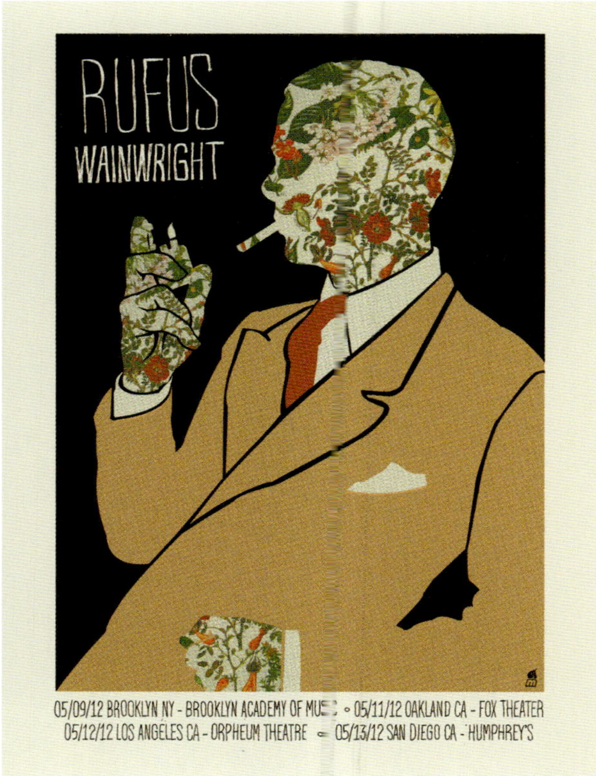

CLIENT: Rufus Wainwright (2 variants)
DESIGN FIRM: Methane Studios
WEBSITE: methanestudios.com

Textured Illustration

The goal of textured illustration is to add a depth and tangible quality to the work. This style utilizes a variety of textures to add detail to the poster. The resulting illustration quality veers toward the realistic or semirealistic, often incorporating photography (either as a base for the poster with illustration superimposed on it or conversely used to add detail on top an illustration).

KEY STYLE CHARACTERISTICS

- Relies heavily on a wide variety of textures
- Texture is used to shade imagery and add detail
- The piece can be illustrative exclusively or can be illustration over photography
- Photography is used as texture in some cases
- High illustration quality creates a semirealistic to realistic effect
- Colors may appear washed-out and bleed into one another to create more texture
- Composition employs flat imagery in combination with texture
- Pieces are very narrative and/or symbolize a place or time period in subject matter

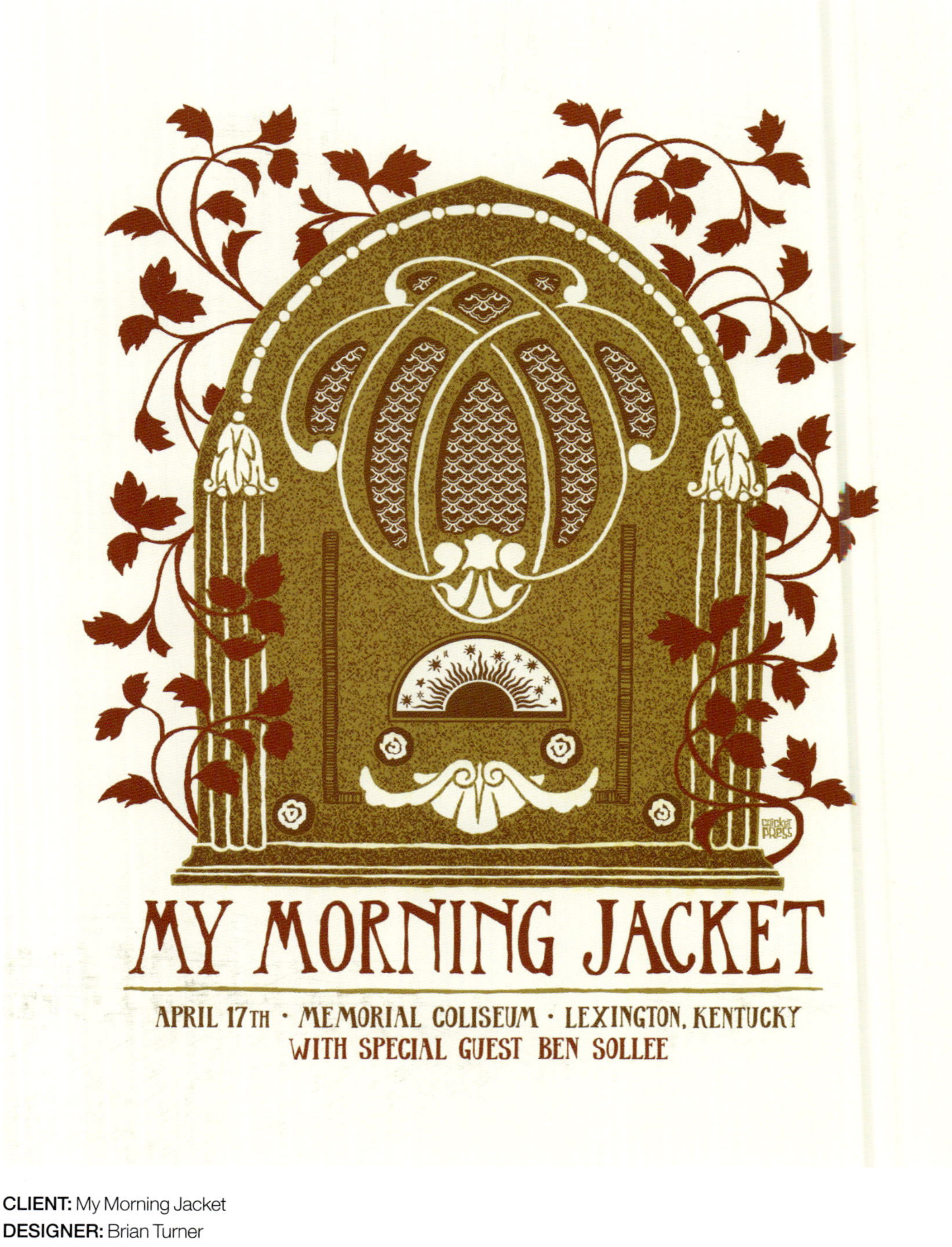

CLIENT: My Morning Jacket
DESIGNER: Brian Turner
DESIGN FIRM: Cricket Press
WEBSITE: cricket-press.com

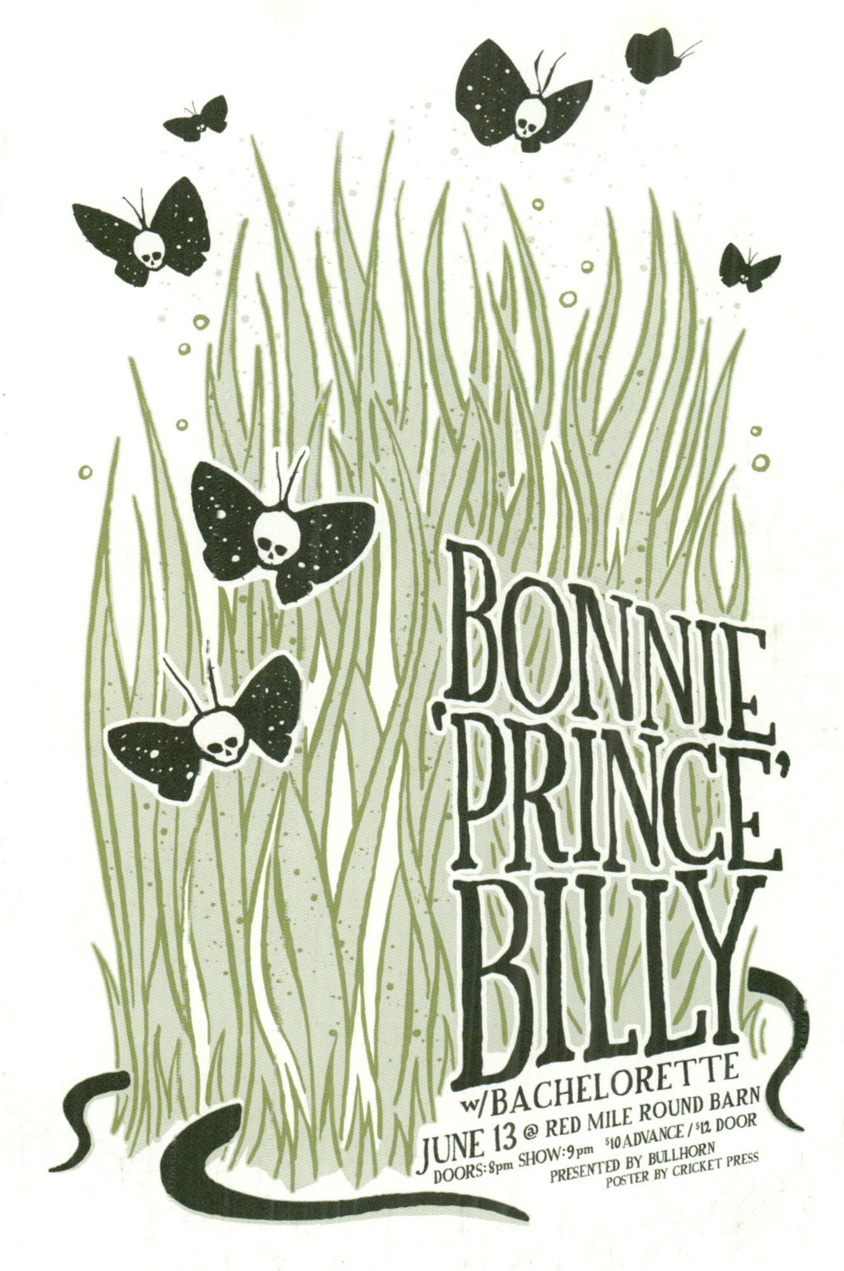

CLIENT: Bonnie "Prince" Billy
DESIGNER: Brian Turner
DESIGN FIRM: Cricket Press
WEBSITE: cricket-press.com

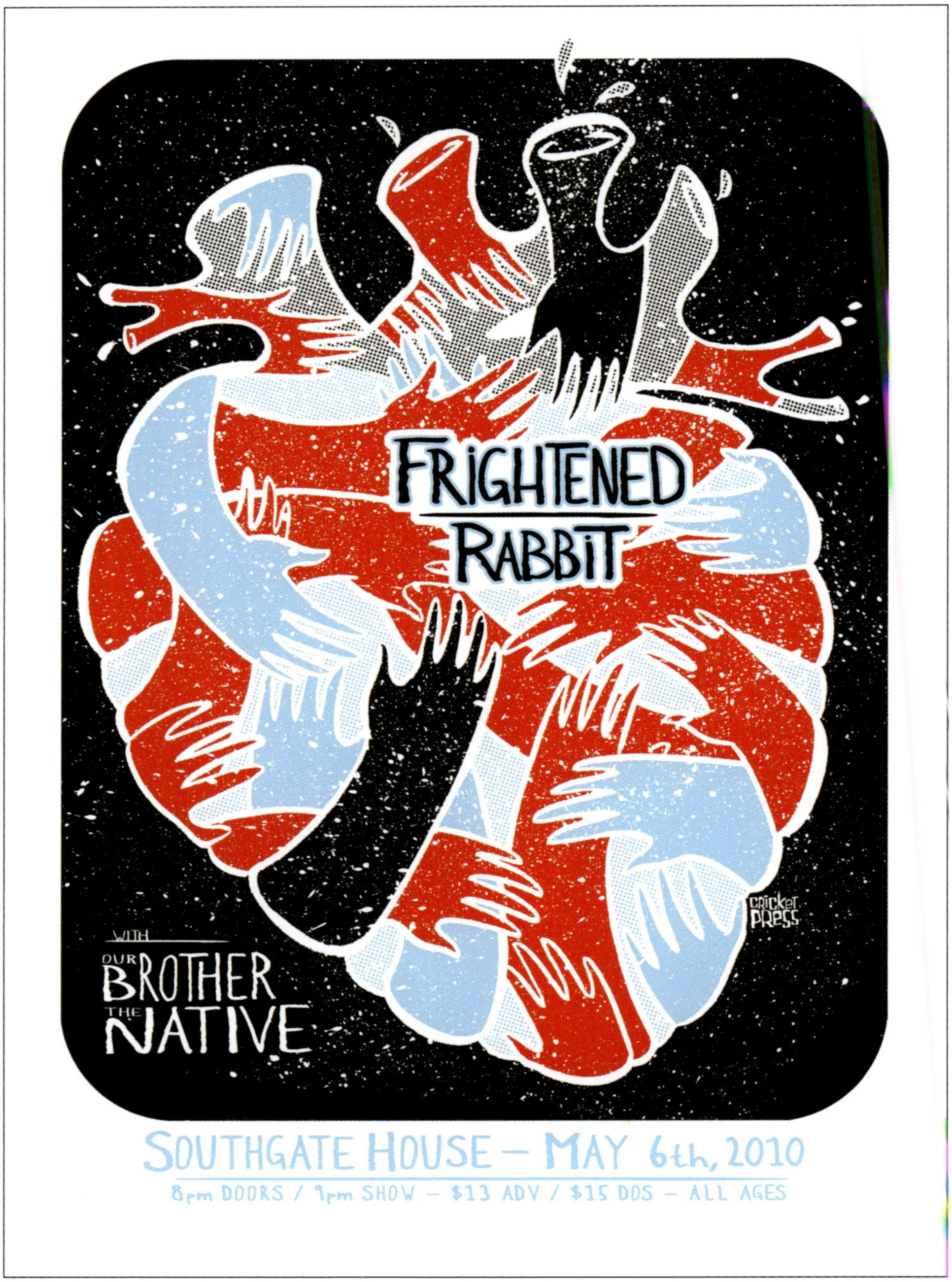

CLIENT: Frightened Rabbit
DESIGNER: Sara Turner
DESIGN FIRM: Cricket Press
WEBSITE: cricket-press.com

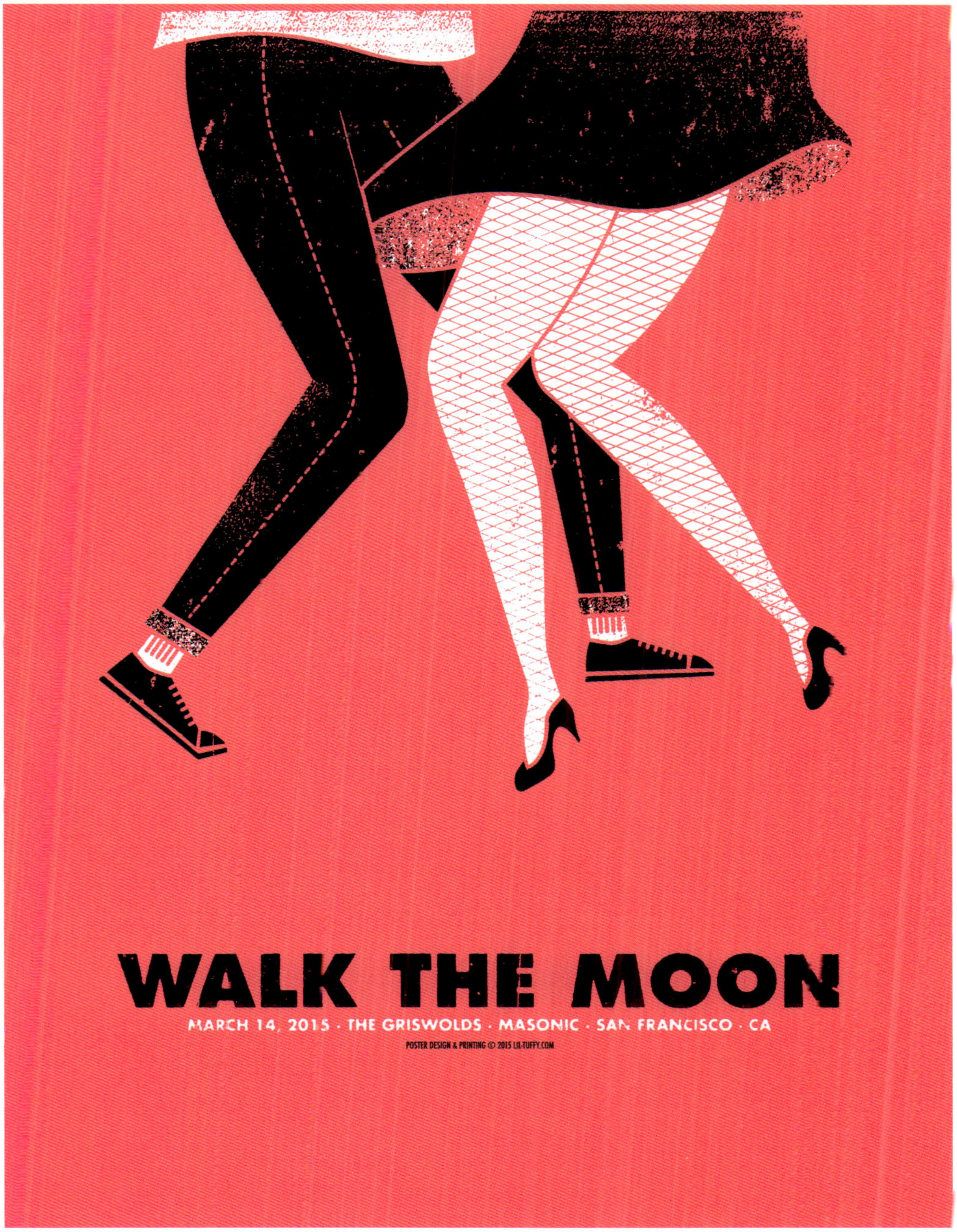

CLIENT: Walk the Moon
DESIGNER: Terrence Ryan
DESIGN FIRM: Lil' Tuffy
WEBSITE: lil-tuffy.com

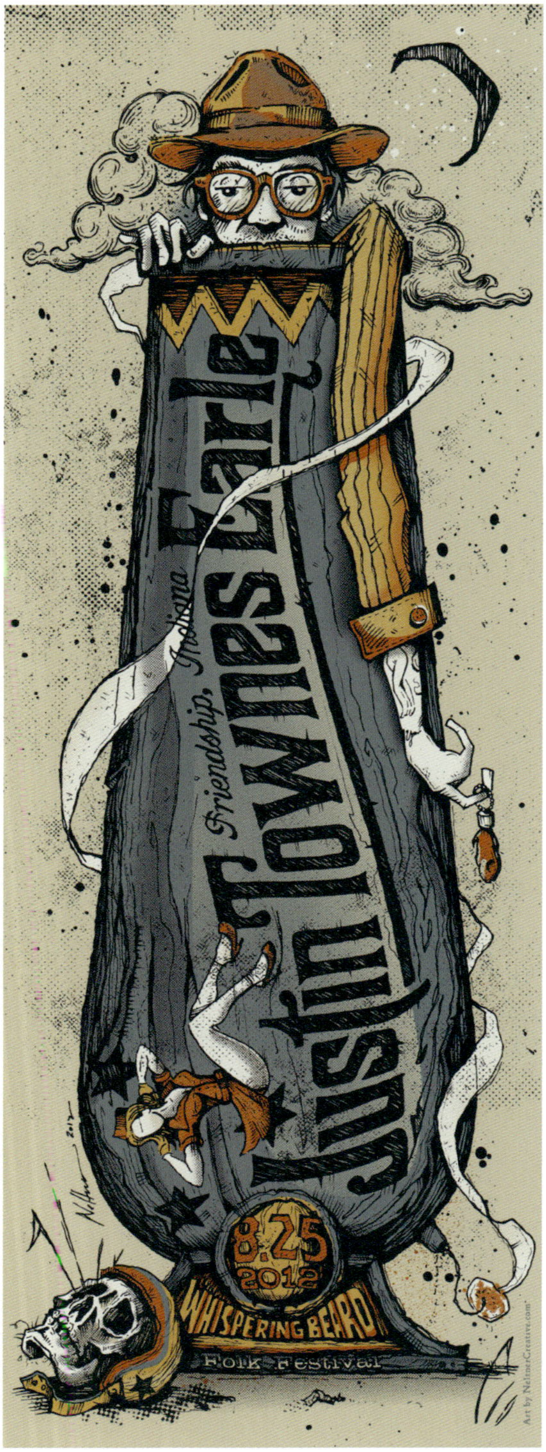

CLIENT: Justin Townes Earle
DESIGNER: Keith Neltner
DESIGN FIRM: Neltner Small Batch
WEBSITE: neltnersmallbatch.com

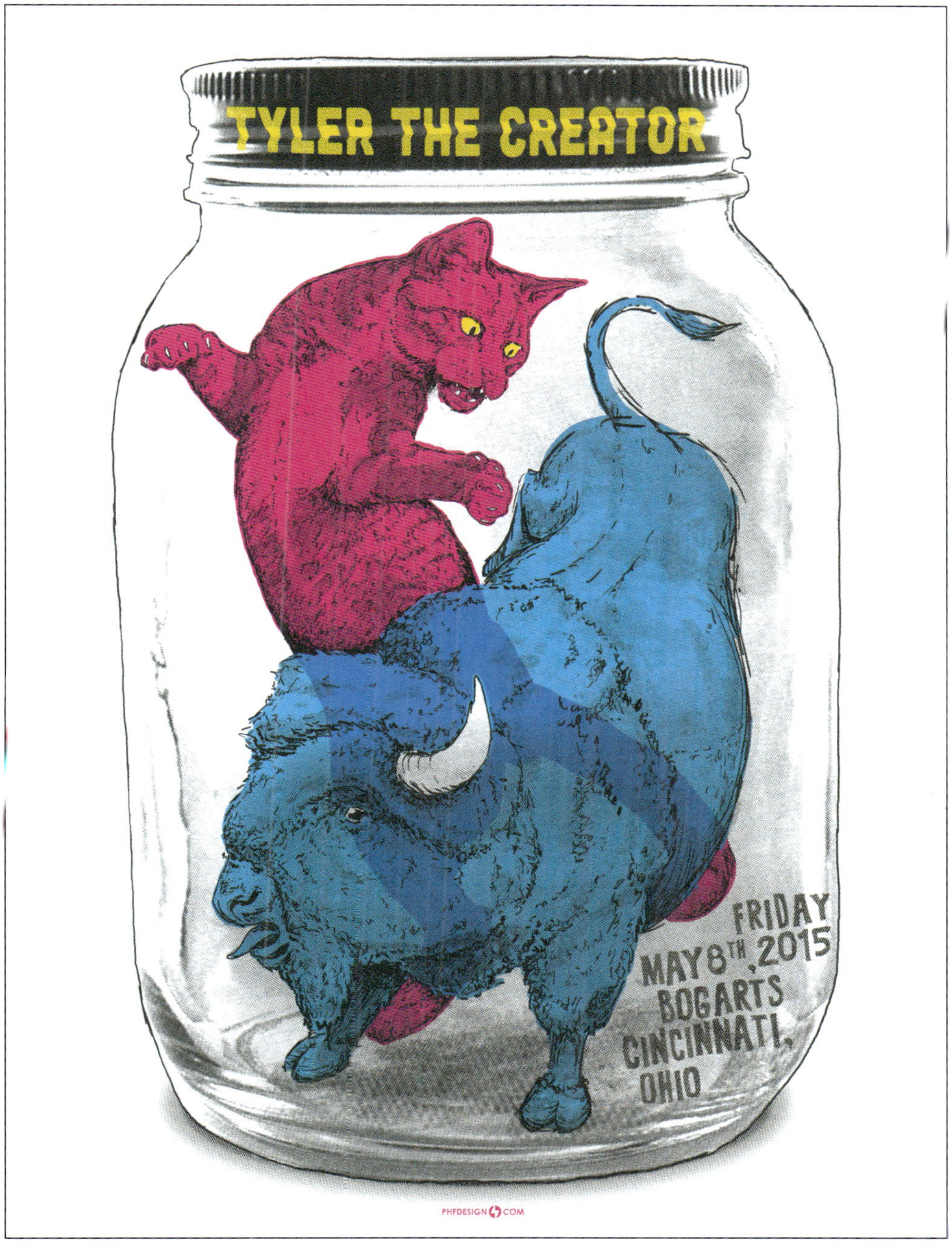

CLIENT: Tyler, the Creator
DESIGNER: Tim Engel
DESIGN FIRM: Powerhouse Factories
WEBSITE: powerhousefactories.com

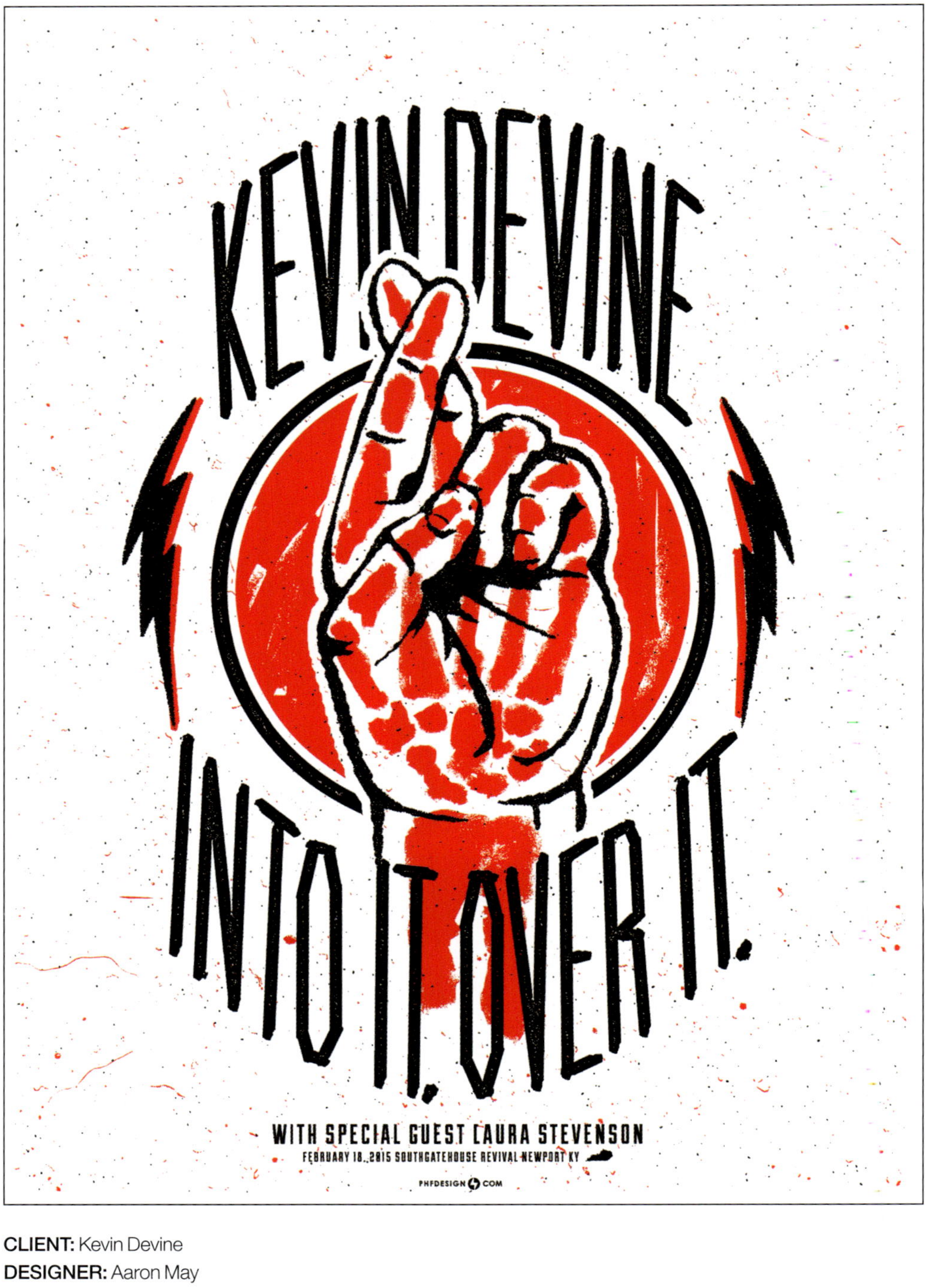

CLIENT: Kevin Devine
DESIGNER: Aaron May
DESIGN FIRM: Powerhouse Factories
WEBSITE: powerhousefactories.com

Psychedelic Repetition

Psychedelic music and the related culture is linked inexorably to the experience of psychedelic drugs. Visual art related with the movement typically has a surreal quality and attempts to mimic the psychedelic experience that follows ingestion of psychoactive drugs. With nods to Indian culture, psychedelic repetition uses bright colors and contrasting patterns to create depth and movement. Shapes, both geometric and organic, are used in full-bleed, complex labyrinthine patterns to guide the eye around the piece, creating a feeling of sensory overload for the viewer.

KEY STYLE CHARACTERISTICS

- Both geometric and organic repeats used heavily to mimic a psychedelic experience
- Tied to Indian cultures using figures with multiple eyes, floral patterns, etc.
- References '70s psychedelic patterns and color selection; colors tend to be bright and contrasting
- Color overlay and colors that mix well, like CMYK, are used to create many colors and heavy depth (even when screenprinted with few colors)
- Full-bleed patterns used and little to no rest for the eye is given
- High contrast and detail is used to show complexity
- Landscapes and faces become labyrinths that trap the viewer

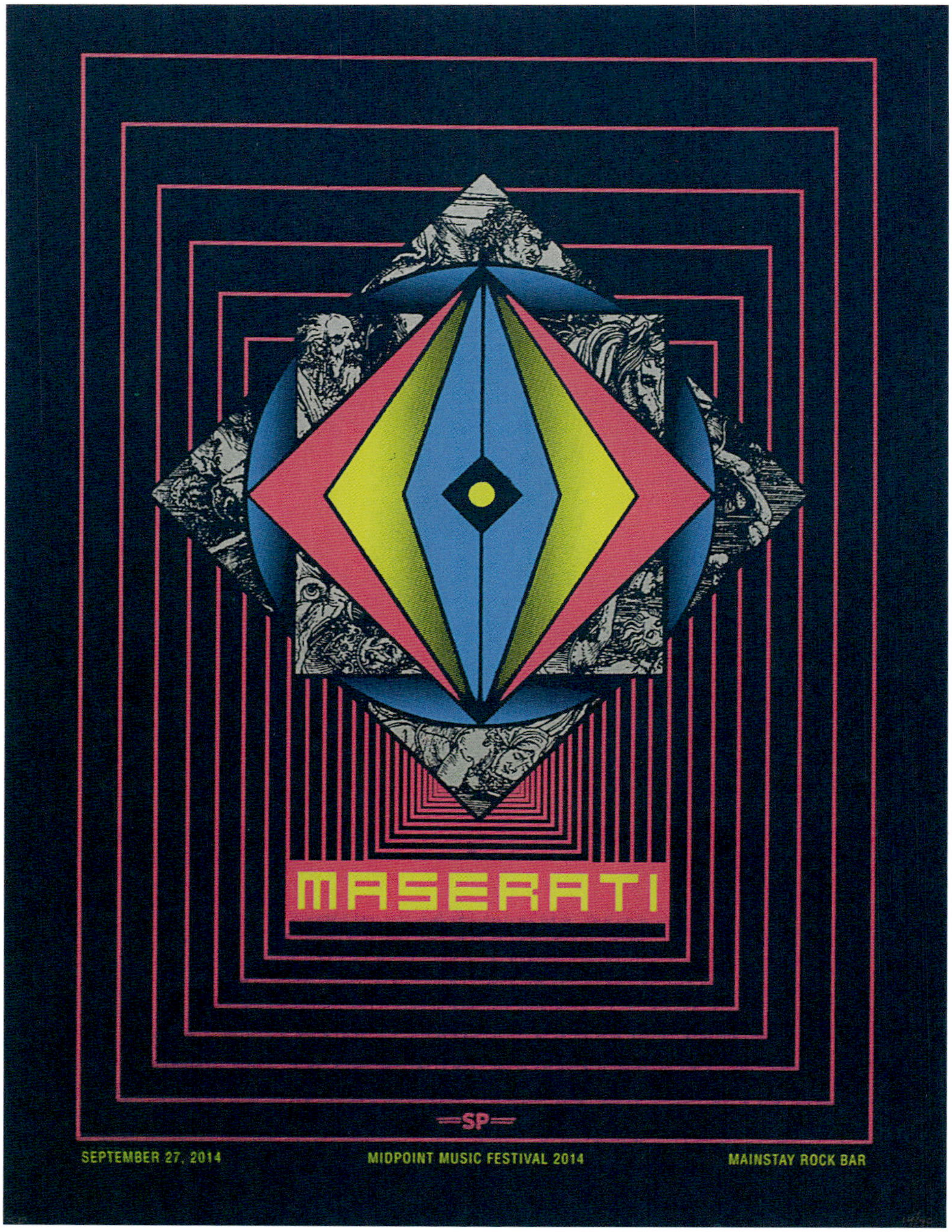

CLIENT: Maserati
DESIGNER: Southpaw Prints
WEBSITE: southpawprints.com

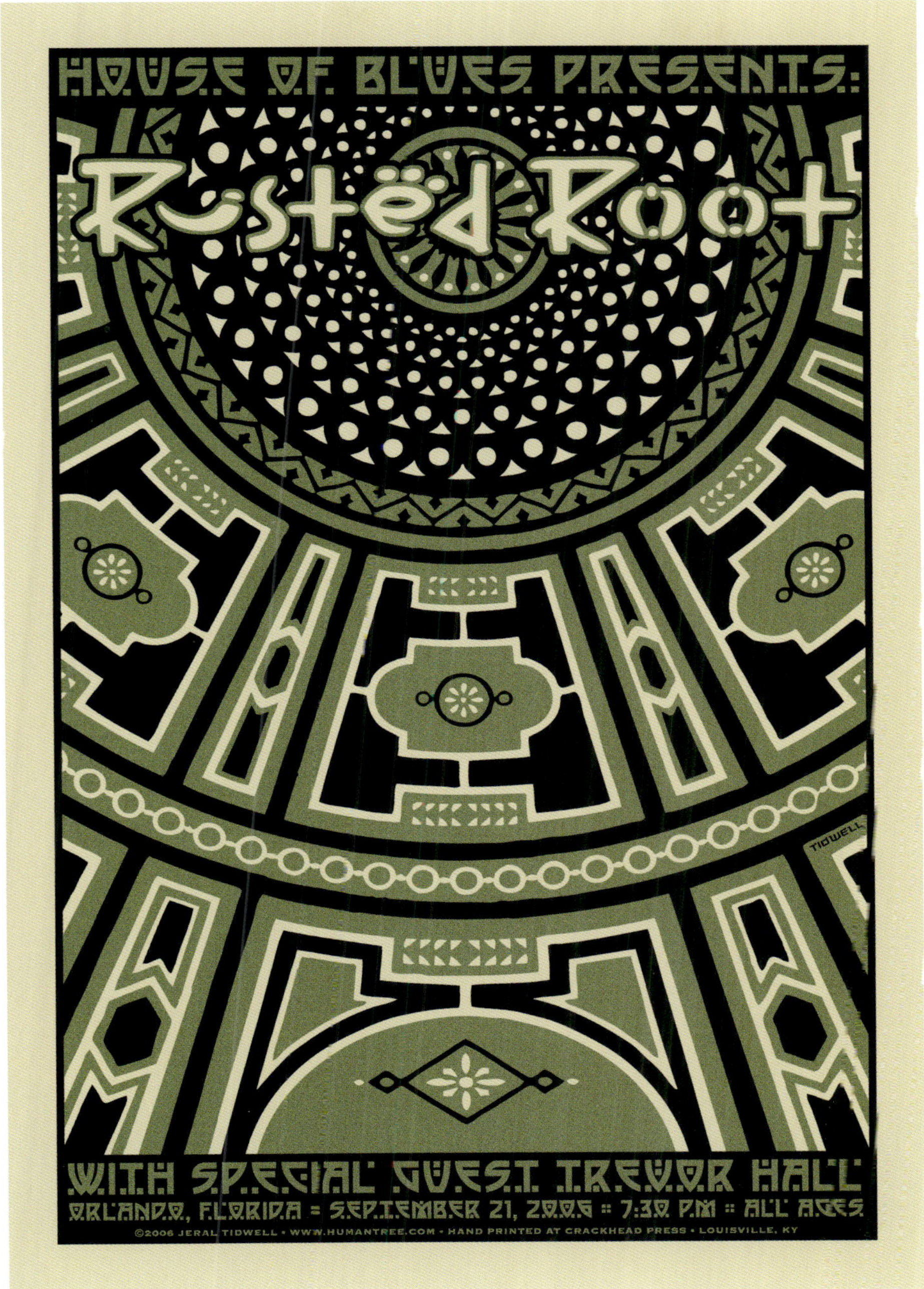

CLIENT: Rusted Root
DESIGNER: Jeral Tidwell
DESIGN FIRM: Humantree
WEBSITE: humantree.com

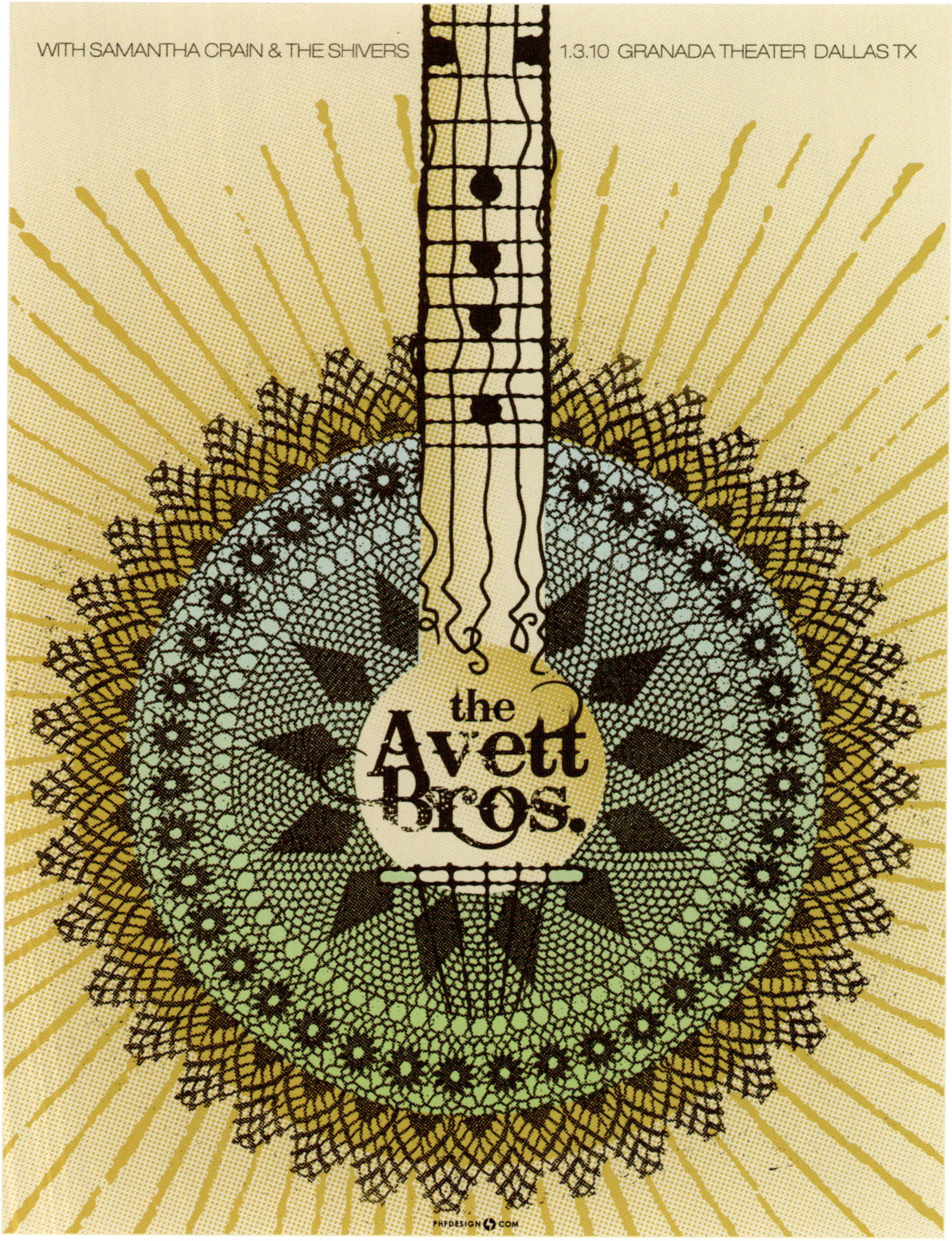

CLIENT: The Avett Brothers
DESIGNER: Ben Nunery
DESIGN FIRM: Powerhouse Factories
WEBSITE: powerhousefactories.com

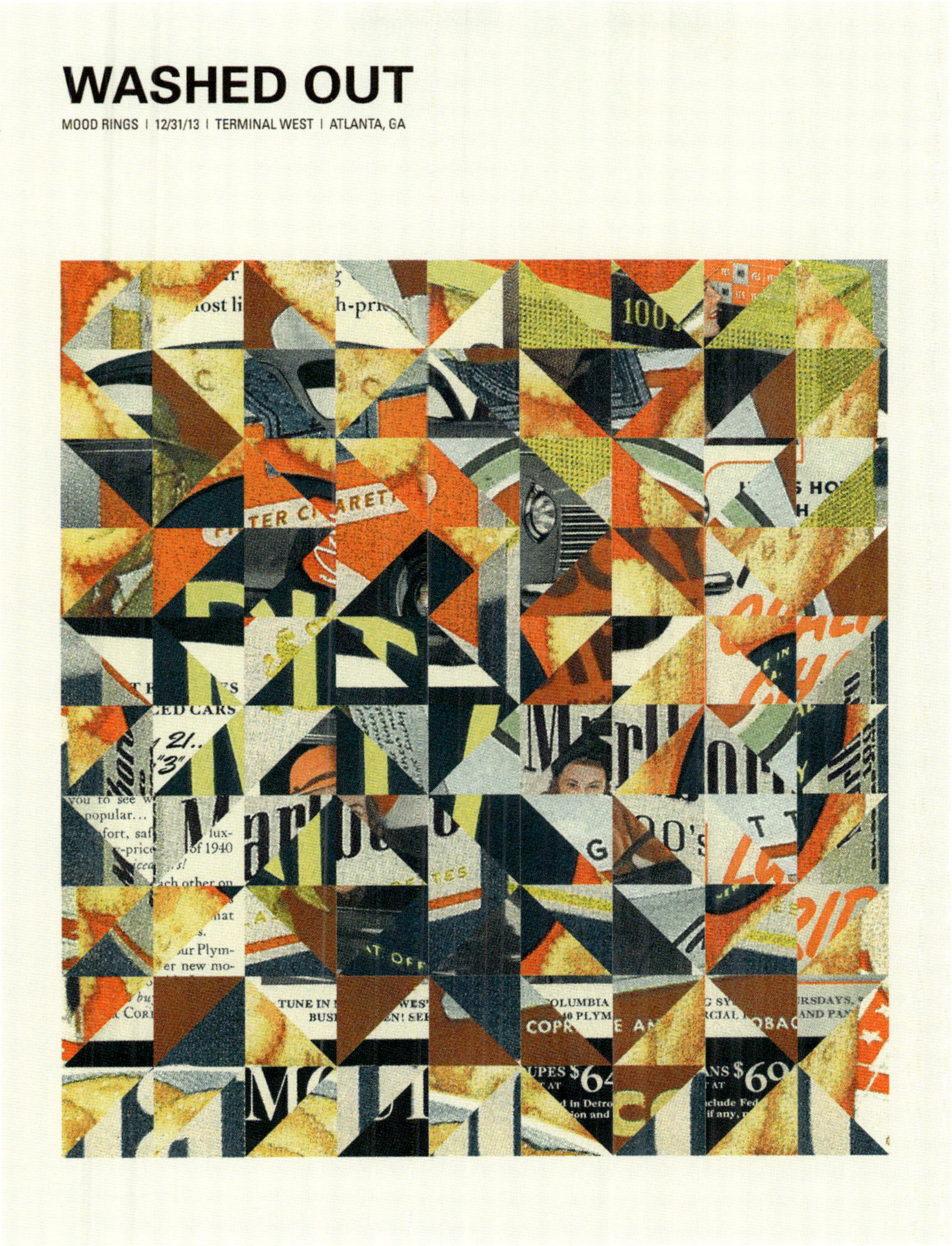

CLIENT: Washed Out
DESIGN FIRM: Methane Studios
WEBSITE: methanestudios.com

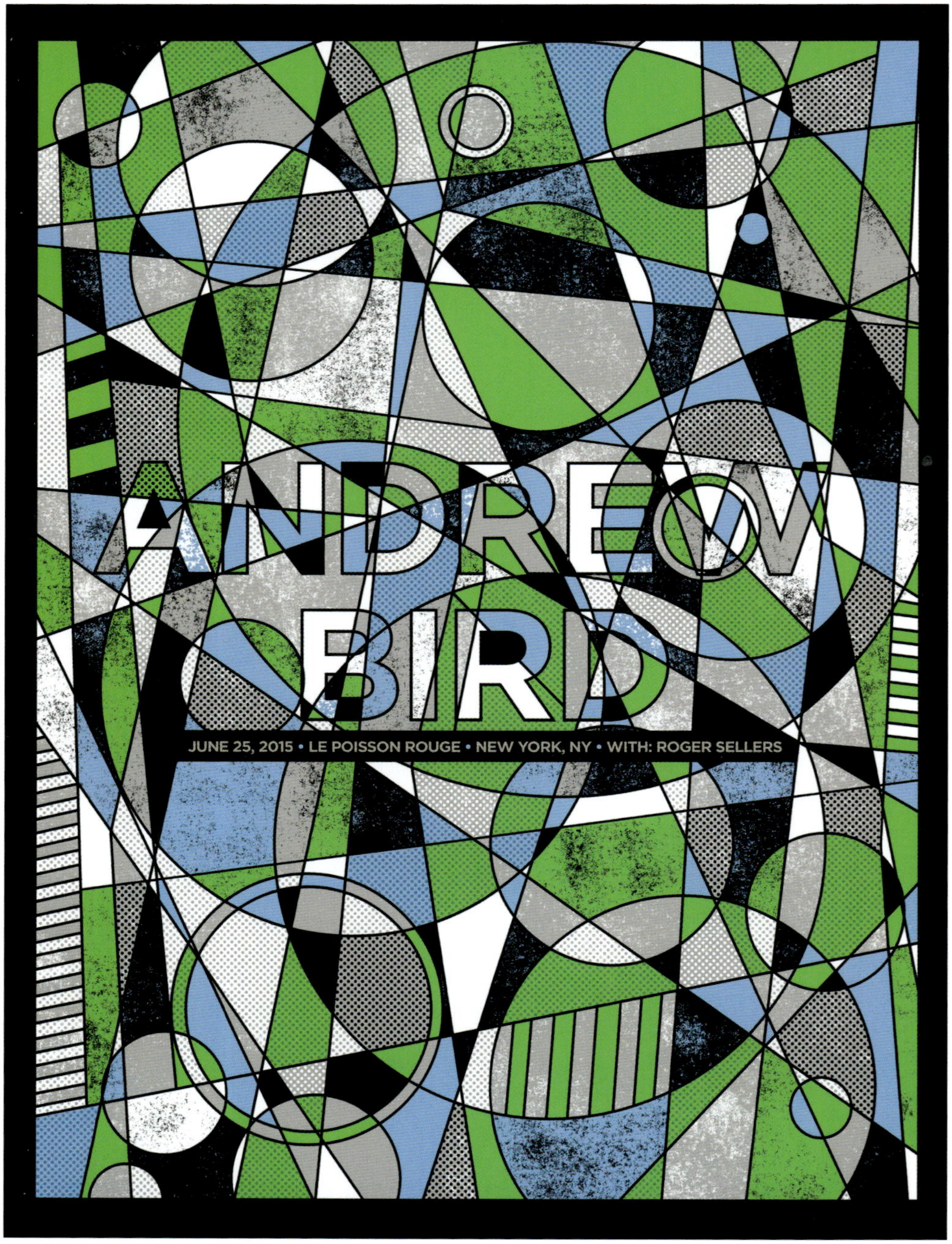

CLIENT: Andrew Bird
DESIGNER: Nate Duval
WEBSITE: nateduval.com

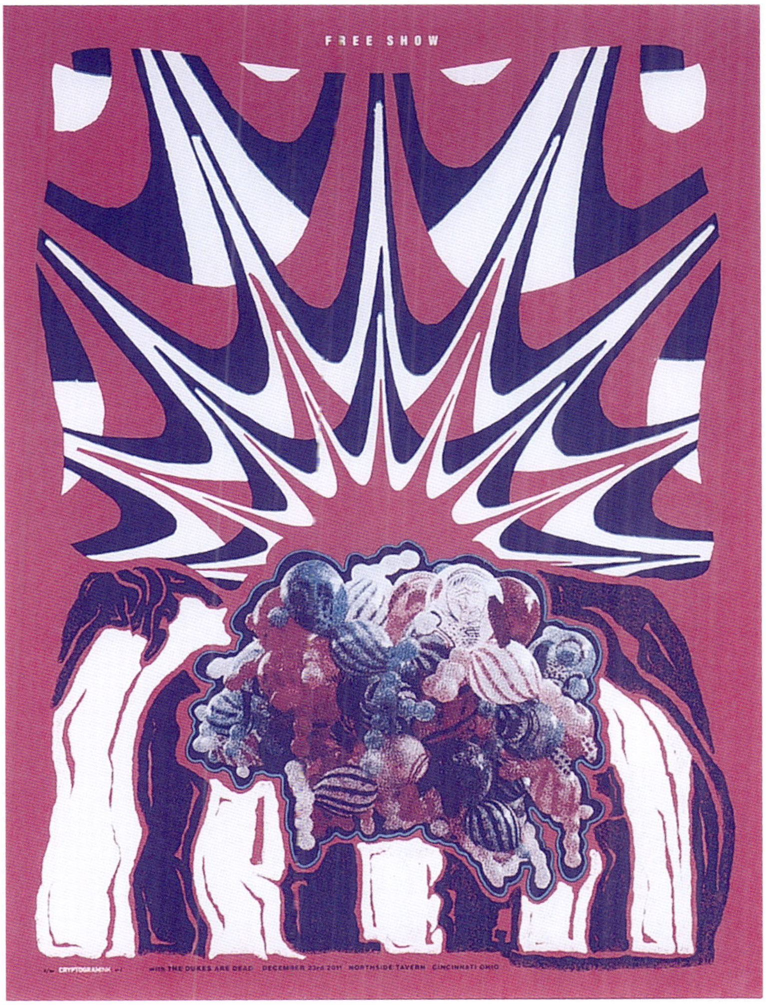

CLIENT: The Harlequins
DESIGNER: Jon Flannery
DESIGN FIRM: Cryptogram

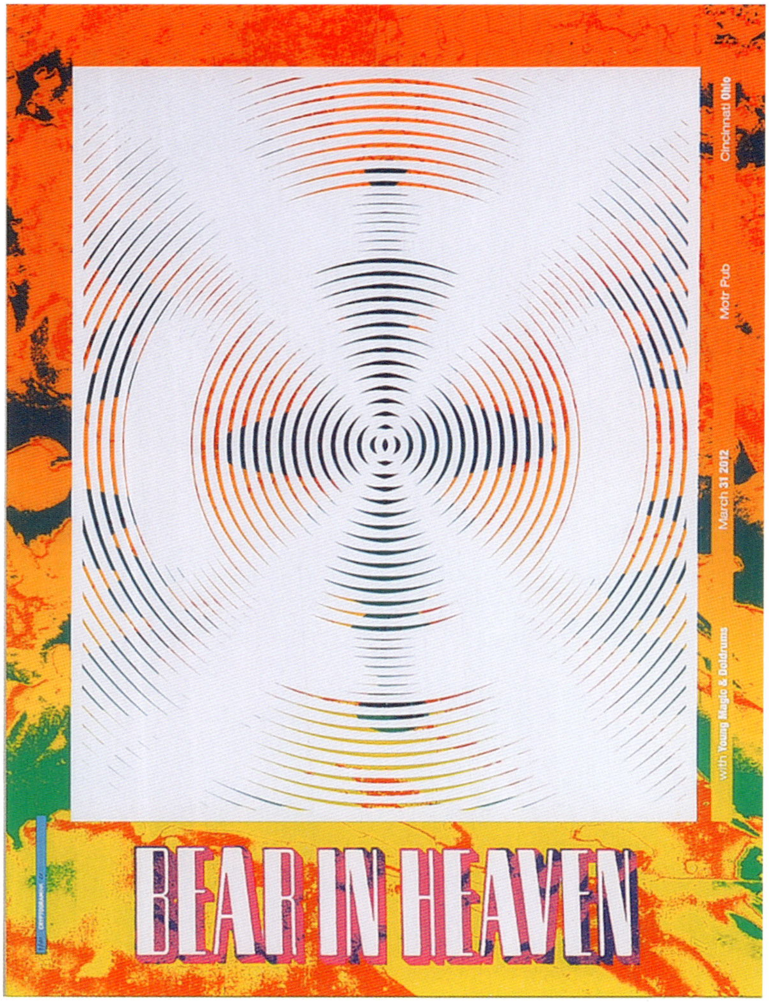

CLIENT: Bear in Heaven
DESIGNER: Jon Flannery
DESIGN FIRM: Cryptogram

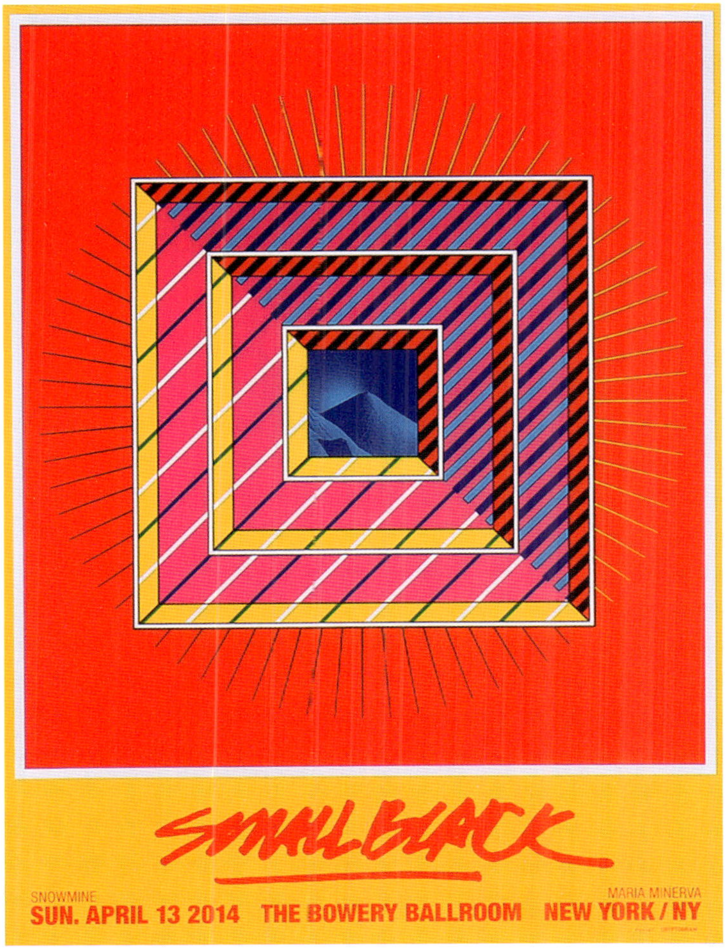

CLIENT: Small Black
DESIGNER: Jon Flannery
DESIGN FIRM: Cryptogram

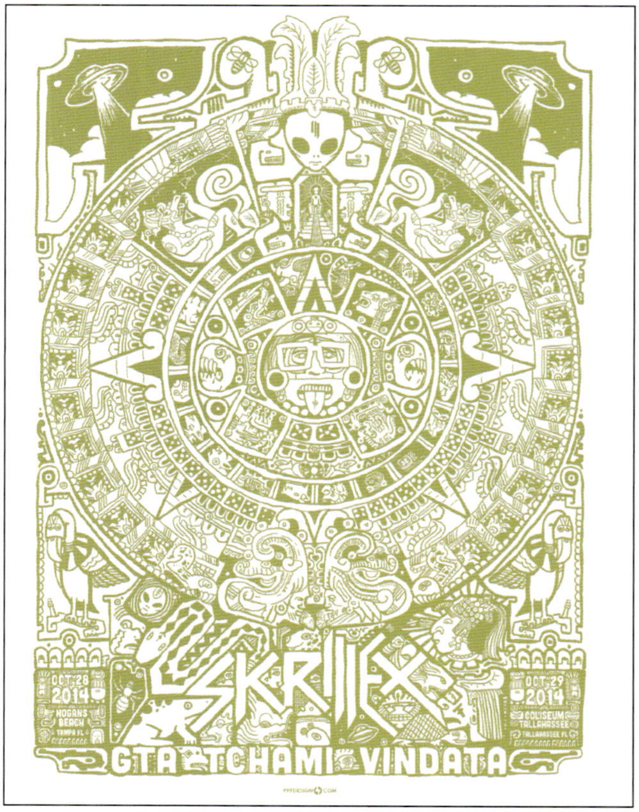

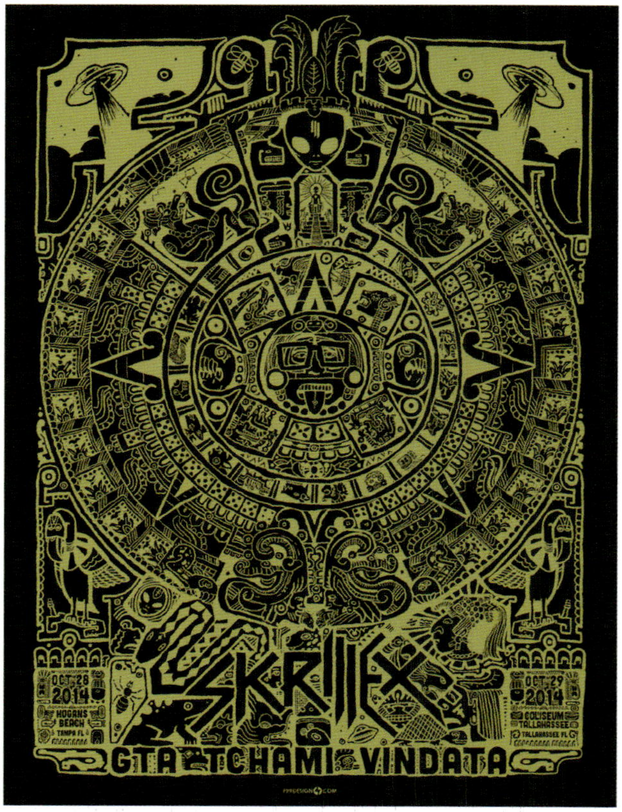

CLIENT: Skrillex (2 variants)
DESIGNER: Tim Engel
DESIGN FIRM: Powerhouse Factories
WEBSITE: powerhousefactories.com

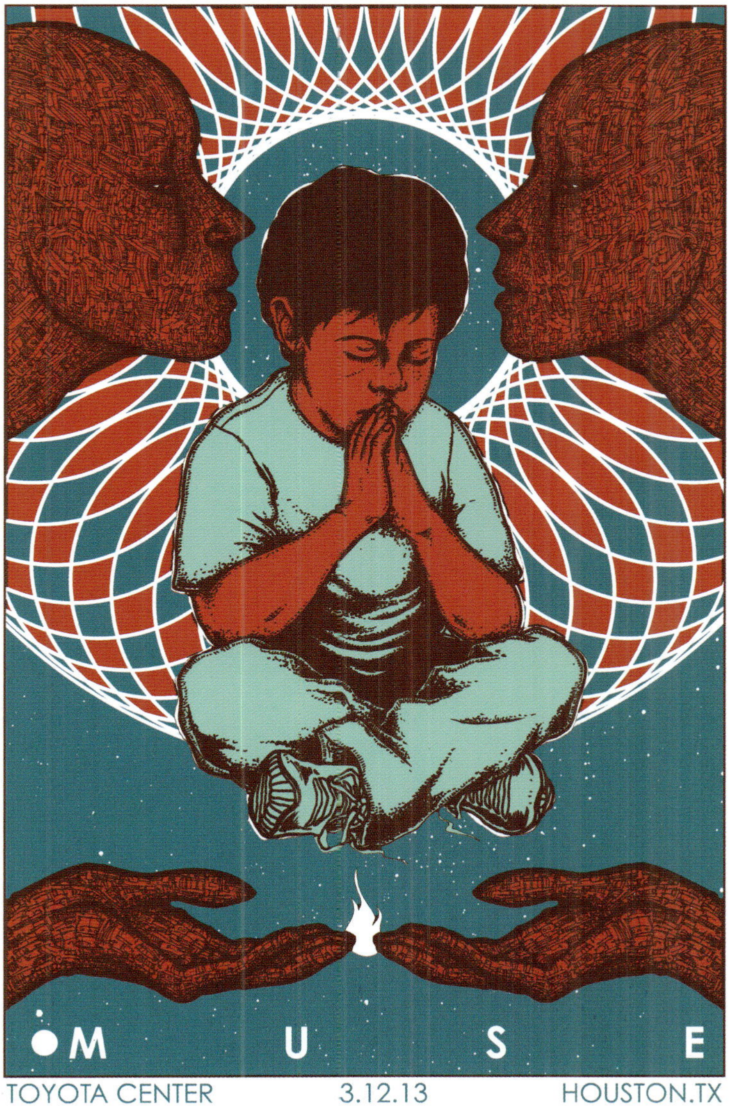

CLIENT: Muse
DESIGNER: Jermaine Rogers
WEBSITE: jermainerogers.com

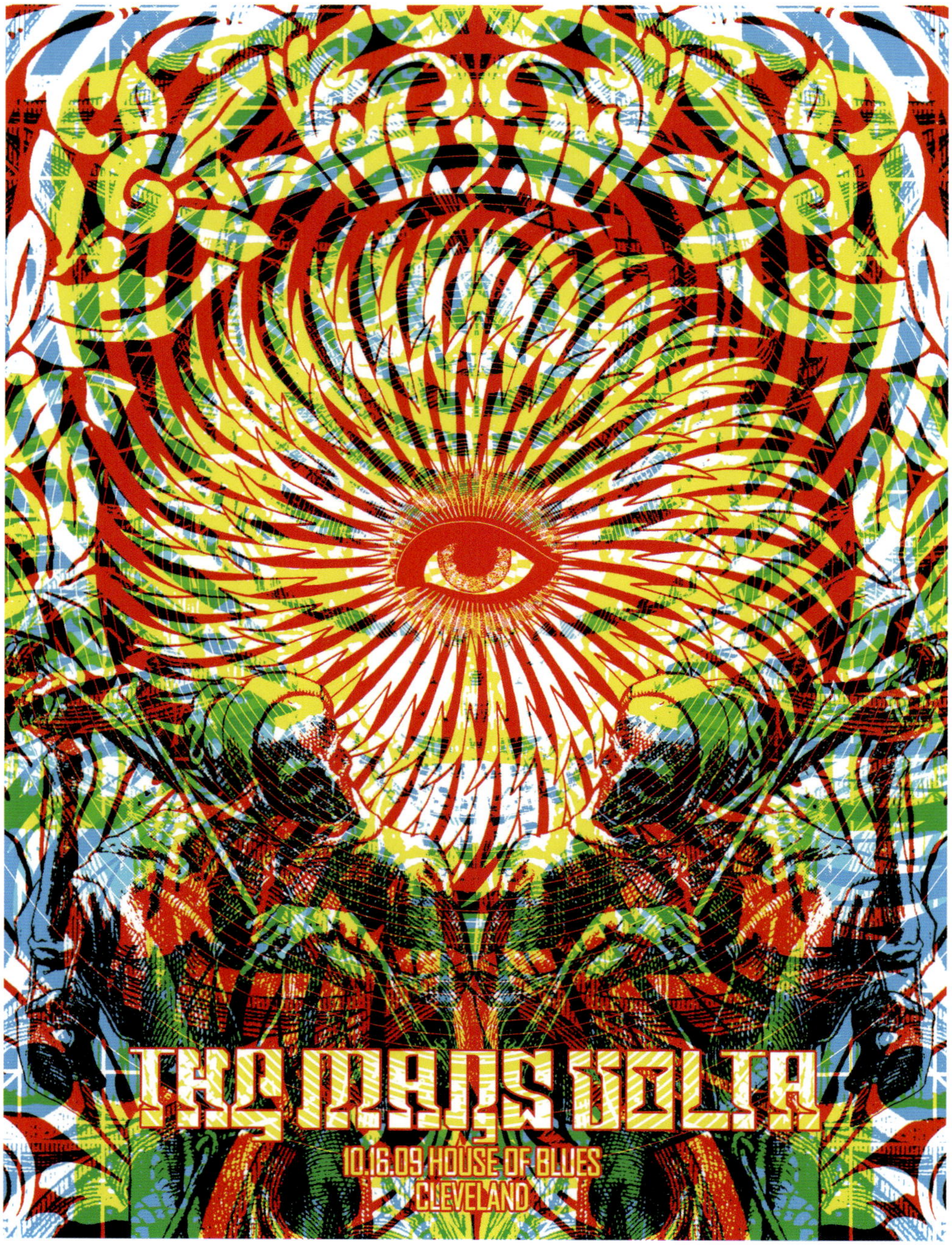

CLIENT: The Mars Volta
DESIGNER: Jared Connor
DESIGN FIRM: Mexican Chocolate Design
WEBSITE: mexicanchocolatedesign.com

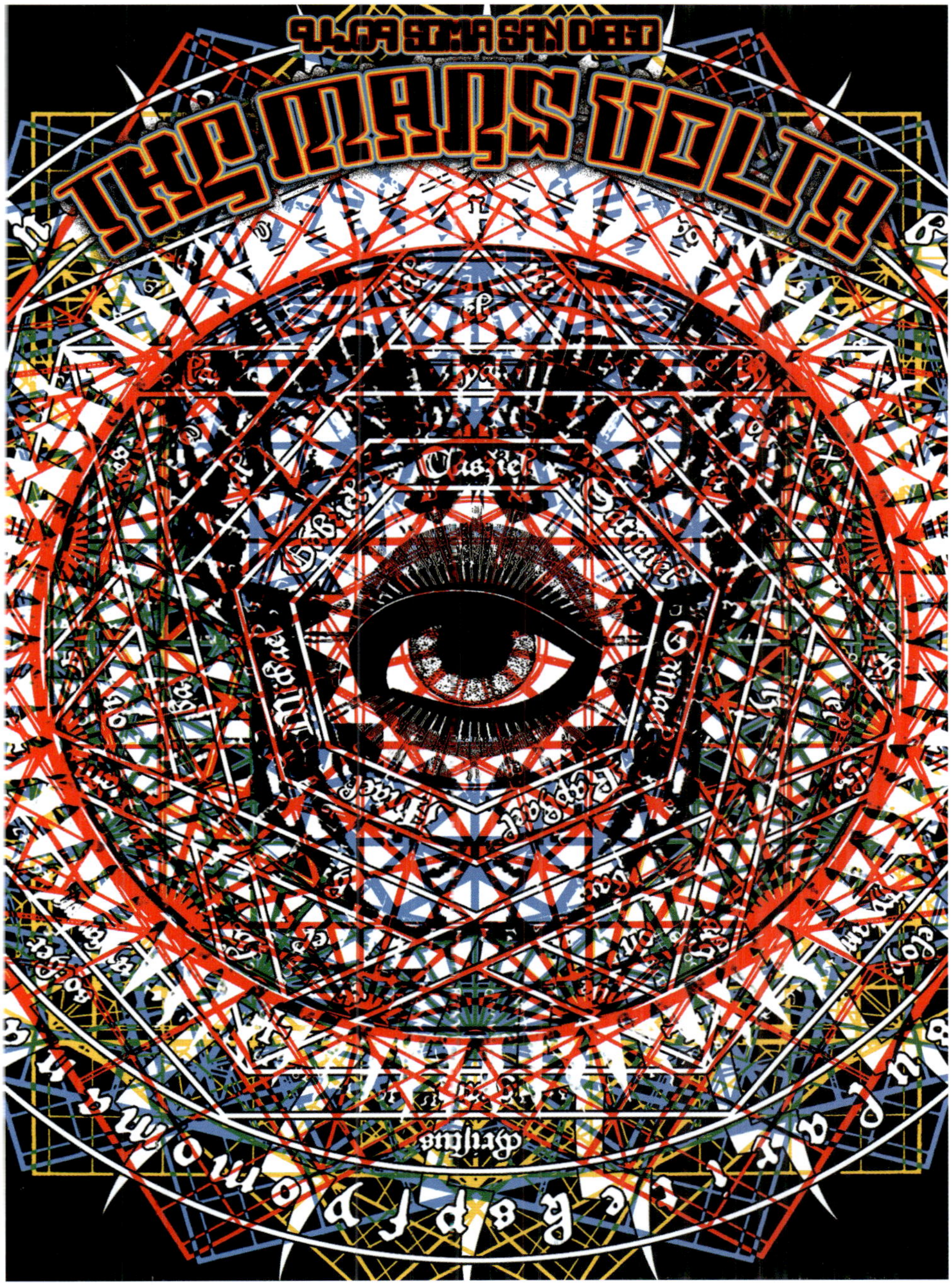

CLIENT: The Mars Volta
DESIGNER: Jared Connor
DESIGN FIRM: Mexican Chocolate Design
WEBSITE: mexicanchocolatedesign.com

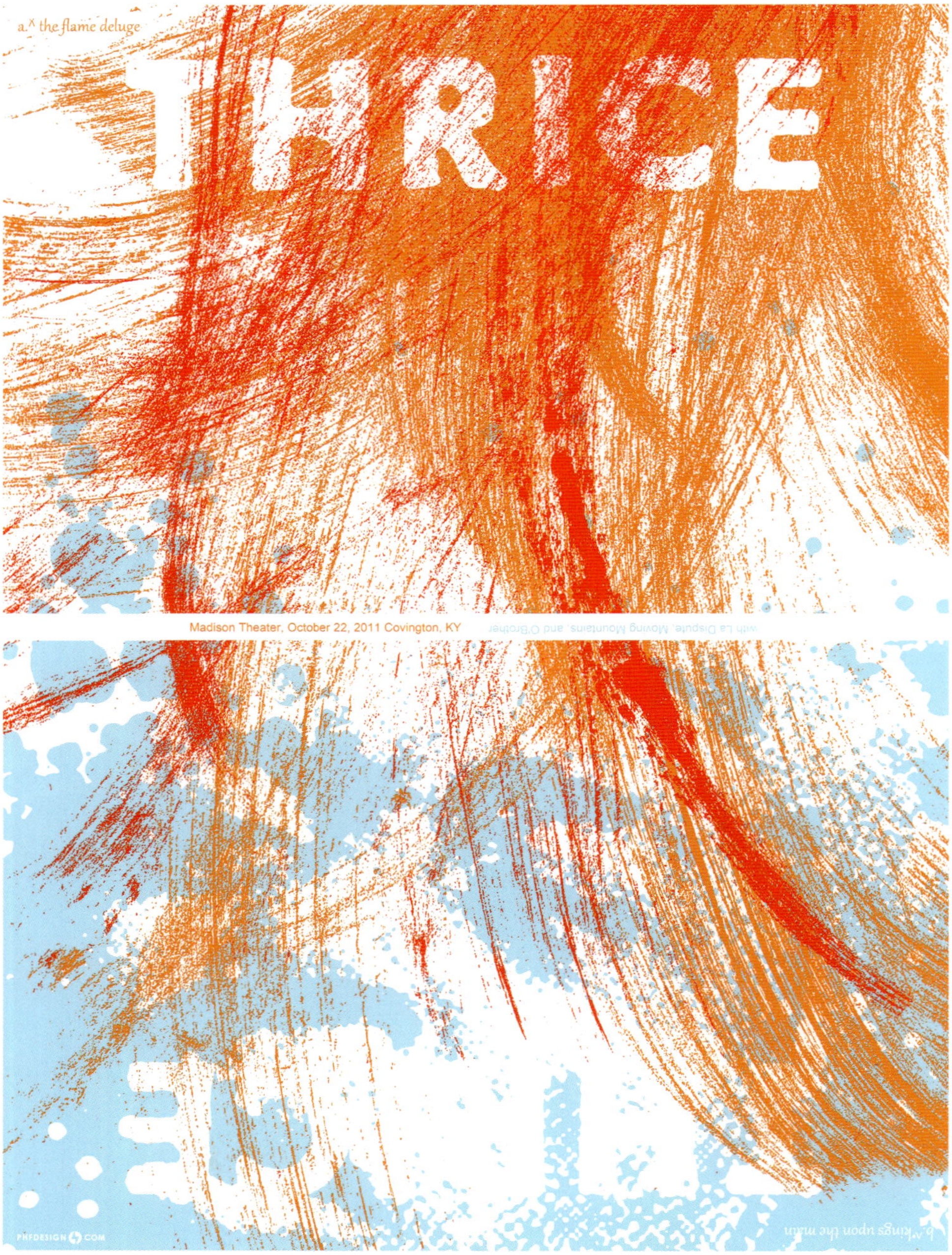

CLIENT: Thrice
DESIGNER: Pat Jones
DESIGN FIRM: Powerhouse Factories
WEBSITE: powerhousefactories.com

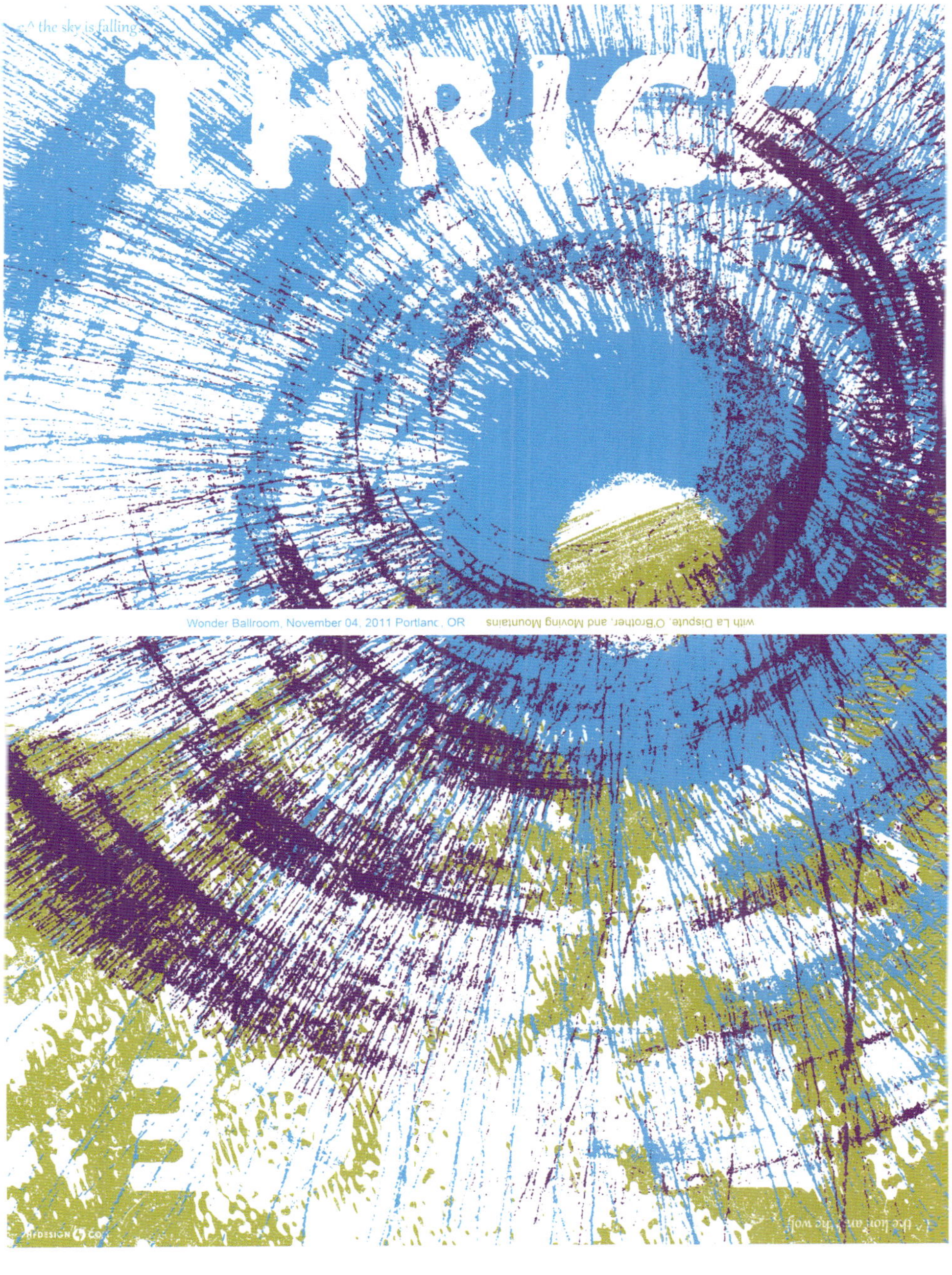

CLIENT: Thrice
DESIGNER: Pat Jones
DESIGN FIRM: Powerhouse Factories
WEBSITE: powerhousefactories.com

Graphic Weight

This style evokes the feel of comic books through the use of thick outlines and heavily saturated color palettes. The emphasis in this style is on hyper-realistic, larger-than-life illustrations. With it's comic book-ish feel, graphic weight is highly narrative and tends to deal with sexually charged imagery or fantastical subject matter such as robots, monsters, and martial arts. Accomplished illustrators saturate this style. They can draw and have been doing so for a while. Not necessarily the "old guys," but this group helped the re-emergence of the gig poster in the mid to late '90s.

KEY STYLE CHARACTERISTICS

- Very similar to a graphic novel or comic book style
- Portrays hyper-realistic, larger-than-life figures and settings
- Heavily saturated and thick color palettes—all solid pantones
- Thick use of outline
- Lots of black used, primarily for negative space or rest for the eye
- Less emphasis on typography; the focus is on the high-quality illustration, composition, and narrative

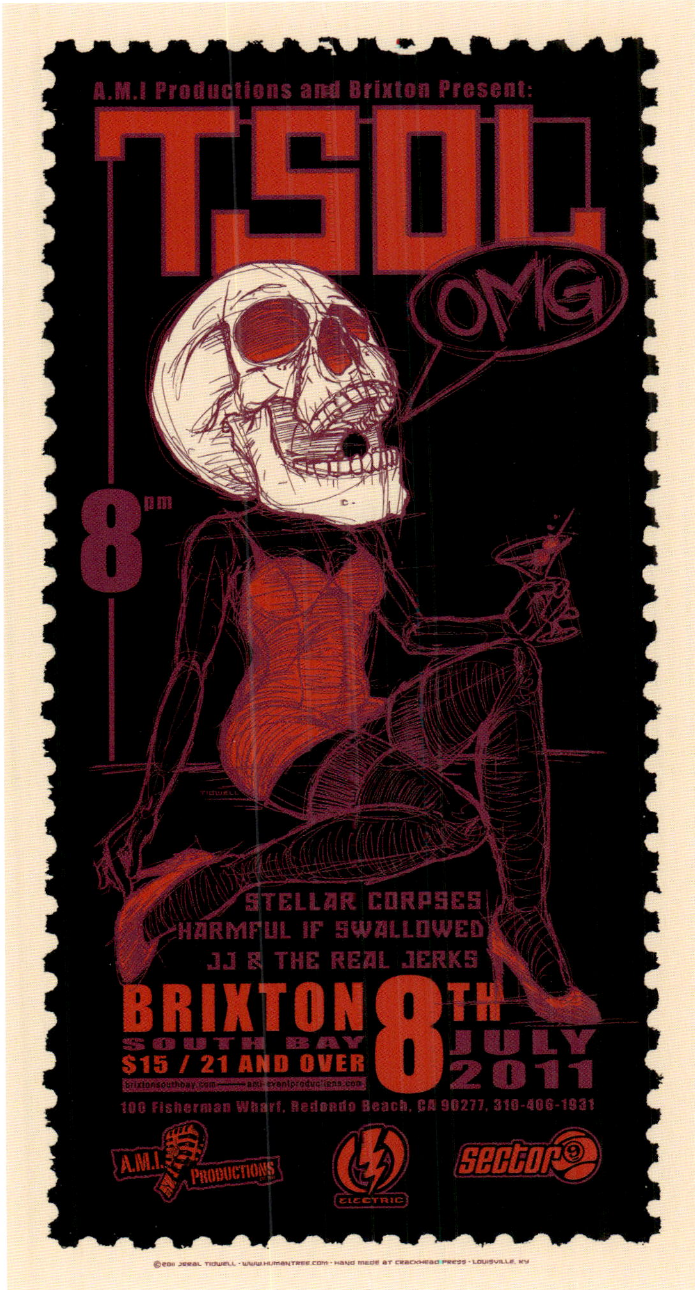

CLIENT: T.S.O.L.
DESIGNER: Jeral Tidwell
DESIGN FIRM: Humantree
WEBSITE: humantree.com

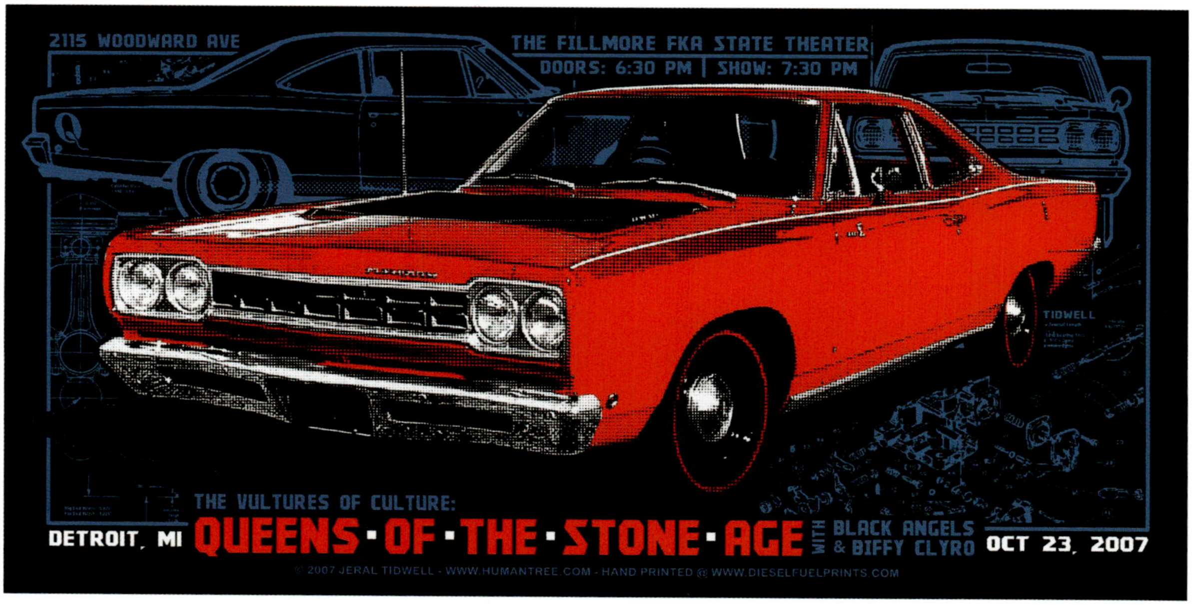

CLIENT: Queens of the Stone Age
DESIGNER: Jeral Tidwell
DESIGN FIRM: Humantree
WEBSITE: humantree.com

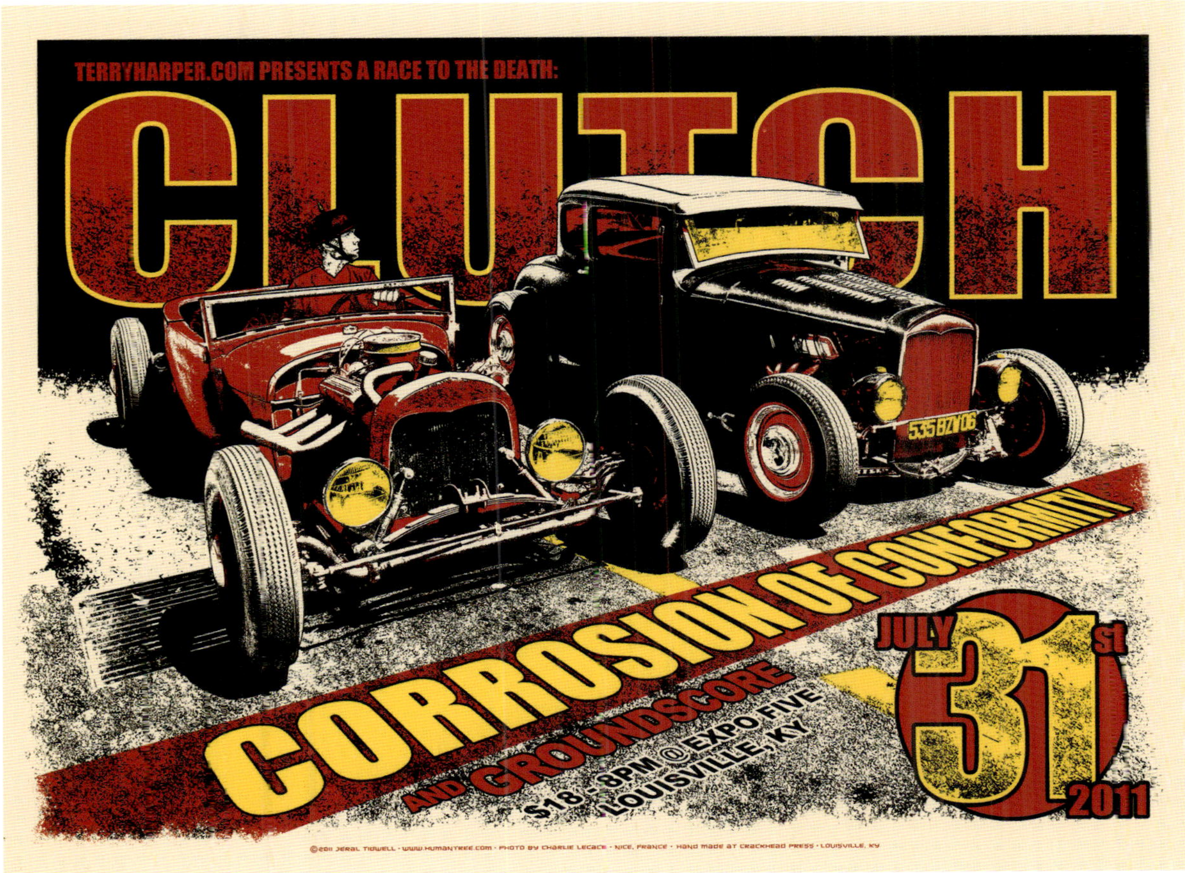

CLIENT: Clutch
DESIGNER: Jeral Tidwell
DESIGN FIRM: Humantree
WEBSITE: humantree.com

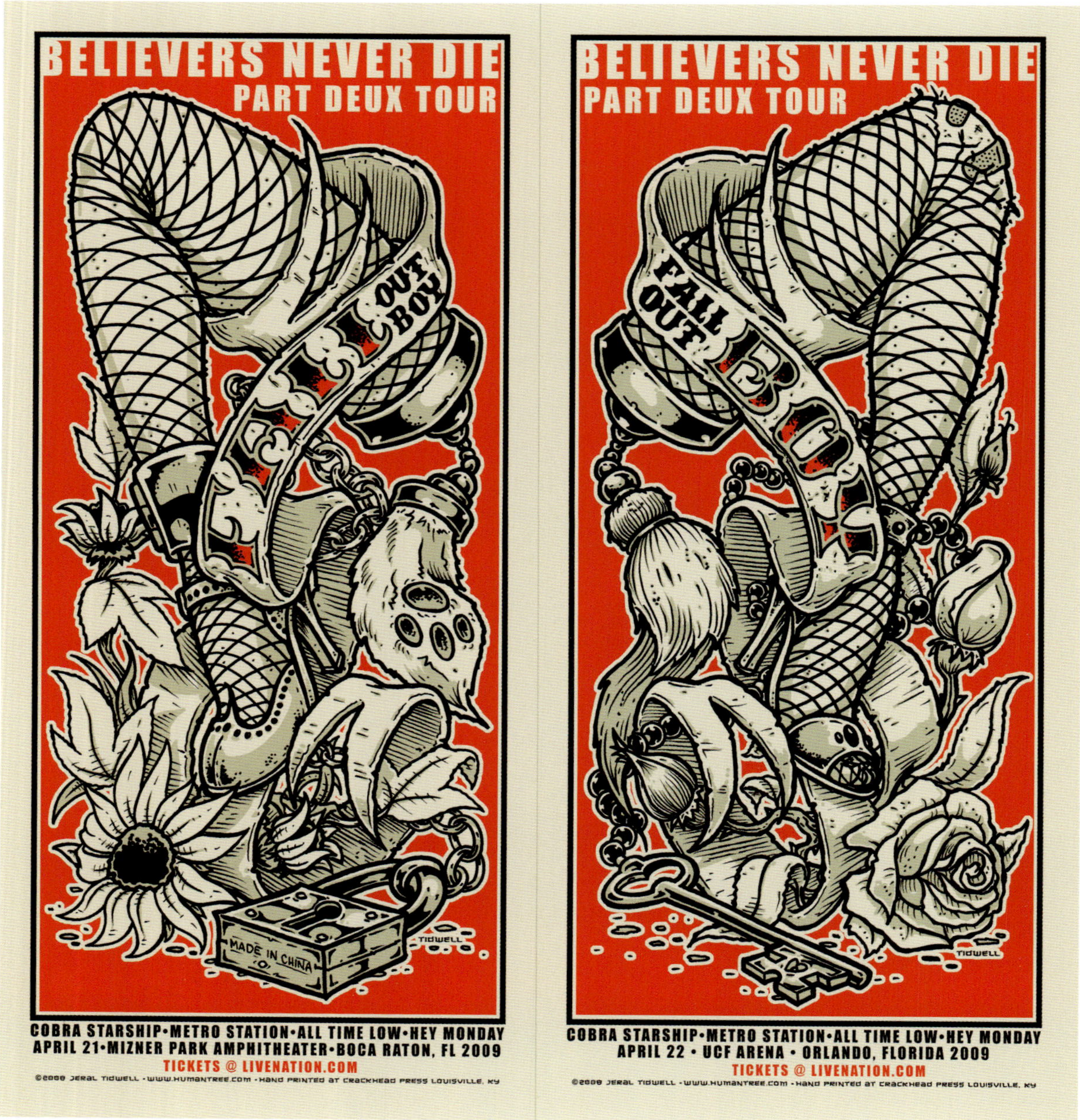

CLIENT: Fall Out Boy
DESIGNER: Jeral Tidwell
DESIGN FIRM: Humantree
WEBSITE: humantree.com

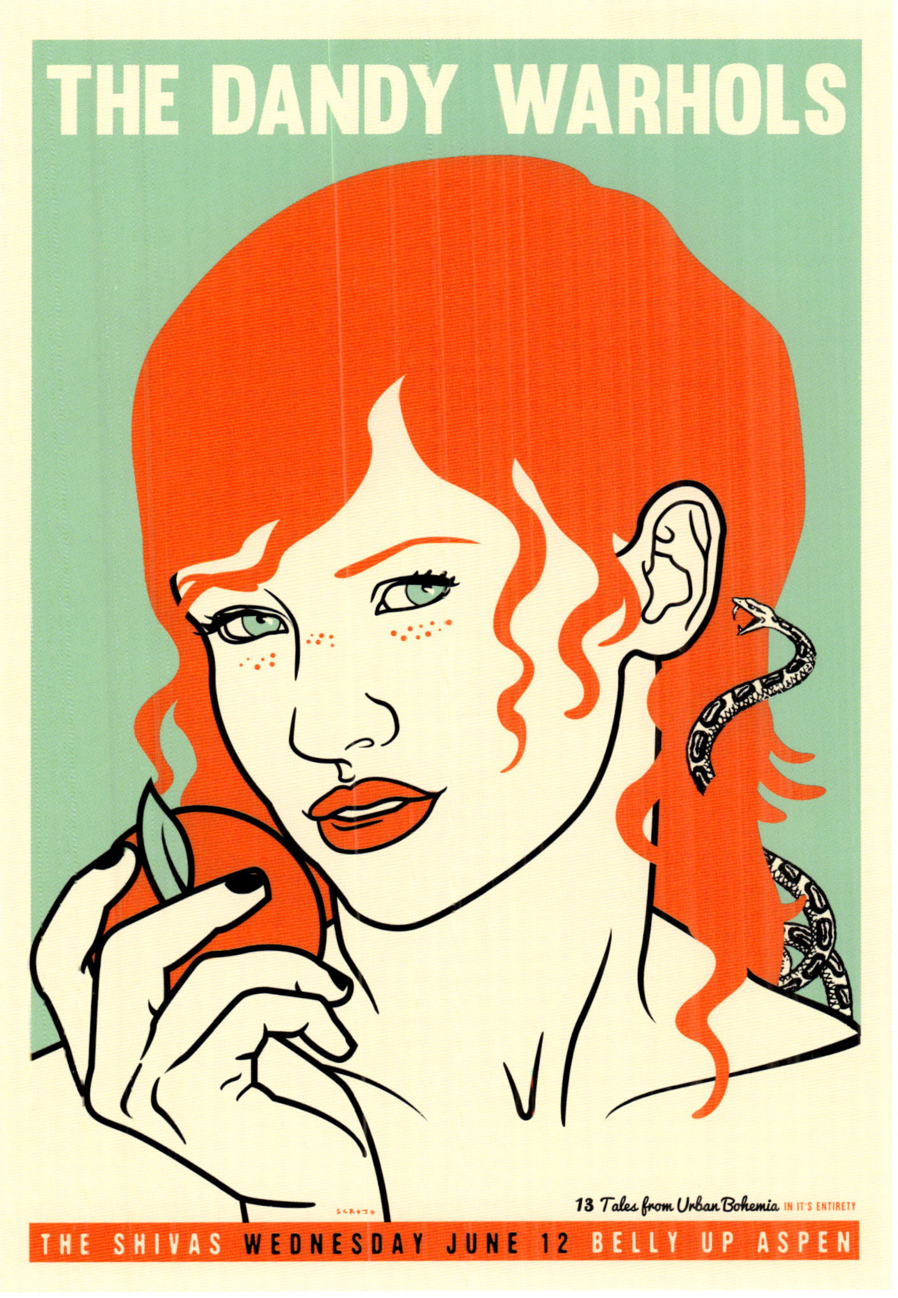

CLIENT: The Dandy Warhols
DESIGNER: Scrojo
WEBSITE: scrojo.com

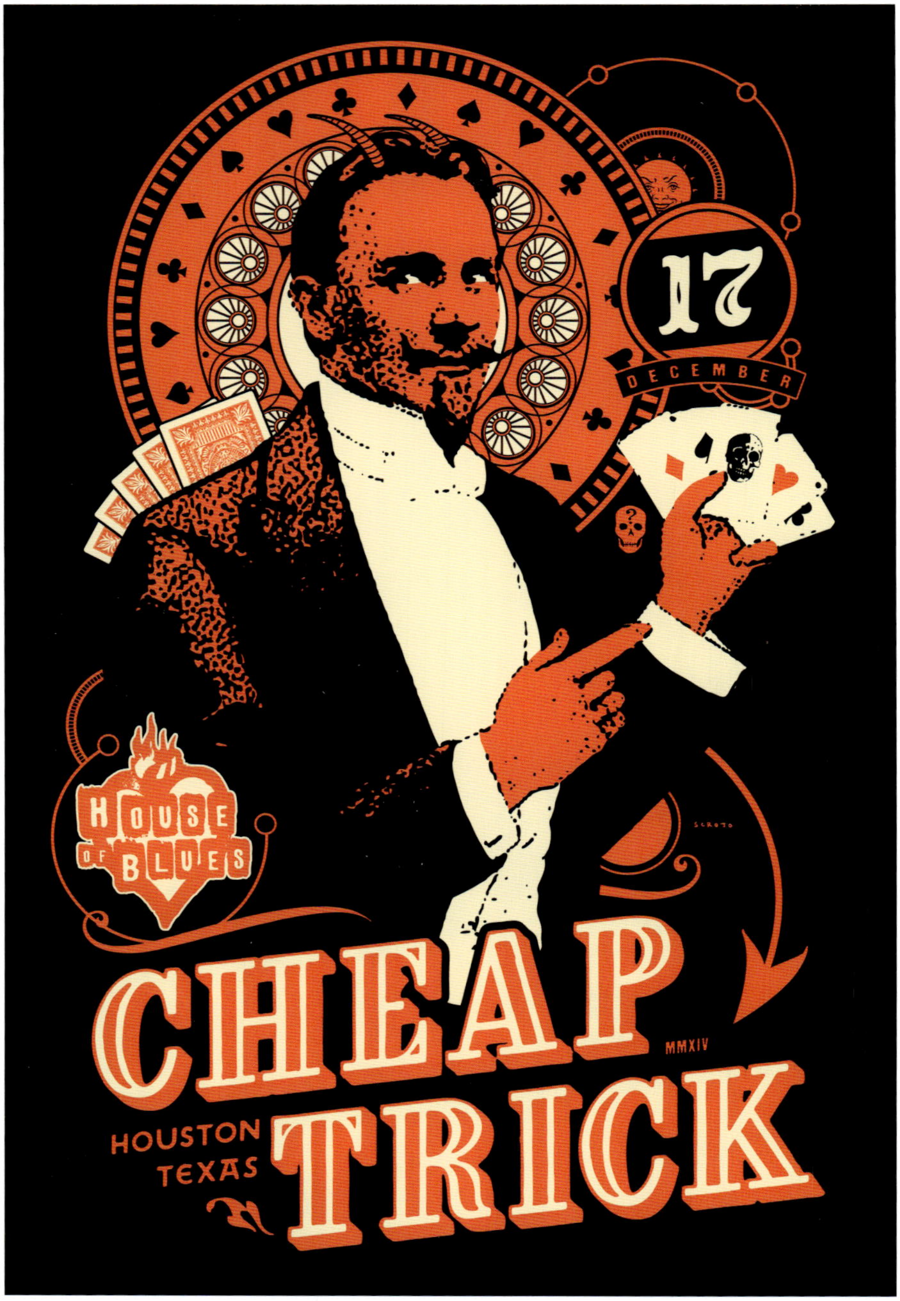

CLIENT: Cheap Trick
DESIGNER: Scrojo
WEBSITE: scrojo.com

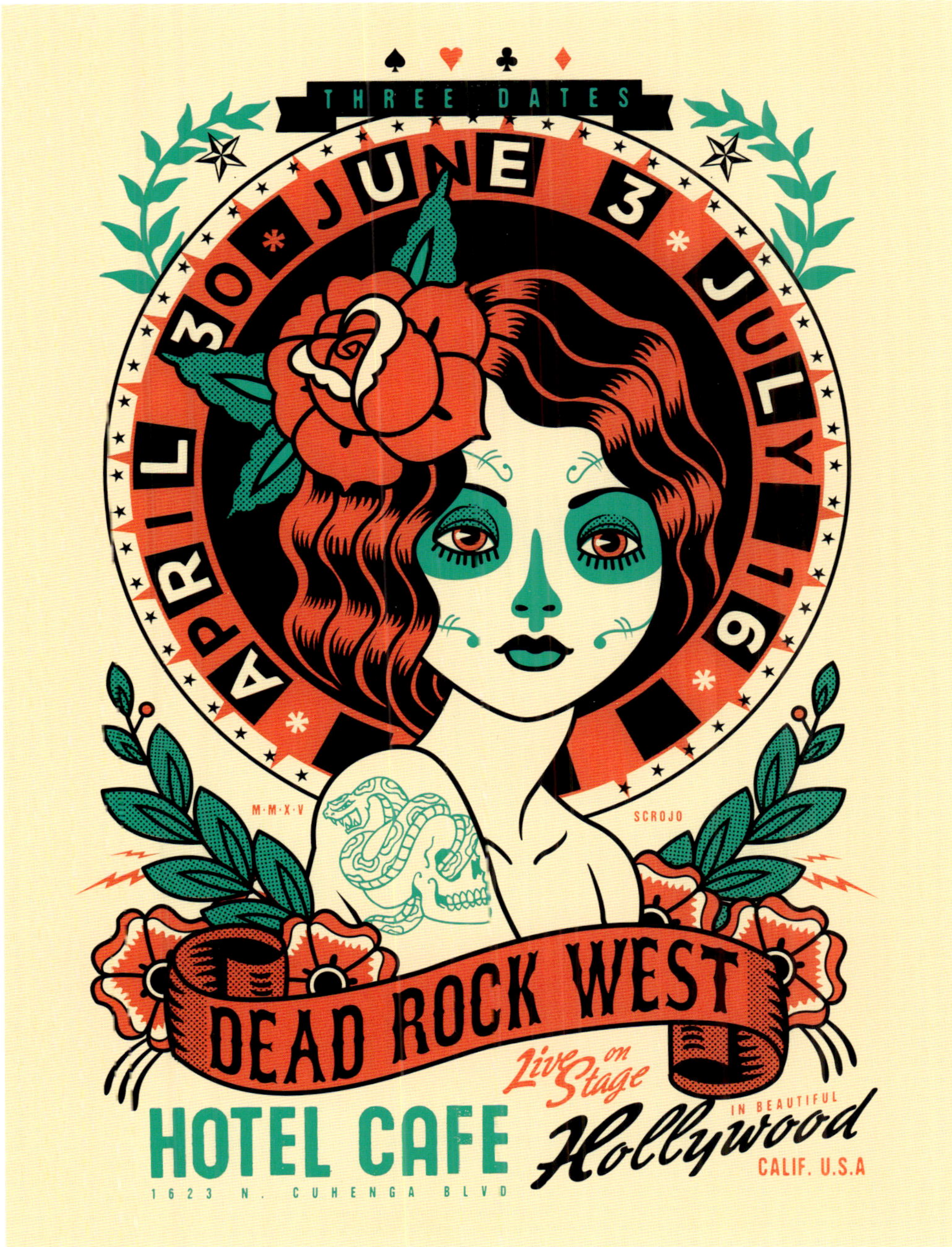

CLIENT: Dead Rock West
DESIGNER: Scrojo
WEBSITE: sarcjo.com

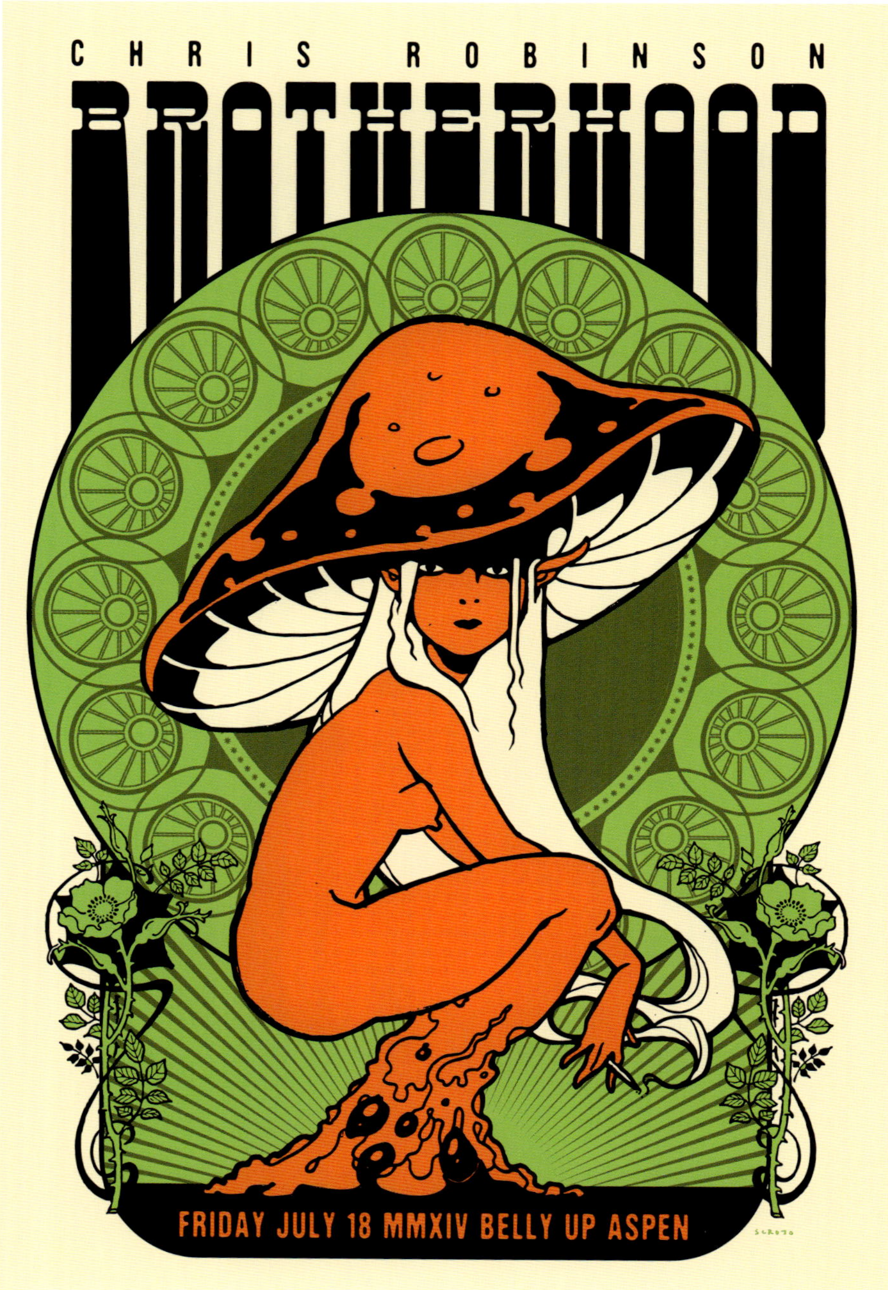

CLIENT: Chris Robinson Brotherhood
DESIGNER: Scrojo
WEBSITE: scrojo.com

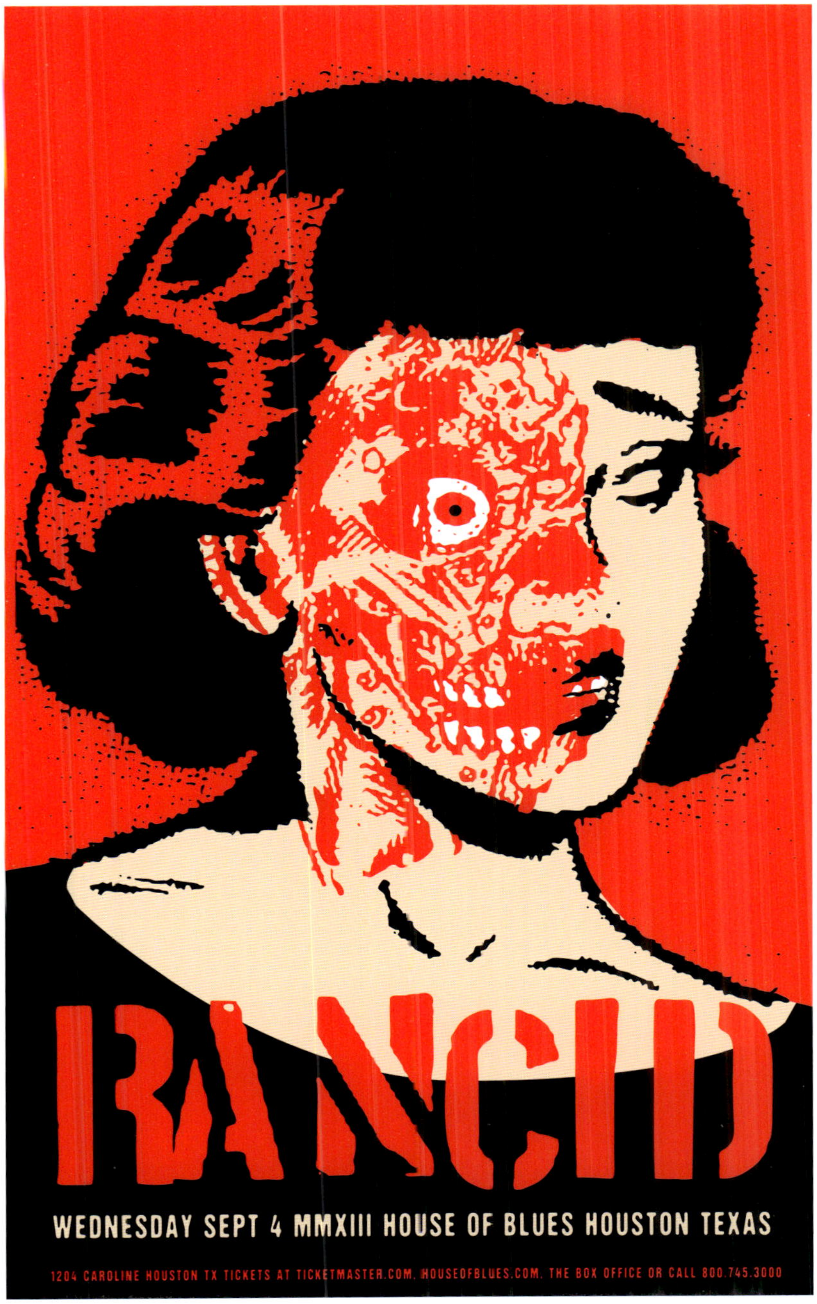

CLIENT: Rancid
DESIGNER: Scrojo
WEBSITE: scrojo.com

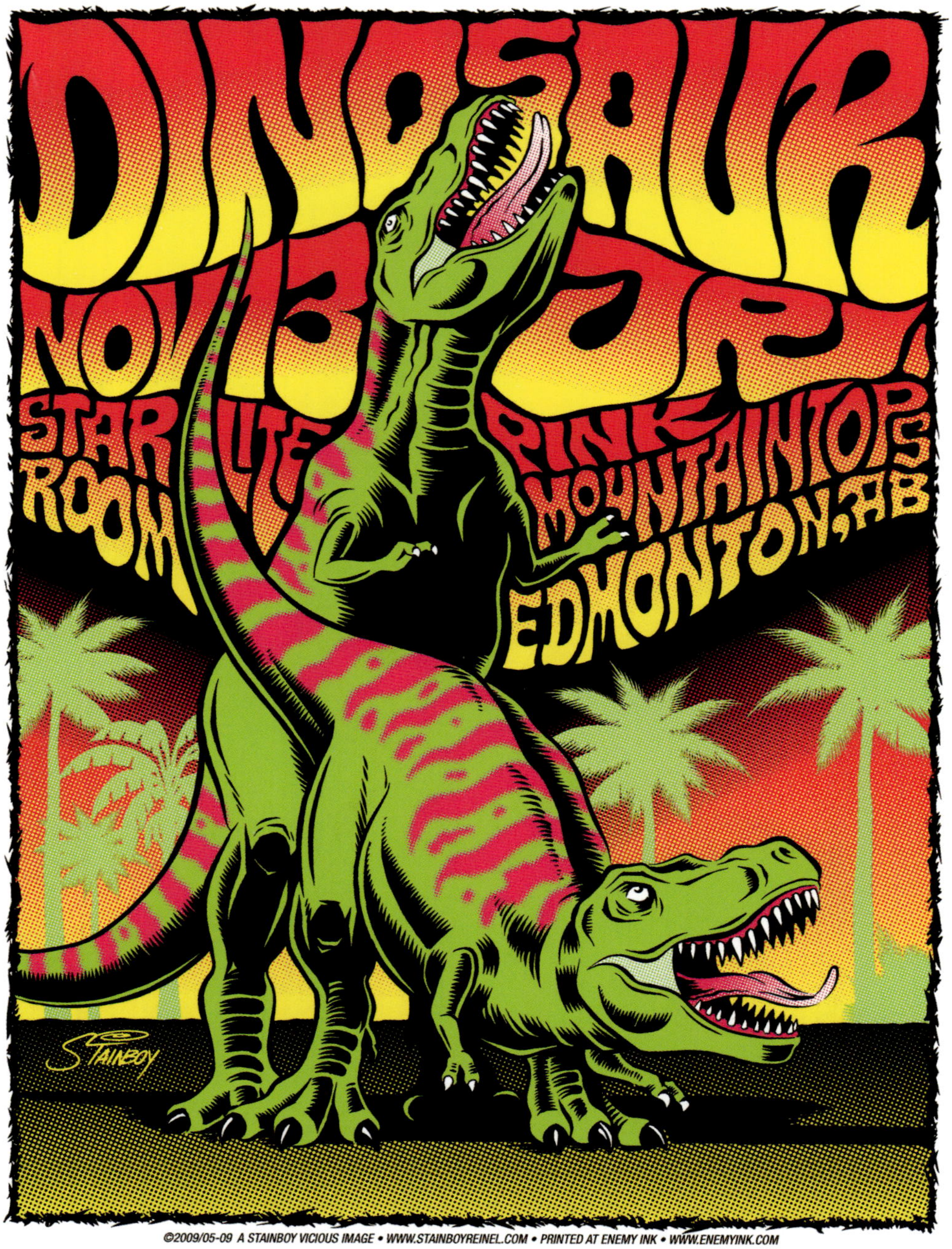

CLIENT: Dinosaur Jr.
DESIGNER: Stainboy

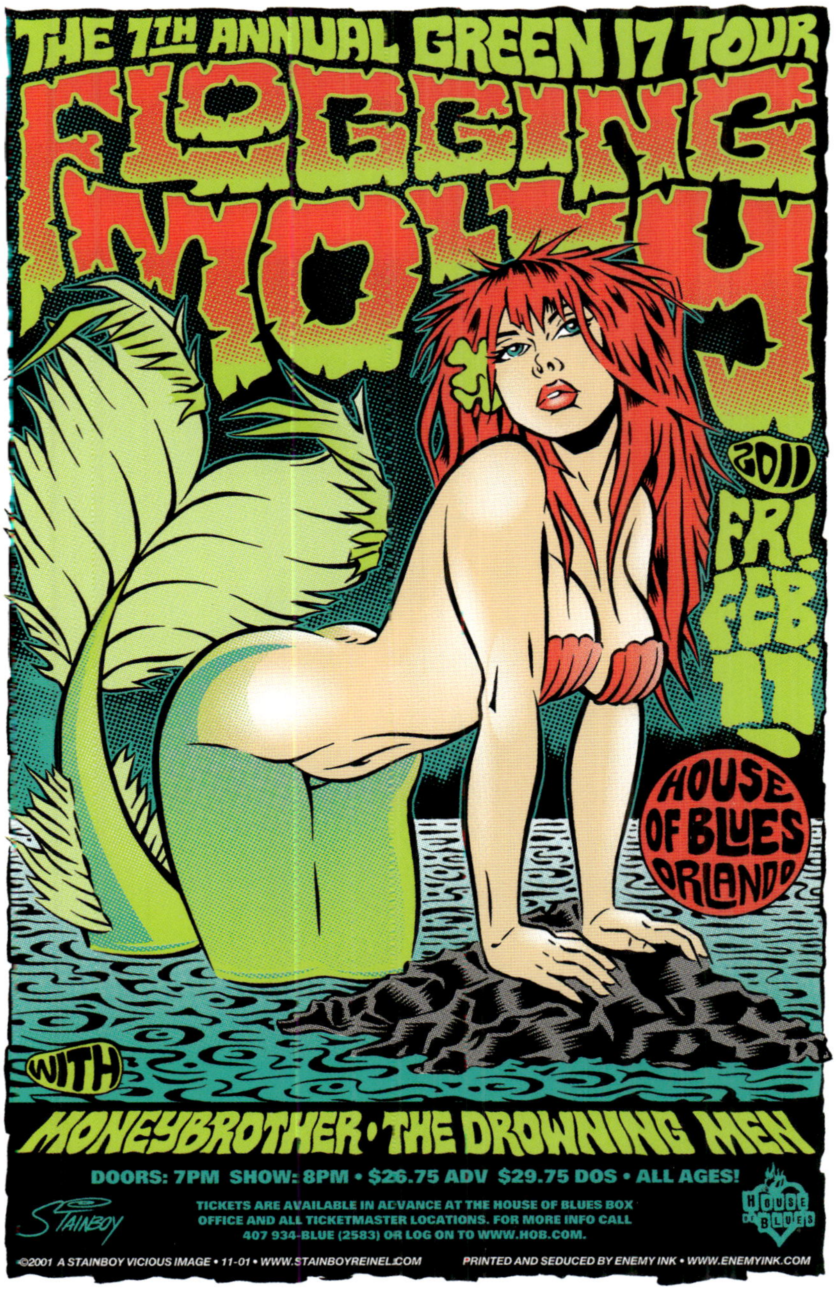

CLIENT: Flogging Molly
DESIGNER: Stainboy

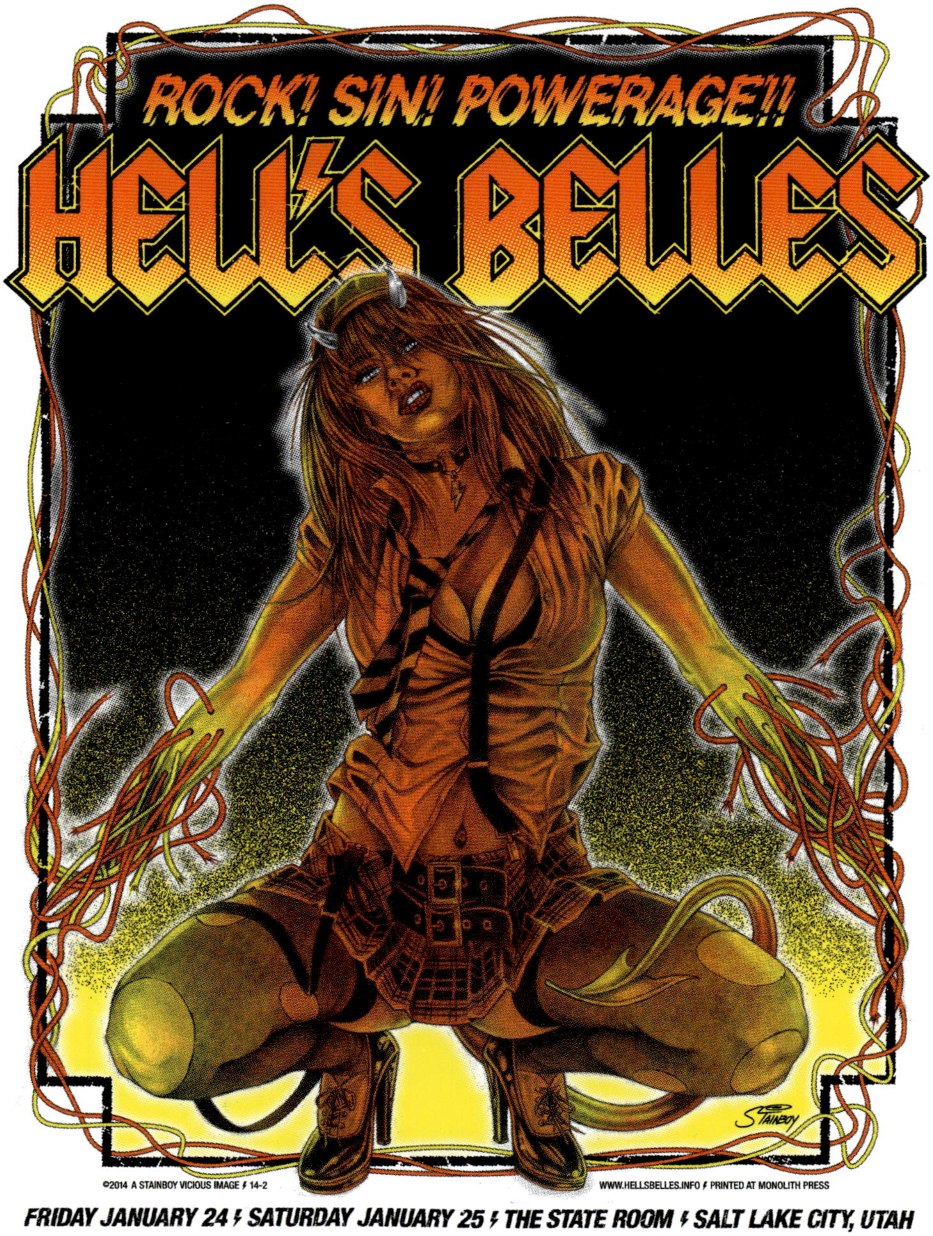

CLIENT: Hell's Belles
DESIGNER: Stainboy

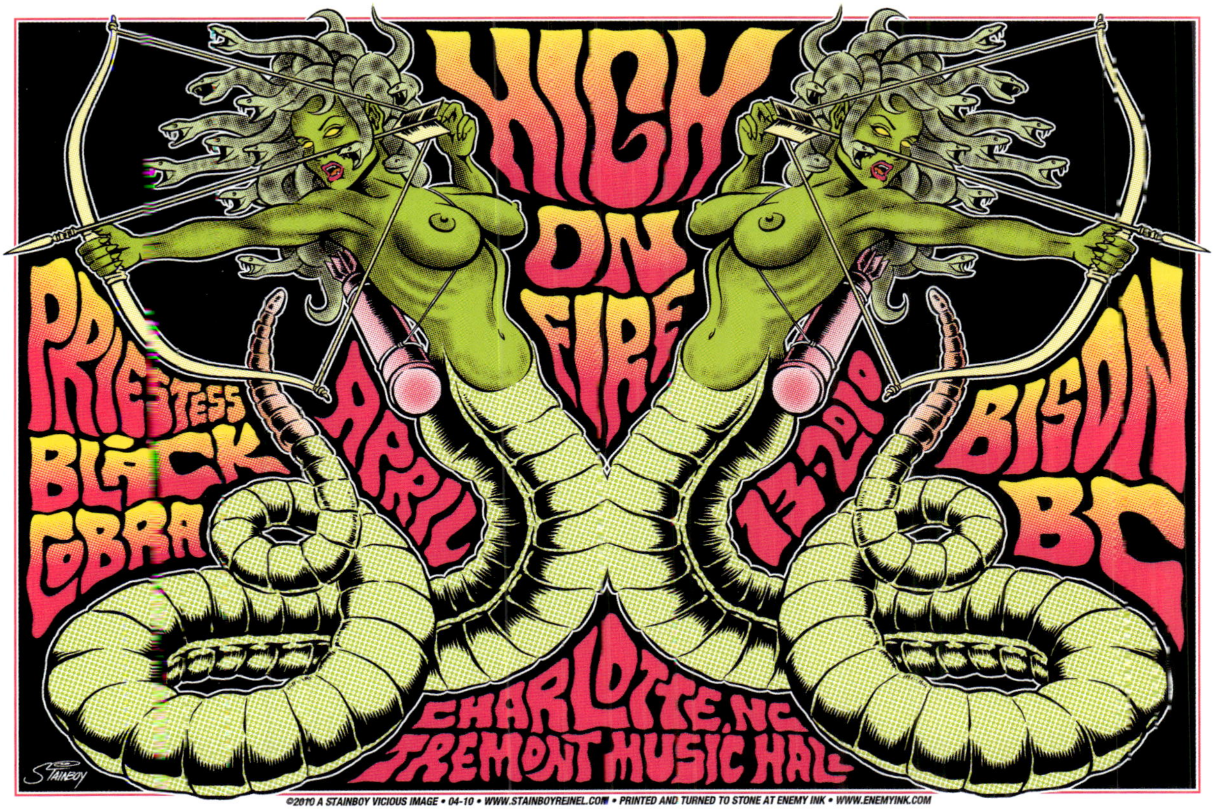

CLIENT: High on Fire
DESIGNER: Stainboy

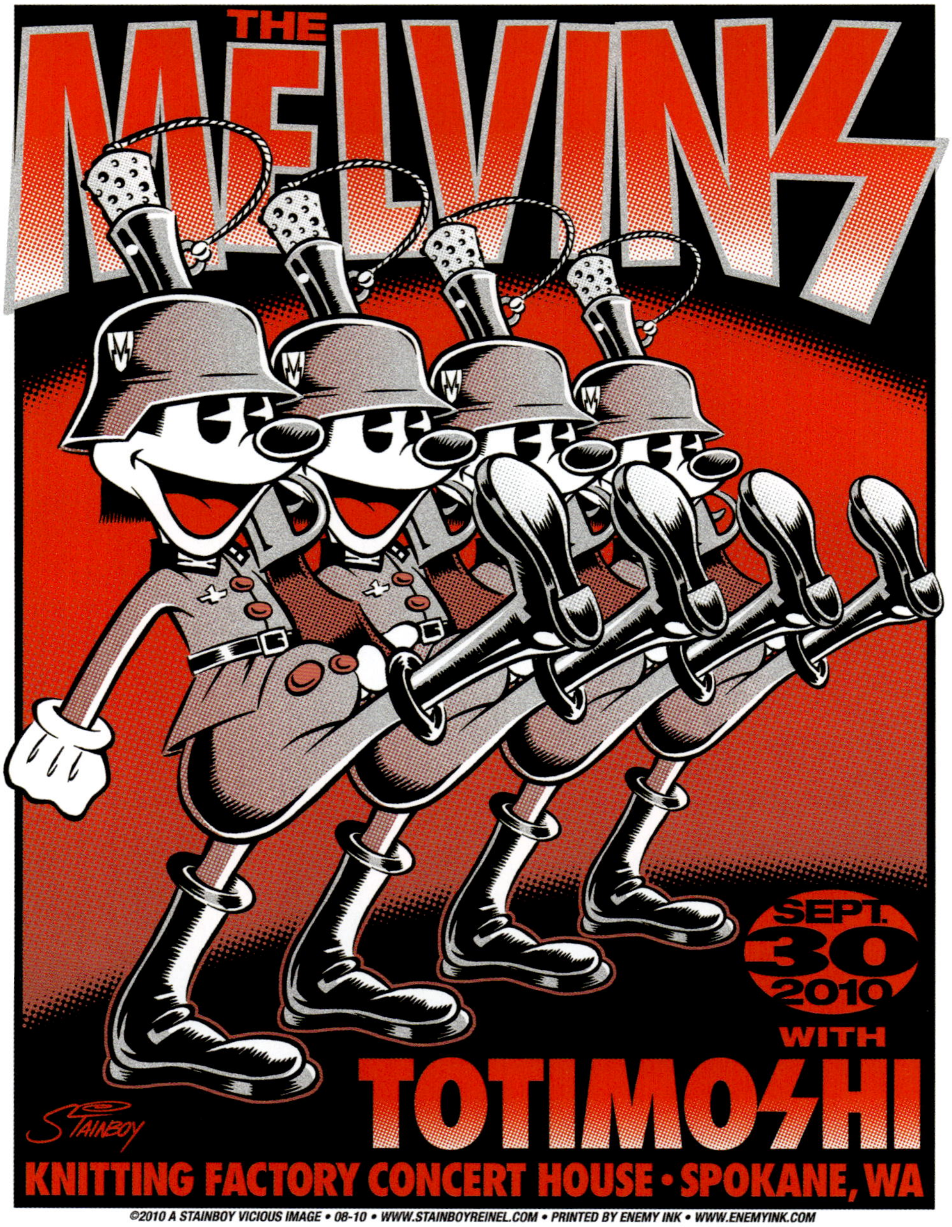

CLIENT: Melvins
DESIGNER: Stainboy

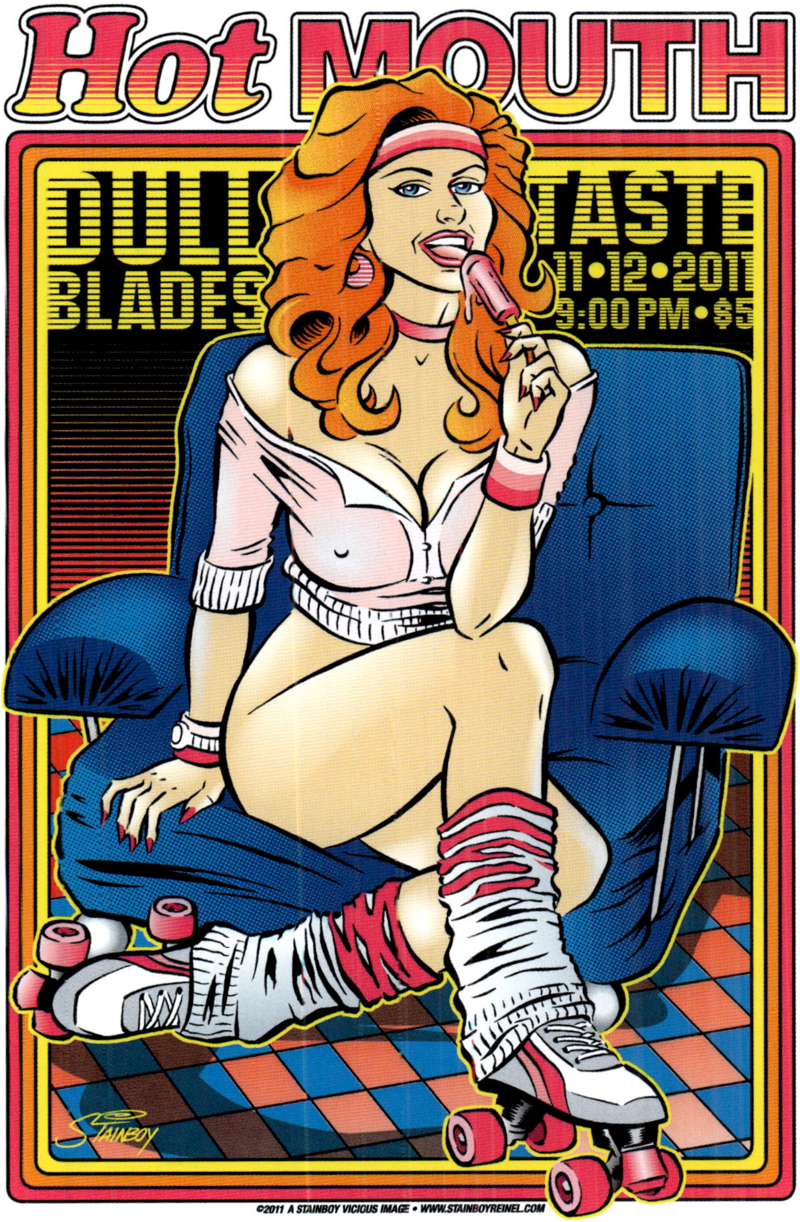

CLIENT: Hot Mouth
DESIGNER: Stainboy

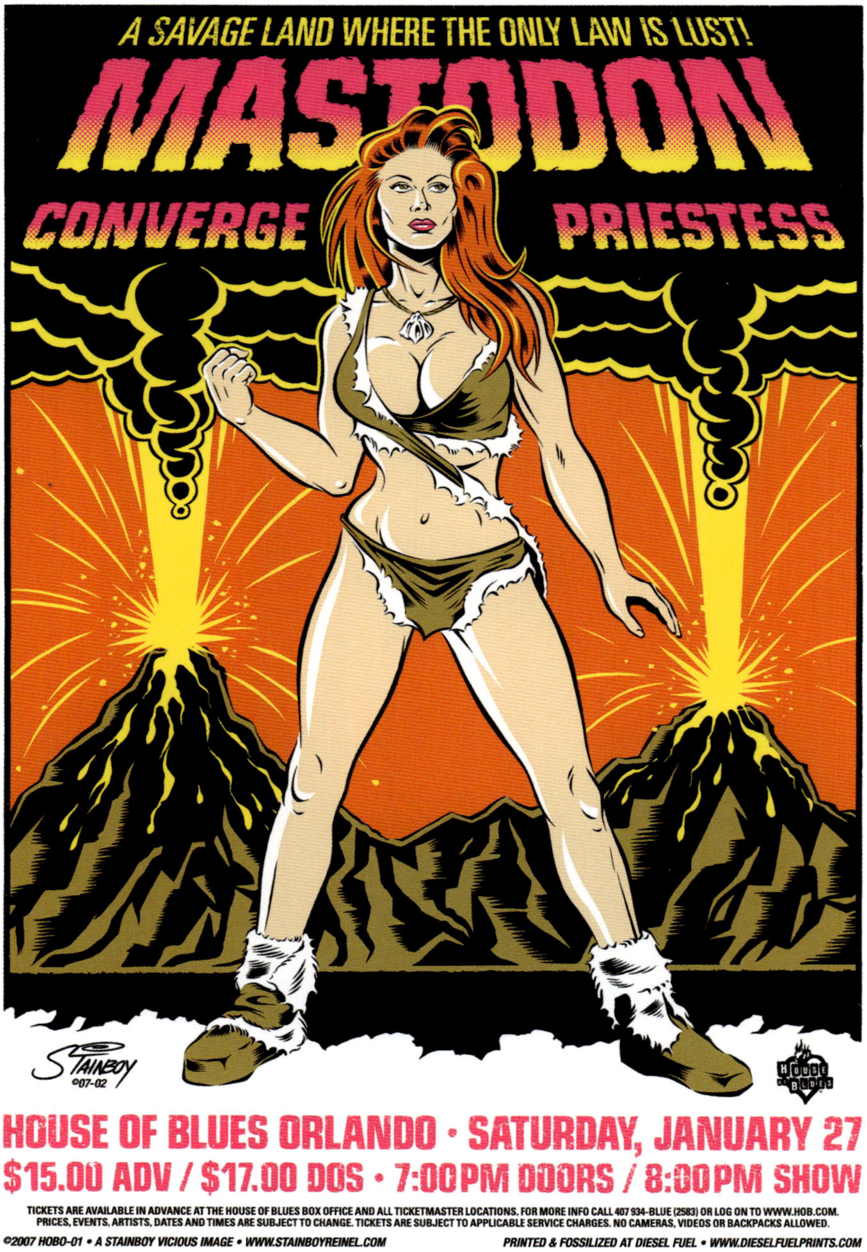

CLIENT: Mastodon
DESIGNER: Stainboy

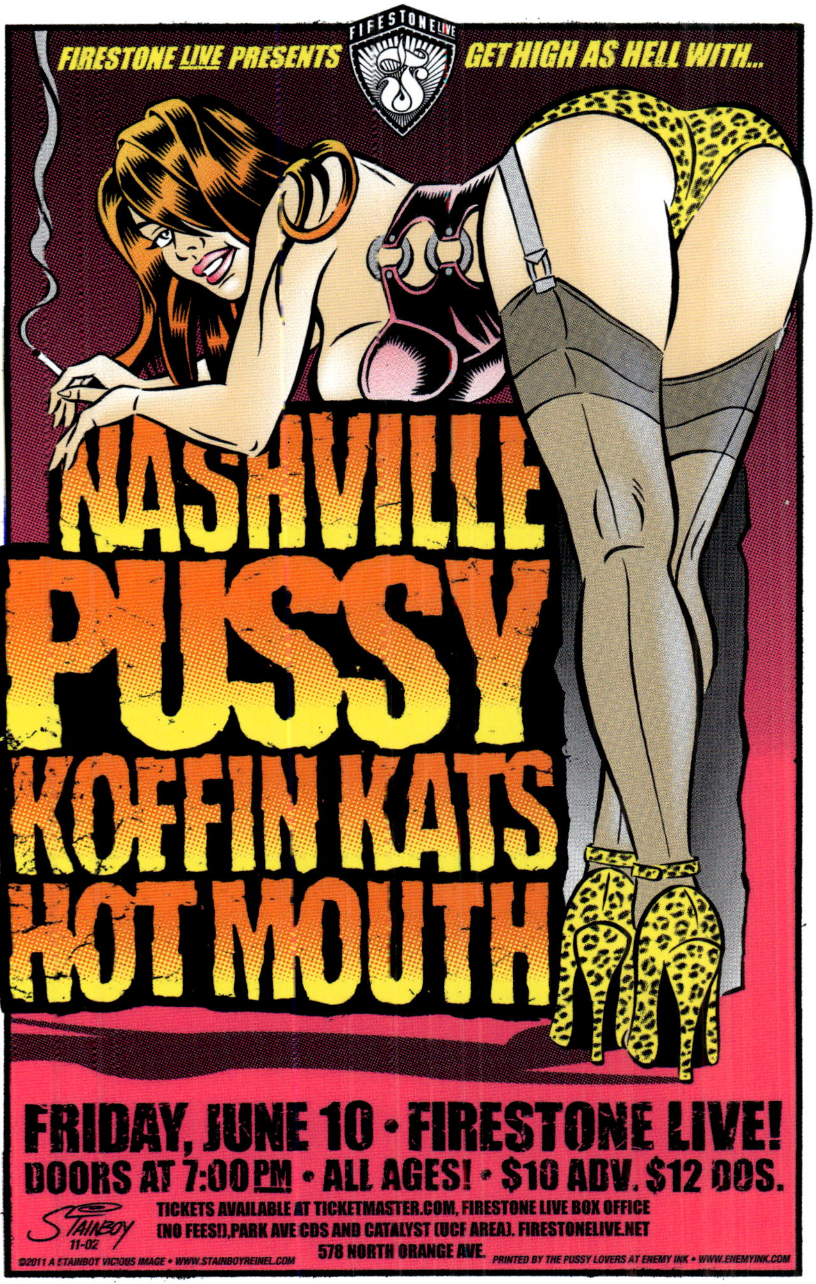

CLIENT: Nashville Pussy
DESIGNER: Stainboy

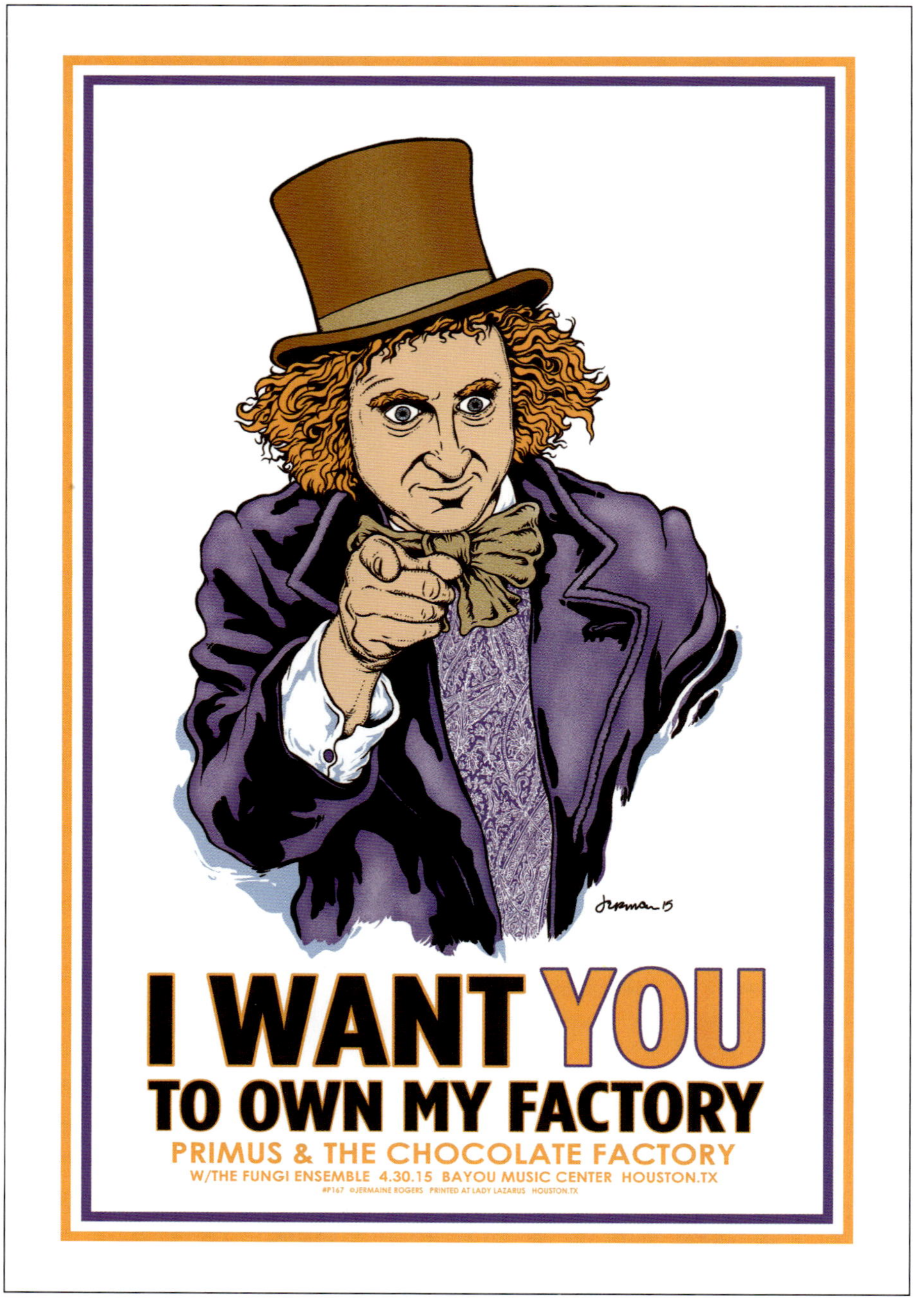

CLIENT: Primus
DESIGNER: Jermaine Rogers
WEBSITE: jermainerogers.com

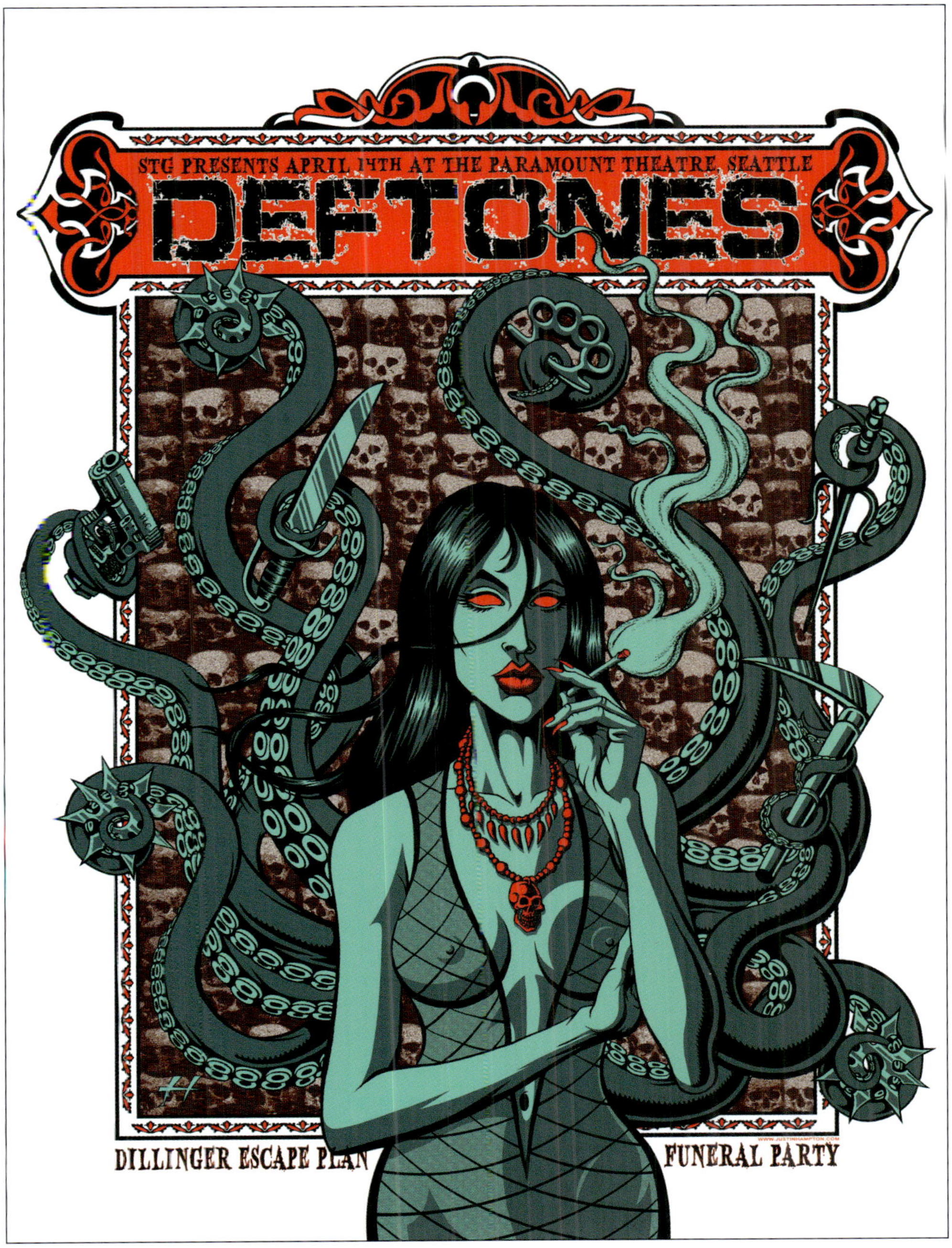

CLIENT: Deftones
DESIGNER: Justin Hampton
WEBSITE: justinhampton.com

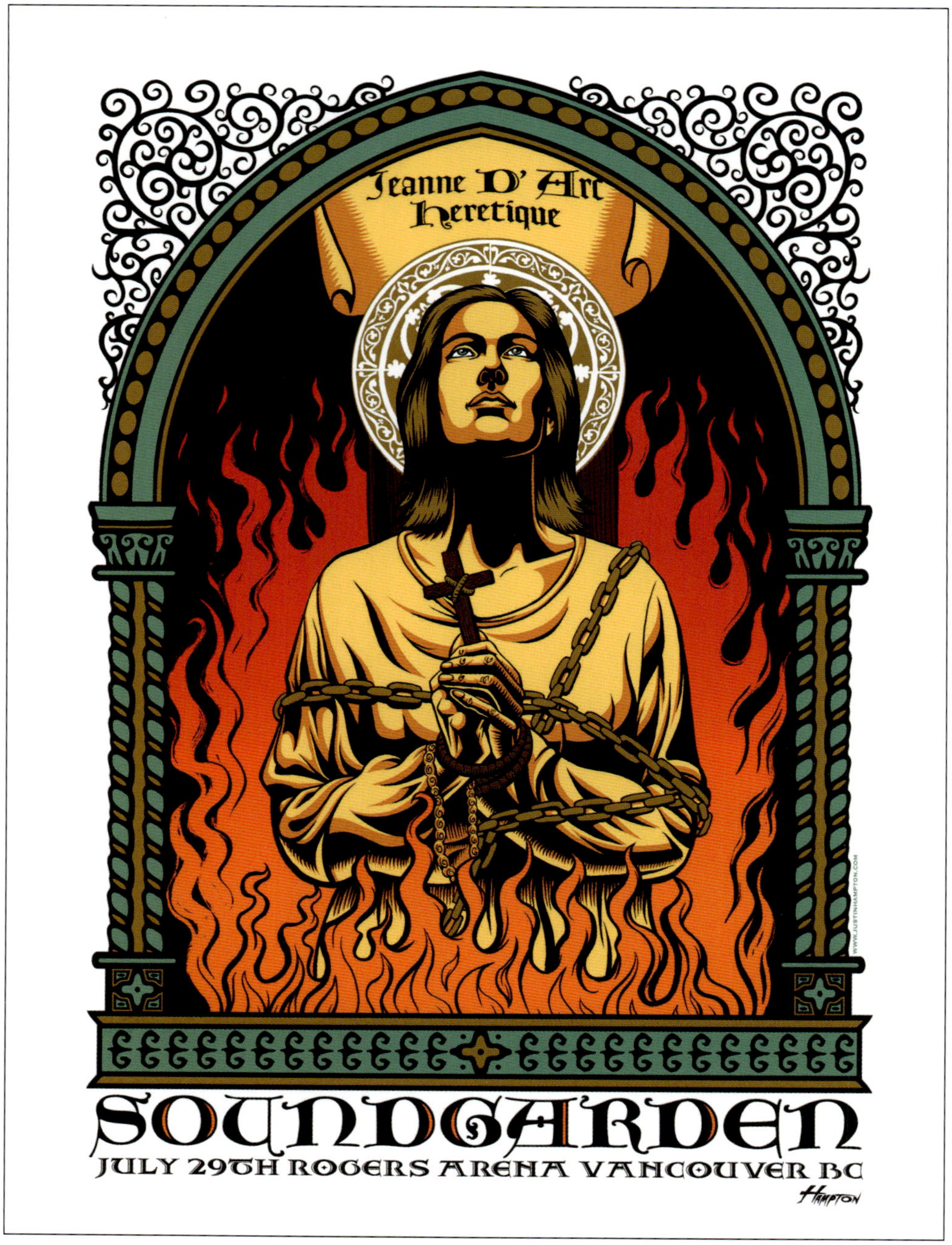

CLIENT: Soundgarden
DESIGNER: Justin Hampton
WEBSITE: justinhampton.com

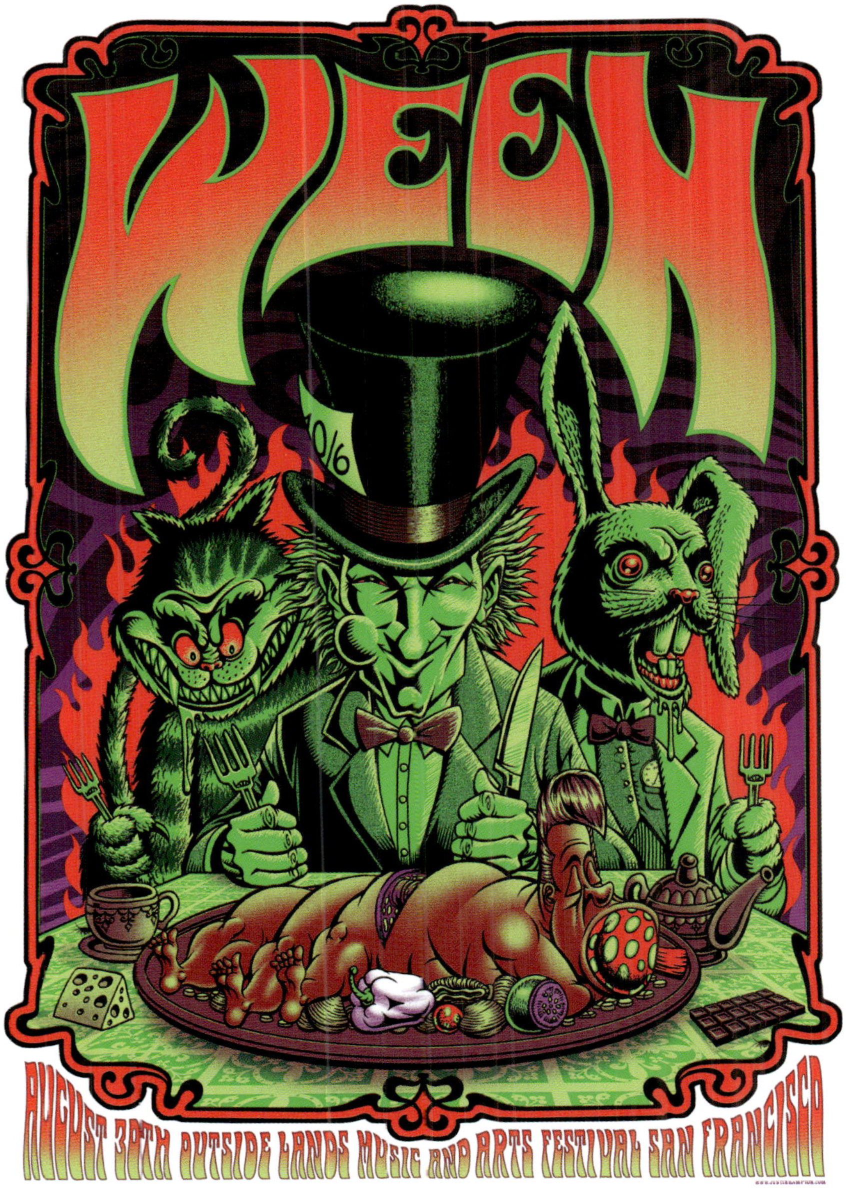

CLIENT: Ween
DESIGNER: Justin Hampton
WEBSITE: justinhampton.com

Newsprint Collage

While the origins of collage can be traced back hundreds of years, the technique truly emerged in the twentieth century and is associated with the beginnings of modernism. The style relies on utilizing multiple images, shapes, and letterforms to create a new cohesive, and often very sophisticated work. Newsprint, type, and handwritten notes are often used as background elements or layered to create patterns. Often vintage source material is used for collage and the effects of aging lend authenticity to the final composition. This has become a popular design style that is employed by a lot of contemporary gig poster artists.

KEY STYLE CHARACTERISTICS

- Composition relies on combining and layering multiple things such as images, letterforms, shapes, and silhouettes
- Patterns, textures, and images are commonly masked within the design's focal point
- Newsprint, type, and handwritten notes are often used as texture and background elements
- De-saturated, old, or processed color is used to show age, layering, and authenticity
- Old Xerox, low-quality copy imagery used or Xerox machine and degradation actually used in the design process
- Utilizes vintage source materials including old ads, magazine models, and maps; well-incorporated/designed type and sophisticated composition/use of space overall

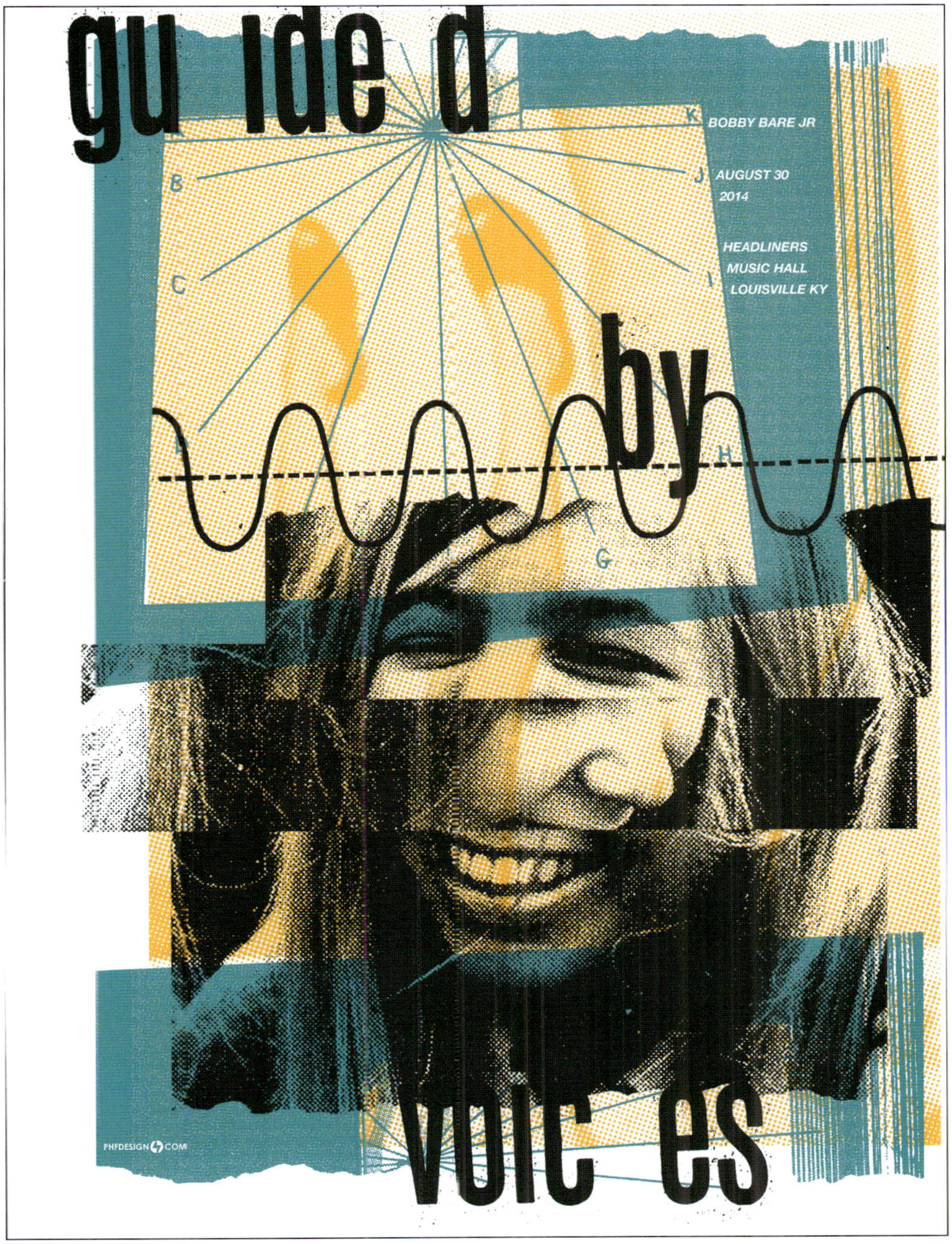

CLIENT: Guided by Voices
DESIGNER: Ben Nunery
DESIGN FIRM: Powerhouse Factories
WEBSITE: powerhousefactories.com

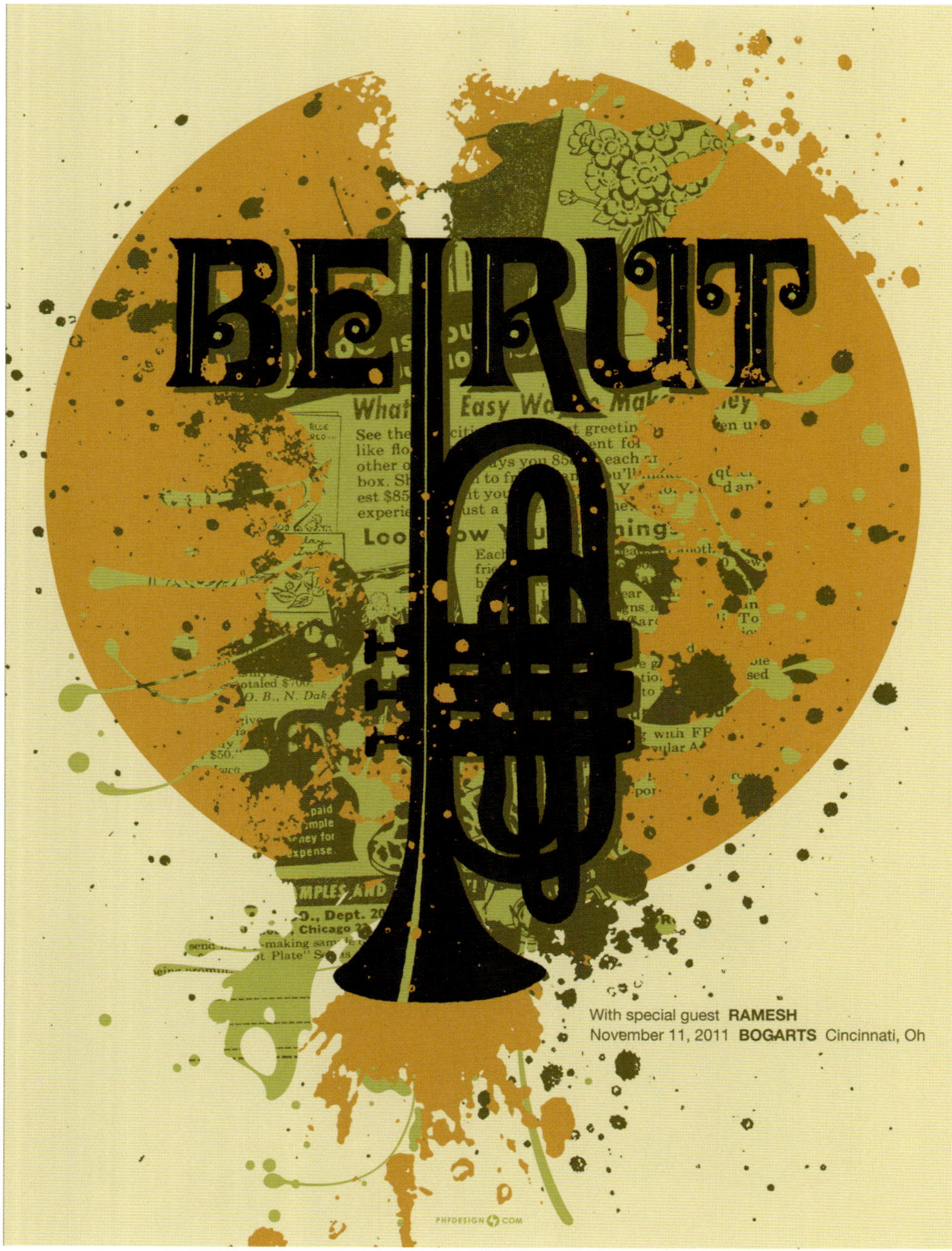

CLIENT: Beirut
DESIGNER: Ben Nunery
DESIGN FIRM: Powerhouse Factories
WEBSITE: powerhousefactories.com

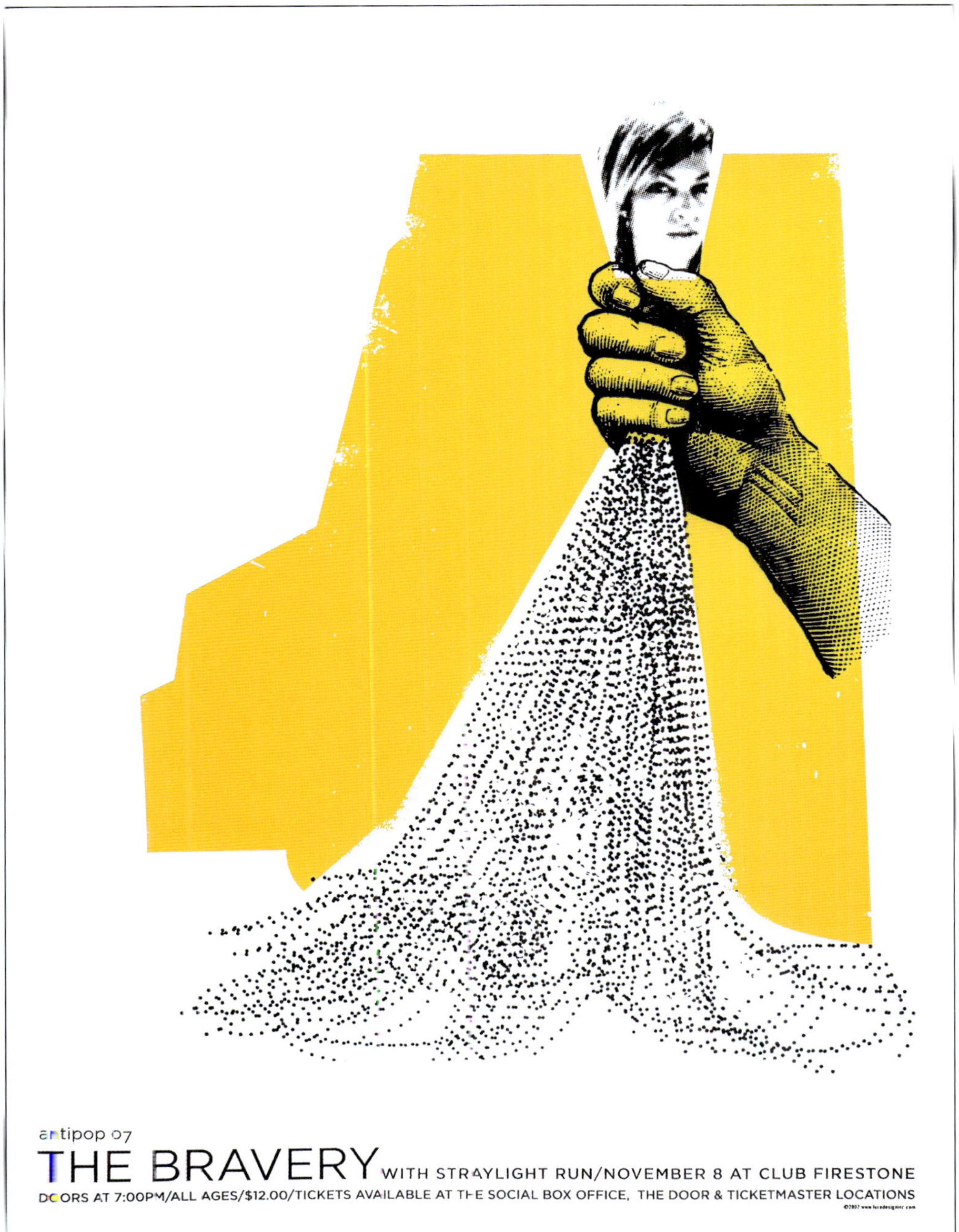

CLIENT: The Bravery
DESIGNER: Jeff Matz
DESIGN FIRM: Lure Design Incorporated
WEBSITE: luredesigninc.com

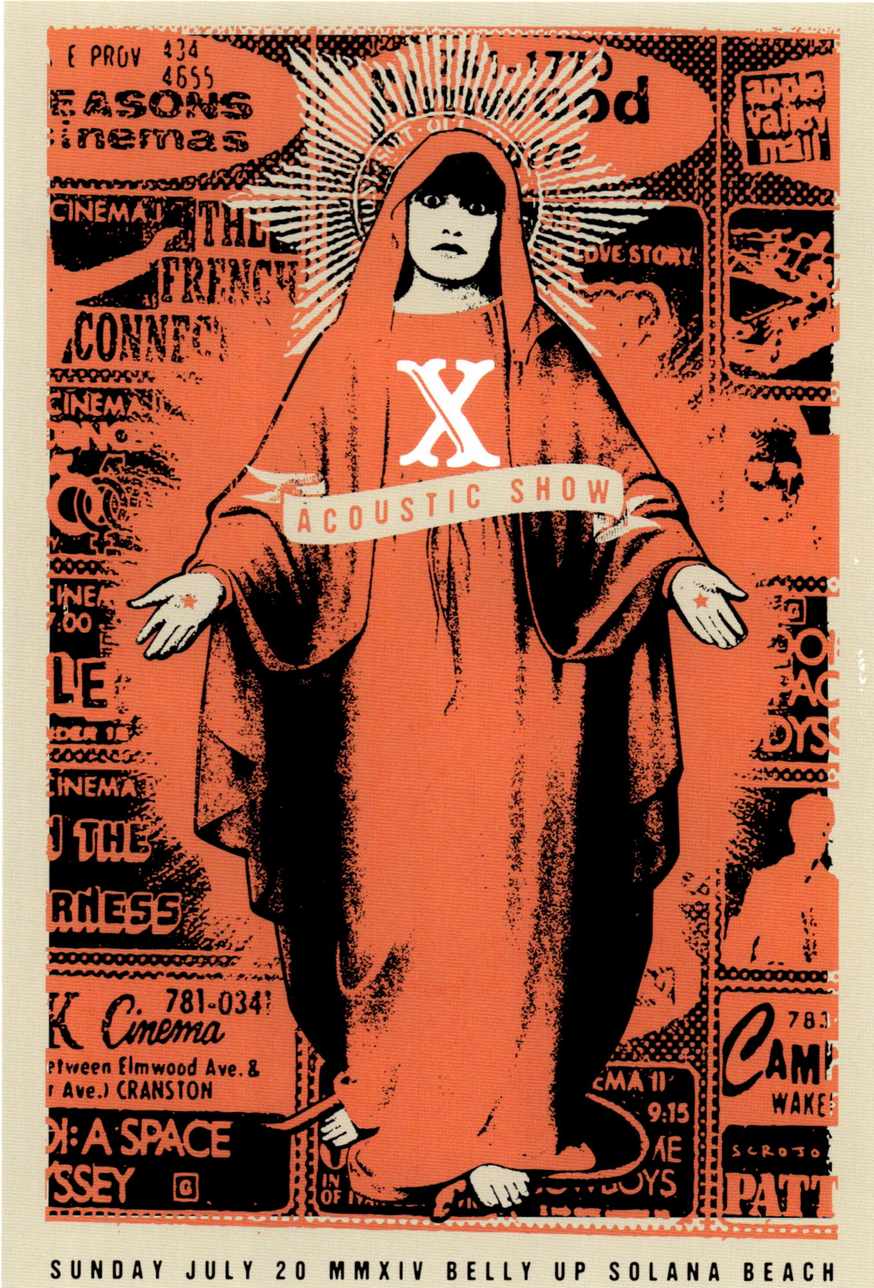

CLIENT: X
DESIGNER: Scrojo
WEBSITE: scrojo.com

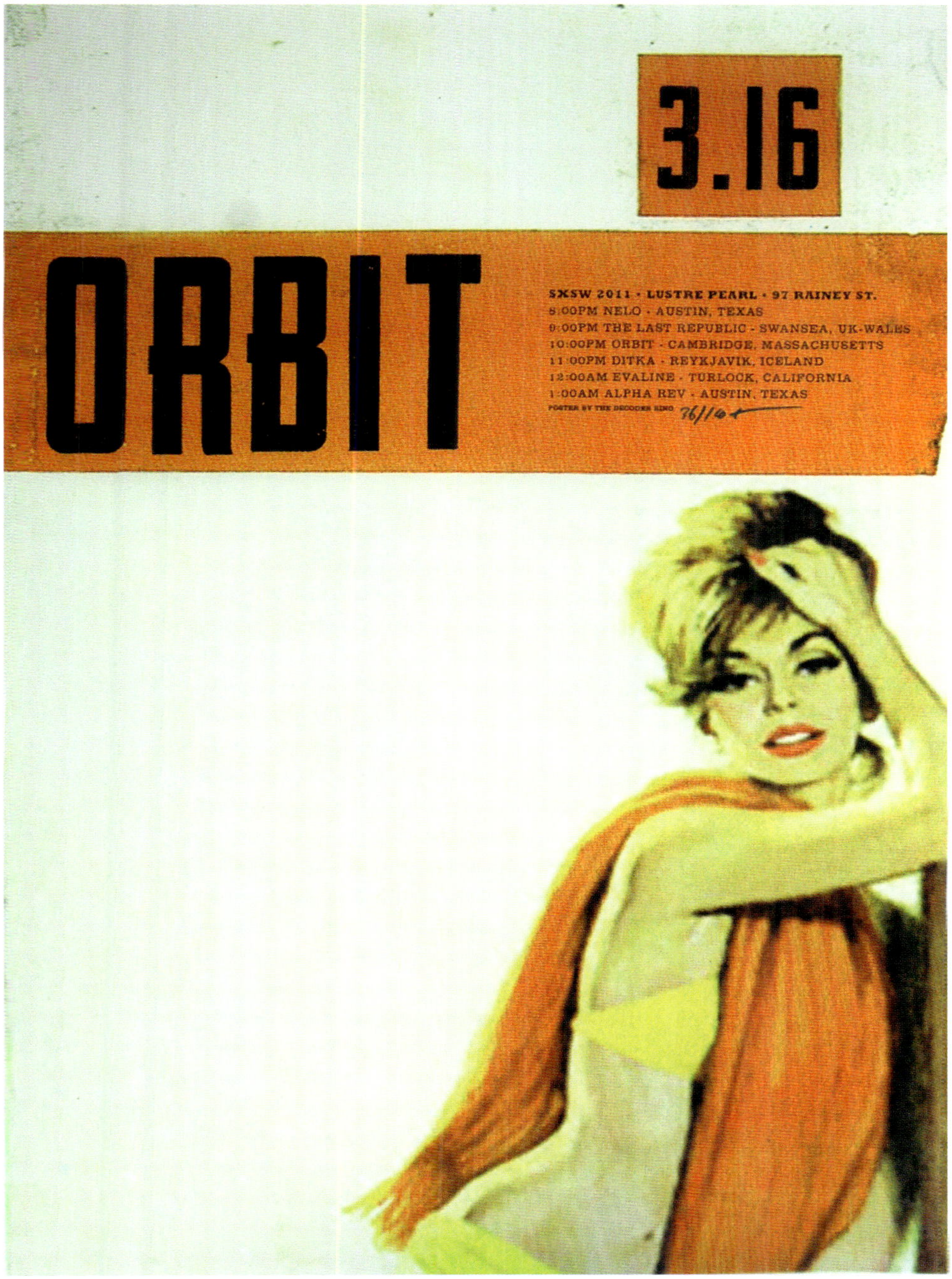

CLIENT: Orbit
DESIGNER: Geoff Peveto
DESIGN FIRM: The Decoder Ring
WEBSITE: thedecoderring.com

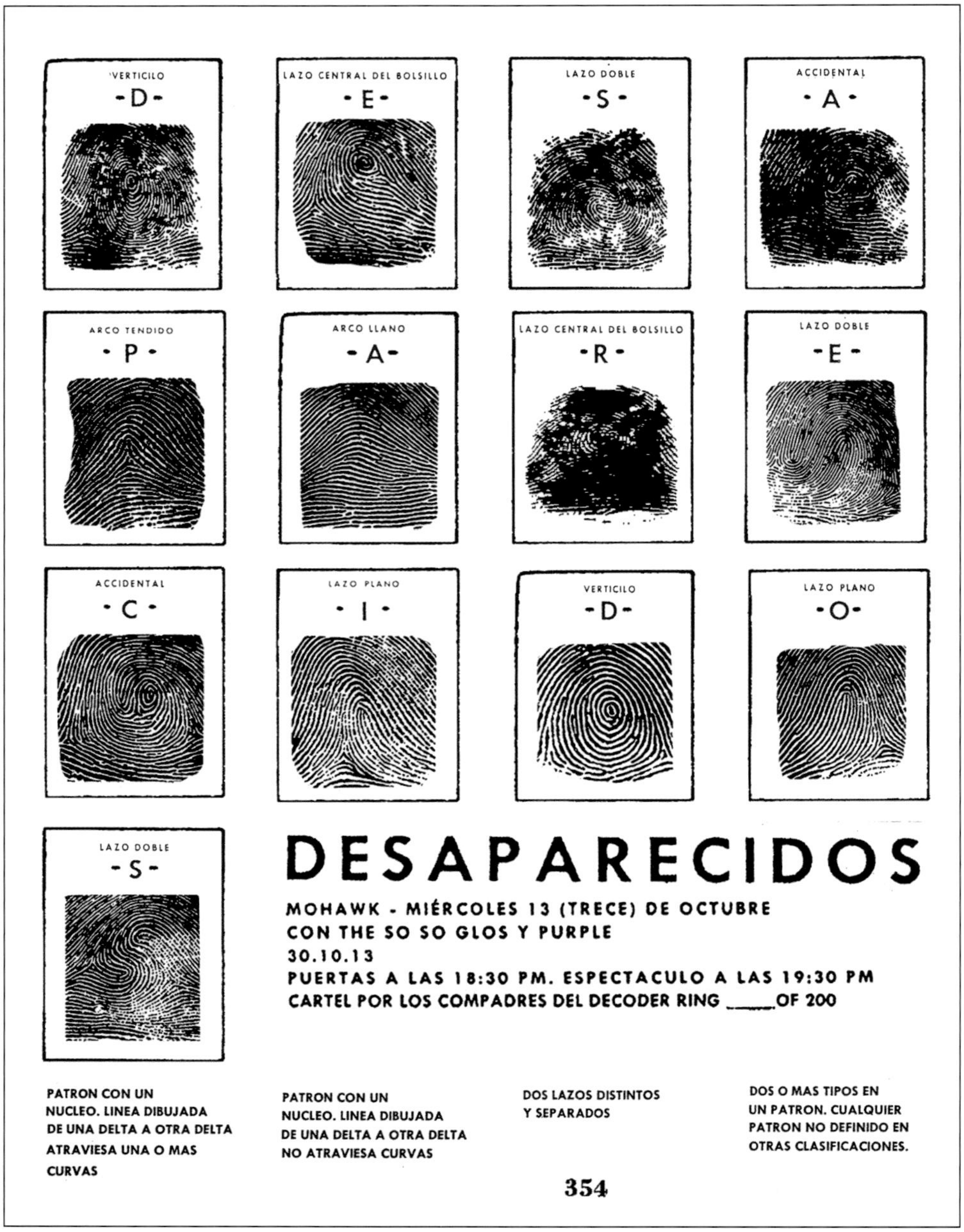

CLIENT: Desaparecidos
DESIGNER: Geoff Peveto
DESIGN FIRM: The Decoder Ring
WEBSITE: thedecoderring.com

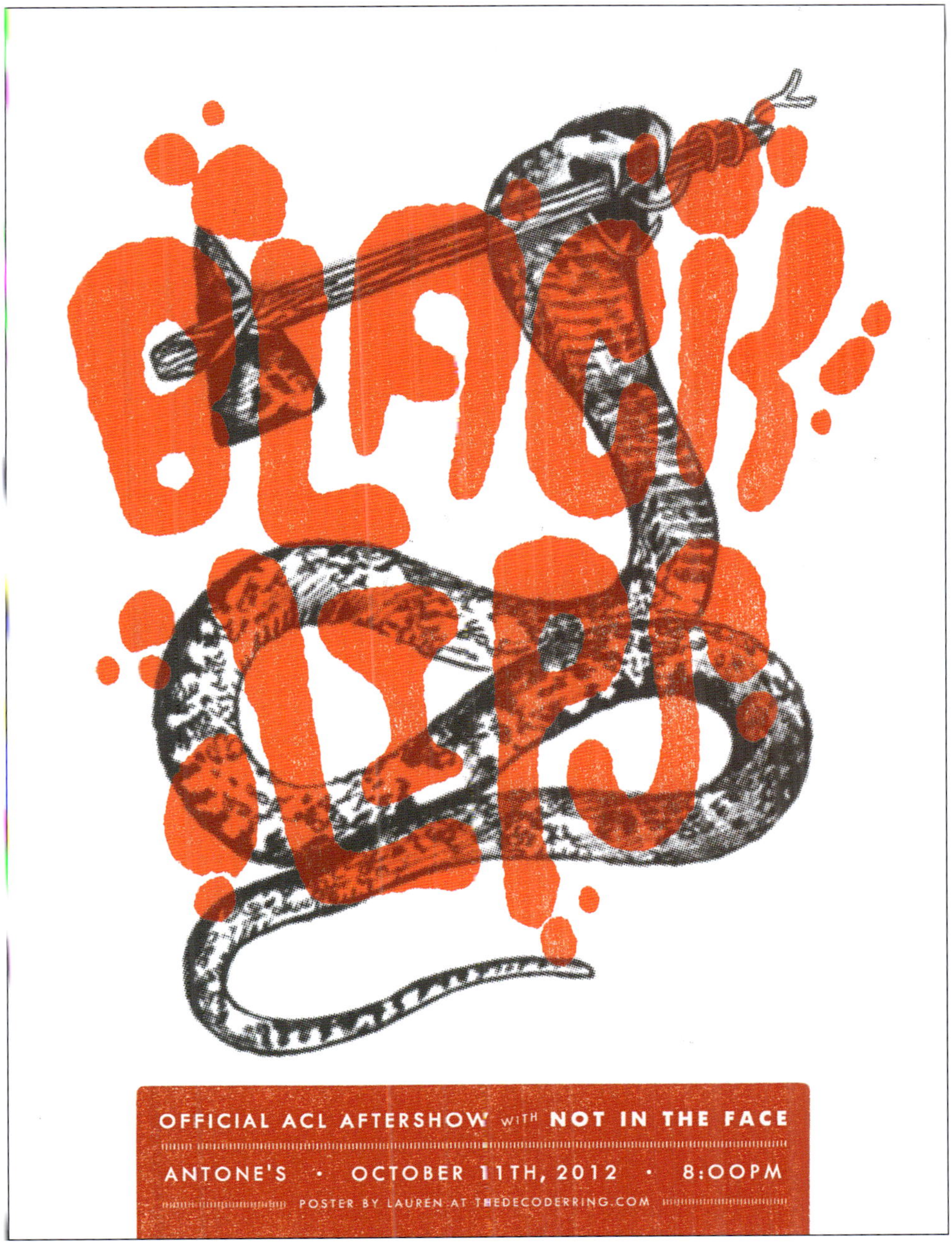

CLIENT: Black Lips
DESIGNER: Geoff Peveto
DESIGN FIRM: The Decoder Ring
WEBSITE: thedecoderring.com

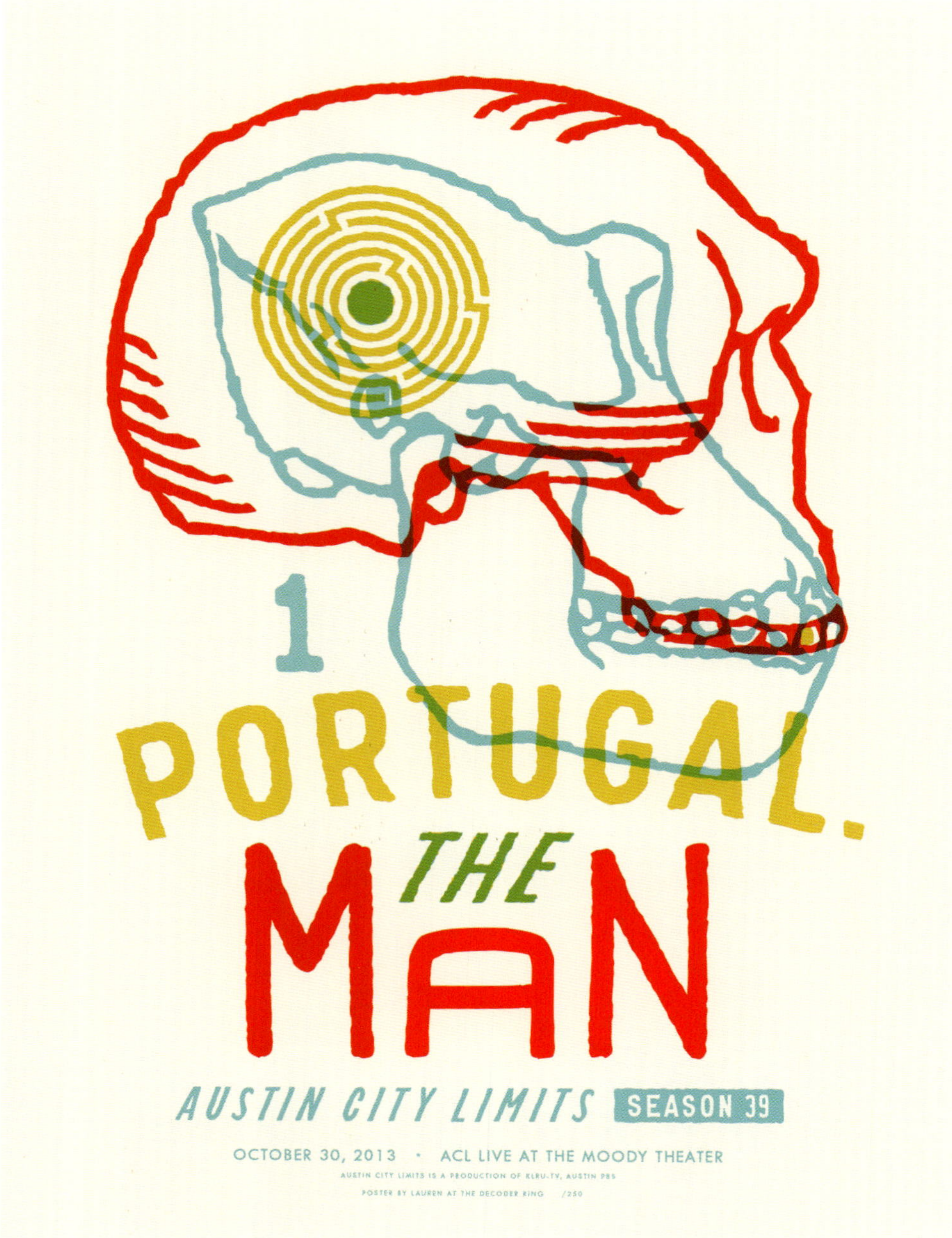

CLIENT: Portugal. The Man
DESIGNER: Geoff Peveto
DESIGN FIRM: The Decoder Ring
WEBSITE: thedecoderring.com

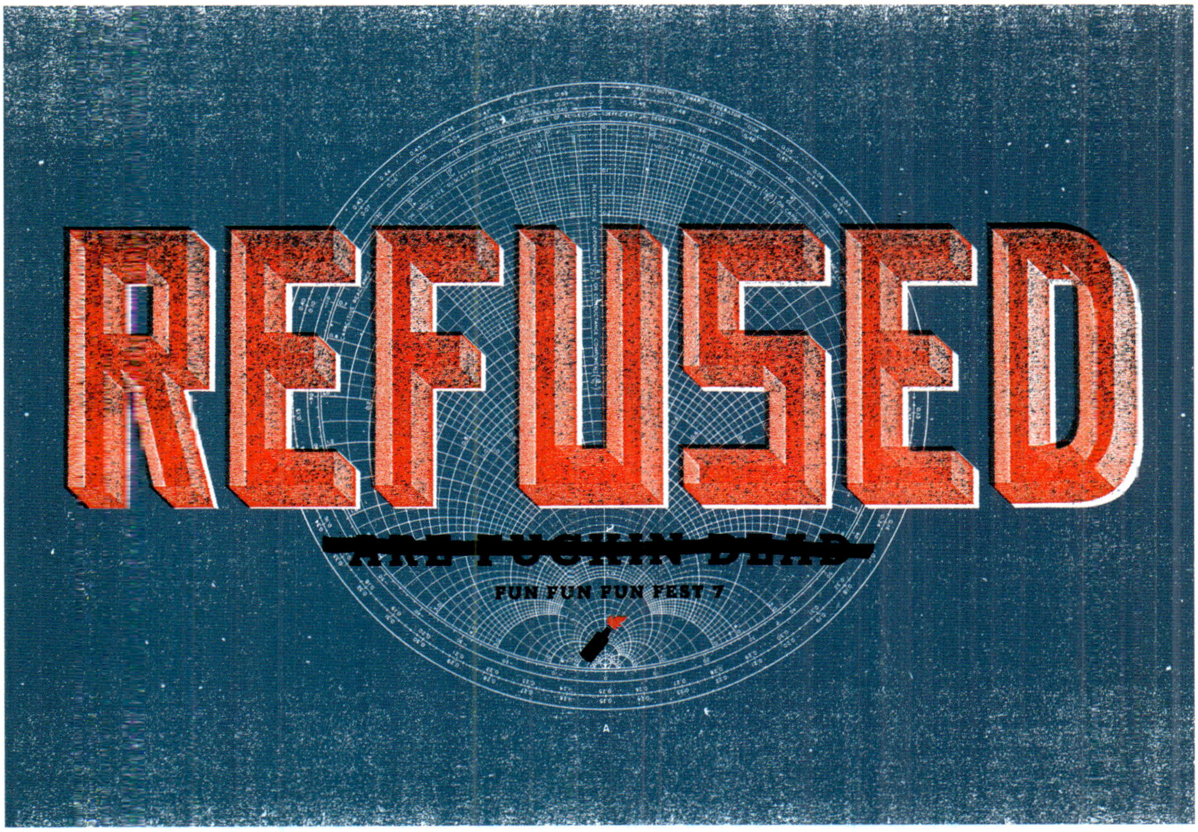

CLIENT: Refused
DESIGNER: Geoff Peveto
DESIGN FIRM: The Decoder Ring
WEBSITE: thedecoderring.com

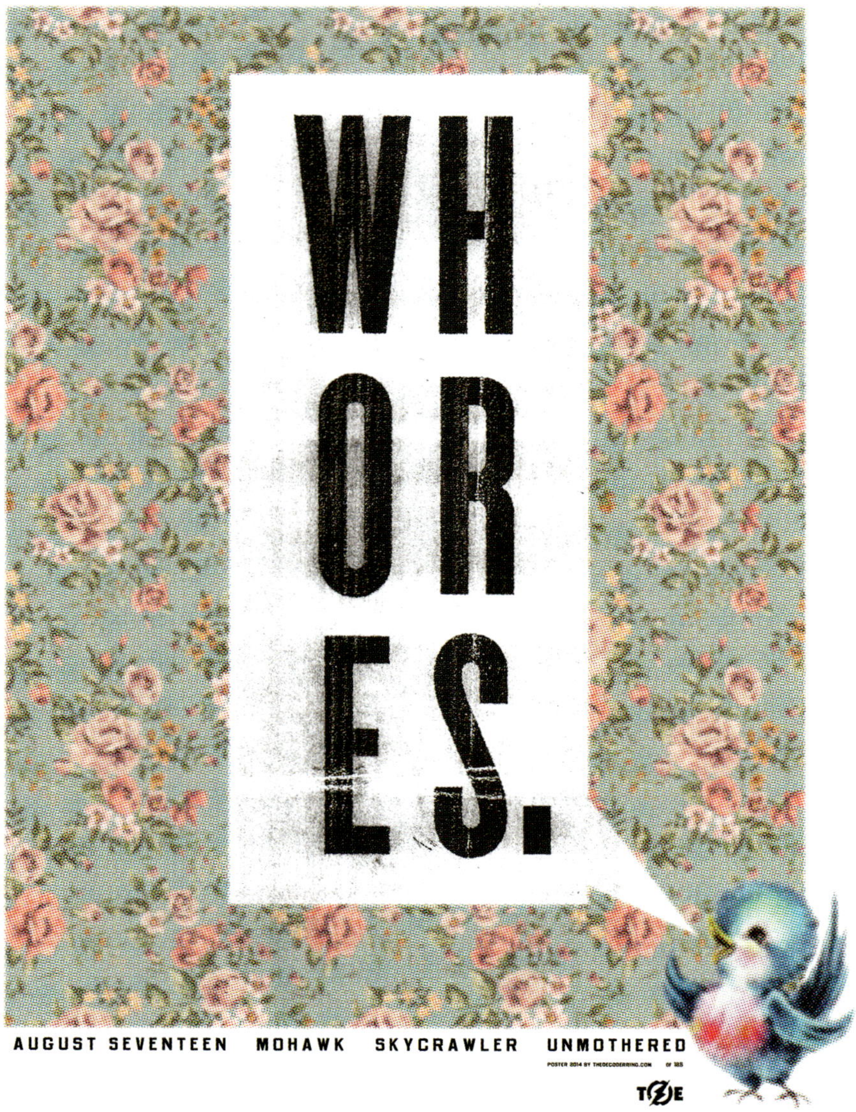

CLIENT: Whores
DESIGNER: Geoff Peveto
DESIGN FIRM: The Decoder Ring
WEBSITE: thedecoderring.com

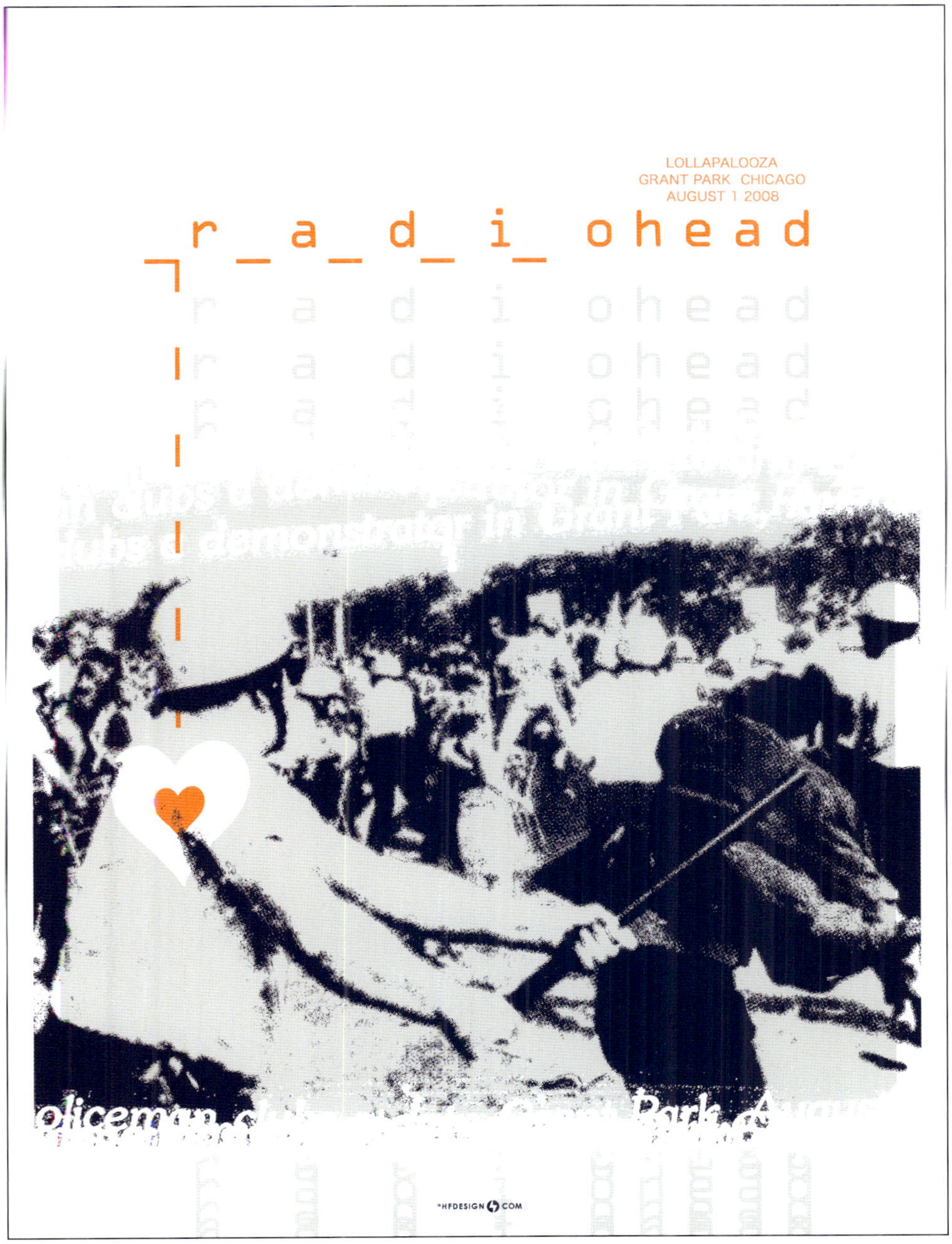

CLIENT: Radiohead
DESIGNER: Pat Jones
DESIGN FIRM: Powerhouse Factories
WEBSITE: powerhousefactories.com

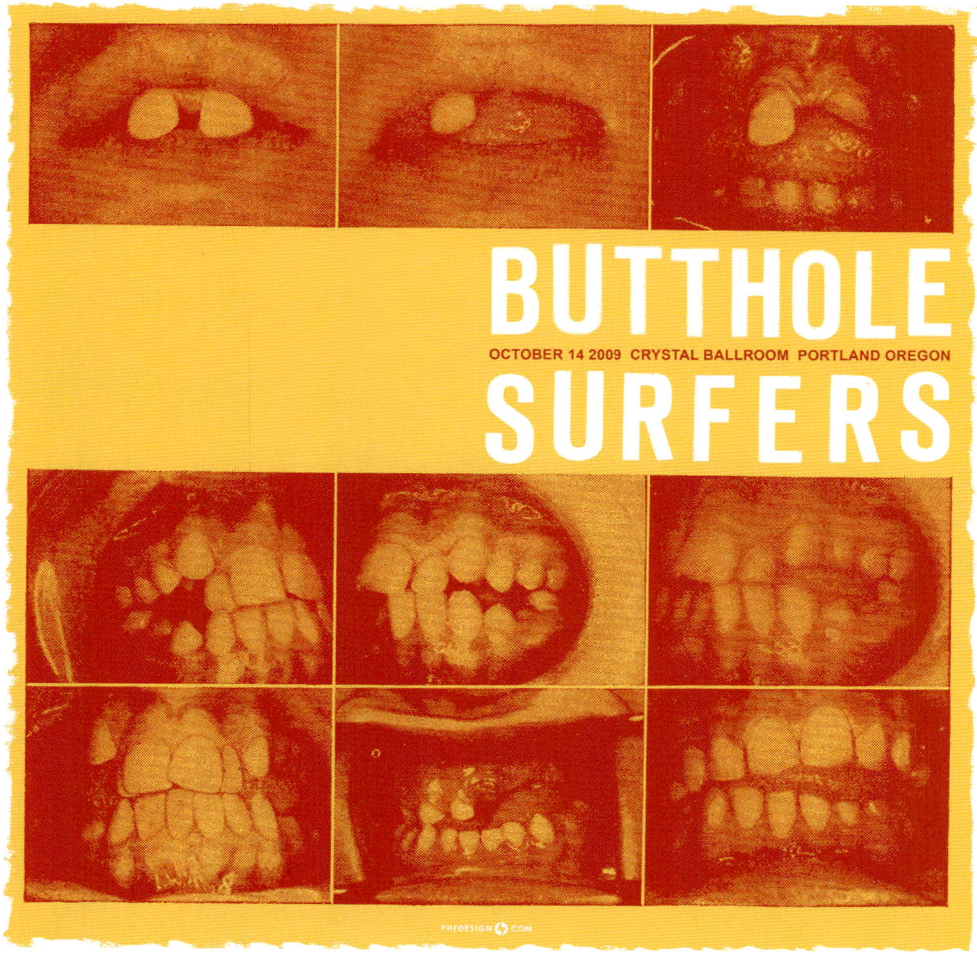

CLIENT: Butthole Surfers
DESIGNER: Pat Jones
DESIGN FIRM: Powerhouse Factories
WEBSITE: powerhousefactories.com

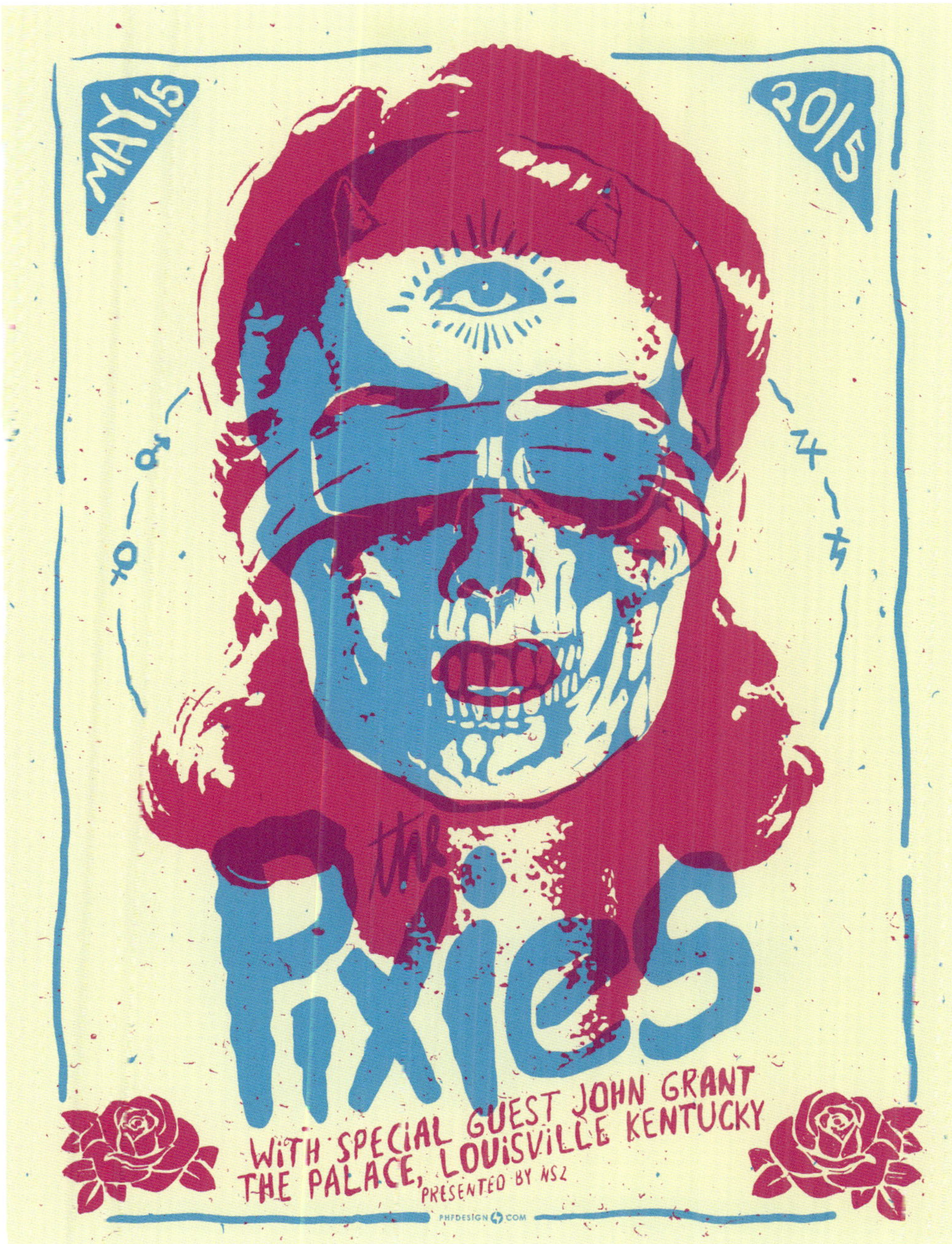

CLIENT: Pixies
DESIGNER: Aaron May
DESIGN FIRM: Powerhouse Factories
WEBSITE: powerhousefactories.com

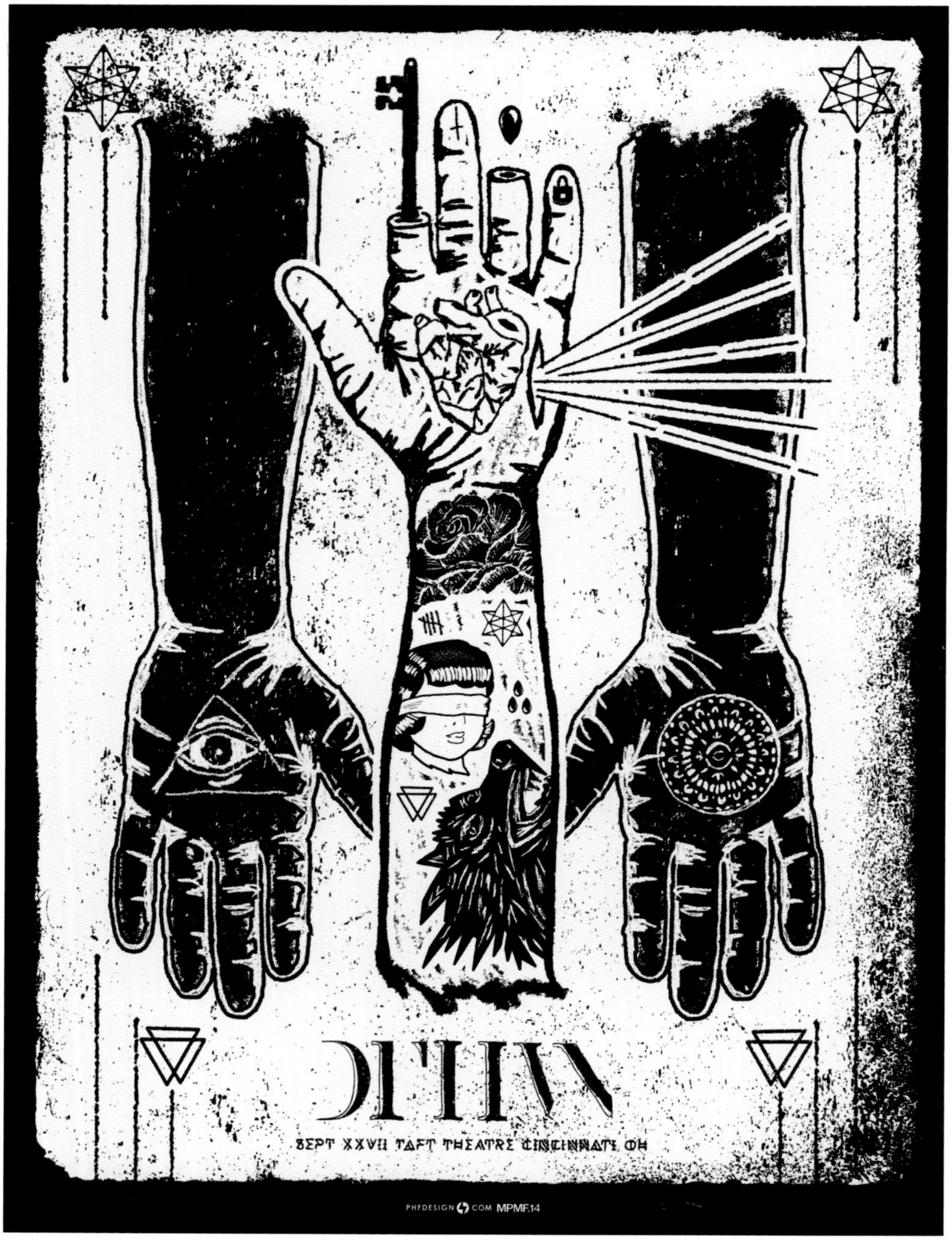

CLIENT: Deafheaven
DESIGNER: Aaron May
DESIGN FIRM: Powerhouse Factories
WEBSITE: powerhousefactories.com

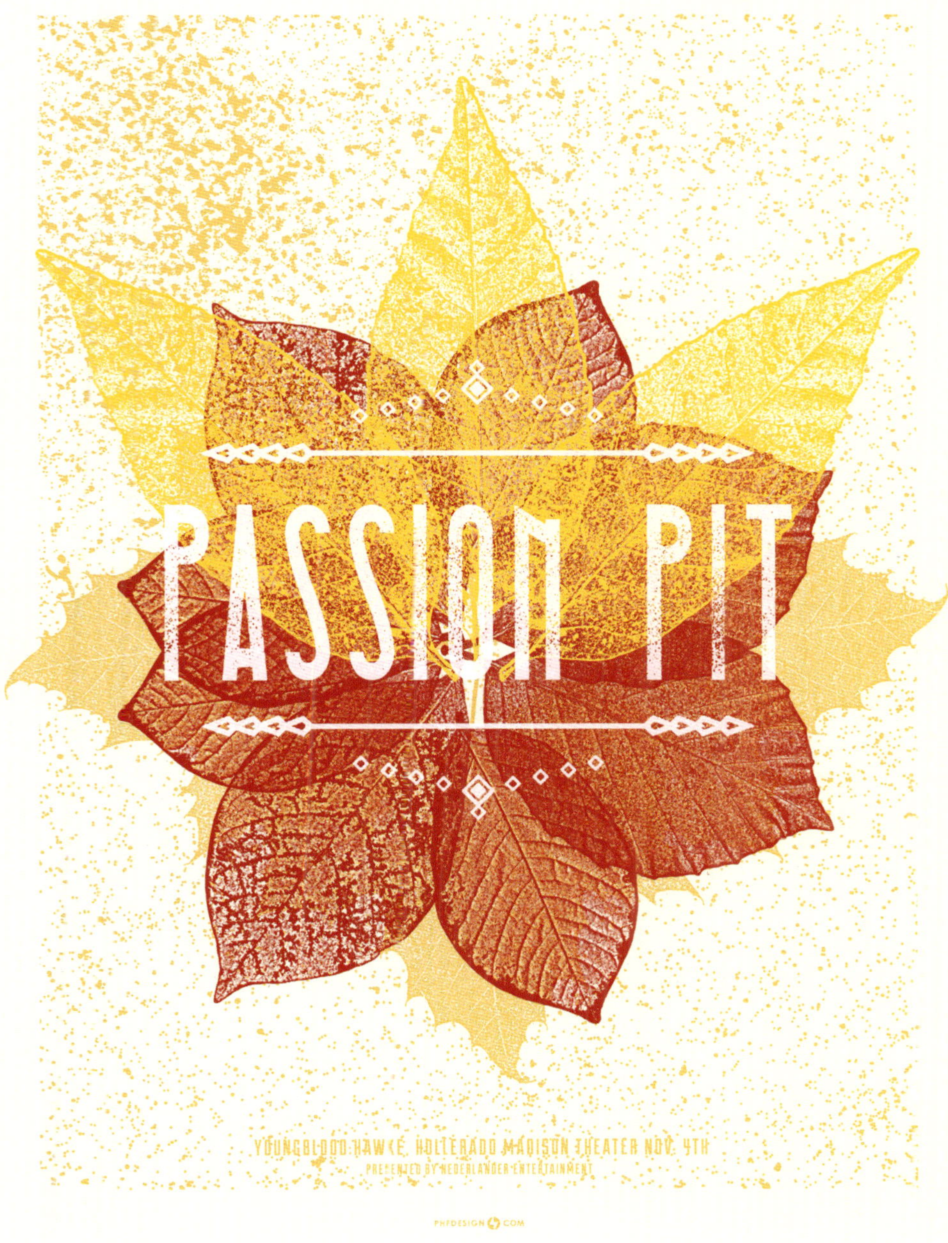

CLIENT: Passion Pit
DESIGNER: Aaron May
DESIGN FIRM: Powerhouse Factories
WEBSITE: powerhousefactories.com

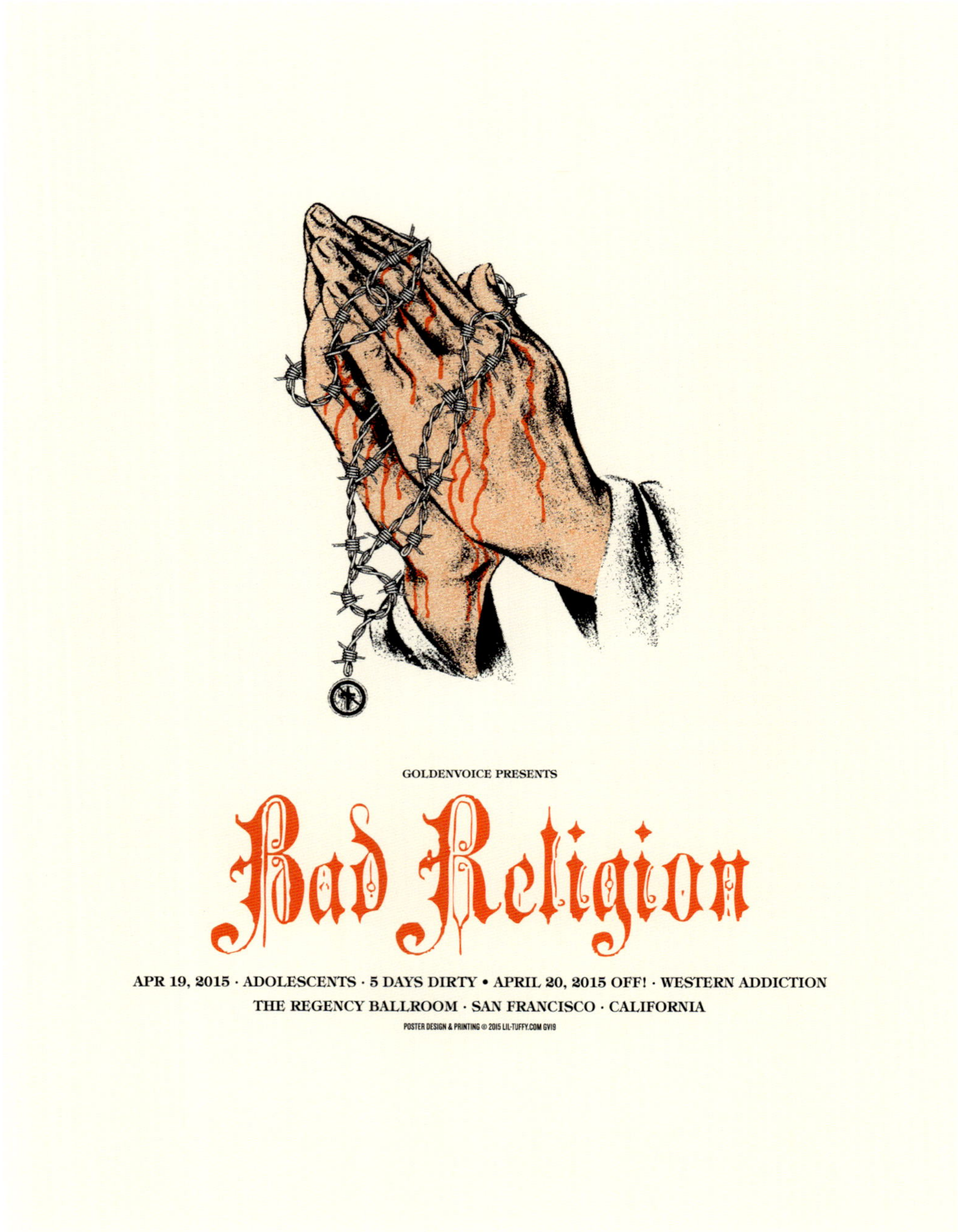

CLIENT: Bad Religion
DESIGNER: Terrence Ryan
DESIGN FIRM: Lil' Tuffy
WEBSITE: lil-tuffy.com

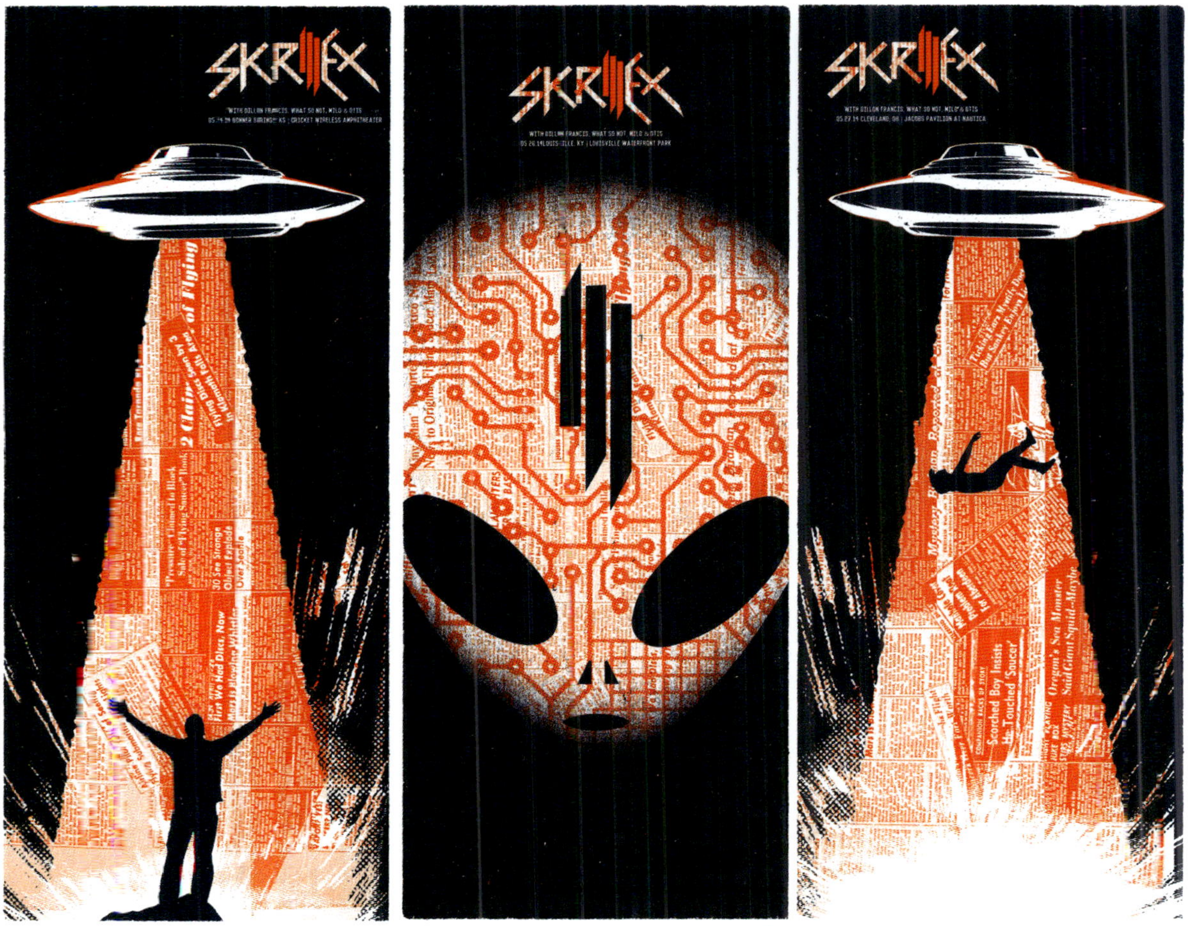

CLIENT: Skrillex
DESIGNER: Andy Vastagh
DESIGN FIRM: Boss Construction
WEBSITE: bossconstruct.com

BEING SUCCESSFUL

MEETING AND WORKING WITH BANDS

For the most part, bands are very interested in the idea of having gig posters made for their upcoming shows, which is good. The problem is how do you actually get in touch with them to get their permission to do a poster, who sets the deal, and how is everyone happy in the end?

The unwritten rule is that in one way, shape, or form, you need the band's permission to use their name and to create a poster for them. If you don't get permission in writing, a band (or their merch company) can send you a cease and desist order forcing you to quit selling the print. This sometimes happens even when you do have permission from a band, but it's pretty rare.

Within the music industry there are four ways that can get you access to a band to discuss doing a limited edition, hand-printed poster for one of their shows or their tour.

BANDS

The first is by directly contacting the band itself. There are multiple ways to do this depending largely on the popularity, or fame, of the band and how much experience you have as a poster artist. A new poster shop may try to hit up local bands, just to get a few designs and prints under their belt, knowing that they may not sell many and/or may have to sell for a reduced price compared to the posters they do for national acts. That said, many shops reach out to their favorite national bands and have success landing a poster gig or two early in their experience. Poster guys that have been in the game for a while obviously have had more access and exposure to larger bands and therefore get more opportunities to do prints for them. As you make connections you'll get to meet bands through promoters, at shows and festivals, or online after a band had searched you out through sites like GigPosters.com, etc. Once a relationship like that has been struck it can be very beneficial to both parties and you might even end up doing the official poster for each individual show on their upcoming tour. This is a big deal when the band is popular and their fans are big collectors (e.g. My Morning Jacket, Phish, or Dave Mathews Band).

BAND MANAGEMENT

The second way is through a band's management. To do this you would typically reach out to the band's manager or tour manager. This can be done at a show when the band comes through town or online through the booking contact info found on a band's website. In this scenario, the manager will act as the agent or broker of the poster deal. Also, it is not unheard of for it to go the other way and a band's manager reaches out to poster artists. In this case the manager and band are willing and wanting to pay a specific artist to do large editions of posters for one or more shows. Typically, they would want the posters to be a part of their merch setup and would sell them throughout the entire tour.

CLUB OWNERS & PROMOTERS

The third way in is through club owners and promoters. They can leverage their connection with bands and booking agents, created when they book bands and shows at their club. Often promoters will mention the idea of doing a gig poster when they are booking bands and this becomes an added value. If not initially discussed, after a show is booked, a promoter can reach out to a band's management (tour manager, booking agent, etc.) to get the idea of doing a gig poster in front of the right people. At the end of the day, you still need permission from a band to do a poster, but if a promoter vouches for a poster artist, it's usually legit. Promoters are rarely, if ever, interested in paying for a poster to be created or interested in buying a stack to sell at the show. This would become another activity that they would have to add to their already busy event, and they usually don't sell enough to justify the time and expense. Not to mention they have even less of a reason to use a band's name than the poster artist. This can be looked down upon by bands and merch companies because it is cutting into the promoters' efforts for the show and club as well as cutting into the merch companies' sales for that night.

MERCH COMPANIES

The fourth way to gain an audience with a band is through their merch company. This way is rare, but it does happen. Basically, you use the merch company's pre-existing permission and agreement it has with the band. The reason this doesn't typically happen is because merch companies have their own designers and don't want to pay an outside artist to design and produce the piece. At times bands and their managers will try to get their merch company to partner up with a poster artist, especially if they want to commission work that can be sold by the merch company along the entire tour, taking the responsibility away from the band. This deal is difficult to work out for the same reasons but does happen on occasion—especially if the band's manager is interested and is driving the deal.

Once you have a connection with the band and permission to do the poster has been established, a deal needs to be struck. The "deal" basically includes what goods and services are being exchanged and what role each party plays. There are three major types of deals that are commonly struck between poster artists and bands:

- a full-commission deal
- each party splits the stack
- free upfront with permission to sell after the show.

Each one works a little differently and sometimes just includes the band, while other times it includes the other parties, like the promoter.

FULL-COMMISSION DEAL

When a full-commission deal is struck with a band it is always done directly through the members of the band and/or their manager. This is similar to any other design or print client a poster artist may have. The band pays you to design and produce a piece. In this case the piece is a poster for a tour or a specific show for that band. Different poster artists work at different rates. A good rule of thumb is that if you are charging them an hourly design rate, then they have complete design control. This means that not only do they inspire the design for the poster, but they direct it initially and critique it throughout the design process like any paying client would. In this situation a separate print cost would be added to the design cost based on the number of colors in the design, size of the print run, etc. In the music industry, working with an hourly design rate is rare, even in a commission deal. More commonly, an upfront total cost is worked out for the design and production of a stack of posters. The design control is shared in this situation, although both parties need to agree on this or the poster artist may end up redesigning a piece or going through multiple rounds of revisions. This can be costly for an artist because the biggest expense when creating a poster is design time. Also, this can become increasingly frustrating for a poster artist if he spends a bunch of time creating the band's vision for the piece versus collaborating with them. You can end up taking shots in the dark until the band sees something they like, which is never good.

SPLIT THE STACK

Another type of deal that is similar to the full-commission deal is what we call "split the stack." In this case the poster artist assumes more of the risk up front, but can also make more money in the end by selling the poster. This type of deal is also nice because the poster artist does get paid a little money upfront from the band. What happens is the poster artist creates the piece at a reduced rate and decides up-front, with the band, what the total edition size will be. Typically bands will want to agree on a per-piece price (like $5/print) rather than working out design and print costs. Once the piece is printed, the poster artist editions the whole stack and then splits them with the band based on whatever percentage they've agreed on. From there, the band sells their stack on tour (and sometimes online) and the poster artist sells her stack through her usual channels.

PRODUCING POSTERS FOR FREE

The third type of deal, and the most common in our experience at Powerhouse, is designing and producing the poster for free in exchange for permission to sell a small stack of posters to recoup costs. The band gets a small stack, around 10–20 copies, and the poster artist gets the rest. The number of copies the poster artist creates for himself or herself can be a pretty wide range and depends on his or her agreement with the band. The reason this is ok with a band and also why it is okay with their merch company is that with any gig poster, the edition is limited, and once the poster has been printed the "mold is broken." Meaning the screen is cleaned out, the film is archived, and no screens are ever shot again. The merch company's biggest hang-up is that it is also trying to sell memorabilia from the band and this competes with that. It's easier for the merch company to palate since the poster is limited, for a specific show, and in most cases not sold until after the show is over.

By no means are these the only types of deals that poster artists have struck with bands; these are just the ones that we are familiar with. As long as the poster artist and band are in agreement, anything goes. Here are some other scenarios of poster agreements from our friends in the industry (Andy Vastagh from Boss Construction, Travis Bone from Furturtle Show Prints, and Lil' Tuffy) followed by some discussion of process and inspiration from Aaron May and Matt Barnes of Powerhouse Factories.

ARTIST PROFILE

Andy Vastagh

BOSS CONSTRUCTION

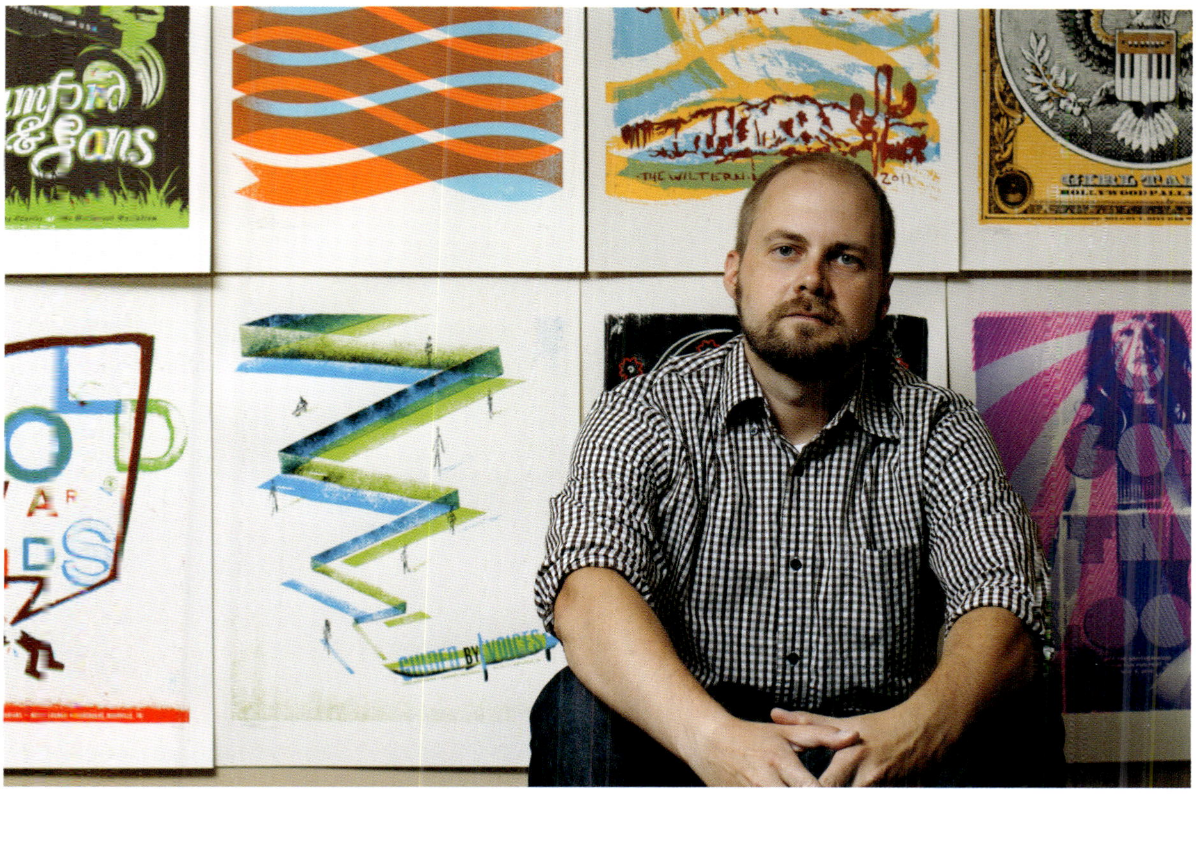

How do you typically work with bands?

A general scenario when working with bands is as follows:

Band (usually management) e-mails me asking availability, interest, rates, and so forth. Nine times out of ten I won't say no for time reasons. No matter how busy or committed to other projects I am, I feel fortunate enough to be considered for the project and will do whatever it takes to make it happen. I may lose some sleep or my hands might be extra sore the next day, but picking up those gigs has turned some of those clients into the most creatively and financially fulfilling long-term relationships I have to date.

Upon committing to the job, we agree upon a timeline for the project. Many times these hard dates are crucial to a project. Showing a client you can make a deadline and take the task at hand seriously will give them a sense of comfort and keep them open and receptive to your ideas. If a client is already frustrated because they are seeing your first round of concept sketches a week later than they were expecting to, it can cause them to possibly overlook a great idea and may even cost the designer the job. If I'm not going to be able to deliver on the day I said I would, I give plenty of heads-up to show that I'm aware of the situation. What some designers can forget is that these people you're dealing with are part of a network of people, a more schedule-oriented network of folks that don't understand or give a damn about the fact that you weren't "inspired" yet to give them your little pencil drawings of their highly involved, time-sensitive, big-budget project. Make the deadlines and stick to them; the project will go much smoother more often than not because of it. Also, clearly communicating your process and rates up front will avoid any unnecessary snags down the road. Communication is key.

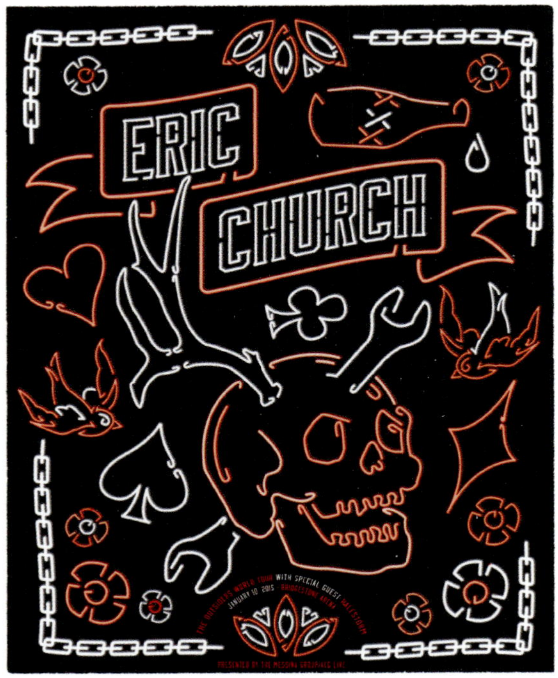

CLIENT: Eric Church
DESIGNER: Andy Vastagh
DESIGN FIRM: Boss Construction
WEBSITE: bossconstruct.com

As far as going from concept to execution creatively goes, I prefer to work like this:

Round One: 3–5 thumbnail-sized pencil sketches to run thru some concepts based on any initial direction the client may (or may not) have provided in the initial conversation. Keep the ideas open and loose; a lot of times the ideas I come to the sketchbook with lead me to better ideas I had no idea were rattling around in my head. Keep the drawings informative without getting too bogged down with details at this phase.

A strong idea clearly illustrated will show through more than a tiny thumbnail with a lot of superfluous details. Another benefit to the quick sketches is to avoid spending too much time with digital comps that have a good chance of not being chosen and constrict the flow a pencil and paper can provide. I'll scan the sketches at a decent size resolution, adjust the contrast for legibility, and then size and label the sketches uniformly. Once sketches are all ready I'll send them to the client with a one- or two-sentence rundown of what each of my chicken-scratch sketches means. A good reason for the anal-retentive aspects of this phase is that much of the time the folks you're dealing with are more on the business-minded side of things and don't necessarily have the vision that other creatives may have. There's nothing wrong with holding their hand and speaking to them in a way that helps them understand what that squiggly doodle in your notebook really means. Also, uniform organization of file names and sizes keeps communication clear and speaks to the possibly more organized and business-minded audience to whom you are speaking to. Trust me, it helps bridge that gap from artist to client.

Round Two: A digital comp (sometimes two) based on what the client responded to. Chances are, if the sketches were what they were supposed to be, this comp is well received and your project is off to a good start.

Round Three: Finalize the art based on final client feedback and get that pup ready to print! If they want to keep changing things more than what's in reason, charge them more. Time is money. Often, if they keep changing things and you tell them it's going to cost more, they'll suddenly think it looks perfect. Funny how that happens.

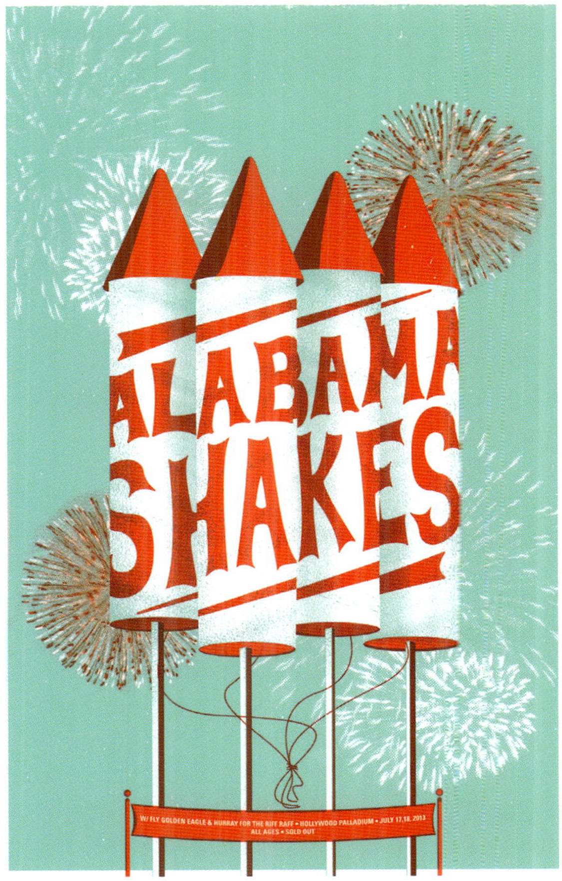

CLIENT: Alabama Shakes
DESIGNER: Andy Vastagh
DESIGN FIRM: Boss Construction
WEBSITE: bossconstruct.com

What are all of the types of "deals" that you have worked with bands?

The majority of the 'deals' I do are the job as requested by the client with an adjusted/discounted design/print rate in exchange for an agreed upon allotment of posters that I get to sell after the show, online or at a poster show in order to recoup any expenses. The bands get a break on their budget and I get the opportunity to make a few more bucks than I would have made without permission to sell my extra copies of the edition.

What is the most lucrative poster gig you ever received?

I am currently working on an estimated 22,000 poster run for a large-scale touring country music act. That is easily the largest collective invoice I have sent to date.

Do you always get permission from the band when selling the poster? How do you get it and from whom?

Absolutely. That is very important to communicate to the client upon the initiation of the relationship. If I am not working directly with the band, I ensure whoever has hired me, be it the promoter, manager, or venue, makes sure everyone involved is on board. If a band says you can't sell the posters, they get charged accordingly and everyone moves on.

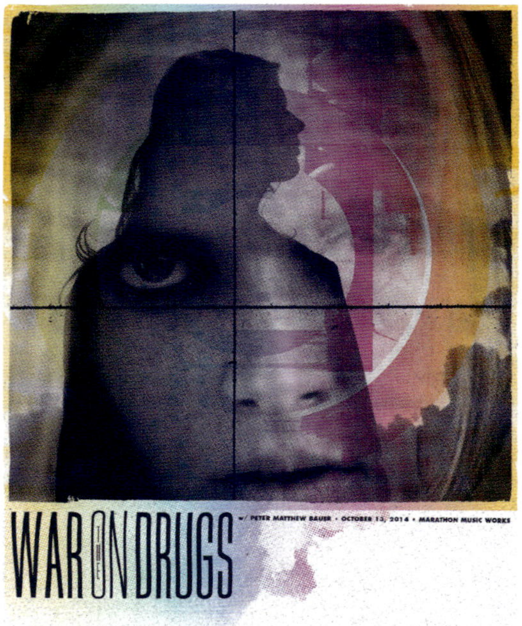

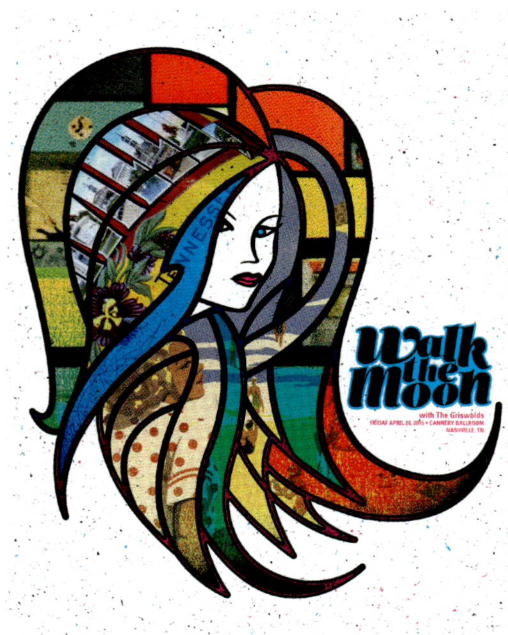

CLIENTS: (TOP) The War on Drugs, (BOTTOM) Walk the Moon
DESIGNER: Andy Vastagh
DESIGN FIRM: Boss Construction
WEBSITE: bossconstruct.com

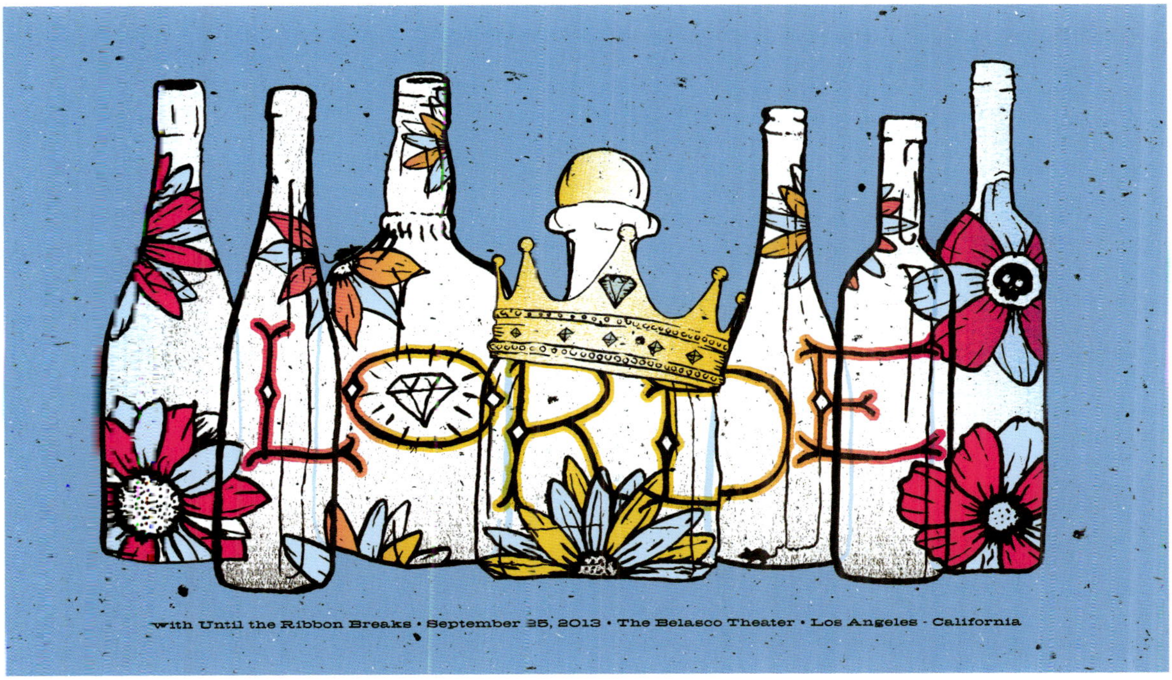

CLIENT: Lorde
DESIGNER: Andy Vastagh
DESIGN FIRM: Boss Construction
WEBSITE: bossconstruct.com

ARTIST PROFILE

Travis Bone

FURTURTLE SHOW PRINTS

On working with bands

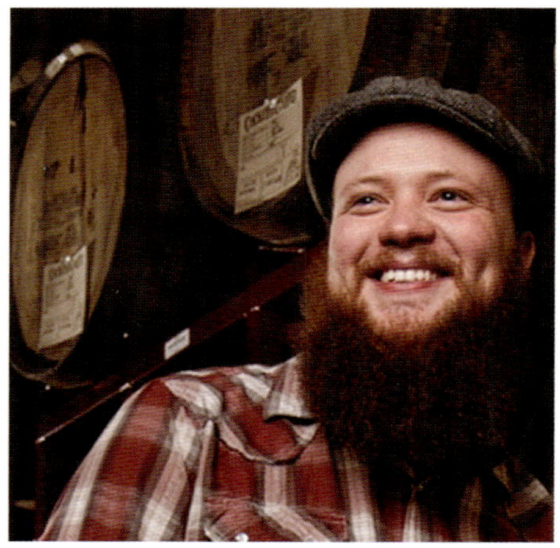

When I first started making posters for bands in 2004 the approach was pretty simple: I liked a band, I would e-mail a proposal and sample drawings from my portfolio to the contact listed on their website or Myspace page, then I would wait to hear back. Most of the time, I never heard a word. Eventually, I got lucky. My first screen-printed poster was for Mogwai (I love them). Barry sent me a response and the deal was on. I felt like I had won the lottery. A musical hero of mine left me voice-mails in a completely unintelligible (to my Yankee ears, anyway) Scottish accent. I honestly could not believe that they were interested in my work. My Morning Jacket's manager responded to an e-mail I sent! I had an opportunity to make a My Morning Jacket poster! It still kind of blows my mind. I thought this must be the way it worked. In some instances, it is still the way it works. I found out pretty quickly, however, that when you deal with a band, especially a large one, there could be an awful lot of cooks kicking around that kitchen. Some of those cooks might even be out of their goddamn minds.

Maybe I get too attached to my little drawings, but if I have been working on a piece every night for a week, late into the morning, just trying to come up with something that I am truly happy with, even sending the finished mockup can be agonizing. Hitting the Send button is like the starting pistol for an anxiety race but getting a positive response back is pure elation. It is all worth it for that feeling.

Now, if that e-mail has to go to a team of folks, odds are pretty good that one of those folks is going to hate it. Maybe I am working with a member of a band that I know personally; he loves the illustration but the merchandise company, or the tour manager, or the lead singer's girlfriend who just graduated from art school has some issues. Things can get complicated but most of the time it is easily manageable.

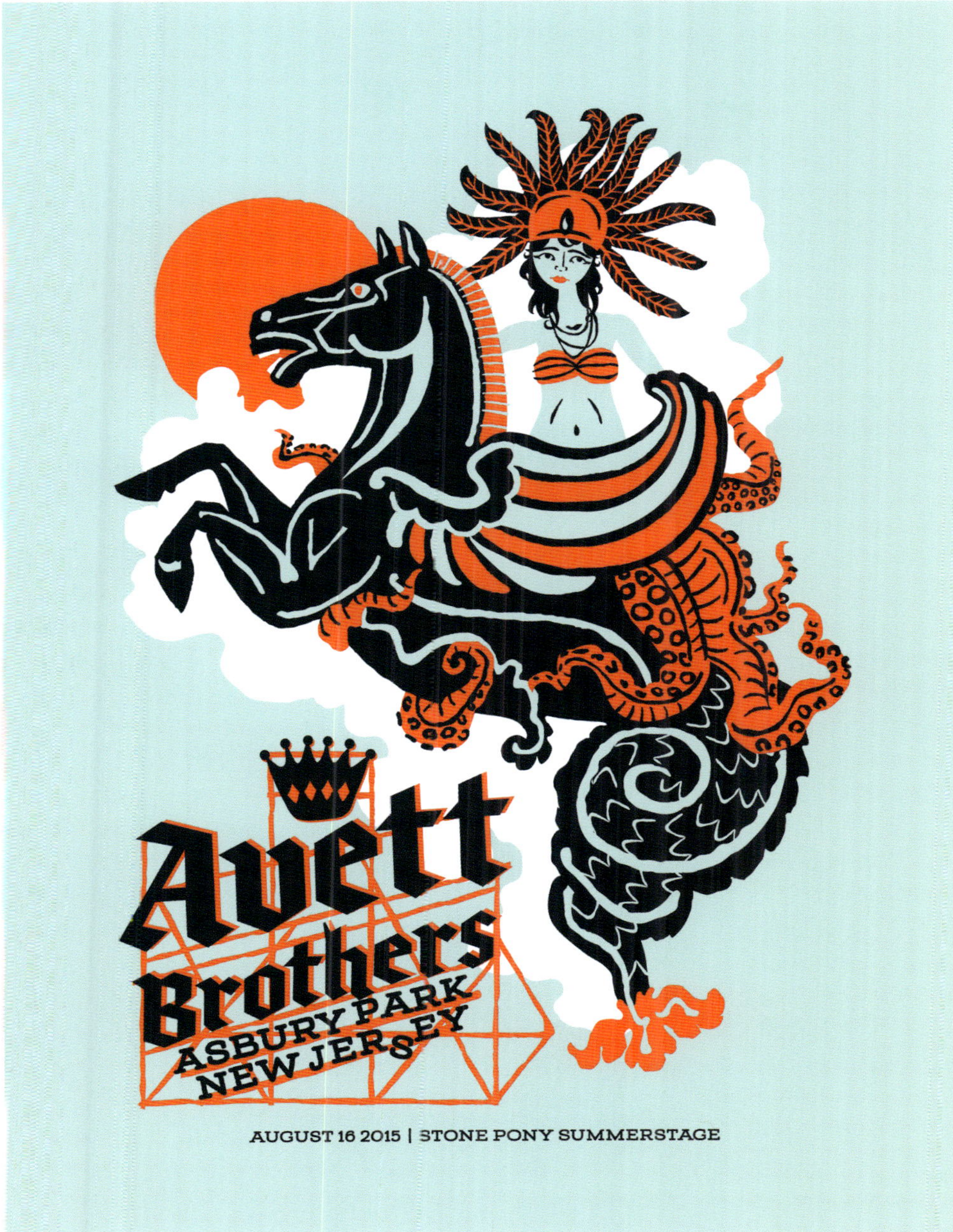

CLIENT: The Avett Brothers
DESIGNER: Travis Bone
DESIGN FIRM: Furturtle Show Prints
WEBSITE: furturtle.com

One time, the merchandise company was concerned about the price of my illustration work despite the deal I made with a member of the band. This company had dealt with another artist who had much cheaper rates. Since the other artist made beautiful posters from vintage clip art pieces and I was spending a bunch of time drawing mine, I could not compete. Despite my explanation, they explained that they felt like I was ripping them off, the job was taken off of my hands, and I have never since been hired to do another for that band.

Another recent job had me working with a tour manager of a band I am particularly fond of. We came up with a fair deal. I went through a few different versions and revisions, but finally came up with something we both felt worked well. When the band's manager was consulted after all that, the deal was quashed with a simple "no" written in an e-mail. At least the response was quick and didn't take too much time to read.

I once had a manager for one of my all-time favorite bands offer me the opportunity to do a show poster for said band. They would need 150 prints and no more than that could be printed or sold by me or anyone else. They would not be paying me anything for the prints or the illustration work, but it would be a pretty awesome thing to be able to say that I had done. I thought it would be an even more awesome thing to say that I didn't, so I declined. Who in their right mind would go for that deal? Some other poster artist would, no joke. The band got their free posters and some lucky bastard got the bragging rights of having made it.

I could go on and on and on but honestly, it bums me out.

Some cases of trouble just can't be avoided but there are some red flags I tend to look for. If a client wants to hire me and they send me samples of a bunch of another artist's work, things will not go well. If "exposure" is mentioned in any part of the negotiation, I can forget about getting paid fairly. If a client wants "several finished illustrations to choose from" and is willing to pay for each, I have found a unicorn client and I will love them forever. In actuality, when a client asks for that, they typically just want an exponential amount of work done for the cost of one illustration and they are not able to ever be satisfied. If I am asked to enter a poster contest with the prize being payment for all the work I did just to enter? No thanks. Is the client someone called Ted Nugent? RED FLAG! Ultimately though, this may sound bad, but I often go with my gut. When I have gone against my gut in a deal, it never ever goes well. I have learned to trust it through a lot of error and pain.

Best advice I can give is just to get all expectations out on the table, from both sides, to begin with. If you are a designer, ask questions and be invested in the project like you have nothing else in the world happening in your life. If you are a person hiring a designer, trust that they know what they are doing. You hired them because you liked their work so let them work. If you hired them because you thought they could do the exact same thing a different artist is doing, then you probably hired the wrong one.

I should wrap up by saying that most of my experiences in doing work for folks like tour managers, merchandise companies, record labels, and the like have been great ones. Bands need these competent people around to handle this stuff because bands are very busy things sometimes and their fans want nice stuff.

Also, you should know that I am very reasonable and easy to work with. Please hire me to draw some stuff... Please.

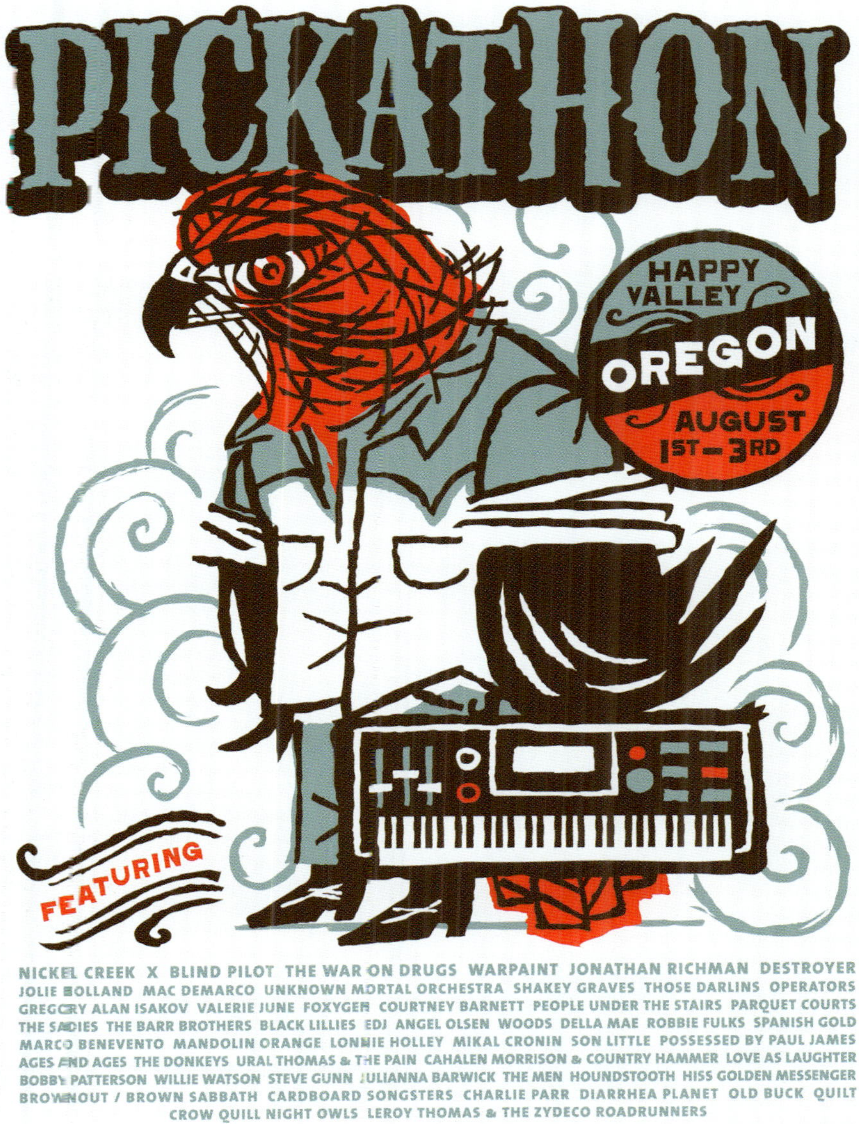

CLIENT: Pickathon
DESIGNER: Travis Bone
DESIGN FIRM: Furturtle Show Prints
WEBSITE: furturtle.com

ARTIST PROFILE

Lil' Tuffy

Each new poster job is different. Sometimes I'm lucky enough to be given free reign over the entire design but usually the band, management, or the promoter will have any combination of style guides, imagery to avoid, sponsor logos, and information.

Once I've gotten a handle on those expectations I'll start listening to the band, especially if I'm unfamiliar with them or their latest album. Next, I'll check out their website and their merch to try and get a feel for what kind of aesthetic they like. I'll also look at other artists' posters on GigPosters.com to make sure my initial ideas aren't treading on overdone themes or cliches. I'll also google recent setlists to make sure I'm not finding inspiration in a song that they aren't currently playing.

I usually find a song or a lyric and build a theme around that and sometimes even include the lyric on the poster. I did a 23-poster run for St. Vincent where every poster was stylistically similar but each one was a graphical interpretation of a song. There were two exceptions for that series: one was a sailor-themed poster for the Treasure Island Music Festival and the other was for a Halloween show.

Sometimes a special date, location, or event will be the focus of the design. I've done a lot of holiday posters for bands including X and the Mother Hips.

Lastly, there's the issue of staying current with design tastes and trends. Almost daily, I'll check out FFFFOUND! and various design blogs and Tumblrs to see what's happening outside of the world GigPosters.com.

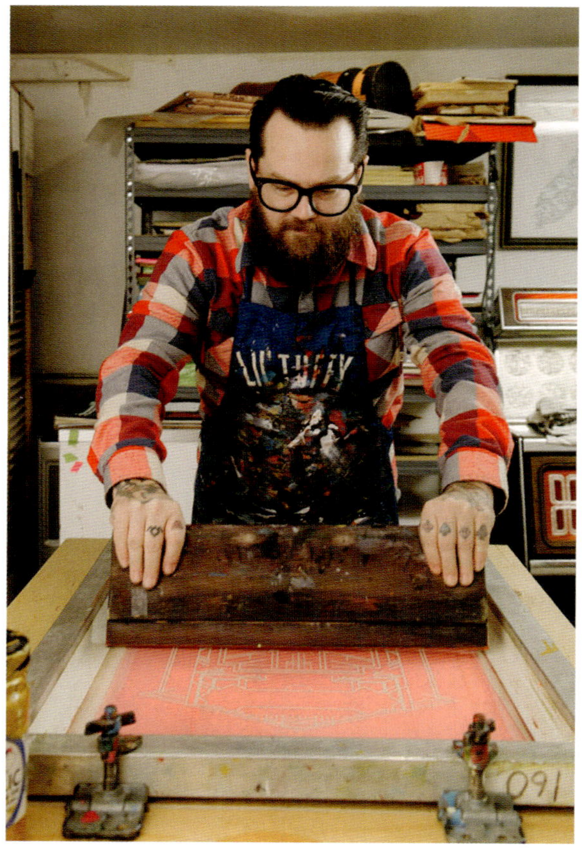

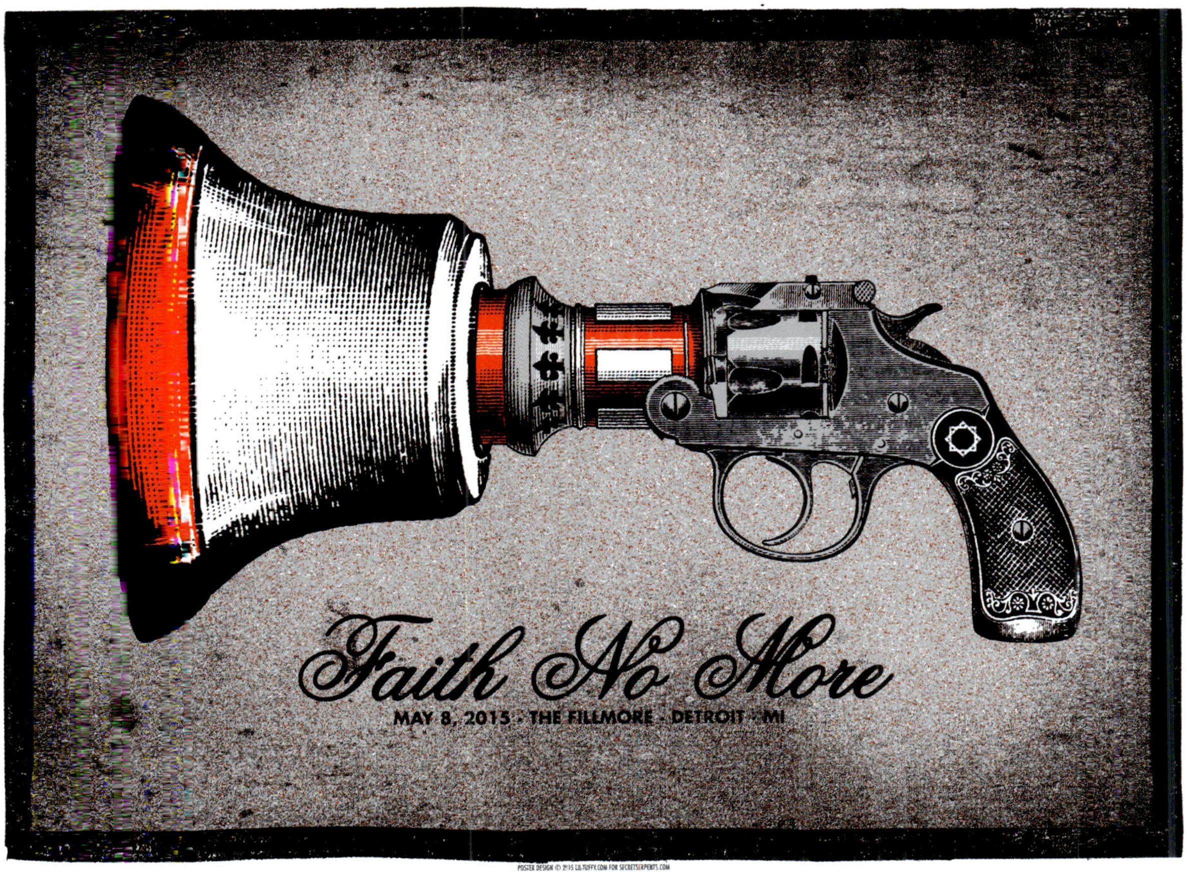

CLIENT: Faith No More
DESIGNER: Terrence Ryan
DESIGN FIRM: Lil Tuffy
WEBSITE: liltuffy.com

ARTIST PROFILE

Aaron May

POWERHOUSE FACTORIES

On being inspired by the music and imagery of the Pixies

It's a tale from the northwest of the country and it's a witch-woman kind of a song. —Frank Black.

Inspiration for the Pixies initially started with the video for the song "Blue Eyed Hexe."

The Pixies have always been so rough around the edges. Classic song writing, great hooks, and a little dark. I tried to make all of that apparent in the artwork.

So I slathered on the occult imagery as a nod to tarot cards, played with some bright transparent ink, and added a dash of hand lettering. The transparent witchy woman reveals her true self in the form of an all-seeing hexe with horns. Ain't she pretty?

Making a show poster or anything for that matter is a process. I like keeping things simple. I often don't start in the same order, but the steps never change. Listen, read, and make and remake. The poster for the Pixies started with my want to make a CMYK poster with tons of overlays. Not photo real. My style is much too loose for something so structured.

Now that I had a color palette set I listened to their latest album over and over. "Blue Eyed Hexe" grabbed me by the short hairs and said I am your fucking muse. I was all like "cool." The song itself is classic Pixies, gritty and melodic with a solid-ass hook, but it was the video that got me.

The video made the song even better. It's slathered in occult imagery and old movie witches. It's a cut and paste, hand-drawn embellishments with rough stop motion. It's killer!

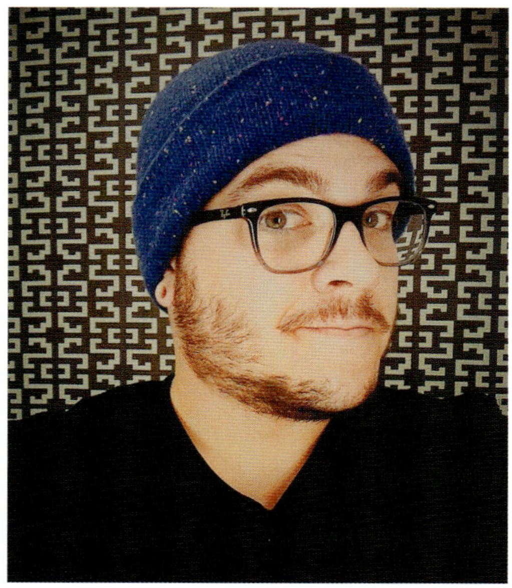

I started drawing as many cliche evil things as I could. Once I had enough symbols and pieces to play with I made version after version of the same theme. A blindfolded witch maybe on a stake somewhere. I fucked with different layer order ratios, redrawing shit until it all made me feel good. The type is based on a font I made this past year. It's showed up in a couple of my posters. The colors were just what stood out to me. I started with CMYK but ended up loving the cyan magenta layers of this particular version of the poster.

Hope you dig.

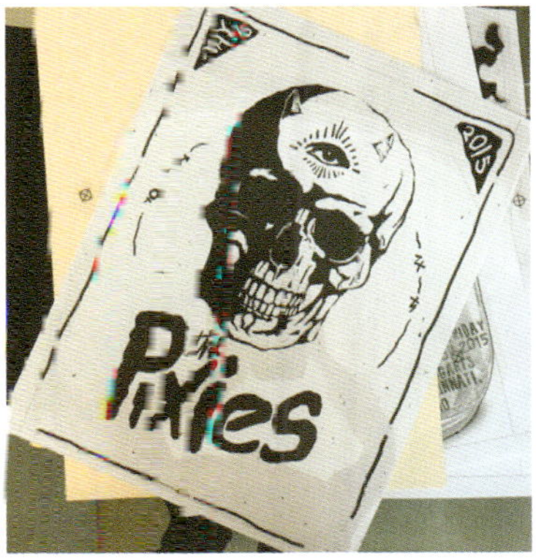
Pixies
2015
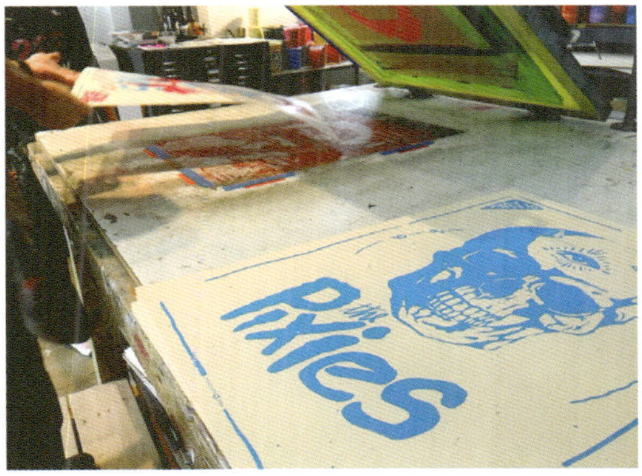
Pixies
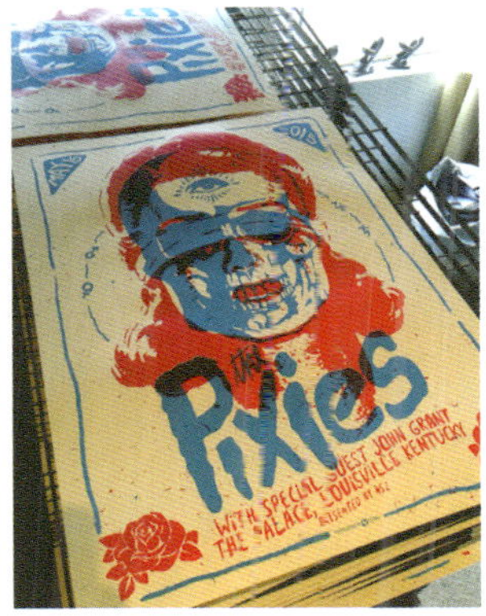
the
Pixies
WITH SPECIAL GUEST JOHN GRANT
THE PALACE, LOUISVILLE KENTUCKY
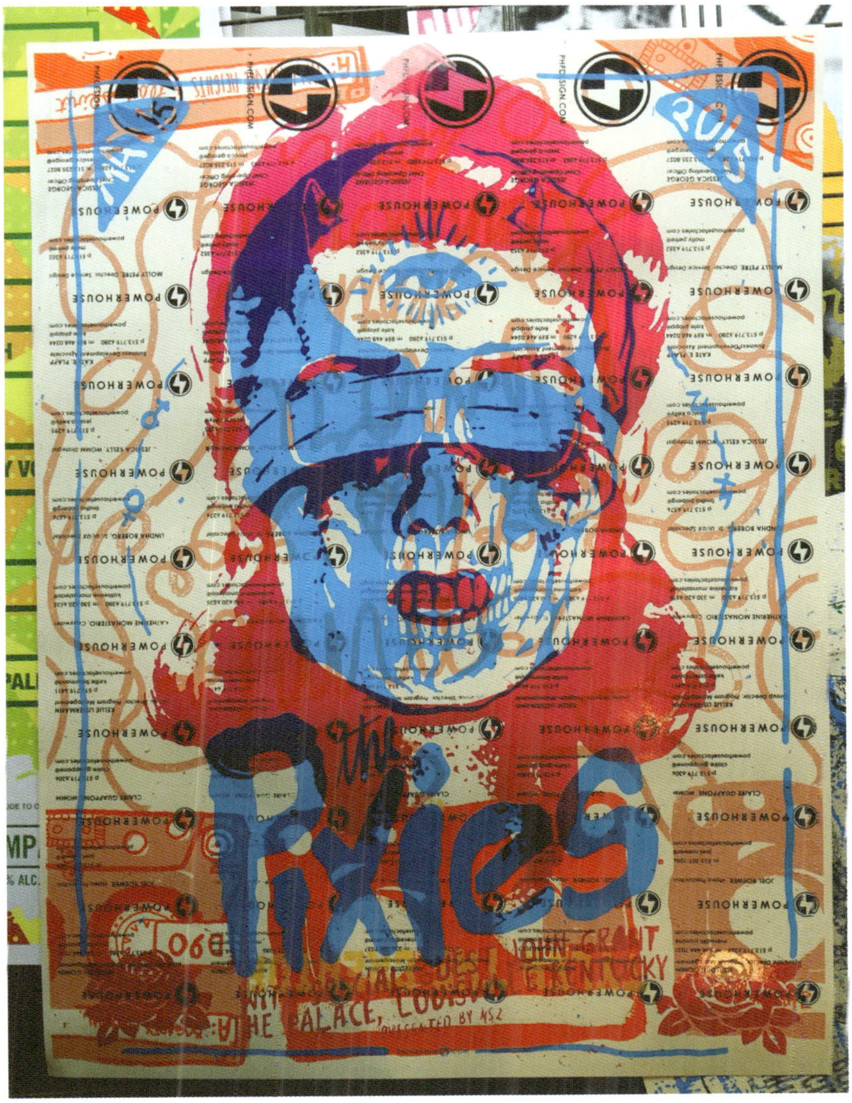
2015
POWERHOUSE
the
Pixies
JOHN GRANT
KENTUCKY
THE PALACE, LOUIS
PRESENTED BY HSZ

ARTIST PROFILE

Matt Barnes

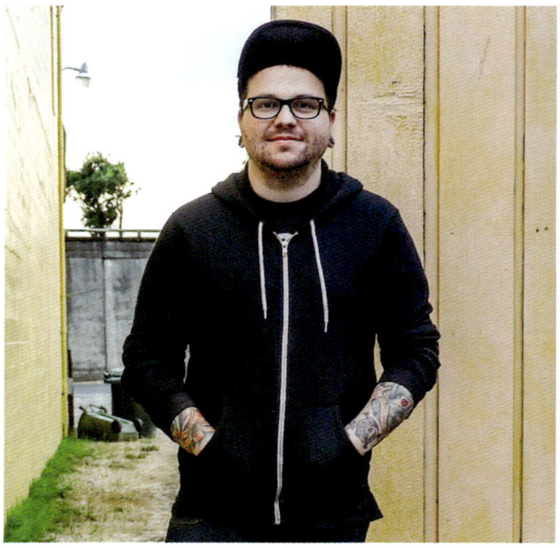

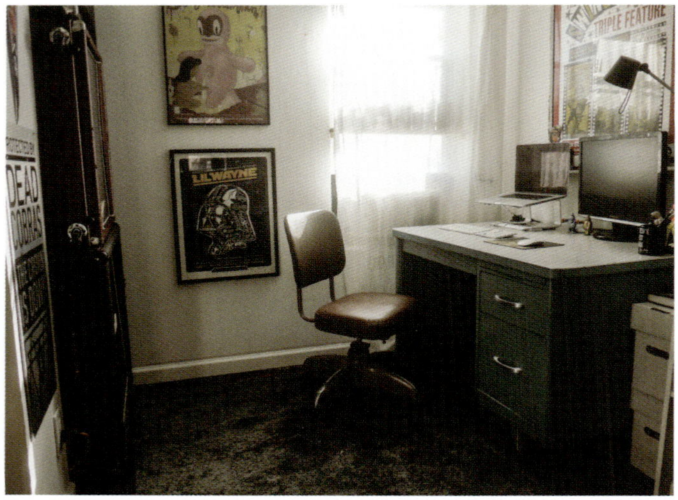

Lightning Bolt

Approaching Lightning Bolt I wanted to produce a concept that was just as chaotic as the music. I wanted to mix a couple of styles and processes to mimic the manipulation that the band does to their music. So instead of distortion pedals and drum synths, I went to hand drawing mixed with found imagery. The typography was created by distorting a Sharpie marker so it would bleed out more than usual. The concept of the poster is the battle of the song; the two members are featured on the poster (right side) battling across the "Magic Mountain." They are up against the antagonist (featured on the left poster). The thought is the aggression and emotion through each track is replicated by the imagery.

Holy Fuck

Creating concepts for instrumental bands has always been a challenge. With Holy Fuck and their methods of producing music it is always taking me to these mental story lines similar to old science fiction movies. I decided to build out the ultimate movie poster that captured the sense of the music. So I pulled Steve McQueen and mashed him against *Yog: Monster from Space*. What is more epic than Steve McQueen facing off with a Kaiju from space!? The type was produced to mimic the *Psycho* type from the *Angels from Hell* exploitation movie poster. The poster was produced by both hand cutting and pasting together as well as edits made in the computer. Final colors were chose by mixing on press.

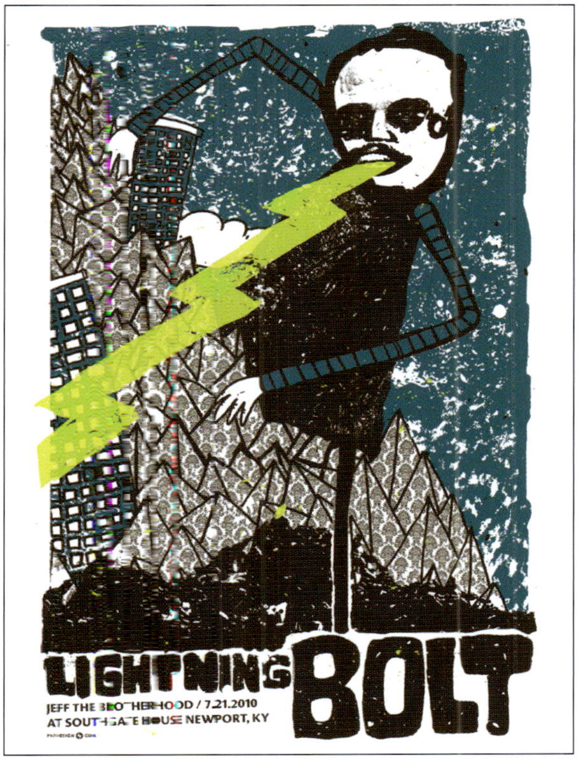

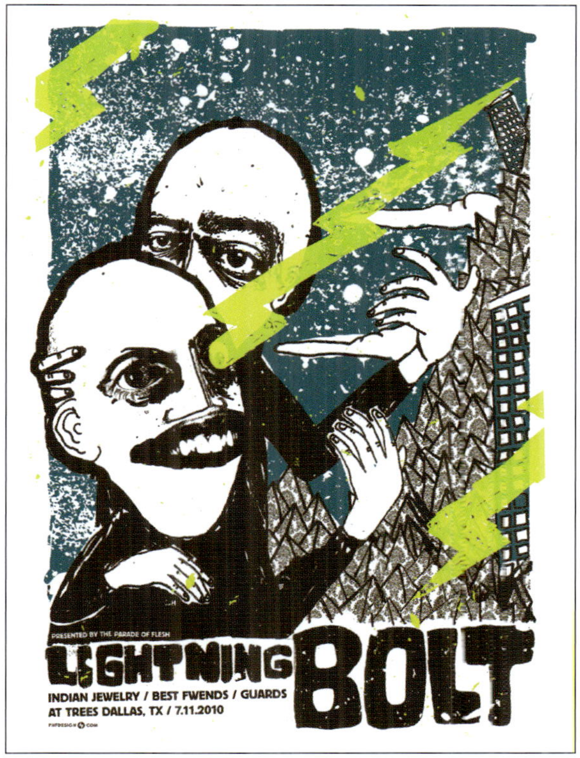

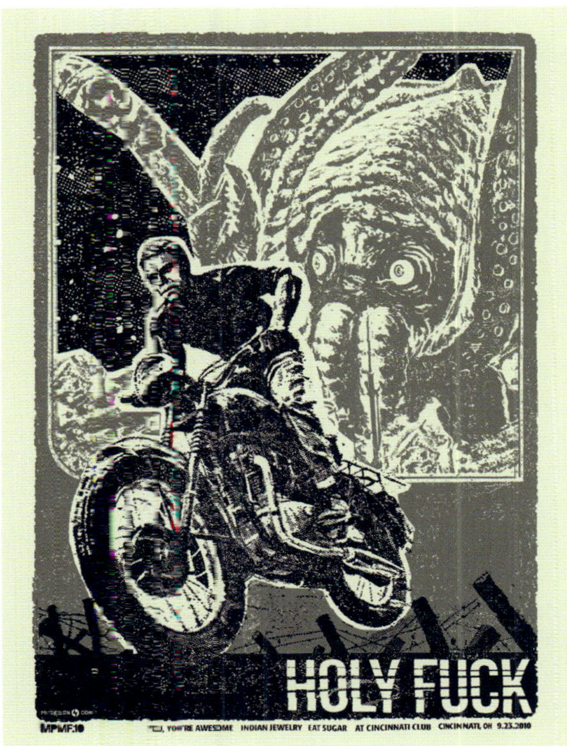

CLIENTS: (TOP) Lightning Bolt, (BOTTOM) Holy Fuck
DESIGNER: Matt Barnes
DESIGN FIRM: Powerhouse Factories
WEBSITE: powerhousefactories.com

PERMISSIONS

Clinton Reno I
My Morning Jacket, The Flaming Lips
Clinton Reno © 2015

Keith Neltner | Neltner Small Batch
Willie Nelson live at Buckle Up; Alice in Chains/ Shooter Jennings live in Asheville; Charlie Louvin live at the Foobar; Justin Townes Earle live at Whispering Beard Folk Festival; Paleface at Arnold's Bar & Grill; Jamey Johnson live at Buckle Up
Neltner Small Batch © 2015

Southpaw Prints |
Man or Astro-Man?, Skeletonwitch, Maserati, the Misfits
© Southpaw

John Matthew Overwine | Powerhouse Factories
Warpaint
John Matthew Overwine | Powerhouse Factories © 2015

Bobby Dixon | Kollective Fusion
Melvins 2013, Melvins Lite 2012, Mudhoney 2013, Melvins 2011, Method Man & Redman, Mastodon 2011
Bobby Dixon/Kollective Fusion © 2015

Daniel MacAdam | Crosshair
Deer Tick, Chicago 2014; Goose Island Block Party 2013; Of Montreal, Chicago 2014; Spoon, Tempe AZ 2014
Crosshair © 2015

Jeral Tidwell | Humantree
Queens of the Stone Age, Wu-Tang, Clutch and Corrosion of Conformity, Rusted Root, T.S.O.L., Fall Out Boy
© Jeral Tidwell, *www.humantree.com*

Mike Davis | Burlesque of North America
Baroness tour poster VII, Arcade Fire Reflektor posters 1–3
© Burlesque of North America 2014 (Arcade Fire) / 2013 (Baroness)

Ben Nunery | Powerhouse Factories
Guided by Voices, Beirut, Phoenix, Blitzen Trapper, Neko Case, Built to Spill, Rage Against the Machine, the Shins, the Greenhornes, the Avett Brothers
Ben Nunery | Powerhouse Factories © 2015

Jeff Matz | Lure Design Incorporated
Wilco-Dallas, Wilco-Indy, Against Me!, the Bravery
© Lure Design Incorporated

Nathan Meyer | Powerhouse Factories
August Burns Red
Nathan Meyer | Powerhouse Factories © 2015

Mark McDevitt/Robert Lee | Methane Studios
Edward Sharpe and the Magnetic Zeros, the Black Keys, Rufus Wainwright, Washed Out
© Methane Studios

Nate Duval |
Father John Misty-Sasquatch Fest; Andrew Bird, NYC; the Decemberists-Los Angeles; Widespread Panic-Richmond, VA; the Black Keys Mountain Jam
Nate Duval © 2015

Tara McPherson |
Beck, Faith No More, Melvins, High on Fire, Kings of Leon
© Tara McPherson

Travis Bone | Furturtle Show Prints
Matt and Kim-The Depot, Pemberton Music Festival, Band of Horses-In the Venue, Lord Huron-The Depot, the Head and the Heart-Pioneer Park, the Avett Brothers-Asbury Park, Pickathon Music Festival
Travis Bone © 2015

Brian Turner | Cricket Press
My Morning Jacket, Bonnie "Prince" Billy, Humboldt State University 2013-2014, Massey Ferguson
Cricket Press © 2015

Sara Turner | Cricket Press
Frightened Rabbit
Cricket Press © 2015

Tim Engel | Powerhouse Factories
TV on the Radio; Deltron 3030; Skrillex; Tyler, the Creator; David Byrne and St. Vincent
Tim Engel | Powerhouse Factories © 2015

Jon Flannery | Cryptogram
The Harlequins 12/23/11, Bear in Heaven 3/31/12, Small Black 4/13/14
Cryptogram © 2011, 2012, 2012, 2014

Jared Connor | Mexican Chocolate Design
The Mars Volta, ISIS, the Dandy Warhols/Spindrift
© Mexican Chocolate Design

Craig "Scrojo" Haskett |
The Dandy Warhols 06.2013; Cheap Trick 12.2014; the Flaming Lips 01.2015; Dead Rock West 06.2015; Sharon Jones & the Dap-Kings 02.2014; Chris Robinson Brotherhood 07.2014; Billy Joe Shaver 03.2015; Styx 07.2013; Rufus Wainwright 12.2013; X 07.2014; Rancid 09.2014
© Scrojo

Stainboy |
Dinosaur Jr, Flogging Molly, Hells Belles, High on Fire, Hot Mouth, Mastodon, Melvins, Nashville Pussy
© Stainboy

Jermaine Rogers |
Ween, Band of Horses, the Black Keys, Deftones, Muse, NIN/Soundgarden, Primus, Foo Fighters/ Motörhead, Feelgood/Queens of the Stone Age
Jermaine Rogers © 2015

Justin Hampton |
Deftones, Queens of the Stone Age, Soundgarden, Ween
Justin Hampton © 2015

Geoff Peveto | The Decoder Ring
Orbit, Desaparecidos, Black Lips, Portugal. The Man, Refused, Whores
The Decoder Ring © 2016

Pat Jones | Powerhouse Factories
Radiohead, Thrice, Metric, 30H!3, Butthole Surfers
Pat Jones | Powerhouse Factories © 2015

Aaron May | Powerhouse Factories
Pixies, Deafheaven, Kevin Devine, Passion Pit
Aaron May | Powerhouse Factories © 2015

Terrence Ryan | Lil' Tuffy
Bad Religion, Best Coast, Dropkick Murphys, Walk the Moon, Faith No More
Lil-Tuffy.com © 2015

Andy Vastagh | Boss Construction
Skrillex, Eric Church, Alabama Shakes, the War on Drugs, Walk the Moon, Lorde, Justin Timberlake
Andy Vastagh © 2015

Matt Barnes | Powerhouse Factories
Lightning Bolt, Holy Fuck
Matt Scott Barnes | Powerhouse Factories © 2015

CONTRIBUTING WRITERS
Matt Barnes, Travis Bone, Scott Francis, Aaron May, Ben Nunery, Pat Jones, Geoff Peveto, Terrence Ryan, Andy Vastagh, Katie Price, Emily Flannery